The New International M

Also by Robert Z. Aliber

MONETARY REFORM AND WORLD INFLATION

NATIONAL MONETARY POLICIES AND THE INTERNATIONAL FINANCIAL SYSTEM

CORPORATE PROFITS AND EXCHANGE RISK

THE MULTINATIONAL PARADIGM

The New International Money Game

Robert Z. Aliber

Sixth Edition

The University of Chicago Press

Robert Z. Aliber is professor of international economics and finance and director of the Center for Studies in International Finance in the Graduate School of Business of the University of Chicago. He is author of *Money, Banking, and Economic Activity* (Norton, 5th ed., 1993) and *The Multinational Paradigm* (MIT Press, 1993), among many other books.

The University of Chicago Press, Chicago 60637
Palgrave Publishers Ltd., Houndmills, Basingstoke, Hampshire RG21 6XS

Printed in Great Britain

11 10 09 08 07 06 05 04 03 02   1 2 3 4 5

ISBN 0–226–01396–0 (cloth)
ISBN 0–226–01397–9 (paper)

Library of Congress Cataloging-in-Publication Data

Aliber, Robert Z.
  The new international money game / Robert Z. Aliber.—6th ed.
    p. cm.
  Rev. ed. of: The international money game. 5th rev. ed. c1987.
  Includes index.
  ISBN 0–226–01396–0 (cloth : alk. paper)—ISBN 0–226–01397–9
  (pbk. : alk. paper)
  1. International finance. I. Title.

HG3881 .A44   2000
332—dc21
                                                          99–055593

Contents

List of Figures, Tables and Boxes

Preface and Acknowledgments

Several individuals have been important in the writing of this book. Martin Kessler provided the necessary condition, for he suggested that serious economic concepts could be discussed in a relatively light manner. Martin was a superb editor and a marvelous friend, and he is greatly missed. Fran Miller provided the sufficient condition; she cheerfully typed the N drafts of the first edition. Without her encouraging feedback, the project would have stalled. Cathy Green has provided substantial support for this edition.

ROBERT Z. ALIBER

List of Abbreviations and Acronyms

ADB	Asian Development Bank
ATM	automatic teller machine
BBC	British Broadcasting Corporation
BIS	Bank for International Settlements
CXT	common external tariff
CIR	Committee of Independent Republics (former USSR)
CPE	centrally planned economy
CPI	consumer price index
EBRD	European Bank for Reconstruction and Development
EC	European Community
ECB	European Central Bank
ECSC	European Coal and Steel Community
EEC	European Economic Community
EMS	European Monetary System
EMU	(European) Economic and Monetary Union
ENEL	National Corporation for Electric Energy (Italy)
ENI	National Hydrocarbon Corporation (Italy)
ERM	European Exchange Rate Mechanism
Euro	common EU currency unit from 1999 (formerly ECU)
EXIM Bank	Export – Import Bank (US)
FDI	foreign direct (direct foreign) investment
FDIC	Federal Deposit Insurance Corporation
FYR	Former Republic of Yugoslavia
G-7(-8)	Group of 7 (now 8) Countries
GNP, GDP	gross national product, gross domestic product
IBRD	International Bank for Reconstruction and Development (World Bank)
IADB	Inter-American Development Bank
IMF	International Monetary Fund
IRI	National Institute for Industrial Reconstruction (Italian)
MBA	Mexico, Brazil, Argentina
Mercosur	Mercado Comun del Sur
MITI	Ministry for International Trade and Industry (Japan)
MOF	Ministry of Finance (Japan)

NAFTA	North American Free Trade Association
NTB	non-tariff barrier
OECD	Organization for Economic Cooperation and Development
OPEC	Organization of Petroleum Exporting Countries
OTC	over-the-counter (market)
P/E	price/earnings (ratio)
PIC	petroleum-importing country
PIN	personal identification number
R&D	research and development
S&L	savings and loan
SAR	Special Administrative Region (of China)
SDR	special drawing right
STO	state trading organization
TVA	Tennessee Valley Authority
UNCTAD	United Nations Committee on Trade and Development
USSR	Union of Soviet Socialist Republics
ZPG	zero population growth

Introduction

International finance is frequently viewed as an esoteric subject, understood by only a few skilled speculators in the German mark and the Japanese yen and the Swiss franc, and a handful of central bankers. In part, the mystery results from the specialized use of everyday language – 'gliding parities' and 'sliding bands,' 'support limits' and 'counterspeculation,' 'SDRs' and 'EMUs,' 'derivatives,' 'zero-coupon bonds,' 'indexed options,' 'cross-rates' and 'intervention limits,' 'tax havens,' and 'transfer pricing.' Most of the words are straightforward, but both the meanings and the significance are elusive. The reader is deterred because of the effort required to learn a specialized language.

Once the jargon barrier is surmounted, a second problem appears – 'recognized experts' frequently disagree about the appropriate explanation for the same event. Is the US dollar 'strong' because US imports have declined owing to a US recession, or because US interest rates are high, or because the US inflation rate is below 2 percent, or because the annual US fiscal deficit, once $300 billion, has been converted to a fiscal surplus or because the United States is viewed as the ultimate 'safe-haven'? Is the market price of gold down because the Russians are selling gold, or because the Chinese have stopped buying gold or because interest rates on US dollar securities are increasing, or because the world inflation rate has declined below 2 percent a year? When the US government reports that the US trade deficit will be nearly $500 billion in 2000, the experts disagree about whether a trade deficit that is more than 2 percent of US national income is caused by an increase in US imports of oil, the loss of a 'competitive edge' in US manufactured goods, rapid economic growth in the United States, the continued closure of the Japanese market to imports from the United States, or the strength of the foreign demand for US dollar securities? And how are foreign purchases of US dollar securities related to the US trade deficit?

And then, even if the experts agree on the analysis, their recommendations about the appropriate policies frequently differ. The experts can't decide whether the US national interest is better served by remaining with the floating exchange rate arrangement adopted in the early 1970s or by returning to a pegged exchange rate system somewhat similar to the one that virtually every country relied on in the

1950s and 1960s. Indeed, the experts can't even agree on how to define the US national interest in international monetary relationships. Some experts propose an increase in the monetary price of gold – the price at which central bankers buy and sell gold with each other and a return to a nineteenth-century gold standard, or at least to a monetary arrangement that would incorporate several of its features. These experts observe – correctly – that national inflation rates were much lower when the growth of national monies was managed by an 'invisible hand' rather than by PhDs in economics. A few experts want to abandon national currencies in favor of a worldwide money, while others want to eliminate the use of the US dollar as an international money. The disagreements among the experts about the policy solutions and even about the facts leave the reader puzzled or bewildered – and skeptical of the value of the experts' advice.

The New International Money Game seeks to break the jargon barrier. Technical issues are presented in a straightforward manner with minimal use of obscure terms. Concepts are clarified by use of metaphor. Explanations are given for why experts disagree. No policy advice is offered – instead the reader is provided with the assumptions that are central to each major position on the crucial policy issues.

The six editions of this book span thirty years. The international monetary arrangements have change sharply during this period – there have been radical changes in the way the foreign exchange market is organized and in the monetary role of gold. In the 1970s the idea that the Europeans would develop their own currency before the end of the century would have seemed preposterous. So would the collapse of the Soviet Union.

The first edition of this book was completed in the early 1970s as the Bretton Woods system of pegged exchange rates – established in the mid-1940s to avoid a repetition of the 'beggar-thy-neighbor' policies of the 1930s – was breaking down, when countries manipulated the foreign exchange value of their currencies to increase their exports. Foreign exchange crises were becoming increasingly frequent, there was intensified concern about a shortage of gold and of international reserve assets. In the late 1960s the United States was beginning to experience a severe peacetime inflation, one that had no good historical parallel since the founding of the republic. The stability of the US dollar as the centerpiece of international financial relationships was being questioned. And the increase both in inflation rates and differences in inflation rates were moving countries toward a floating exchange rate arrangement.

The second edition was completed in the mid-1970s as the international economy was moving from an inflationary boom to recession, at that time one of the most severe of the postwar period. The increases and decreases in the price of the US dollar in terms of the German mark and the Japanese yen in the foreign exchange market were much larger than anticipated by virtually all of the proponents of floating exchange rates. But the spin at the time was that traders and investors required some time to adjust to the new floating exchange rate system, which had replaced the pegged rate system in 1973; thereafter changes in exchange rates would more or less track differences in national inflation rates. Herstatt Bankhaus in Frankfurt failed because of foreign exchange losses, and a few larger banks incurred foreign exchange trading losses in the $50–$100 million range. International money flows seemed unsustainable: the Organization of Petroleum Exporting Countries (OPEC) countries earned several hundred billion US dollars as a result of the surge in oil prices in late 1973 and the resulting massive increase in their export earnings,. The major international banks seemed threatened by statements that individual OPEC countries might withdraw their deposits unless the banks were more 'sympathetic' to the interests of these countries.

At the time of the third edition in the late 1970s, the key concern was whether the United States could significantly reduce its inflation rate, then approaching 15 percent. Investors were rushing to buy gold and silver and other 'hard assets' and even collectibles like rare books and antiques in search for hedges against declines in wealth due to the increase in the inflation rate. The price of gold increased from $100 an ounce in 1976 to nearly $1000 an ounce in January 1980. The supply of US dollars was increasing more rapidly than the demand, and the foreign exchange value of the US dollar was declining; in a relatively few years the US dollar had lost half of its value in terms of both the German mark and the Japanese yen. The central banks in Western Europe and Japan increased their purchases of US dollars – reluctantly – to limit the increase in the price of their own currencies in the foreign exchange market. The US President and other American policymakers were put on notice that their economic policies lacked credibility. The need to regain confidence in the value of the US dollar prompted the US Federal Reserve to adopt a 'tight money' policy in the autumn of 1979 to reduce the US inflation rate – interest rates on US dollar securities surged.

High interest rates on US dollar securities depressed the housing and auto industries and led to a large increase in the foreign exchange value of the US dollar as investors again purchased US dollar securities. Magazine articles highlighted the 'Superdollar.' Because of the increasingly high value of the US dollar in the foreign exchange market, US imports soared while US exports increased only slowly. The US unemployment rate reached 10 percent, the highest level since the Great Depression of the 1930s. Business bankruptcies also were at record high levels. The smell of financial disaster was in the air.

The disaster hit in mid-1982 when Mexico announced it could no longer pay the interest on its foreign debt of $90 billion. All of a sudden, the market value of the $800 billion owed by governments and government-owned firms in the developing countries declined sharply. Few investors were willing to pay 60 or 70 cents of good US money for $1.00 of a Mexican loan, or $1.00 of a Polish loan, or $1.00 of an Argentinean loan; some of these loans traded at 20 or 30 cents for each $1.00 of their face value. The shock that triggered the Mexican debt crisis – a decline in the price of oil from $36 a barrel to $29 a barrel – effectively caused Penn Square, a small shopping center bank in Oklahoma, to collapse. Suddenly the $1 billion of oil loans that had been acquired by Continental Illinois Bank in Chicago – the largest bank between New York and San Francisco, identified by *Fortune* magazine a few months earlier as one of the best managed US firms – from Penn Square appeared to have questionable value. Depositors – particularly other large banks and large firms – withdraw $10 billion, the first run on a major bank since the Great Depression. The savings and loan crises began to develop as interest rates increased and real estate prices began to decline (investors learned that 'a real estate loan in Houston is an "oil loan" in drag'). Eventually the US government was stung with a $140 billion bill to ensure that the guaranteed depositors in US banks and thrift institutions would not incur any losses.

Within the last several decades the threat of financial crises has appeared with increasing frequency. Such crises have blurred the usual distinction between economics and politics. The Shah of Iran favored a high price for oil – and after he was forced from the Peacock throne, the future darkened. The oil price shot up again, from $12 to $36 to $40 a barrel, first as a result of the decline in Iranian production and then as a result of further supply cuts owing to the Iraqi invasion of Iran. There was great fear that the world would 'run out of oil' – indeed that the world would run out of many depletable resources, and even foodstuffs. Every time the prices of basic commodities increased The Club of Rome and the ZPGers (Zero Population Growth) came out of the woodwork to announce that there was a major shortage of basic raw materials just over the horizon.

By the mid-1980s a major economic recovery was under way in the United States. Employment was up by more than 10 million from the recession lows. The annual US inflation rate ranged between 3 and 4 percent – the twist on the usual textbook presentation was that the inflation rate was declining as employment was booming. The dark clouds had moved elsewhere – the annual US fiscal deficit was about as large as total US government spending had been a decade earlier. The United States had the largest trade deficit that any country ever had. The smell of protectionism in the land was stronger than in any period since the early 1930s.

The remarkable US economic expansion that began in the early 1980s ended in 1989; 20 million more Americans were at work in 1989 than in 1981. But the US government's debt had increased from $1000 billion to $3000 billion. President Reagan had a conservative spiel, but his administration cut taxes and in effect adopted a Keynesian-type pump-priming policy of large fiscal deficits. The supposed rationale was that large government fiscal deficits would lead to pressures to reduce government spending and hence the role of the government in the economy.

The United States, once the world's largest creditor country, became the world's largest debtor, a change without any good historical precedent. One remarkable feature of this change is that the US Treasury did not borrow in a foreign currency. Moreover US firms continued to invest abroad; few US firms borrowed in a foreign currency to finance their activities in the United States. This change in the US international investment position occurred because foreign investors – and especially investors in Japan and Germany – had become large buyers of US dollar securities, and US real assets like Rockefeller Center, the Pebble Beach Golf Course, the Steamboat Springs Ski Area, Firestone Tire, Columbia Records, Columbia Pictures, and MGM–Universal.

The US recession of the early 1990s was triggered by the sharp collapse of real estate values, which was especially severe on the East Coast and in the coastal areas of California. Prices of many office buildings in New York, Chicago, and Los Angeles and most other large US cities declined by 30–40 percent. Some real estate developers went bankrupt. The lenders to these real estate developers, including many of the largest US banks, incurred tens of billions of dollars' losses. The prices of the stocks of some of these banks declined sharply; one- third of the US savings and loan associations went bankrupt or were acquired by healthier firms. More US commercial banks failed than at any time since the Great Depression. American business went through a remarkable period of restructuring, downsizing, and outsourcing – and this was especially true of those firms that earlier had been the pace-setters in their industries – IBM, General Motors, Eastman Kodak, and Sears.

The collapse of commercial real estate values was a worldwide phenomenon – prices of office buildings in Toronto, Tokyo, London, Paris, even Frankfurt were declining. Economic events in Japan appeared to be following those in the United States – with a lag of 18–24 months. By mid-1992 Japanese stock price indexes had declined to slightly more than one-third of their December 1989 value. Economic activity was slowing, and Japanese exports increased rapidly, while its imports fell sharply.

One remarkable change from the first edition to the sixth has been the most far-reaching financial revolution since the development of paper money. There is a large number of new financial instruments – futures contracts in foreign exchange, options on futures contracts in foreign exchange, foreign currency swaps, interest rate swaps, zero coupon bonds, collateralized mortgage obligations; the list goes on and on. Exchanges for trading futures contracts and options were established in more than 20 countries. Because more and more financial transactions have occurred in unregulated markets, financial regulations have been extensively liberalized to reduce the handicap imposed on the firms that customarily dealt in regulated markets. The rapid increase in the number of new financial instruments is traceable to the information revolution: the costs of storing, manipulating, and transmitting financial data have declined sharply.

One consequence of the financial revolution is that New York, London, Frankfurt, and Tokyo have moved much closer to each other as a result of sharp declines in the costs of economic distance. More and more investors believe that German mark securities and Japanese yen securities are closer substitutes for US dollar securities. The buzzwords are 'globalization' and 'liberalization.' A thousand mutual funds are now engaged in helping investors obtain the higher returns believed to be associated with the 'emerging markets.' US investors can readily compare the returns on securities available in these foreign centers and, by use of one or several of these new instruments, can readily hedge their exposure to the risk of loss if the foreign currency should depreciate. Similarly, US borrowers can readily compare the costs of sourcing funds in these foreign centers with the cost of obtaining funds in the United States.

The second big development since the earlier editions is the dramatic change in political landscape. The Berlin Wall is down; the two Germanies have been reunified. The Union of the Soviet Socialist Republics is dead and transformed into 15 independent countries. Poland, Hungary, and their neighbors in what had been Eastern Europe have moved toward much greater reliance on the market – in some cases under the guidance of the same fellows that ran the command economies; these countries have also moved geographically from Eastern to Central Europe. (Eastern Europe is probably getting too crowded, with a host of new countries including Estonia, Latvia, Lithuania, and Belarus.) Yugoslavia has fractured into five countries – Slovenia, Croatia, Serbia, FYR Macedonia, and Bosnia and Herzegovina and, perhaps soon, Kosovo. What was Czechoslovakia is now the Czech Republic and Slovakia.

The European Union has moved further to economic unification, with the commitment by 11 of the 15 members to adopt a common currency to replace their national currencies. Canada and the United States formed the North America Free Trade Area (NAFTA), then Mexico joined; from time to time it looks as if Chile may join as well. Argentina, Brazil, Uruguay, and Paraguay have formed Mercosur, their own free trade area.

China has liberalized its economy and has achieved double-digit rates of economic growth for nearly 20 years – a remarkable accomplishment.

The sixth edition of this book provides one more opportunity to reflect on recent events. The breakdown of the system of pegged exchange rates was inevitable once the US and foreign inflation rates began to increase at rates approaching 10 percent a year, as they did in the early 1970s, a pegged exchange rate system is incompatible with significant differences in the inflation rates of major countries. The 'date of no return' for the move to floating exchange rates occurred early in 1969, soon after Richard Nixon became US President. If the United States had successfully obtained a change in the alignment of parities for the Japanese yen and the German mark, the payment imbalances in 1970 and 1971 would have been much smaller, with the result that there would have been a much less rapid growth of money supplies in Europe and Japan. As a result, the world inflation of the 1970s would have been much less severe, and much of the instability of the 1970s and the 1980s might have been avoided – or as a minimum, would have been significantly smaller.

The last 30 years have proved to be a period of much greater instability than had been foreseen. Floating exchange rates, while not the disaster that some of the critics had suggested, had proven to be less of a panacea than the proponents had thought. The smooth, gradual adjustments predicted by their proponents of floating rates have not materialized – the movements in exchange rates were sharper, and within a substantially larger range, than had been anticipated. Moreover, the dominant position of the US dollar has declined because securities denominated in the German mark and the Japanese yen have proved to have superior attributes as stores of value.

There has also been a reorganization of financial relationships in the international economy – the system centered on the US dollar has been breaking down, and a new currency bloc centered around Germany has been developing; the new money for the members of the European Union, the Euro, is the economic manifestation of this change.

The decline in inflation rates in the United States, Europe, and Japan in the late 1990s presages a move toward greater monetary stability – and perhaps a smaller range of movement in exchange rates, at least among the currencies of the industrial countries; inflation rates in these countries have generally been below 2 percent a year – levels not seen since the 1950s and the early 1960s. By any reasonable test US goods seem remarkably inexpensive compared to the prices of comparable goods produced in Japan and in Europe. Yet the US trade deficit has remained in the range of 1–2 percent of US national income; the apparent puzzle is between the seeming price advantage of US goods and the persistence of large US trade deficits.

One of the major surprises in the 1990s is that Japan has been in the economic doldrums – the growth rate has averaged 1 percent a year, with a surge in 1996, and then a move to a severe recession in 1998. The contrast with the 1980s has been sharp; at the end of the 1980s, the pundits in Tokyo were counting the years until Japan would become the number one country. Banks headquartered in Tokyo and in Osaka dominated the list of the world's largest banks; their foreign branches were expanding at a rapid rate. The Japanese stock market was on a roll, and Japanese firms were aggressive investors abroad. The Japanese firms were dominant players in autos, electronics, photo-optics, and steel.

The slowing of the Japanese economy in the early 1990s has been explained by the decline in stock prices and real estate prices, and large losses incurred by the banks and other financial institutions. Perhaps the sluggishness in the economy could be explained by the long delay in recapitalizing the banks. Or perhaps some other explanation will prove more compelling – the rapid aging of the Japanese population or the very low return that many Japanese firms have earned on their domestic investments. The contrast between the United States and both Europe and Japan in the 1980s and the 1990s has been sharp. In the 1980s, the theme appeared to have been that American firms were falling behind, and that productivity in Japan and Europe was higher than in the United States. In the 1990s, the United States pulled ahead in terms of the creation of new jobs; moreover the US government moved from a large fiscal deficit to a small fiscal surplus while most of the government in Europe and Japan had modest or large fiscal deficits. US firms seemed to be increasingly dominant in the new industries concerned with the information revolution and as well with biotech. Moreover US stock prices surged.

Concern about the stability of the world economy began to heighten in the summer of 1998 as a result of the external impacts of the Asian financial crisis, which had started more than a year earlier with the collapse of stock prices and currency values in Thailand, Indonesia, Malaysia, Korea and their neighbors. In the mid-1990s these countries had been achieving rapid rates of economic growth; their success was captured by the term 'Four Dragons,' more or less the next generation of the 'Four Tigers' – the city-states of Hong Kong and Singapore, and Korea and Taiwan. The chatter was that the post-millennium years would become known as the 'Pacific Century.' Perhaps. But the advent of the Pacific Century appears likely to be delayed by the bankruptcy of many industrial firms and most of the domestic banks in this group of countries.

In some ways the débâcle in Thailand and Korea and their neighbors is similar to the collapse of real estate prices and stock prices in Japan in the early 1990s after a period of rapid expansion of domestic credit. But there are several important differences: one is that the implosion of asset values in Japan was associated with an appreciation of the yen whereas the Thai baht and other currencies depreciated sharply once their domestic asset prices declined. Another is that the collapse of asset values in Thailand and elsewhere appears to have larger external impacts than the implosion of asset values in Japan, even though GDP in Japan was nearly three times as large as GDP in Korea, Thailand, Malaysia, and their neighbors combined.

Because GDPs in these countries have declined sharply, their demand for imports also fell, with the result that the price of oil declined; the currencies of the oil exporting countries such as Russia,

Venezuela, Indonesia, Nigeria, and Mexico have in consequence depreciated. Other countries that have been major exporters of primary products – Chile, Australia, Canada, and New Zealand – similarly experienced significant declines in the foreign exchange values of their currencies. The imports of capital equipment of the Asian countries declined, with adverse impacts on Japan and the United States. The decline in the price of oil led to a financial disaster in Russia; most of the foreign investors in Russia incurred large losses. As a result the risks attached to investments in individual emerging countries and the transition countries have increased, and the decline in asset values has been spilling over into the stock markets in the United States and other industrial countries.

The decline in GDP in Japan and its Asian neighbors and the sharp declines in the prices of oil and other primary products have focused attention on the possibility of global deflation. US and European imports increase, while their exports decline, employment and profits in export- and import-competing firms will then decline, followed by stock prices and household wealth.

The paradox is that the declines in the costs of transportation and communication identified with the buzzword 'globalization' have brought national markets much closer together. The decline in the costs of economic distance is evident in a thousand ways – in the moves to the European Union, NAFTA and Mercosur, in the competition between London and Frankfurt to become the financial capital of Europe, in the development of global brands like Coca-Cola, Kodak, Sony, Ford, Toyota, and of global banks like Citibank, Deutsche Bank, ABN–AMRO.

Yet the politics of money is becoming increasingly decentralized. In the late 1940s when the International Monetary Fund (IMF) was established there were less than 50 member countries; now there are more than 150. The United States remains a dominant financial power, but it is less dominant now than then; and one of the many motives for the establishment of the European Community and now the European Union is that a United Europe will prove to be a more effective challenger to US hegemony than 15 or 20 independent countries.

ROBERT Z. ALIBER

1
A System is How the Pieces Fit

The goal of every science is a conceptual model that shows how the pieces of its universe are related. An economist who seeks to become the Copernicus or the Einstein of the international financial system finds the task complicated because the arrangements have changed substantially in the last 100 years, and the pace of change has quickened since the early 1970s.

Relationships among the key components

Before the First World War the system was described as the 'gold standard.' Then a change in concept led to a change in name, and the term 'gold exchange standard' was applied to the monetary arrangements for the period between the First and Second World Wars – although the changes in the arrangements belied the term. From 1947 to 1971, the term 'Bretton Woods system' was applied to exchange market and reserve arrangements. Since 1971, these arrangements are so ad hoc and varied that the most descriptive term has been 'post-Bretton Woods arrangements' – which is no more than a statement about an extended interval. These changes in the key arrangements have been more than cosmetic, for the systemic relationships among the key components – the mechanisms for determining exchange rates and for supplying the money that central banks in different countries use in payments with other central banks – also have been revamped.

Changes in the system have usually been precipitated by a crisis over the relative values of different national currencies; the established arrangements for financing payments imbalances were about to break down. Thus the move to the gold exchange standard in the 1920s reflected an anticipated shortage of gold; the new arrangements were

1

intended to economize on the use of gold in payments – in effect,to reduce the demand for gold. The gold exchange standard failed in the Great Depression of the 1930s because changes in the foreign exchange values of different national currencies were too frequent: individual countries had concluded that maintaining parities for their currencies seemed too costly in terms of their domestic economic objectives. The Bretton Woods system collapsed in 1971 because it was unable to cope with the large payments imbalances partly generated by the US inflation associated with the Vietnam War. The pattern is one of crisis, breakdown, and innovation.

There has been no significant innovation at the global level since the collapse of the Bretton Woods arrangements. At the regional level, however, there has been a remarkable innovation as the member countries of the European Union (EU) – initially 11 of the 15 members – moved to adopt a common currency as a replacement for their national currencies.

The Copernicus of the international financial system must resolve two issues. First a model must be developed of the relationships among the major components of the arrangements: the foreign exchange market in which one national money is traded for other national monies, the monetary and fiscal policies of various countries and especially of the large industrial countries like the United States, Germany, and Japan, and the supply of international monies such as gold and US dollars and German marks. (Thus the US dollar and the German mark do 'double duty' as national and international monies.) Then the Copernicus must explain why these relationships change over time, and whether the changes in these relationships follow a pattern or are random. This chapter discusses the relationships among these components, while Chapter 3 reviews the changes in the arrangements over the last 100 years.

Fitting the pieces: the foreign exchange market

International transactions have one common element that makes them uniquely different from domestic transactions – one of the participants must deal in a foreign currency. When Americans buy new Mercedes and new Volkswagens, they usually pay US dollars to the dealers who in turn pay US dollars to the German producers; the German firms must then exchange the US dollars for German marks, so they will be able to pay their workers and their suppliers. If instead the German automobile firms want to be paid in German marks, the

US buyers must first exchange the US dollars for marks. At some stage in the chain of transactions between the American buyers and the German producers, someone must use US dollars to buy German marks: either the American buyer or the German producer takes the US dollars to the foreign exchange market to buy German marks.

Floating exchange rates

The foreign exchange market is a market in national monies; the exchange rate is the price in this market. There are two basic types of exchange rate systems – two basic ways of organizing this market. One involves *floating exchange rates*: the price of foreign monies in terms of domestic money rises and falls in response to changes in supply and demand, much as the prices of IBM shares on the New York Stock Exchange or the price of wheat futures contracts at the Chicago Board of Trade vary in response to changes in the supply and demand relationships. If the Americans decide to buy more Mercedes and Volkswagens, the increase in the demand for German marks leads to an increase in the US dollar price of the German mark – or, what is the same thing, a decrease in the German mark price of the US dollar.

The concept of a floating exchange rate system is simple: the exchange rate or price moves freely in response to market forces of changes in the relationship between supply and demand. The central banks in individual countries may participate in the exchange market, usually to limit the increase or the decrease in the price of their currency; they might seek to dampen daily or weekly movements in this price.

Despite the simplicity and neatness of the concept, few countries permitted their currencies to float for extended periods – that is, until the early 1970s. Among developed countries, Canada has the record for permitting its currency to float (1950–62 and 1970 to the present). Lebanon holds the record for developing countries (1950 to the present). On three occasions, a substantial number of countries permitted their currencies to float at the same time; at least two of these occasions have been interim arrangements pending changes in the relationship between national price levels and the foreign exchange values for national currencies rates that would facilitate a return to pegged exchange rates. The first of these interim arrangements was between 1919 and 1926 when most European countries were adjusting to the inflationary impacts of the First World War. Each country wanted to peg its currency to gold, and in most cases at the same parity that had been prevailed before the war; the implication was that the national price levels in most countries would have to decline. The second interim arrangement occurred between August 1971 and December 1971; most Western European countries and Japan permitted their currencies to float while a new set of parities was being determined. In this case, the foreign exchange values adjusted to the change in the price level relationship. Finally, the currencies of the major industrialized countries have been floating since early 1973; time will tell whether this extended period will be shown to have been an interim arrangement as countries attempted to achieve low and similar inflation rates

Pegged-rate system

The alternative to a floating exchange rate is a *pegged-rate system*. This system has two main features. First, a government authority, usually the central bank, limits variations in the prices of foreign currencies in terms of its own national money within a narrow range – perhaps as little as 1 percent and rarely more than 3 or 4 percent. The price at the center of this range is the parity, or peg, or central rate for the currency, a reference point for the price of domestic currency in terms of some other asset, perhaps gold or some other national currency. In the nineteenth century the US dollar and the British pound were both pegged to gold; indeed, the first act of the First US Congress in 1793 was to state the value of the standard US $20 coin in terms of a given weight of gold. The US gold parity of $20.67 per fine ounce of gold prevailed for the next 140 years, until 1933 (although payments in gold were suspended during the Civil War and for some years thereafter); the $35 parity was adopted in 1934. Alternatively, some countries state the parity for their own currency in terms of the currency of another country, usually one of their large trading partners; thus many countries pegged their currencies to the US dollar in the 1940s, the 1950s, and the 1960s.

The second feature of a pegged-rate system is that on occasion – perhaps once a generation, or once a decade, or even more frequently – the government may change the peg for its currency, as the British did when they devalued the pound in November 1967; the US dollar price of the British pound declined from $2.80 to $2.40.

Pegged-rate arrangements are more complex than floating-rate arrangements, for the authorities must limit variations in the price of their currencies in the foreign exchange market so that this price does not differ significantly from parity. Usually each central bank buys its own currency to prevent the price from falling substantially below its parity; conversely, each sells its own currency to prevent its price from rising substantially above its parity. Such purchases and sales are undertaken to limit any significant deviation of the market exchange rate from parity. The boundaries within which the market price of the currency may vary before the central bank is obliged to intervene are known as the 'support limits' or 'margins'. For example, the Bank of England bought the British pound in exchange for US dollars when the demand for the pound was weak, thus limiting the decline in the price of the pound in terms of the dollar. And the Bank of England sold pounds when the demand for pounds was strong to limit the increase in the price of the pound. In the 1960s, when the pound was pegged at $2.80, the support limits were $2.78 and $2.82, or about 0.75 percent on either side of parity. When the pound was pegged at $2.60 at the end of 1971, these limits were widened to 2.25 percent, or to about $2.54 and $2.66.

In the 1980s France and Germany took the lead in developing the European Monetary System (EMS); participating countries agreed to limit the range of movement of the prices of their currencies in terms of the currencies of other countries, initially by about 5 percent. Subsequently these support limits were narrowed.

Under a pegged-rate system, countries incur payments imbalances – payments surpluses and payments deficits – as a result of central bank purchases and sales of an international money in terms of their own currencies in the foreign exchange market. A payments surplus occurs when the central bank sells its currency in the foreign exchange market and buys gold or some other international money (the concept of international money and the assets that are considered as international money are discussed later in this chapter). Conversely, a payments deficit occurs when the central bank buys its currency and sells an international money.

From time to time, the authorities in a country may change its parity to reduce a large payments deficit – or, much less frequently, a payments surplus. A country with a payments deficit devalues its currency by increasing the price at which it buys and sells foreign money in terms of its own money. Conversely, a country with a payments surplus revalues its currency by reducing the price at which it buys and sells a foreign money in the foreign exchange market.

During the 1960s, most countries were reluctant to change their parities (the basis of their concern is discussed in Chapter 4) despite increasingly large payments imbalances; thus the parities tended to become 'frozen'. Still governments had to take measures to limit their payments deficits because they lacked the ability to finance these deficits indefinitely, so on occasion they raised tariffs and imposed controls on foreign payments, and they also subsidized exports. Some importers found that they had to pay more for foreign exchange than they would have if the currency had been devalued. In effect, such controls devalued the currency on a selective, 'backdoor' basis. Conversely, countries with large payments surpluses reduced controls on foreign payments rather than revalued their currencies.

Central bank transactions in the foreign exchange market under a pegged-rate system are the counterpart of changes in the exchange rate under a floating-rate arrangement – these transactions match the supply of foreign exchange with the demand. If a central bank does not intervene in the exchange market under a floating-rate system, payments surpluses and deficits will not occur; instead the exchange rate would change more or less continuously to balance supply and demand. The floating-rate arrangements' equivalent of a payments deficit is an increase in the price of foreign monies in terms of domestic money – or, what is the same thing, a depreciation of the domestic currency.

The distinction between a system of pegged and a system of floating exchange rates can become fuzzy, for the more frequently the currency parities are changed, the more nearly the pegged-rate system would seem to resemble a floating-rate system. Conversely, the more frequently authorities in countries with floating exchange rates intervene in the exchange market to dampen the movements in the foreign exchange price of their currencies, the more nearly the floating-rate system resembles the pegged system.

Changes in the parities for national currencies when currencies are pegged and variations in the price of foreign exchange when currencies are not pegged are not economic accidents. Such changes are primarily the result of differences in national inflation rates, or of major disturbances such as crop failures and sharp changes in the price of oil. These sudden movements in foreign exchange values are generally a response to a sudden change in the volume, or even the direction, of international capital flows.

Fitting the pieces: national financial policies

One approach toward the formulation of national monetary and fiscal policies involves managing these policies so the prevailing parities for the national currency can be maintained. A competing approach is to aim these policies in the direction of high levels of employment, or price-level stability, or more rapid economic growth. If the second approach is followed, then changes in currency values are likely to be necessary; the authorities may alter their parities and their controls on international payments, or instead permit their currency to float.

Monetary and fiscal policy

The monetary policies of the central bank and the fiscal policies of the national Treasury have a major impact on each country's international financial position – affecting, for example, whether a country with pegged rates will be in deficit or surplus or whether the currency of a country with a floating rate will appreciate or depreciate. A change in a monetary policy leads to changes in the amount of money held by the public; central banks increase the money supply to induce an increase in the public's spending for goods and services, and they decrease the money supply to induce a decline in spending. Usually a move to a more expansive monetary policy is associated with a decline in interest rates, while the move to a more contractive monetary policy is associated with an increase in interest rates.

Fiscal policy involves changes in the government's expenditures relative to its revenues. Monetary and fiscal policies are managed to help governments achieve their employment, income, and price level objectives.

Changes in monetary policy and changes in fiscal policy affect a country's payments balance by altering the demands of domestic residents for foreign goods and foreign securities. These policies lead to changes in GNP or national income: the demand for foreign goods increases when national income increases, and exports may increase less rapidly or even decline. Moreover, the increase in income may cause domestic prices to increase; and if prices of domestic goods rise relative to prices of foreign goods, the country's international competitive position becomes less favorable. Then imports increase even more rapidly while exports increase less rapidly. Changes in monetary and fiscal policies also cause changes in interest rates; as domestic interest rates rise relative to interest rates abroad, the demand for foreign securities is likely to decline while exports of domestic securities may increase.

Some countries have changed the parities for their currencies relatively infrequently because their monetary and fiscal policies were geared to maintaining a particular value for their currency. Thus the Mexican peso was pegged to the US dollar for more than twenty years, from the mid-1950s until the mid-1970s; the central objective of Mexican monetary policy was to maintain the parity of 12.5 pesos per US dollar. In the mid-1970s, Mexican monetary policy became more expansive, and eventually the more rapid increase in the Mexican price level led to a progressively larger payments deficit, so the established parity was no longer viable.

In contrast, Brazil, Israel, and Denmark changed their parities frequently because their monetary and fiscal policies were directed to achieving domestic objectives, whether they be economic growth, full employment, or fighting wars in the Sinai and the Golan Heights. For these countries the retention of a particular parity for their currency was neither an important policy objective nor a significant constraint on the choice of domestic policies. Thus, for many years Brazil adjusted its monetary and fiscal policies to maintain a rapid rate of economic growth, Israel to finance its defense expenditures, and Denmark to pay for its welfare programs. Instead of adjusting its domestic economy to the prevailing parity for the currency, each of these countries adjusted its exchange rate peg so that international payments and receipts would be roughly equal. The monetary policies of these countries were independent of their balance-of-payments positions.

The priority in a country for different national economic objectives changes over time. US history provides a good example. During the Civil War, monetary policies in both North and South were highly expansive, and money supplies in both North and South were increased rapidly to finance war expenditures. Commodity prices rose rapidly. After the war, the objective of the US government was to peg the dollar at its prewar parity with gold – which finally happened at the end of 1878 after a massive reduction in the US price level.

During the First World War, as in the Civil War, the US money supply grew rapidly; again commodity prices increased sharply. Price stability level did not become an important objective of US policy until the 1920s; substantial up-and-down price-level variations, tolerable in the largely agricultural society of the nineteenth century, were unacceptable in an industrial society because falling prices led to large increases in business failure and high levels of unemployment. During the Second World War, full employment became an important US objective of national policy – and full employment was generally associated with an unemployment rate of 4 percent. In the 1950s, largely in response to the threat of Soviet economic and technological achievements, economic growth became an important objective. The realization of the Great Society – raising the economic welfare of the millions of Americans who lived below the poverty line – became a prime objective in the mid-1960s. Shortly thereafter, the preservation of freedom and the stability of the 'dominoes' in Southeast Asia meant that security expenditures went to the head of the list. In the late 1970s, the emphasis was on getting the US economy and the world economy moving again. In the early 1980s, the objective was a return to price level stability; full employment was then viewed as an unemployment rate of 6–7 percent. By the mid-1990s, full employment was viewed as an unemployment rate of 5 percent. As the priority among these US objectives have changed, so did the targets for monetary and fiscal policies.

Currency boards

In the last 10 or so years, several countries have adopted currency boards; they have pegged their currency to that of a major trading partner, and changes in the domestic money supply have varied with changes in the countries' holdings of international monies. In effect, the central bank gives up any semblance of monetary independence; the money supply increases when the country has a payments surplus and falls when the country has a payments deficit. The motivation for the adoption of a currency board arrangement is that traders and investors had lost confidence that the central bank could manage the growth of the money supply on a discretionary basis without soon moving into a period of inflationary finance.

National economic policies

Several themes emerge. Wars lead to inflation, and inflation leads to large payment deficits. No payments deficit can persist forever; ultimately an adjustment is needed. As populations have becomes industrial and urban, governments have become increasingly concerned with economic welfare. Full employment, rarely a problem in an agricultural economy, became a matter of crucial importance as societies have become increasingly urban. The fiscal role of governments has increased; taxes in some countries now amount to 50 percent or more of national income. As expectations of higher living standards have become more widespread, raising the economic growth rate has grown increasingly important.

National economic policies have stressed domestic objectives in recent years; the importance of a particular exchange rate peg has been slighted. The international system has had to accommodate these increasingly inward-looking national policies. At first, the combination of domestically-oriented financial policies and a pegged-rate system led to increasingly large international payments deficits – and surpluses. The size of these imbalances was limited by the ability of individual countries to finance large payments deficits and, eventually, the inability to finance deficits forced changes in parities.

Now, to the extent that each country allows its currency to float in the foreign exchange market, the diversity in national policies is reflected in movements in exchange rates; the currencies of countries with relatively high rates of inflation tend to depreciate. The paradox is that although the movements in exchange rates have been continuous, there have often been periods when these movements have been abrupt – and much larger than would have been forecast on the basis of the difference between the domestic inflation rate and the inflation rates in the major trading partners.

Fitting the pieces: the supply of international money

A central bank can buy its own currency in the foreign exchange market only by selling some other asset, and it can sell its own currency only if it buys some other asset. By definition, any asset that a central bank buys and sells when it supports its currency in the exchange market is an *intervention asset*. And the securities that central banks acquire with intervention assets comprise the set of international monies. An international money is a necessary component of a pegged exchange rate system; a floating-rate system, in contrast, has no need for an international money.

What is 'international money'?

One key question is: what determines which securities qualify as international money? Why is gold an international money, while silver is not? Why are US dollar securities considered international money, while Canadian dollar securities are not? A related question involves how much of each security is held as international money.

Given that central banks need to hold an international money once they are committed to peg their currencies in the foreign exchange market, each central bank must decide which security has the most attractive combination of attributes in the form of interest income, stability of purchasing power, and low transaction and storage costs.

Until the mid-1960s, holdings of gold were the largest component of international money (see Figure 1.1). Then holdings of foreign exchange, largely short-term securities denominated in the US dollar,

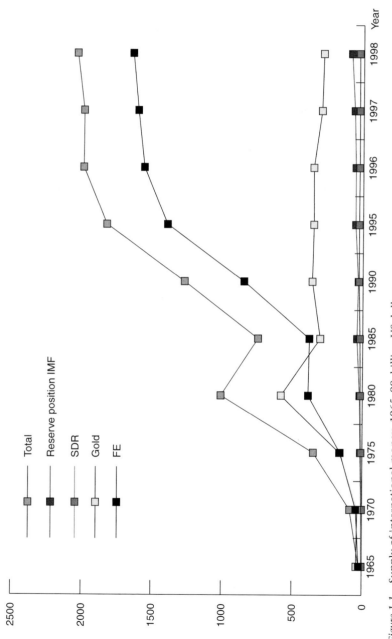

Figure 1.1 Supply of international money, 1965–98, billion US dollars
Source: International Financial Statistics.

surged. Because of the ten-fold increase in the market price of gold, the gold component of reserves has increased sharply; the value of these holdings fluctuates with changes in the market price of gold. The third and the smallest component of international monies are those produced by international institutions, primarily the International Monetary Fund (IMF). Such institutions are groups of countries acting jointly; negotiations among the members determine how much of each type of money will be produced each year and how the newly produced money will be distributed among the member countries.

The role of gold

The use of gold as an international money is explained by its history. (Chapter 5 examines gold's past and future as an international money.) For centuries, gold was the world's principal money. Gold bullion and then gold coins were used to make payments, both within countries and across national boundaries. Because gold was used in so many countries, payments between countries frequently did not involve any foreign exchange transactions, for within many countries foreign coins circulated together with domestic coins.

The volume of gold held as an international money represents the cumulative acquisitions of national central banks, or the difference between the amount of gold produced and the amount absorbed by jewelry, the arts, dentistry, industry, and private hoards. New gold discoveries led to increases in national price levels as money supplies increased. Gold mining costs then increased, and gold production tended to decline.

For most of the last 300 years, central banks have bought and sold gold at their parities. If the amount of gold produced during a period exceeded the amount demanded by private parties at the central bank's parity, the mining companies sold their gold to the central banks, because the companies could obtain a higher price from these banks than in the commodity market. When private demand for gold was weak, central banks acquired a large share of new production; when private demand was strong, they acquired a smaller share.

Several factors explain the central banks' historic preference for gold. A central bank acquired gold because it believed it would be able to sell gold to some other central bank when the need arose. Even if this expectation proved wrong, gold could still be sold in the commodity market, perhaps at a price not far below the price paid by the central bank.

Over the last several hundred years, gold's role as a money in domestic economies has declined as national currencies have become more important. Initially, national monies in the form of bank notes and deposits could be easily used to buy gold from central banks. But as the amount of national money increased relative to the amount of gold, sovereigns found it difficult to maintain the national money and gold in circulation at the same time. Gold was often hoarded, especially during inflationary periods. The policy response to the hoarding problem was to eliminate the use of gold in domestic transactions. In the last 50 years, monetary gold transactions have been increasingly restricted to transactions among national central banks. For example, the Bank of England would sell gold to the US Treasury to get US dollars to support the British pound in the exchange market; conversely, the Bank of England would acquire dollars in the foreign exchange market knowing that it could use these dollars to buy gold at the US Treasury.

The increasingly severe gold shortage of the 1950s and 1960s led to renewed efforts to reduce the demand. US citizens, who in 1933 had been prohibited from owning gold in the United States, were prohibited from owning gold abroad in 1961. Foreign central banks were encouraged to acquire US dollar securities rather than gold to meet their demand for international money. A major international negotiation to produce a 'paper gold' – a security which was supposed to have all of the attributes of gold except its weight, durability, and glitter – was initiated in the mid-1960s. The objective of all such measures was to forestall the surefire cure for the shortage of gold – an increase in its price in terms of national currencies.

These measures proved ineffective. As long as private parties could buy gold in private markets at $35 an ounce, central banks were obliged to let private demand determine how much newly produced gold would flow into private uses and how much would accrue to central banks and thus add to the stock of international monies. Indeed, maintaining the same price of gold for private parties as for central banks meant that central banks were required to sell gold from their own holdings to private parties if private demand in any period exceeded new production.

The inevitable occurred: by 1965, the private demand for gold exceeded new production, and sales from central banks as a group mounted to $2 billion by early 1967. The major central banks, following the US lead, arranged a two-tier market: central banks would continue to buy and sell gold with each other at $35, while private parties would buy and sell gold in a free market. The price of gold in the private market might rise above the $35 parity or fall below it. Gold producers would be tempted to sell new gold output to private parties if the price in the private market was higher than the price that central banks would pay.

Soon after this two-tier system was adopted, the price of gold in private markets began to rise modestly above the official price. Paradoxically, the gold shortage intensified: central banks were reluctant to sell gold to other central banks at $35 if the price of gold in the private market was $40. The usual economic response to resolve any shortage is to permit a price increase. The gold price rose slowly in the late 1960s, and then very rapidly in the early 1970s. The price increase led to a very sharp increase in the value of gold held by monetary authorities. At a price of $200 an ounce, central bank gold holdings exceeded $225 billion; at a price of $300 an ounce, central bank gold holdings were about $350 billion, and the gold shortage had disappeared.

US dollar securities

The gold shortage of the 1960s was similar to that of the 1920s; then, too, central bankers were concerned that there wasn't enough gold to go around, not enough gold was being produced, and too much of the production was going into various private uses. There was a similar search for substitutes for gold. Some countries began to acquire securities denominated in the US dollar. The Bank of Canada and the Bank of Mexico, for example, held most of their international money in the form of US dollar securities – US Treasury bills and time deposits in US banks.

US dollar securities had several attractive attributes for foreign central banks: they provided interest income, and they could be used to buy gold at the US Treasury. For a long time, US dollar securities appeared more likely to remain acceptable and retain value than securities denominated in any other currency. The US dollar could be used to buy goods and securities in a country with a large, productive economy that seemed militarily secure and politically stable. And the US dollar had (remember, this is still the 1950s and the 1960s) – and still has – a better long-term record for retaining its purchasing power than most other currencies. Whether US dollar securities in the future will continue to have these qualities is examined in Chapter 6.

As foreign holdings of US dollar securities increased, however, countries became increasingly reluctant to acquire more dollar securities – in part, because the US Treasury's ability to convert these securities into gold was increasingly questioned. Nevertheless, US dollar holdings of foreign central banks surged in 1970 and 1971, for business firms, banks, and private investors began to anticipate that the price of the West German mark, the Swiss franc, and the Japanese yen would rise in terms of the US dollar, either because the US dollar would be devalued in terms of gold or because these currencies would be revalued in terms of gold. So foreign central banks ended up with the US dollar securities these other investors were selling; the foreign central banks were caught between their reluctance to acquire more US dollar securities and their reluctance to revalue their currencies. The indecision proved costly, since these central banks first acquired the dollar securities and then subsequently revalued.

One of the ironic aspects of international monetary developments in the 1970s and the 1980s was the surge in the supply of international money. In the 1960s the view developed that the demand for international money would decline sharply once central banks stopped pegging their currencies in the foreign exchange market, since they would have no need to intervene in this market when currencies were floating. But, in fact, intervention has been more extensive because central banks have wanted to limit the appreciation of their currencies in terms of the US dollar.

The use of gold as money, because of its underlying value as a commodity, points to a unique problem of the international economy. In the domestic economy, paper money (in the form of bank notes and demand deposits) has value because the government declares that it has value – sellers and tax collectors are obliged to accept it. No government has similar power in the international economy; no sovereign can compel another sovereign to accept a security as money, and neither can any international agency. Some countries may be reluctant to acquire a particular security as an international money unless they are confident that it will retain its value and remain acceptable for payments in other countries.

The persistent gold shortage, together with the reluctance of central banks to acquire more US dollar securities, led some observers to suggest that the demand for international money should be satisfied by increased reliance on the monies produced by international institutions. Perhaps. But the question remains whether countries would have confidence in this money, an issue discussed in Chapter 12.

Who fits the pieces together?

The gold and exchange crises of the 1960s, 1970s, and 1980s can be explained by the absence of institutions to ensure that the growth in the supply of international monies matched the growth in demand.

The larger problem is that there is no mechanism to ensure that the three major components of an arrangement – the exchange rate mechanism, national monetary and fiscal policies, and the supply of international monies – are consistent with each other. The move to floating exchange rates in the early 1970s occurred because of significant differences in national inflation rates, and in particular because of the increase in the US inflation rate relative to the inflation rates in Germany and Japan. National financial policies were increasingly oriented to domestic objectives, even as it was becoming easier and less costly to move money from one country to another. Political forces within the individual countries explain the change in orientation: the large variations in currency values in the 1970s and the 1980s were responses to changes in inflation rates and to differences in national inflation rates.

In the 1990s, inflation rates in the United States and its major trading partners again converged at the low levels last seen in the 1960s; price-level stability again has become a major objective of national economic policies. These low inflation rates are the necessary condition for a return to a pegged exchange rate arrangement. A major question is whether initiatives will develop to move back to some type of pegged exchange rate arrangement at the global level; this initiative would reflect that the conclusion that the costs of the extremely variable movements in exchange rates are too high relative to the benefits. Such a move would have significant implications for the demand and supply of international money.

2
The Name of the Game is Money

International finance

International finance is a game with two sets of players: the politicians and bureaucrats of national governments, and the presidents and treasurers of giant, large, medium-large, medium, medium-small, and small firms and banks and hedge funds, and other financial institutions. The government officials want to win elections and secure a niche in the histories of their countries. A few aspire to get their portraits on the national currency. And to do so, they want to be able to manage their economies to provide more jobs and better-paying jobs and financial security for their voters. They want to avoid sharp increases in inflation rates and sharp declines in the foreign exchange value of their currencies. The corporate presidents and treasurers want to profit – or at least avoid losses – from changes in exchange rates, changes that are inevitable in a world with more than 150 national currencies.

Dollar/yen relationships, 1970–99

Consider the changes in the relationship between the US dollar and the Japanese yen over the last 30 years. Throughout the 1950s and the 1960s the Japanese currency was pegged at 360 yen per US dollar, which had been set in the late 1940s when Japan was still occupied by US military forces; the productive power of the economy was still much below that in the early 1940s. In the early 1970s, the yen began to float and increased to 175 yen per dollar by the end of the decade. In contrast, in the early 1980s the yen declined sharply; in the second half of the 1980s the yen again appreciated, and by 1994, had climbed to 80 yen per dollar. Three years later, the yen traded in the range of

125–150 yen per dollar. Japanese politicians generally were displeased by the stronger yen, because exports from Japan were less profitable and grew less rapidly. So the Bank of Japan often limited the rate of appreciation of the yen. A lot of money could be made by identifying the factors that led to these wide swings in the value of the yen in terms of the US dollar. The counterpart was large changes in the Japanese trade surplus with the United States. So US producers of a wide range of products – textiles, steel, autos, electronics – complained, especially in Washington, that the Japanese followed unfair trading practices, and were much more eager to sell to Americans than to buy from them.

Receipts and payments

The inevitability of the changes in exchange rates reflects the fact that differences among countries in their rates of population growth, family structures, tax rates, and educational standards lead to differences in their inflation rates, investment rates, and rates of economic growth. As a result, payments to and from foreigners tend to differ. Either measures will have to be adopted so that these payments and receipts are more or less equal at the prevailing exchange rate, or the exchange rate must change to bring payments and receipts into balance. And it's generally easier to rely on changes in exchange rates to bring payments and receipts into balance.

Every economic unit needs to keep payments more or less matched with receipts. This budget constraint holds for individuals, families, firms, and governments as well as for regions within a country. West Virginia has a budget constraint and even New York City has one – although that lesson was learned slowly. At the global level, an array of shocks – changes in inflation rates, in savings rates, in rates of growth of national income, in productivity gains in export industries, in import prices, and in the rates of return on securities denominated in the domestic currency–cause payments to foreigners to differ from receipts from them at the prevailing exchange rates.

Within a domestic economy, there is only one currency, so by definition the necessary adjustments cannot occur through changes in exchange rates; instead, these adjustments occur in the relationship between prices and wages and rates of growth of income in different regions or through changes in the unemployment rate. The shocks across countries may be much, much larger than the shocks among the regions within a country, so that the adjustment problem is much larger.

Foreign exchange management

Each country has to decide how to manage the foreign exchange value of its currency. If the country ignores the problem, then its currency will float, by default; market forces will lead to changes in the value of its currency in terms of other currencies, just as market forces lead to changes in the price of wheat as supply and demand conditions change. Alternatively, the country may peg the value of its currency in terms of some other currency because the costs of the changes in the exchange rate are deemed too high. While there are modest variants of each arrangement, there really are no other choices. When currencies are pegged, as they have been for most of the last 200 years (although not for the last 25 years), then when payments imbalances are extended the problem that arises is which countries should take the initiative in changing the value of these pegs. The only point that national authorities agree on is that it is highly preferable that the authorities in some other countries take the initiative in changing the exchange rate – those in the countries with the payments surpluses believe that the authorities in the countries with the payments deficits should take the initiative, because they have mismanaged their economies.

The bankers – especially the foreign exchange traders in both large international banks and in hedge funds – seek gains from volatile movements, and even from gentle movements in exchange rates.

Parities and shocks

The result is that necessary changes in parities almost always have been delayed. From 1970 on political leaders believed that any initiative they might take to change the parity would be criticized by their supporters. Thus it seemed obvious to both many Americans and many Japanese that, at a price of 360 Japanese yen to the dollar, the Japanese yen was too cheap. The view in Washington was that the Japanese would have to reduce the yen price of the dollar because they were not permitting their imports to grow to match the increase in their exports. The view in Tokyo was that the Americans should devalue the dollar to offset the trade consequences of the increase in the US inflation rate above the inflation rate in Japan. In both cases, Japanese autos would cost more in the United State – and fewer US workers in autos, steel, and textiles would lose their jobs because US imports from Japan would increase less rapidly. Eventually, the US government took the initiative and forced a revaluation of the Japanese yen in August 1971 – an event recorded in Japanese monetary history as Nixon Shockku II (Nixon Shockku I was the US opening to China).

Three times in 10 years (1961, 1969, and 1971) Germany raised the parity of the mark in terms of the US dollar to reduce its balance-of-payment surpluses. The Germans acted to further their self-interest – they wanted both to reduce inflationary pressures at home and to reduce the likelihood that substantial numbers of American troops would be withdrawn from Europe to reduce the US payments deficit. In the 1960s, French President Charles de Gaulle bought $2 billion of gold from the US Treasury in an attempt to force the US government to increase the dollar price of gold. De Gaulle believed that this increase would have benefitted his domestic supporters, restored the prestige of France and its record of monetary stability, and demonstrated that the US dollar was a weak currency and the United States an untrustworthy ally. The increase in the US dollar price of gold that General de Gaulle anticipated occurred after an extended delay. The first step occurred in December 1971, when the US dollar price of gold was raised to $38 an ounce (effectively a devaluation of the US dollar by 12 percent), and the second step took place in February 1973, when the US dollar price was increased to $42 an ounce. But since the US Treasury kept its 'gold window' closed and would not sell gold to foreign central banks, these price increases were somewhat academic. Private investors ignored the changes in the US Treasury's gold parity, and bid the price to nearly $200 in 1974 and then to about $1000 in January 1980. De Gaulle appeared prescient. Throughout the 1970s, the 1980s, and the 1990s, the US Treasury continued to value US gold holdings at $42 an ounce, even though the market price varied extensively; in the 1990s gold has traded in the range of $280–$400.

Pegging and floating

In February 1973, the United States, Germany, Japan, and the other major industrial countries abandoned the system of pegged exchange rates, which had more or less naturally evolved from the reliance on gold as money and that had been around for most of the previous 200 years. Previously a country had stopped pegging its currency when involved in a major war, which almost always led to significant increase in the domestic inflation rate: maintaining a fixed price or a parity for the national currency when the domestic price level was increasing by 10 or 15 percent a year would have been impossible. The unique aspect of the move to floating exchange rates in the early 1970s was that this change occurred when the major industrial countries were not at war. Since the early 1970s, the foreign exchange value of the currencies of the major industrial countries has been set primarily by market forces, and the price of the US dollar in terms of the German mark, the British pound, and the Japanese yen has varied within a wide range. From time to time central banks have intervened in the foreign exchange market to limit these swings, usually because of a decline in the competitiveness of domestic goods associated with too rapid an appreciation of the domestic currency. Paradoxically, central bank intervention in the foreign exchange market – purchases and sales of US dollars and German marks and other foreign currencies – has been more extensive when currencies have been floating than when they were pegged.

Devaluations and revaluations

Business fortunes are made on the ability to forecast changes in the prices of national currencies (George Soros is reported to have earned more than $1 billion from the depreciation of the British pound in the autumn of 1992). In contrast, political futures became frayed as a result of these changes. Under a pegged rate system, the national monetary authority 'fixes' the foreign exchange value of its currency. The direction of the change in currency parities (and, frequently, the approximate amount of the change) has generally been predictable. What has been less readily predictable are the dates when the change in the parity would occur. At one time, periodic cycles could be discerned. The British pound was devalued in 1914, 1931, 1949, and 1967; it seemed as if there was an 18-year 'cycle'. But the cycle was interrupted by the sharp depreciation of the pound in 1975 and 1976. Still, the British pound hit a low against the US dollar in 1985, so the 18-year 'cycle' remained valid. The French franc has generally been devalued every 10 years – in 1919 (the devaluation that might have come in 1929 was delayed until 1936), 1939, 1949, 1959, and 1969. In 1979 the French franc along with the other European currencies began to depreciate rapidly relative to the US dollar.

Devaluations and revaluations of national currencies were more frequent in the late 1960s and early 1970s than in the 1950s. Exchange rate crises occurred in November 1967 (British pound), May 1968 (French franc), September 1969 (German mark), June 1970 (Canadian dollar), May 1971 (German mark, Dutch guilder, and Swiss franc), August 1971 (Japanese yen, British pound, and French franc), and June 1972 (British pound and Italian lira). The increase in the frequency of changes in currency parities was closely associated with greater divergence in national inflation rates, and especially with the surge in the US inflation rate relative to the inflation rates in Germany and Japan.

The changes in the price of the US dollar in terms of the German mark and several other European currencies and the Japanese yen are shown in Figure 2.1. One feature of the data is that the range of movement in the price of the US dollar in terms of the German mark and the Japanese yen has been large – and much larger than would have been forecast on the basis of the contemporary difference in national inflation rates. The mark and the yen appreciated sharply in the late 1970s, depreciated sharply in the first half of the 1980s, and then appreciated again in the second half of the 1980s. Both the mark and the yen depreciated in the mid-1990s. A second feature of this data is that the mark and the yen have tended to appreciate and depreciate at more or less the same time. Indeed for a long while, it seemed as if 100 yen would buy 1 mark, more or less. A third feature of this data is that when the US inflation rate increases, the US dollar tends to depreciate, and conversely when the US inflation rate tends to decline, the US dollar tends to appreciate: note the word 'tends'.

The relations among countries and the positions of political leaders within those countries are affected by movements in exchange rates and the measures adopted to reduce payments imbalances. During the 1960s Germany had large payments surpluses and the United States had nearly as large payments deficits. The US government kept leaning on the German government to take measures to offset some of the costs of keeping American troops in Germany; these pressures eventually forced the downfall of Ludwig Erhard as German Prime Minister. The 10 percent surcharge on US imports adopted by the US government in August 1971, followed by the 17 percent revaluation of the yen, advanced the date of Prime Minister Sato's resignation in Japan.

British government – especially Labour governments – resisted devaluing the pound in the 1960s because of the perceived costs in declining domestic political support. The Labour Party had been in power when the British pound was devalued in 1931, and Labour was again in power at the time of the 1949 devaluation (Paradoxically, the constituency of the Labour Party would almost certainly have benefitted when the pound was devalued, since a cheaper pound meant that

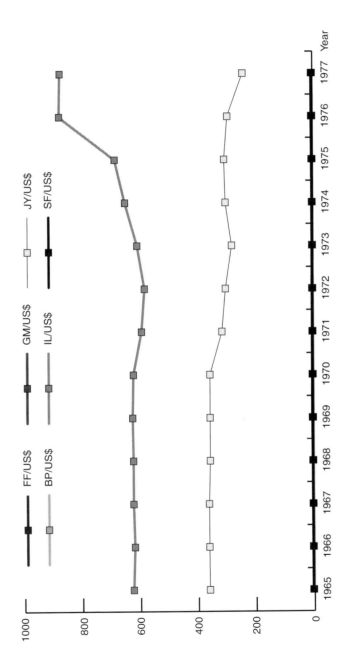

24

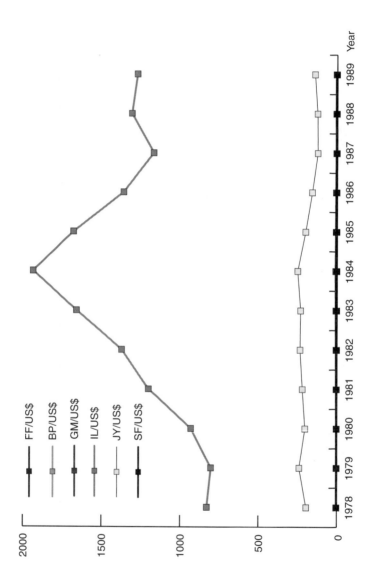

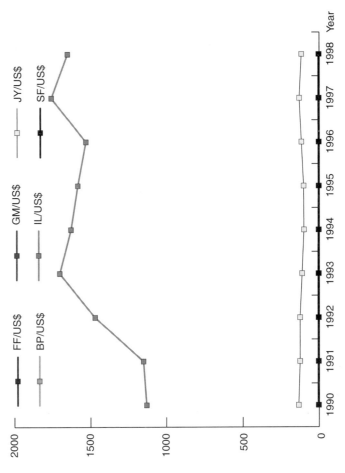

Figure 2.1 Foreign exchange value of US dollar, 1965–98
Note: SF = Swiss franc, JY = Japanese yen, IL = Italian lira, GM = German mark, BP = British pound

British manufacturing goods would be more competitive in foreign markets; the stronger the competitive position of British goods, the larger the number of jobs in British manufacturing industry – or what was left of it.) The devaluation of the pound that was inevitable and that should have occurred in 1964 was delayed until 1967.

Throughout the 1960s US government officials were extremely reluctant to recognize that an increase in the US dollar price of gold was inevitable. The monetary authorities in Great Britain and France in effect forced the increase in 1971. An increase in the US dollar price of gold was much more than a US problem. The gold producing countries including South Africa and the Soviet Union would benefit from an increase; the value of their existing production would be higher and production would increase. (Many economists were strongly against a gold price increase, because they did not want these countries to benefit from an increase in the price of gold, given their oppressive governments.) Moreover, the large gold holding countries such as France, Switzerland, and Italy and Germany would benefit, since the value of the gold owned by their central banks would be much higher. And the United States would benefit, since the US Treasury's gold holdings were much larger than those of any other country.

Every finance minister is continually concerned with changes in the price of the national currency relative to the US dollar because of the implications for the profits and the employment in the domestic firms that produce exports and import-competing goods. In the late 1970s, European governments complained that the price of the US dollar in the foreign exchange market was too low, and that US exporters had a tremendous competitive advantage in international markets. In the early 1980s, these same finance ministers complained that interest rates on US dollar securities were too high, which greatly handicapped their ability to follow policies that might offset their own high levels of unemployment. (They didn't complain about the marvelous profits their exporters were earning on their US sales when the US dollar was strong.) Part of the job of being a finance minister in Europe involves complaining about US policies.

Similarly, whether the Japanese yen price of the US dollar should be higher involves not only the United States and Japan but also other countries such as Germany and Korea which produce goods competitive with those produced in Japan. Toyota's profits vary inversely with the foreign exchange value of the yen. When the yen is weak, Japanese auto firms have a tremendous competitive advantage in foreign markets; as the yen becomes stronger, the export competitiveness of

Japanese auto firms declines. Either the Japanese firms will experience a decline in their profit rate if they fail to raise the selling prices of their autos in foreign markets (indeed, some may incur losses); if, however, they raise their selling prices to maintain their profit rates; their sales and their market share will decline

Exporting national problems

Changes in exchange rates redistribute both payments surpluses and payments deficits and jobs and profits among firms and workers in different countries. The immediate consequence of a strengthening of the Japanese yen was to lower profits and wage bonuses in Japanese export industries and to raise profits and permit more rapid wage increases in competing US industries. In the late 1980s and early 1990s, the profitability of Mercedes Benz, BMW, and Porsche from their North American sales declined because the price of the US dollar was low in terms of the German mark. Indeed, both Mercedes and BMW established plants in the United States because production costs were lower than those in Germany.

Exporting national problems is a classic form of international behavior. Foreign votes are not counted in domestic elections. The political costs of domestic measures that might solve an unemployment problem, an inflation problem, or a 'depressed industry' problem are frequently higher than the political costs of exporting the problem. Yet if one country exports its unemployment problem, some other countries are likely to experience a loss of manufacturing jobs. In the Great Depression, nations exported their unemployment with 'beggar-thy-neighbor' policies – tariffs were raised to reduce imports and currencies were devalued to increase exports. Few countries were – or are – eager or willing to import unemployment.

In the 1990s, countries once again appear to be adopting policies that might qualify as 'beggar-thy-neighbor'. Japanese trade surpluses have been more than 3 percent of its GDP, which has proved very useful in maintaining employment in Japanese manufacturing firms when domestic demand growth was extremely sluggish. Taiwan wants a large trade surplus. China prefers large trade surpluses; indeed, its trade surplus has been second only to Japan's. Many other countries want large trade surpluses to compensate for sluggish growth of domestic demand. Obviously not every country can run a large trade surplus at the same time; to the extent that one country achieves trade surpluses, then another country will incur the counterpart trade deficits. Recently that country has been the United States.

The politics and technology of money

The costs of communication and control have declined sharply in the last 30 years as a result of remarkable advances in computing power and telecommunications. The costs of economic distance have declined sharply, and national markets are much more closely linked. Tokyo and London have moved much closer to New York in economic terms, even though the geographic distances are unchanged. At the end of the twentieth century there are several dozen global financial firms with a significant trading activities in these three major national financial centers, as well as in regional centers such as Frankfurt and Singapore.

International financial coordination

The politics of international money is decentralized. Each of the 100+ countries has its own national interests and its own economic objectives. Each national central bank wants to control the rate at which its money supply grows so as to achieve its own employment, price level, and growth objectives. Because the objectives and economic structures of countries differ, so the preferred rates of growth of money supply growth also differ. Germany and Switzerland, for example, are at the top of the hit parade of countries that want a low inflation rate. Other countries seem more concerned about maintaining low levels of unemployment.

International monetary arrangements must somehow accommodate these divergences in the priority attached to low inflation and high levels of employment. International institutions such as the International Monetary Fund (IMF) in Washington, the Bank for International Settlements (BIS) in Basle, Switzerland, and the Organization for Economic Cooperation and Development (OECD) in Paris provide frameworks for coordinating national policies. Finance ministers meet twice a year at the IMF. Presidents and Prime Ministers of the Group of Seven Countries (G-7, née G-3 and now G-8) meet twice a year to discuss the coordination of their policies – or at least to talk about how they might coordinate policies if they were to coordinate them. And small groups of finance officials meet bilaterally to discuss problems of common interest – which almost always means the size of the trade imbalances and the value of the currencies.

The forms of international financial coordination are varied. Central banks borrow national currencies from each other when their holdings of foreign currencies decline, and from time to time they intervene jointly in the foreign exchange markets. Some modest steps have been taken to develop substitutes for gold in central bank holdings of international reserve assets. Such coordination, while useful as a counter to the decentralized decisions of national governments, is rarely an effective substitute for centralized decisionmaking.

In December 1991 the member countries of the then European Community committed themselves to develop a common currency by the late 1990s, in what has become known as the Maastricht Agreement. These countries agreed to a set of criteria to facilitate the move to a common currency; each agreed to reduce its inflation rate below 3 percent, to reduce the ratio of its fiscal deficits to national income to 3 percent, and to hold the ratio of government debt to national income below 60 percent. Soon after most of the Europeans began to learn of the costs of accepting this commitment when interest rates in Germany climbed to very high levels as the Bundesbank adopted a contractive monetary policy to reduce the inflation associated with the costs of reunification of what had been East Germany with West Germany. Great Britain, France, and the other European countries imported these high interest rates from Frankfurt because their currencies were pegged to the German mark; indeed their interest rates were modestly higher than those in Frankfurt because investors were concerned that their currencies might be devalued relative to the mark. Since they did not have the economic stimulus of a large fiscal deficits such as that in Germany associated with reunification, their inflation rates were below those in Germany; as a result, real interest rates in these countries were higher than real interest rates in Germany. So Germany's neighbors in the European Union imported sharp recessions. In September 1992, Great Britain and Italy stopped pegging their currencies within the European Monetary System (EMS); they were then able to reduce interest rates significantly. Spain and Portugal and the Scandinavian countries followed this lead.

Still, the train ride to a common currency has been moving on schedule and 11 of the 15 countries in the European Union are committed to the move to the first phase of a common currency by 1999. In effect, the national central banks will become branches of the new European Central Bank (ECB). The move to a common currency will – if it succeeds – eliminate uncertainty about currency values on intra-European payments. (In the short term, the uncertainty may become transformed into uncertainty about whether countries will continue to abide by their treaty commitments.) The underlying concern is that unemployment in one country (or several countries) may increase to high levels, and the political authorities may be feeble in their responses because they have no control over monetary policy and only a modest ability to use fiscal policy.

The commitment to move to a common European currency has meant that governments in Europe have had to raise taxes relative to expenditures. So unemployment rates in France and some other countries have been above 10 percent. President Chirac of France called an election, and the Socialists won – on the basis of promises of less severe policies. But the contractive fiscal policies have been continued.

The international money game

The 'rules of the game' – the set of commitments that countries have accepted – also may not be effective in setting patterns for national policies. These rules seek to ensure that conflicts among the nations' authorities are resolved in accord with established procedures. When the rules constrain national policies, countries sometimes ignore the rules unilaterally and search for a legal justification later, as did President Nixon when the US Treasury closed its gold window August 1971. During the 1970s, the rules and procedures governing exchange market practices of central banks eroded and monetary practices were increasingly based on ad hoc decisions. Exchange crisis were less frequent, yet the conflicts between Ministers of finance in different countries about currency values – and about trade imbalances – became more severe.

In the 1950s and the 1960s the proponents of floating exchange rates had suggested that import protectionism would decline if countries were to stop pegging their currencies; their reasoning was that governments would no longer feel obliged to adopt tariffs or quotas or other measures to limit imports so as reduce their payments deficits. The evidence of the last 20 years is that trade protectionism has increased, in part because governments have adopted a variety of measures to limit imports when their currencies became overvalued and in part because of the move toward regional trading arrangements.

Firms and individual investors play their own games against this background of changing values for national currencies in the foreign exchange market. They borrow currencies that they expect to fall in value, and acquire securities denominated in currencies they anticipate will appreciate. Sharp foreign exchange traders and corporate treasurers earned millions of dollars – and German marks and Swiss francs – for their companies in the late 1960s and early 1970s by correctly anticipating changes in currency parities. The hedge funds earned billions in

1992 from selling British pounds and Italian lira in anticipation that these currencies would be devalued; these funds lost money in 1994 when they bet that the US dollar would appreciate. Investors made billions of dollars from their bet that the Mexican peso would be devalued in 1994.

Not all corporate treasurers, however, participated in these profits. In the 1960s, some of them believed the statements of the authorities that parities would not be changed, invested accordingly, and lost their jobs – and others deserved to. Corporate treasurers get paid big bucks – and lots of pounds and marks – from doing smart finance. During the mid-1970s, some firms reported losses in the tens of millions of dollars because of changes in exchange rates. In 1992 several Japanese oil firms reported losses of more than $1 billion as a result of their (misguided) foreign exchange transactions. The corporate treasurers of international firms are supposed to know all about profiting from differences in interest rates in various countries, from changes in exchange rates, and from the misfortunes of ministers of finance. Many foreign exchange traders developed great confidence in their ability to predict changes in exchange rates during the pegged-rate period. Their confidence led them to continue speculating on a large scale during the period of floating exchange rates. Some did well. Some did not – Banque du Bruxelles reported losses of $60 million; Franklin National, $42 million; Herstatt, $70 million. These were the last large losses ever reported by Franklin and Herstatt, for they then went bankrupt.

Bankers and corporate treasurers learn and adapt. By the 1980s the large international banks were reporting profits of several hundreds of millions of dollars a year from trading foreign exchange. These banks reported profits on their foreign exchange transactions when the US dollar was appreciating, and they reported profits when the US dollar was depreciating. A key question became the source of these profits – the foreign exchange market is a zero-sum game, so that if banks are consistently securing profits in their foreign exchange transactions, some other groups must be incurring the counterpart losses – or so it would seem.

In addition to predicting exchange rate movements, the international money game involves firms and individuals circumventing the regulations of their countries. Indian peasants hoard gold because they believe gold is a better store of value than the rupee. Shoppers in Warsaw hold US dollars and German marks as stores of value; indeed, the prices of apartments in Warsaw, Moscow, and Tel Aviv are quoted in the US dollar, and the sellers will accept payment only in US dollars. The US dollar holdings of Russians are almost as large as their holdings of roubles. American banks have established branches in London and Nassau to avoid the regulations of US monetary authorities. Italians once carried suitcases loaded with lira notes into Switzerland because they want to reduce the government's tax bite. All these moves are designed to increase personal income.

Interdependence of business and currency values

One view about the game – a view reinforced by the daily newspaper columns – is that changes in currency values and international business competition are independent of each other. A competing view – the view of this book – is that these events are related, and that patterns of international trade and investment are affected by changes in exchange rates. Changes in exchange rates in turn result from changes in investor views about inflation rates and especially changes in anticipated inflation rates and the international capital flows undertaken in response to changes in these views.

In the 1950s and even more in the 1960s, US firms were on a global march, and rapidly expanded their sales abroad and their ownership of productive facilities in many foreign countries. US companies competed aggressively in Canada, Europe, and Latin America, buying out some of their host-country competitors and forcing others into insolvency. Machines Bull, the last independent French-owned computer firm, could not survive in the competitive international league because the world price level for computers, set by IBM, was too low relative to French production costs. Nor could Rolls-Royce continue to compete in jet aircraft engines, for the prices set by its US competitors – General Electric and the Pratt and Whitney division of United Technologies – were too low relative to British production costs. Rolls went bankrupt and then was restructured. British Leyland, the largest auto firm in Great Britain, was forced into bankruptcy because British costs were rising much more rapidly than the world price of automobiles.

In the late 1970s and even more in the late 1980s, Japanese firms were expanding their foreign investments. The Japanese auto firms were extremely vigorous competitors; within a span of 15 years they had upgraded the size, styling, and quality of their product lines. Japanese consumer electronics firms dominated the global industry and especially the production of quality components; the pace of new product development was exceptional. The banks headquartered in

Tokyo and Osaka dominated the hit parade of the world's largest banks. For a while, the quip was that the value of the real estate in Japan was twice the value of US real estate – even though GDP in Japan was less than half GDP in the United States. The market value of Japanese stocks was twice the market value of US stocks. Alas, it was not to be. Early in 1990, asset prices in Japan began to implode. Then Japanese banks incurred massive losses on their real estate loans and their loans to construction companies, and had to be bailed out by the Japanese government.

The Asian Tigers – Taiwan, Korea, Hong Kong, and Singapore – have experienced rapid growth, much like Japan. Then the dragons – Thailand, Malaysia, Indonesia and, to a lesser extent, the Philippines, achieved high rates of growth. China realized growth rates of more than 10 percent a year beginning in the late 1970s, and the growth rate was significantly higher for the seacoast provinces.

These remarkable economic achievements led to the view that a Pacific Century was dawning, and that the US role as the dominant economic power in the twentieth century would be displaced. But the bloom about Japan faded in the early 1990s as prices of Japanese equities and Japanese real estate fell sharply. By the mid-1990s the Japanese banks were retrenching, and reducing both their foreign loans and their foreign offices.

The politics and technology of money

The drama of international finance reflects the contrast between the politics and the technology of money. All the financial securities in the world – currency notes, bank deposits, government bonds, mortgages – are denominated in one national currency or another; each currency – the US dollar, the German mark, the Japanese yen, the British pound – is a brand name, more or less like the brand names on automobiles, cigarettes, toothpastes, detergents, and cornflakes. The advantages of having a national money are rarely questioned. Some these advantages may seem obvious. A national money – like a national airline, a steel mill, and, at one time, a branch of the Playboy Club – brings prestige. Control of the production of a national money brings profit. Kings and presidents finance wars in Algeria and Vietnam and build monuments to themselves with newly produced money.

Control over the production of money frequently means that the supply of money increases more rapidly than the demand, which leads to debasement of the money as its purchasing power declines. Inflation is an indirect or backdoor form of taxation: the US price level in 1995 was more than four times higher than the US price level in 1970. Debtors benefitted greatly from the decline in the purchasing power of money, especially in the 1970s – and the biggest debtor of them all is the US Treasury. Taxation through the printing press and inflation is easier and less messy than raising tax rates; the inflation tax appears hidden, at least for a while. Sovereigns manipulate monetary policy because they want to secure full employment, speed growth and development, fight wars, or accomplish some other worthy objective that will win the approval of their constituents.

Central bankers and finance ministers may not be able to make their country's economic policies effective unless they can isolate their national market for money and credit from the international market. The US military draft of the 1960s provides an analogy: if too many potential draftees moved to Canada or Sweden or failed to register, the draft would not have been effective. Similarly, if too many holders of US dollar securities, or British pound securities, or French franc securities, anticipate the actions of the authorities and move their money abroad, their governments' policies will be frustrated.

Over the last several decades the links among national monies have become even stronger as a result of changes in technology, and the sharp reduction in the costs of transportation and communication across national borders. As these costs of information continue to diminish, the effectiveness of national monopolies in the production of money declines. As knowledge about foreign investment opportunities grows and the cost of taking advantage of these opportunities declines, differences in national monetary systems become increasingly important.

In a world of isolated countries, kings had monopoly power over their subjects' monies; there was no other place for these subjects to send their wealth and no other currency in which they might hold their funds to escape the sovereign's taxes. So the politics of money was largely national. But the monopoly power of kings and presidents has been declining, and the constituents of various governments are adjusting to this new world more rapidly than the governments. Governments frequently need international agreements to revise established institutions, and negotiating these agreements takes years.

Today, because of low-cost transportation and instantaneous communication, the several national markets for monies, bonds, deposits, and shares denominated in the various currencies are – in fact – parts of one international market. At any given moment, the price of IBM shares in Amsterdam and the price of IBM shares in London – and in the other foreign centers where IBM shares are traded – differ only by pennies from the price in New York. A particular group of traders known as 'arbitragers' buy these shares in the centers where they are cheap and sell them where they are dear to profit from the difference, thus keeping prices in line. The technology of money is international.

The plan of this book

Part I of the book examines the structure of national monies, focusing on the tension between economic pressures toward integration of national monetary policies and political pressures toward decentralization. The concern throughout is with the basic components of the international financial system – gold, the US dollar, the foreign exchange market, the Eurodollar market – and with the problems created by changes in the price of oil and in the relationship among the inflation rates in different countries. One major concern is how the increasing economic integration in Europe will affect the United States; a counterpart question involves the impacts of changes in the rates of economic growth in Japan, China, and in Southeast Asian countries on the competitiveness of US goods.

Part II of the book discusses some of the direct and indirect consequences of segmenting the world into multiple currency areas. Each chapter focuses on a particular issue. Thus, Chapter 16 on taxation considers the impact of differences in national rates on the competitive position of firms headquartered in different countries. Chapter 17 on commercial banking asks whether, as the technology of the banking industry changes so that the distance between banks and their customers becomes less important, banks in the United States, Europe, or Japan will have a competitive advantage in the international marketplace.

During the last 100 years, changes in technology have widened the marketplace for goods, services, and securities. For generations the market was smaller than the nation-state; at one time there were more than 12 different regional stock exchanges within the United States; now there are six; even now, there are five stock exchanges in Germany, and two in Japan. The expansion of the boundaries of the market beyond the fixed boundaries of the state has threatened the viability of national economic independence and the future of many national industries. Adjustments to the problems created by efforts at national monetary independence are inevitable, but the form that this adjustment will take remains in doubt. One adjustment involves harmonizing national policies to reduce the competitive advantage – or disadvantage – encountered by firms in various countries as a result of policy differences. Thus initiatives have been taken to establish uniform capital requirement for banks headquartered in each of the industrial countries. Banks in some countries will no longer have a competitive advantage of lower levels of capital requirement; the alternative adjustment involves protecting national firms against more successful foreign competitors. A variety of discriminatory barriers could block or retard the movement of goods and capital, thus protecting the efficacy of national policies.

Both types of adjustment are likely. Yet 20, 50, perhaps even 100 years from now, the problems created by the multitude of national monies will remain. For, inevitably, the national authorities will manage their economies and develop regulations for their national constituents. And firms and investors will seek to profit from differences in national regulations and national policies.

Part I

International Monetary Arrangements, Money, and Politics

3
'The Greatest Monetary Agreement in History'

International agreements

The Smithsonian Institution in Washington, DC is the repository for America's artifacts. Lindbergh's *Spirit of St Louis* hangs from the rafters. The Hope Diamond is there. So are George Washington's uniforms and the largest blue whale ever caught. In December 1971 the US Secretary of the Treasury met with the finance ministers of Great Britain, Canada, Japan, Germany, and a few other industrial countries at the Smithsonian and agreed to a new set of foreign exchange values for the various European currencies and the Japanese yen in terms of the US dollar. President Nixon called the Smithsonian Agreement 'The Greatest Monetary Agreement In History.' The remarkable accomplishment of the agreement was that more exchange rates were simultaneously realigned in a multinational framework than ever before.

By mid-summer 1972 Great Britain ceased pegging the pound, and the pound almost immediately depreciated by 10 percent. Then, early in 1973, Germany permitted the mark to float, and it began to appreciate sharply. Most other industrial countries followed Germany and also ceased pegging their currencies. Once these countries stopped pegging their currencies, the semi-revived Bretton Woods agreement was dead, replaced by a floating exchange rate arrangement. The 'Greatest Monetary Agreement in History' lasted for a year and a month – more or less. In effect, the breakdown of the agreement meant that the existing machinery for resolving disputes about trade imbalances and exchange rates could be sent to some monetary counterpart of the Smithsonian Institution to take its place alongside earlier monetary agreements as another historic artifact. The International Monetary Fund (IMF) which had been established to manage the system of adjustable parities was instantly obsolete – and a thousand well-paid international civil servants scrambled to find another *raison d'être*.

In December 1991 the Prime Ministers of the member countries of the European Community met at Maastricht – the capital of a relatively small province in the South of the Netherlands – and agreed to adopt a common European currency by the end of the 1990s. In the 1980s each of these countries had agreed to peg its currency to those of other members to facilitate the trade and investment with neighboring countries. In the late 1980s changes in the parities among their currencies were less and less frequent, so the commitment to move to a common European currency in the 1990s seemed like an extension of earlier commitments to maintain parities for currencies.

In September 1992 Finland – not a member of the European Union – devalued its currency by more than 30 percent, in response to a sharp decline in its exports to what had been the Soviet Union. Investors – speculators – then began to sell the Swedish krona in anticipation that Sweden's competitive position would weaken as Finland's competitive position improved, since Finnish exports and Swedish exports were somewhat competitive in foreign markets. Investors also began to sell the British pound, the Italian lira, the Spanish peseta, and other currencies in anticipation that these currencies might also be devalued. By the end of 1992, more than half of the currencies of the members of the European Community had been devalued or allowed to float. Maastricht seemed barely alive – still it survived and subsequently Germany and France and their neighbors returned to the timetable for the move to a common currency.

Both the Smithsonian and the Maastricht Agreements were efforts to reduce uncertainty about exchange rates. The premise of both agreements was that international trade and investment would be enhanced if traders and investors had greater confidence about currency values in the future. Some of the countries that had participated in the Maastricht Agreement had a more ambitious agenda, for they believed that a common currency was a necessary complement to a 'single integrated market' and both were necessary steps in the move toward greater political integration within Europe.

Rules and myths of the gold standard

The attraction of the gold standard

A hundred years ago, according to popular economic history, the world was on the gold standard. Participation in the gold standard was open to any country which agreed to buy and sell gold at a fixed price – the mint parity – in terms of its own currency. The gold standard was not based on a formal international agreement; instead, individual countries believed that their own economic well-being would be enhanced if they pegged their currencies to gold, for they then would be able to borrow on more favorable terms in London, the world's principal financial center. Once several countries had established parities between their currencies and gold, the exchange rate between any two national currencies was set by the ratio of their mint parities, adjusted for any difference in the gold content of their coins. For example, the mint parity for the US dollar was $20.67 in 1900, while the mint parity for the British pound was 3 pounds, 17 shillings, 10 pence (£3.17s.10d.). The US dollar–British pound exchange rate was $20.67 divided by £3 17s 10d, or $4.86 per pound after adjustment for the somewhat greater gold content of US coins than of British coins.

Moreover under the gold standard each central bank was ready, on demand of private parties, to buy and sell gold at its mint parity. Whenever exporters within a country acquired gold from their foreign customers, they could sell the gold to their central bank in exchange for domestic money. The central bank would then print more money to pay for its gold purchases; the domestic money supply and the central bank's gold holdings would increase at the same time – indeed, as part of the same transaction. Conversely, the domestic money supply would decline whenever importers, in order to make payments abroad, sold domestic money to the central bank to buy gold to ship to their foreign suppliers.

The attraction of the gold standard – the reason a return to this type of arrangement appears so attractive to Jack Kemp, formerly a quarterback for the Buffalo Bills and later a candidate for the Republican Presidential Nomination in 1996 and again in 2000 – is that under the gold standard consumer price levels were remarkably stable in the long run. The US consumer price level in 1900 was only two-thirds as high as in 1800 – although there had been sharp changes (both increases and decreases) in the price level during various decades. The US consumer price level increased modestly in the 1850s, and then nearly doubled during the Civil War – but the United States had gone off gold at the beginning of the war. After the war the price level decreased slowly. And during various financial crises – 1847, 1873, 1884, 1890, 1893, 1907 – the price level frequently fell but usually by no more than 3 or 4 percent a year.

Under the gold standard market forces automatically and simultaneously answered two important questions: how rapidly should the domestic money supply increase in each country, and how rapidly should the international money supply grow? The 'rules of the game' of the gold standard held that a country's money supply increased when it achieved a payments surplus, and declined when it had a payments deficit. Exchange rate arrangements and monetary policies were compatible; there was never any risk that the rate of growth of the domestic money would be so rapid that the central bank might sell so much of its gold that it would no longer be able to maintain the value of its currency in terms of foreign currencies.

The flow of gold from each year's new production meant that the gold holdings of all central banks could increase together; conceivably every country could have a payments surplus at the same time. In the 1850s, after the discovery of gold in California, and again at the end of the nineteenth century following gold discoveries in the Canadian Yukon, Alaska, and South Africa, the more rapid growth in gold holdings led to increases in the supply of domestic monies and to worldwide increases in commodity prices. Increases or decreases in price levels were accepted as a natural part of economic life, much like the weather. But these increases were rarely larger than 3 percent a year.

Market forces also determined how rapidly the supply of international money should grow. The amount of gold produced during any period depended on the relationship between the price that central banks would pay for gold and the costs incurred by the gold mining firms in discovering and producing gold. These costs in turn varied with changes in the consumer price level; when the price level increased, these costs would increase. Gold production would then decline, since producers were squeezed between rising costs and a fixed selling price, the mint parity. Gold holdings would then increase less rapidly – and national money supplies also would increase less rapidly. On the other hand, when the commodity price levels declined, the costs incurred in mining gold would decline, and gold mining firms then would then find it profitable to increase production. Money supplies would grow more rapidly, and the decline in the commodity price levels would be dampened or stopped. So, changes in the amounts of gold produced and changes in the consumer price level were components of a stable, self-correcting system. The pieces fit, at least in theory. And the stability of the consumer price levels in both the United States and Great Britain in the long run led to the inference that the pieces fit in practice.

The gold standard in practice

The gold standard in practice was never as systematic as this descriptive model suggests. Changes in the gold production and gold supplies often reflected the chance of new gold discoveries and innovations in gold ore refining processes rather than changes in the consumer price level and gold mining costs. Changes in the money supplies in individual countries did not follow the lock step, mechanical linkages that the model suggested.

Moreover during the infrequent wars in the nineteenth century (infrequent compared with the wars in the twentieth) the management of money was directed at financing military expenditures. But the fact that the countries went off gold when they went to war should not be viewed as a criticism of how the system worked when countries retained their parities. The automatic, anonymous, and consistent attributes of the gold standard attracted numerous supporters who advocated adherence to the system as a basis for managing national monies.

Several developments associated with the First World War reduced the relevance of the gold standard model. The war demonstrated that nationalism was a powerful force in Britain and France as well as in Germany and Central Europe. The monetary counterpart of nationalism was that central banks managed monetary policies to help finance their own war efforts. The cohesiveness of the international monetary arrangements was becoming fragmented even as the costs of economic distance were declining.

Wartime inflation, moreover, pushed commodity price levels in the 1920s to levels at least twice as high as in 1913. Higher price levels meant increased demands for both money and for gold and, because of higher gold production costs, a reduced level of gold output. There were persistent fears of a gold shortage. Few countries were willing to accept the substantial reductions in commodity price levels that would have been needed to raise gold production – and no one contemplated that central banks would pay higher prices for gold than the prices they paid before the war. Still if the demand for international money was to be satisfied, either the price of gold in terms of national currencies would have to be increased or substitutes for gold as an international money would have to be developed or national price levels would have to decline.

Finally, the war brought about a sharp increase in US economic power in both absolute and relative terms. The stimulus of the war tied the regional economies of the nation together, linkages that would otherwise have developed more slowly. The United States, moreover, escaped both the material destruction and the postwar financial turmoil that befell most of the countries in Europe. After the First World War, the US economy was about as large as the combined economies of the 10 next largest countries – a much more dominant position in the world economy than Great Britain had ever enjoyed.

The breakdown of the gold standard

The monetary problems of the decades following the First World War revolved around these three themes: nationalism, the shortage of international money, and shifts in economic power toward – and, much later, from – the United States. The disintegration of the international system in the 1930s resulted from the failure to adjust institutional arrangements to the changes in the economic realities.

The breakdown of the gold standard became starkly evident in the economic behavior of nations during the 1920s and 1930s. At the beginning of the First World War, most European countries left the gold standard, since their rates of inflation were much higher than the US inflation rate; indeed, the US dollar was the only major currency that remained convertible into gold. During the early 1920s the European currencies floated in the foreign exchange market, and many of them depreciated sharply in terms of both gold and the US dollar. The reliance on floating exchange rates was viewed as an interim measure, for most governments in Europe wanted to return to the gold standard and again peg their currencies at their prewar gold parities. But this objective could be achieved only if they permitted their domestic price levels to decline substantially – or if there was a substantial increase in the US price level. Few countries were willing to adopt the policies to reduce their price levels by the amounts necessary so that a return to the 1913 parities would be feasible, and the United States was unwilling to increase the US price level to facilitate the necessary adjustment.

By the mid-1920s, most European currencies were again pegged to gold. The British pound, the Swiss franc, and a few other currencies – those of countries that were neutral during the war – were again at their 1913 parities. Many more currencies had been devalued extensively in terms of both gold and the dollar – for example, the French franc, which had been worth 18.3 cents in 1913, sold for 3.9 cents in 1926.

This system of pegged rates held together for several years. But there were too many inconsistencies among the pieces for the arrangement to be viable for long. The British pound was overvalued; the British price level had not declined sufficiently so that British goods could be competitive in foreign markets and the prewar gold parity again viable. In contrast, the French franc was undervalued; the decline in its foreign exchange value as a result of a speculative attack in the 1924–6 period was much greater than was justified by the increase in the French price level relative to the price levels of its major trading partners.

In the late 1920s, the central banks in Argentina and Chile and other primary-product producing countries experienced a sharp decline in export earnings as the prices of farm products fell sharply; these countries again stopped pegging their currencies. Then in May 1931, Austria went off gold, because the high interest rates adopted to attract funds from other countries were causing high levels of domestic bankruptcy. In July 1931, Germany went off gold, and for very much the same reason: the costs to the domestic economy in terms of the high level of unemployment of maintaining the parity were deemed too high. Then, in September 1931, the Bank of England stopped selling gold, and the pound depreciated sharply.

In 1933, immediately after President Franklin D. Roosevelt took office, the US government ceased pegging the dollar to gold at the $20.67 parity as one measure to limit the run on the banks for gold and to reduce the likelihood that additional banks might fail. The US dollar floated until early 1934, when a new $35 parity was established. Two years later, other currencies – the French and Swiss francs, and the Dutch guilder – were also devalued in terms of gold. Within a six-year period, nearly every currency had been devalued in terms of gold, many by as much as 50 to 70 percent, and the alignment of currency values in 1939 was not very different from the alignment 10 years earlier.

This sequence of currency devaluations in the 1930s by the industrial countries – Great Britain, the United States, France, the Netherlands, and Switzerland – resembled a sequence of falling dominoes. Each country devalued its currency because the interest rates necessary to maintain its established parity led to high levels of domestic unemployment. Each country was concerned that more expansive monetary policies that might be adopted to lead to higher levels of employment would lead to large gold outflows at the established parities. Some countries sought to stimulate domestic employment by measures to increase exports and to limit imports, including increases in tariffs. Each country wanted to import jobs by reducing the price of its goods in foreign markets and raising the price of foreign goods in its domestic market. But no country wanted to export jobs at a time of substantial domestic unemployment. So the world economic system disintegrated behind higher trade barriers because of increasing priority to national economic objectives.

The Bretton Woods system

The fragmentation of monetary and trading arrangements in the inter-war period demonstrated the need for an institutional framework that would enable countries to follow policies directed toward domestic objectives without exporting their problems. The economic institutions were unable to cope with the problem of obtaining consistency among the financial policies of the major countries. During the Second World War, the United States and Great Britain took the initiative in developing an international treaty that would reduce the likelihood that countries would adopt policies in the postwar period similar to those in the interwar period, and particularly in the 1930s. This treaty – the Articles of Agreement of the International Monetary Fund (informally called the Bretton Woods Agreement after the New Hampshire mountain resort where the final negotiations took place in July 1944) – had two major components.

The IMF Agreement

One was a set of rules or constraints directed at the exchange rate behavior of member countries; these rules required each country to state a parity for its currency in terms of gold or the US dollar and limited the ability of each country to change its parity. The thrust of the IMF Agreement was that unnecessary changes in exchange rates should be avoided, while desired and justifiable changes should take place in an orderly manner. The rationale was that once currencies were no longer pegged, some central banks would seek to manage the foreign exchange value of their currencies to enhance achievement of their domestic economic objectives.

The second major component of the IMF treaty led to the establishment of a pool of member countries' currencies – the US dollar, the British pound, and the French franc as well as the currencies of every other member. The IMF would be a 'lender of last resort,' the currencies in this pool would be available to its members to help them finance payments deficits, provided they complied with certain conditions; access to these currencies were expected to reduce the need to devalue their currencies. The rules about procedures for changing exchange rates and the pool of national currencies were part of a package; it was believed that member countries would be more likely to accept the constraints on changing their parities if they were assured that they could borrow foreign currencies from the Fund to finance their payments deficits.

Shortcomings and increasing stress

The IMF Agreement proved to have two shortcomings. first, there was no mechanism to induce countries to change their parities when they became inappropriate, which proved especially relevant for countries with persistent and large balance of payments surpluses. Second, the components of the system were not compatible: the agreement focused on the behavior of individual member countries, but not on consistency among the monetary policies of the major industrial countries, the exchange rate system, and the supply of international money.

The emphasis of national monetary policies on domestic objectives and the reluctance of countries to alter their parities subjected the Bretton Woods system to increasing stress, especially in the second half of the 1960s. Changes in currency parities became inevitable, with most industrial countries pursuing independent national monetary policies. But national authorities were reluctant to recognize the implications of their monetary policies for their exchange rate parities: they retained the exchange market arrangements of the gold standard even though they were unwilling to accept the increases and decreases in the national price levels that enabled countries to maintain their parities in response to various shocks. The IMF rules sought to minimize unnecessary changes in exchange parities but, in fact, changes in parities proved too infrequent and especially too long-delayed: the adjustable parities of the IMF system were 'sticky' or 'frozen'.

During the 1950s and 1960s, the supply of international money increased less rapidly than the demand. The analogy with the 1920s is strong – in both periods, the problem was aggravated by sharp increases in national price levels during and after a world war; the higher price levels led to an increase in the demand for both international money and for gold. At the same time, the increase in price levels meant higher levels of mining costs, which deterred increases in gold output.

The increase in the central bank demand for gold was greater than the increase in monetary gold stocks resulting from new production. As a result, individual central banks could satisfy their demand for gold only by buying gold from other countries. Between 1950 and 1970, US gold holdings declined from $23 billion to $11 billion in response to the increase in the demand for gold from other countries, and especially those in Europe.

One alternative to increased central bank holdings of gold was increased holdings of short-term securities denominated in the US dollar, the British pound, and other major currencies. Foreign countries could add to their holdings of liquid dollar securities if they achieved payments surpluses – but the purchase of US dollar securities by countries in Western Europe and Japan meant that the United States would incur payments deficits. Foreign holdings of US dollar securities increased from $8 billion in 1950 to $47 billion in 1970.

The US payments deficit

The United States could supply dollar securities to meet the international money demands of other countries without limit; there was a virtually inexhaustible supply of US Treasury securities and deposits in US banks. (Whether the US national interest or the system's interests would be served by the continued exports of these bills and deposits is a different issue.) But the US ability to supply gold to foreign central banks was limited; each billion dollars of gold sold to foreign central banks meant the gold holdings of the US Treasury declined by a billion. The US dilemma was that it was unable to distinguish, in the design of its balance-of-payments policies, between those foreign countries that wanted to add to their holdings of US dollar securities and those countries that wanted to add to their gold holdings.

For most of the 1950s and the 1960s (probably until 1967 or even 1968), foreign holdings of dollars increased and the US Treasury's gold holdings declined, not because US goods were too expensive or foreign goods were too cheap, but because foreign central banks wanted to add to their holdings of international money. During this period, the United States became the principal source of international money because other sources were inadequate. But the United States could not sell US dollars and gold to foreign central banks without incurring a payments deficit, at least as a payments deficit had been traditional defined.

Numerous explanations were offered for the US payments deficit, including increased US imports of Scotch whisky, French brandy, and German beer; increases in US military expenditures in Western Europe and Southeast Asia; and decreases in US exports of automobiles and steel. But these stories about larger US payments and smaller US receipts were the result of the persistent strong foreign demand for US dollar securities and for gold. The logic is that if other countries wanted to add to their holdings of gold and US dollar securities, they were obliged to reduce the prices of their goods relative to the price of US goods so they would achieve payments surpluses.

Policy responses to payments imbalances

Reducing demand for gold

The implication of the worldwide gold shortage was that central banks were buying and selling gold at prices that were too low relative to the costs of gold production. One solution was an increase in the price of gold in terms of all currencies. Gold production would be stimulated; more gold would be mined each year and the value of gold output would increase even more rapidly. The private demand for gold would be lower because gold would be more expensive, so a larger share of the newly produced gold would be sold to central banks. In this way, the central banks in Europe would be able to satisfy their demand for gold without coming to the US Treasury. Instead, they could purchase it from South Africa, the Soviet Union, and other gold producing countries. At some price – $40, or $50, or $70 – everyone's demand for gold could be satisfied.

If, on the other hand, the monetary price of gold were to remain unchanged, then the gold shortage would disappear only if the demand for gold declined. One way to reduce the demand would be to stem the flow of dollars to foreign central banks, thus reducing their ability to buy gold from the US Treasury. During the 1960s the US authorities adopted a series of measures to reduce the flow of dollars abroad. Foreign recipients of US government aid were obliged to spend the money on US goods, even though foreign goods were cheaper. US government agencies were directed to buy their goods from domestic sources unless the prices of similar foreign goods were lower, first by 6 percent, then by 12 percent and then by 50 percent; the US Army began to ship Milwaukee beer to Munich. Purchases of foreign securities by US residents were taxed, initially at a rate of 1 percent, then 2 percent. Purchases of foreign securities by US firms and financial institutions were subjected to 'voluntary' controls in 1965; the controls became mandatory in 1968. Measures were adopted to increase US receipts from foreigners – for example, US airlines offered special low fares to foreign tourists visiting the United States. Germany and several other countries were induced to buy more military equipment in the United States; if they did not, US authorities indicated than they might reduce the number of US troops stationed overseas.

These measures effectively devalued the dollar by the 'back door,' because taxes and other barriers to US purchases of foreign goods and securities raised their prices to US residents. Individually these measures reduced US payments abroad for particular types of purchases. Yet the annual US payments deficit remained about as large in the mid-1960s as it had been in the late 1950s and early 1960s. These measures appeared to affect the composition of US payments and receipts, but not the size of the US payments deficit.

One explanation for the apparent failure of these measures was that US tourist expenditures abroad were increasing; another, that US firms were investing more abroad; the length of the list of special explanations was long. An alternative explanation is that, as a group, other countries wanted to increase their holdings of international money at an annual rate of $2–$3 billion a year – and so the United States passively adjusted to supply the increase in these holdings. Whenever the payments surpluses of other countries were too low, they adopted measures to increase receipts or reduce payments. So the measures taken by the United States to reduce the US payments deficit were more or less neutralized by offsetting measures adopted by other countries to maintain their payments surpluses (Figure 3.1).

The US authorities adopted somewhat different measures to reduce the official foreign demand for gold. US Treasury secretaries cajoled their foreign counterparts not to buy gold. The level of US troops in Germany was tied to Germany's commitment not to buy more gold. The US Treasury developed new securities for sale to foreign central banks; these securities were denominated in the German mark, the Swiss franc, and other foreign currencies in the hope that foreign central banks would find these securities more attractive than US dollar securities, and good substitutes for gold.

By 1965 the US government began to recognize that the US balance of payments deficit could better be explained by the foreign demand for gold and US dollar securities than by the overvaluation of the dollar. Devising new institutional arrangements that would satisfy the foreign demand for international money without forcing the United States to incur payments deficits year after year was a complex undertaking. The countries with the balance of payment surpluses were not convinced that the US deficit was a problem of the system; rather, they believed that mismanagement of US monetary and fiscal policies had led to the large deficits. Moreover, some countries – France, the Netherlands, Belgium, Switzerland, and, to a lesser extent, Italy and Germany – preferred to hold most of their international money in the

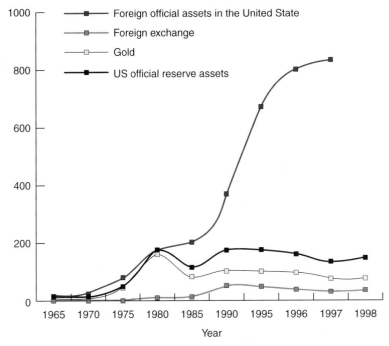

Figure 3.1 US international monetary position, 1965–98, billion US dollars

form of gold. They favored a worldwide increase in the price of gold, primarily for political reasons. The US authorities, in contrast, were reluctant to increase the US dollar price of gold, primarily for political reasons. US voters might conclude that a devaluation of the US dollar in terms of gold reflected poor financial management; and, internationally, revaluation profits would go to South Africa and the Soviet Union, countries not high on the list of those that the United States wanted to benefit from windfalls. Moreover speculators in gold would also be rewarded.

Special Drawing Rights

The US government wanted the IMF to produce a security that would satisfy the demands of other countries for international money. This security, colloquially termed 'paper gold,' would have the monetary but not the physical attributes of gold – it would not glitter, nor would it have a high value-to-weight ratio. Political negotiations would determine the appropriate rate of production of paper gold. European governments – especially the French – were reluctant to accept the US initiative until the US payments deficit was eliminated, but the conundrum was that the US payments deficit could not be eliminated until the foreign demand for international money declined.

The US view eventually prevailed, and an international treaty was signed providing for the production of a new international money, known as Special Drawing Rights (SDRs), within the IMF framework. Some 10 billion of SDRs were produced between 1970 and 1972.

Perhaps the SDR arrangement would have been successful in resolving the system's needs for an increasing supply of international money at the end of the 1960s in the absence of any major shocks. But with the Vietnam war and the increase in US and world inflation rates, the SDR arrangement became irrelevant even before it became operational.

The monetary impact of Vietnam

The irony of the late 1960s was that just as the Europeans came to accept the view that their demand for payments surpluses might be connected with and, perhaps even be the cause of, the persistent US payments deficit, the cause of the deficit changed. In 1969 the US payments deficit of $6 billion was substantially larger than could be explained by the demands of other countries for international reserve assets. The overseas spending of US military forces increased sharply – and, more importantly, US prices rose rapidly, reducing the competitiveness of US exports. As US incomes and US prices rose, so did US demand for imports.

The United States wanted other countries to take the initiative in restoring the payments balance. Whenever the international money holdings of one or two countries increase at a faster rate than they wish – a not unlikely event in a world of more than 100 currencies – these countries have an exchange rate problem, which they can resolve either by revaluing their currencies or by other measures to increase their international payments. From time to time in the 1960s, Germany and perhaps Switzerland were in this position; so, in 1969 and 1970, were Canada and Japan. When a few countries have excessively large payments surpluses, it does not follow that the United States should limit its payments to all countries as a group, as it did from 1960 on. But when many countries have excessively large payments surpluses at more or less the same time, there is a much stronger case for the US government to take initiatives to reduce the payments imbalance.

Altering currency parities

The European governments were in a delicate position. They wanted to force the United States to reduce its payments deficit. They might threaten to buy gold from the US Treasury using the funds acquired from the sale of some of their US dollar securities; many central banks had initially acquired these dollars in the belief that the US Treasury would convert them into gold on demand at a price of $35, but this premise obviously was no longer tenable. A few countries might buy small amounts of gold – $10 million or $25 million at a time – from the US Treasury. But for Germany, Italy, Japan, and other countries with large dollar holdings, the US dollar was effectively inconvertible into gold even though ostensibly the US Treasury remained ready to sell gold to foreign central banks on demand. The European threat to convert dollars into gold was no longer credible, for then the US Treasury might stop selling gold.

If the Europeans could no longer buy gold from the US Treasury with their dollars, the wisdom of their acquiring substantial amounts of both gold and dollars would be questioned. Their purchases of US dollar securities would be criticized because the dollars would no longer be convertible into gold. And their purchases of gold would be criticized because a decision by the US Treasury not to buy or sell gold would cloud the future of gold as an international money.

From 1969 through the summer of 1971, the underlying issue was whether the United States or the European countries and Japan would take the initiative in altering currency parities, for it was increasingly obvious that the parities would have to be changed. Germany revalued the mark in October 1969. Canada returned to a floating rate in June 1970. Through late 1970 and the beginning of 1971, speculative pressure against the US dollar mounted, as it became more and more evident that the European currencies and the Japanese yen would increase in price in terms of the US dollar; the payments imbalances were too large to be sustained indefinitely. What remained unclear was when the change in the alignment of currency values would take place, and which country or countries would take the initiative in changing this alignment.

In May 1971 speculative pressure increased still further; Germany and the Netherlands followed the Canadian example and permitted their currencies to float. Switzerland revalued its currency by about 5 percent, and so did Austria. But investors were not assuaged, and continued to move billions and billions from dollar securities to securities denominated in the German mark, the British pound, the Swiss franc, and the Japanese yen.

Devaluation of the dollar

The crisis came to a head in early August. The then leading US congressional authority on international finance suggested that the US dollar price of gold be raised slightly – that the US dollar should be devalued. Speculative pressure against the dollar greatly intensified. Finally, on August 15, President Nixon announced that as part of his New Economic Policy, the US Treasury would suspend gold sales and purchases. (Once it became obvious that the $35 parity would not remain viable until November 1972, it was in President Nixon's domestic political interest to advance the suspension of US gold sales as far as possible before the 1972 election if closing the gold window could not be delayed until after the election.) However, the decision to suspend gold transactions did not automatically lead to changes in the alignment of currency values. Most foreign countries were reluctant to revalue their currencies because of the adverse impacts of any revaluation on jobs and profits in their export industries. Because of this concern, the US government also adopted a surcharge of 10 percent on all imports subject to tariffs as a way to raise the dollar price of these goods – and to reduce US purchases. US government officials made it clear that this import surcharge would remain in effect until currency parities were realigned, discriminatory trade barriers against US imports were reduced, and Europe and Japan agreed to begin negotiations toward a new international monetary system. The Europeans and Japanese stopped pegging their currencies to the US dollar, and their currencies began to rise in price in terms of the dollar.

Much of the monetary history of the 1970s is traceable to the delay in not changing the alignment of parities in 1969. Because of this delay, the United States incurred a $40 billion payments deficit in the 1969–71 period. The counterpart of this US payments deficit was that other countries as a group had balance of payments surpluses. Their purchases of $40 billion led to a very rapid expansion in their money supplies, which in turn contributed greatly to worldwide inflation.

Much of history has a 'what if' quality. Assume the US government had been much less resistant to raising the monetary price of gold in 1961 and altering the exchange rate alignment in 1969. Both changes were made – but long after they should have been made. If these changes had been made earlier, the monetary history of the 1970s would have been different, and probably very different.

Monetary artifacts and the Smithsonian agreement

The suspension of US gold sales was inevitable at some time; the 10 percent surcharge was not. The surcharge was levied when most countries were in a recession – and, as in the 1930s, these countries found it attractive to import jobs by increasing their exports of goods. But they could do this only by maintaining undervalued currencies. In the first test in 20 years of its ability to prevent 'beggar-thy-neighbor' policies, the Bretton Woods system failed.

Political and economic issues

Two complex questions complicated the realignment of exchange rates. One was whether European and Japanese currencies should be revalued around the US dollar while the dollar remained pegged to gold at $35, or whether the US dollar price of gold should be increased so that the dollar would depreciate in terms of some of the European currencies. The second question concerned the amount of the revaluations of individual foreign currencies in terms of the US dollar. The first question involved political issues, the second, economic issues.

The political aspect was especially clear in the context of US–French relations. President Nixon's standing with US voters would decline if the US dollar were devalued in terms of gold, while President Pompidou would gain support with his Gaullist followers if it appeared that the dollar had been dethroned as the center of the international system. An increase of 10 or 15 percent in the US dollar price of gold and other currencies would have no significant impact on gold output, but such an increase would win points for Pompidou.

The economic issues involved the effect of changes in the exchange rate structure on the competitive position of firms with plants in different countries. Germany, for example, would not set a new parity for the mark until Japan had set a new parity for the yen. The Germans wanted to be sure that the yen would be revalued by a larger amount than the mark, so that German producers would be in a more favorable position relative to their Japanese competitors in world export markets.

And the French would not set a new value for the franc until the rate for the mark had been set.

Currency realignment

In mid-December 1971, agreement was reached on a currency realignment: the United States would increase the US dollar price of gold by 8 percent to $38 and the other countries would realign their currency parities about the dollar. The Japanese yen was revalued by 17 percent from its May 1971 parity, the German mark by 14 percent. But US authorities would still not sell gold.

Thus, the Smithsonian Agreement – 'The Greatest Monetary Agreement in History' – may have resolved the imbalances resulting from the US inflation associated with the Vietnam war, but it did not solve the gold problem or the inconsistencies between national monetary policies and the exchange rate system. While it was agreed that a new monetary system was needed, there was no agreement on the key features of such a system.

Adoption of floating rates

Any new system, regardless of its name, had to accommodate itself to several realities. Most countries continued to prefer pegged to floating exchange rates as a way to reduce the uncertainty associated with international trade and investment. More and more countries gave greater priority to independent monetary policies, countries then adjusted to external disturbances by altering controls to increase or reduce net international payments. There was a widespread belief that the international role of the US dollar would have to be diminished – a euphemism for attempting to reduce the economic power and influence of the United States. And somehow the new system would have to be built through multilateral negotiations and agreement.

In June 1972 a speculative attack on the British pound forced the British authorities to stop supporting the pound, which promptly depreciated to its pre-Smithsonian parity. Speculation against the US dollar increased in early 1973; in less than a day, the Bundesbank was obliged to buy $6 billion to maintain the parity for the mark. The German monetary authorities were concerned that they were losing control over the changes in their money supply and so they stopped pegging the mark to the US dollar. Other countries followed the German lead.

A new Smithsonian-style accord was virtually out of the question. While the national monetary authorities might again commit themselves to a new set of currency parities, few investors would believe that these parities were credible – that the national monetary authorities would be willing to incur the costs necessary to ensure that these parities would be viable. National treasuries were obliged to adopt floating rates because there was no feasible alternative. And so, beginning in late February 1973, the major currencies began to float relative to the US dollar.

The changes in the price of the US dollar in terms of European currencies and the Japanese yen since the early 1970s have been much sharper than had been anticipated. The Bundesbank, the Bank of Japan, and other central banks intervened extensively in the foreign exchange market to limit the variations in the foreign exchange values of their currencies. One of the ironies was that central bank purchases and sales of foreign exchange were much more extensive under the floating-rate than under the pegged-rate system. Despite this extensive intervention, the price of the dollar in terms of the German mark, the Swiss franc, and the Japanese yen varied by as much as 50 percent. The system of floating exchange rates proved to be far less of a panacea than its proponents had suggested. But that's another story – and another chapter.

EMU is not a bird – but the euro is a money

One feature of the second half of the twentieth century has been a series of agreements among Germany, France, Italy, and other European countries leading to increased integration of their economies – a response to the reduction in the costs of economic distance. There was the European Coal and Steel Community (ECSC). Then there was the European Economic Community (EEC), which involved a common agricultural policy, a common tariff on external trade (CXT), and the elimination of tariffs and other barriers on internal trade. Over the years the number of member countries has increased from six to 15 (and numerous others in Central Europe seek to join), and more and more initiatives have been adopted to integrate national markets in goods and services, making professional qualifications in one country acceptable in others for example.

One feature of the movements in exchange rates in the 1970s and the 1980s was that the value of most European currencies increased and decreased more or less together in terms of the US dollar. The similarity in the changes in the value of these currencies relative to the dollar reflects two factors. One is that many of the shocks that have led to changes in exchange rates have originated in the United States, and have involved changes in the US inflation rate and changes in interest rates on US dollar securities. The second is that an increasing share of the trade of most European countries is with other European countries.

The changes in the name from the European Economic Community to the European Community (EC) to the European Union (EU) is suggestive of the increase in ambitions for integration. The motives for integration differ, and overlap somewhat. Thus the French and the Dutch have sought to wrap Germany into a web of economic and military and other relationships so that the likelihood that German armies would again march west would be sharply reduced. Those in the smaller countries have often concluded that their countries are too small for their domestic markets to be competitive, and that their consumers would be better off if their firms were forced to compete in a larger setting.

The French view a larger integrated Europe as a much more effective counterweight to the United States in the management of international economic affairs than individual countries could be on their own. One symbol of this challenge that a united Europe could offer to the United States is the Airbus, which has proved – after many years and billions of marks and francs of subsidy – a remarkable challenger to Boeing's dominance of the world market for large commercial aircraft. The Maastricht Agreement was established to prepare the way for the move to a common currency. Eventually a new European Central Bank (ECB) would be established, and the existing national central banks would in effect become branches, much as the Federal Reserve Bank of Boston and the Federal Reserve Bank of San Francisco are branches of the Federal Reserve System in Washington.

The future of monetary agreements

There are two dominant features of monetary agreements. One is that there is persistent desire to adopt them to limit the movements in national currencies, which is what Bretton Woods and Maastricht are all about. The second is that these agreements do not last forever; the Bretton Woods system in effect lasted about 25 years.

The implication of the first feature is that there will be another monetary agreement to limit the variability of the Japanese yen and the Euro in terms of the US dollar. The implication of the second feature is that Maastricht agreement will break down.

Go figure.

4

The Gnomes of Zurich Play in the Largest Market in the World

Foreign exchange transactions

On a busy day, the volume of trading in the foreign exchange market is $400 billion – and since there are 250 trading days in a year, the yearly volume is $100,000 billion – which is three or four times world GDP. The volume of daily transactions in foreign exchange is 20–40 times larger than the volume of international trade and investment, which leads to the question of why the transactions volume is so large.

Most foreign exchange transactions – probably 90–95 percent – are between foreign exchange traders in different large international commercial banks; only a relatively small part of these transactions are between the foreign exchange traders in the banks and the treasurers of the large and small firms engaged in importing and exporting and in international investments. Moreover, the US money center banks have reported increasingly large revenues and profits on their foreign exchange transactions in the 1980s and the 1990s; it's a safe bet that the trading revenues and profits of other large international banks have also increased, although perhaps not so rapidly. It must follow that if the money center banks are earning exceptional profits from trading foreign exchange, then the source of this income must be from the transactions of others that participate in the market.

To some extent, the source of this income is that central banks support the value of their currencies at the established parity – and then, after repeated denials, they change it. In the long run, however, central banks report profits on their foreign exchange transactions. The implication is that the incomes of both the large commercial banks and the central banks must be at the expense of importers and exporters. Still no participants in the foreign exchange has been heard to complain that they are 'paying for' these profits.

It is an axiom that the large international banks would not earn profits from trading foreign exchange if the exchange rates were more or less fixed. It follows from this axiom that the revenues and the profits of the large international banks must be systematically related to the scope of changes in the exchange rates. But the revenues and profits of these banks might reflect that the traders in these banks buy and sell to limit the range of movement in exchange rate, or alternatively they might reflect that they buy currencies when they are appreciating and sell these currencies when they are depreciating

Buy low and sell high

Pegged currencies

In Autumn of 1993 George Soros' Quantum Fund reported profits of $1000 billion from betting that the British pound and the Italian lira would be devalued relative to the German mark – in effect that the pound and the lira would leave the Exchange Rate Mechanism (ERM) of the European Community. Quantum didn't own British pounds. Quantum might have borrowed British pounds, say at the market interest rate of 10 percent, and then sold the British pounds to buy US dollars in the spot exchange market; the US dollar would have been used to buy US money market securities that might have paid 4 or 5 percent. So Quantum would have 'lost' 5 or 6 percent a year because its interest payments would have exceeded its interest income. But Quantum's bet was that the British pound would be devalued, so fewer US dollars would be required to repay the British pound loan – and the profit on the combination of the two foreign exchange transactions would have been larger than its loss from paying a higher interest rate on the funds borrowed than on its interest income.

Quantum also sold British pounds in the forward exchange market. A forward exchange transaction is like a spot exchange transaction with two principal differences. The first is that the transfer of bank deposits denominated in the domestic and the foreign currency occurs at a more distant date than the transfer of deposits associated with a spot exchange transaction and so there is no immediate need for cash. The second is that the forward exchange rate is likely to differ from the spot exchange rate. Quantum intended to buy the British pound when the British pound would be less expensive. So its profits would be the difference between the price at which Quantum sold the British pounds, and the price at which it repurchased them, less the loss or difference between the two interest rates. The counterpart of Quantum's profits was that the Bank of England incurred losses on its foreign exchange transactions. The Bank of England sold US dollars when they were cheap in terms of British pounds, and subsequently bought US dollar when they were more expensive. The Bank of England was committed to maintaining a fixed parity for the British pound in terms of the German mark – a political commitment.

Non-pegged currencies

The more difficult question concerns the source of the revenues for the banks when currencies are not pegged. When the news suggests the oil price will increase, investors buy the British pound; when the news suggests the oil price will decrease, they sell it. Changes in the foreign exchange value of the pound – and of the currencies of other oil producing countries – tend to be strongly correlated with changes in the price of oil.

Speculation

Few banks or firms admit that they speculate; it sounds anti-social. Rather, they maintain that they are solely engaged in hedging their risks, or satisfying the needs of their customers. Everyone points instead to the 'Gnomes of Zurich' as the speculators. The brotherhood of Gnomes is worldwide. There are chapters in London, Paris, Tokyo, New York – indeed, in every financial center where banks and firms and investors deal in foreign exchange. Membership in the brotherhood is open to anyone willing to take the risks; all that is necessary is a willingness to play by the rules of the market economy. The Gnomes are on *Fortune's* lists of the 500 largest US corporations and the 300 largest foreign corporations.

Successful currency speculation can be profitable. Speculators who bought US dollars with British pounds near the $2.80 parity, just before the November 1967 devaluation, and then repurchased the pound near the new $2.40 parity made a 16 percent profit – in some cases for an increase in their holdings of US dollars which they might have purchased only a week or two before the devaluation. In the months prior to the revaluation of the German mark in September and October 1969, speculators sold dollars to get marks at a parity of about 4 marks to the dollar. After the revaluation they bought dollars at about 3.67 marks, giving them a profit of 8 percent. Note that many speculators secured these profits in a month or two, so on an annual basis their profit may have been as high as 50 or 100 percent. If, for example, a speculator sold the British pound for dollars in the middle of September 1967, about two months before the mid-November devaluation, the profit of 16 percent on an investment of two months equals an annualized profit of 96 percent. In a world in which annual rates of return of 8 or 10 percent are the norm, these high annual rates of profit attract risktakers – and the greedy.

Profits can be earned by playing the movements in the floating exchange rates – by buying currencies when they are cheap and selling them when they are dear. Some commercial banks have reported that they have earned as much as $100–$200 million each quarter from foreign exchange trading. Part of these profits may have been earned from acting as brokers in transactions with the petroleum companies and drug companies and the thousands of other firms engaged in foreign trade and investment. Most of their profits, however, were made from being quicker than others in predicting whether the US dollar would become stronger or weaker, and positioning the bank to take advantage of these movements.

Someone must pay for the revaluation profits earned by the Gnomes; for every winner there's a loser, or two or three. In part, one Gnome loses what another wins; speculators deal with each other. But any Gnome that loses money trading foreign exchange one week after the next polishes his résumé and seeks a new career.

The revaluation losses of the Bank of England–and of the Bank of Japan, the Bank of France, the Bundesbank, and numerous other central banks–fall on their stock holders. And since these institutions are owned by their governments, the taxpayers foot the bill. Despite massive losses, the taxpayers rarely complained; most after all are ignorant.

Foreign exchange speculation is not without risk. Nor is it costless – anticipated changes in exchange rates may not occur, or they may occur long after the investors altered their holdings of foreign exchange in anticipation that central banks would alter their parities. But under the exchange market arrangements that prevailed until the end of 1971, the risks and costs were low.

The Gnomes of Zurich were a handy scapegoat for the problems besetting the British pound in the mid-1960s, problems that had their source in London, not Zurich. The pound's weakness was a result of British monetary policy; $2.80 had ceased to be a viable parity by 1964, if not by 1962 because the British inflation rate was too high and its productivity gains too low relative to those of its trading partners. Speculators sought revaluation profits at low risk because the British authorities retained an increasingly overvalued currency.

With the move to floating exchange rates in early 1973, central banks greatly reduced their subsidies to business firms that speculated in the exchange market, at least initially. Many firms and banks had developed confidence in their ability to predict changes in exchange rates during the pegged period. When currencies began to float, they continued to speculate. In the summer of 1974, several private banks began to report substantial foreign exchange losses. In some cases, including Herstatt Bankhaus, Westdeutsche Girozentral, and Franklin National, top management participated in the decisions to seek profits from changes in exchange rates. In other cases, exchange speculation occurred at the distant branches or by surreptitious activities of the bank's traders. Altogether, some privately owned banks lost over $1 billion, not large by the standards of central banks, but enough to force Herstatt and Franklin National out of business. And the foreign exchange traders associated with the losing banks changed careers. A few went to jail.

Gnomes and non-gnomes

Gnomes (and non-Gnomes) who deal in foreign exchange buy and sell bank deposits denominated in different currencies. A turn of events – an election, the quarterly report on exports and imports, a dock strike, this month's report on changes in the wholesale price level – can alter expectations about the future price of a currency. Gnomes sell and buy to profit from anticipated changes in exchange rates.

Traders in the market

The traders in the large international banks often specialize in a particular segment of the foreign exchange market. Small groups of traders in the very large banks are 'market-makers' -- they provide both a buy price and a sell price to other banks and to large commercial customers, not knowing whether the customer is likely to be a seller or a buyer. Often the banks will provide the quotes to the customer through a foreign exchange broker, who acts as a silent intermediary. These price quotes are valid for transactions of a standard size and are valid for a few seconds. A few of the traders in some of the banks are proprietary traders; they have 'strong views' of how the currency values are likely to change over the weekend or over the next several weeks based on their interpretation of both the political and the economic news.

Most of the traders in the banks are 'day-traders' – during the course of the day, they might undertake 50 or 100 transactions, buying the currencies that are increasing in value and selling those that are declining in value. They seek profits from small trendlike movements in the exchange rates; they follow the cliché that 'the trend is my friend.' Profits once earned are banked, and they repeat the process. At the end of the day, these day-traders close their positions and go home; they start trading the next day without a position.

Particular individuals have skills that are better suited for one type of trading activity than another. Still, it follows that each of these trading activities must be profitable – or else they wouldn't occur.

Round-trip profits: arbitrage

A market in national monies is inevitable as long as there are separate national currencies. Domestic monies – primarily bank deposits – are traded against similar deposits denominated in other currencies. In New York, US dollars are traded against Canadian dollars, British pounds, French francs, Swiss francs, German marks, and more than 100 other currencies. In the United States, there are foreign exchange dealers in New York, Chicago, San Francisco, and Los Angeles; in Switzerland, in Zurich, Geneva, and Basle. But in reality, New York, London, Brussels, Zurich, and the other financial centers are the geographic extensions of one international market.

Because the costs of foreign exchange transactions are extremely low, at any moment the British pound-US dollar exchange rates in New York and in Zurich are virtually identical with the rates quoted in London, which is the principal center of trading in the dollar–pound market. The deposits are not moved from one country to another; rather, the ownership of British pound deposits in London changes as the banks trade with each other. Foreign exchange traders find it financially rewarding to buy a currency in one center if it is fractionally cheaper than in others. Assume an extreme example: the price of £1 is $2 in New York and $3 in London – that is, the pound is cheap in New York and dear in London. Foreign exchange traders buy British pounds with US dollars in New York: they receive a British pound deposit in a bank in London that they pay for with a US dollar deposit in New York. Each British pound costs them $2. At the same time, they buy US dollars with British pounds in London and receive $3 for each British pound; they receive a US dollar deposit in New York and pay with a British pound deposit in London. Thus, their profit per 'round trip' for each $2 investment is $1. Their activity is riskless, for the two transactions occur simultaneously. Riskless transactions undertaken to take advantage of differences in prices in various geographic centers are known as *arbitrage*.

Investors continue this pattern of transactions until the British pound price of the US dollar rises in New York and falls in London, and the remaining spread between them is too small for arbitrage to be profitable. In practice, this means that the spread can be as low as several thousandths of 1 percent.

Arbitragers also ensure that the exchange rate between the Dutch guilder and the German mark is consistent with the price of the US dollar in terms of the guilder and the price of the dollar in terms of the mark. Once the price of the dollar in terms of each of these currencies is known, then the guilder price of the mark (the *cross-rate*) can be determined arithmetically. Arbitragers see to it that the arithmetic is correct. Assume, for example, that the dollar costs 4 marks, the mark costs 2 guilders, and the dollar costs 6 guilders. These rates are inconsistent; the cross-rate for the mark in terms of the guilder, given the price of the US dollar in terms of both the guilder and the mark, is 1.5 guilders to the mark. So the arbitragers sell guilders to buy dollars, then sell the dollars to buy marks, and finally sell marks to buy guilders; 6 guilders buy $1, which buys 4 marks, which in turn buy 8 guilders. Not bad – a profit of two guilders for each round trip – but remember this is only an illustrative example. Arbitrage continues until the riskless profit opportunities are eliminated. The mark price and the dollar price of the guilder decline, while the dollar price of the mark rises.

Spot and forward dealings

Some foreign exchange dealings are *spot* transactions: buyers and sellers agree to transfer bank deposits immediately after they enter into the contract, which in practice means two days later. Most transactions in foreign exchange, however, involve trades in *forward* contracts, which differ from trades in spot transactions in two important respects – the exchange of deposits occurs at a more distant future date, often 30 days or 90 days after the date of the contract. And because the exchange of deposits occurs at various dates in the future and time is money, the exchange rate on forward contracts usually differs from that on spot exchange contracts.

Gnomes prefer forward transactions because they can buy a foreign currency without having to make immediate large cash payment. But Gnomes can buy forward contracts only if some non-Gnomes sell forward contracts. If, for example, the Gnomes believe that the British pound will depreciate, they may want to sell the British pound forward, which means they will want to buy US dollars forward. Most participants in the exchange market would be reluctant to buy British pounds in the forward market if they thought that the pound might depreciate. Some arbitragers, however, may buy forward pounds, but only after selling pounds in the spot market. By combining a sale of British pounds in the spot exchange market with the purchase of British pounds in the forward exchange market, they protect themselves against a loss from a depreciation of the British pound. Thus, the arbitragers might sell spot pounds at $1.50 and at the same time buy forward pounds at $1.45. Regardless of changes in the dollar price of the pound, they would profit from the difference in the two exchange rates. While speculators seek to profit from anticipated changes in the exchange rates, arbitragers (who by definition are reluctant to bear the risk associated with such changes) profit from the differences in the price of foreign exchange in the spot exchange market and in the forward exchange market.

The government's role

The foreign exchange market (Box 4.1) is distinguished from the commodity, stock, and bond markets by the pervasiveness of the government's role, especially the central bank's intervention to maintain the foreign exchange price of its currency.

Under the Bretton Woods system, exchange rates were free to float within a narrow 'band' around par values. Under the IMF rules of the 1960s, support limits of the band could be no greater than 1 percent on either side of par; these limits were increased to 2.25 percent under the Smithsonian Agreement of 1971. Speculation about changes in the exchange rate then centered largely on changes in the central bank's parity. Exchange speculators bought and sold foreign exchange with the large commercial banks, but these banks were not eager to hold large amounts of currencies that might be devalued. They were more likely to be sellers of the weak currency; indeed, many qualified for senior membership in the Brotherhood of Gnomes. Since for every seller there must be a buyer, the central banks were obliged to buy their own currencies to prevent them from deviating significantly from their parities.

While countries were reluctant to change the parity formally, they could not avoid or even postpone changes in the effective exchange rate. So ad hoc measures were adopted to prevent exceptionally large and persistent losses in central bank holdings of international money. Purchases of foreign exchange were restricted, taxed, delayed, and licensed. Supplemental tariffs were levied on commodity imports. Ceilings and taxes were placed on overseas spending by tourists. Government agencies were directed to supply their needs from domestic sources even though foreign sources were cheaper. Such taxes and restrictions increased the effective price of foreign exchange; in

Box 4.1   10 Things your Mother Never Knew About the Foreign Exchange Market

1   **The foreign exchange market is the largest market in the world.** On a busy day, the volume of transactions may reach $400 billion, 50 times the volume on the New York Stock Exchange.

2   Most foreign exchange transactions (90–95 percent) **involve only banks**: interbank transactions are undertaken to adjust their positions in currencies in order to offset the imbalances caused by purchases and sales with customers.

3   For the major currencies the larger banks act as **market makers**: they hold inventories of foreign currencies and stand ready to deal in large amounts at stated prices. In other currencies, in contrast, banks operate as brokers and avoid the price risk.

4   The exchange market is the **most efficient market in the world**, at least as judged by transactions costs. Assume you started with $1 million US dollars and bought Canadian dollars. Then you realized you had made a mistake, so you sold the Canadian dollars for US dollars. You would end up with less than $1 million US by the amount of two commissions – equal to the bid – ask spread. How much less?*

5   The foreign exchange market **never (well, hardly ever) closes.** When it is 3 p.m. Tuesday in Tokyo, it is 2 p.m. in Hong Kong; when it is 3 p.m. in Hong Kong, it is 1 p.m. in Singapore. When it is 3 p.m. in Singapore, it is noon in Bahrein; when it is 3 p.m. in Bahrein, it is 1 p.m. in Beirut. When it is 3 p.m. in Beirut, it is 1 p.m. in London; when it is 3 p.m. in New York, it is noon in San Francisco; when it is 3 p.m. Tuesday in San Francisco, it is 9 a.m. Wednesday in Sydney. The center of trading moves with the sun around the world (see also Box 13.1).

6   About 99.44 percent of all trades **involve the US dollar**. If a Swiss importer wants to pay his German supplier, the bank calculates the Swiss franc–German mark rate as the combination of the Swiss franc–dollar rate and the German mark – dollar rate. Most trades in Frankfurt are marks against dollars.

Box 4.1   continued

7   The largest volume of foreign exchange trading **occurs in London.**

8   Most customer transactions in foreign exchange involve **forward transactions** – the corporate client makes a commitment to buy or sell forward exchange at a future date at a rate agreed to today.

9   Since 1973, about 20 firms have been established to sell **forecasts on exchange rate movements**. One inference is that they can make more money selling forecasts than using them.

10   A good foreign exchange trader can earn $250,000 a year – and **lose $1 million in a day.**

*   The cost is 230 Canadian dollars. The comparable estimates for other currencies are: mark, $503; sterling, $514; yen, $1041; Swiss franc, $1229.

effect, as we saw in chapter 2, the currency was being devalued through the 'back door'.

Once the ability to buy foreign exchange freely at the established price is restricted or taxed, a black market in foreign exchange almost inevitably develops. Rather than pay the taxes or wait in line at the central bank to buy the foreign exchange at the legal parity, some importers decide that it is cheaper to buy the currency they need in the black market. Some exporters increase their income by selling their foreign exchange earnings in the black market, some governments profit by offering to sell foreign exchange to importers at the artificially low price, and then taxing their purchases. And various government officials in the agencies which ration foreign exchange and import licenses may place individual importers in a favored position, in return for side bets, private payments, commissions, or promises or suggestions of future employment opportunities.

Surprisingly, most governments tolerate black markets in foreign exchange. Legal penalties are rarely imposed in spite of the pervasiveness of apparently illegal transactions; few people have gone to jail because they've been caught violating the currency regulations. In many cases the black market permits the government to delay the political costs of formally devaluing the parity, while minimizing the economic costs of maintaining an overvalued currency.

The source of exchange crises

Crises in the foreign exchange market reflect two underlying factors. The first – and necessary – factor is the desire of many countries to pursue independent monetary policies. Price levels rise rapidly in some countries and slowly in others. The resulting changes in the relationships between the prices of domestic goods relative to the prices of comparable foreign goods affect patterns of imports and exports. The imports of countries whose prices are rising increase rapidly while their exports increase at a slower rate or may even fall. The international money holdings of their central banks decline, and ultimately a devaluation is necessary. Meanwhile, in the countries with more stable prices, exports grow more rapidly than imports and holdings of international money increase. A revaluation of the currency may be necessary in countries with payments surpluses.

The second factor in the exchange crises of the past is that the IMF rules for regulating exchange rates were archaic, if not when they were adopted in the 1940s, then certainly by the early 1960s. These exchange rate provisions – a combination of narrow support limits around the parity and measures that sought to constrain countries from changing their parities by too large an amount – proved unworkable when changes in parities became necessary as national price levels began to increase at divergent rates.

The anomaly of the Bretton Woods system, which ultimately led to its breakdown, was that the exchange market arrangements of the gold standard were retained even though many central banks had switched from dependent monetary policies appropriate for the gold standard to independent monetary policies – that is, producing money at rates which satisfied their domestic economy objectives. Predictably, an exchange rate system designed in accordance with the gold standard worked less well in a period when central banks gave higher priority to domestic employment and growth.

The politics of parity

The decision to change a currency parity is ultimately political. Necessary changes in parities have often been delayed because of the perceived political costs. One holdover from the gold standard era is the notion that there is something sacrosanct about a parity and that devaluation is an admission that domestic financial policies have failed. The monetary authorities always hope that events will somehow save them from the need to devalue–the next month's trade data will show a healthy rise in exports, or other countries will revalue their currencies making their own devaluation unnecessary.

No one needs any private knowledge to recognize when a currency is overvalued or undervalued. Because changes in parities are usually delayed, investors do not need remarkably accurate foresight to anticipate them. The cost of guessing wrong is minimal as long as the band between the support limits is narrow, since the transactions can easily be reversed and at modest cost. And because the authorities are often reluctant to change the parities by small amounts, speculators can be confident that the eventual changes will be substantial.

The British pound, 1964–7

Take the British pound. By 1964 the pound was clearly overvalued. British prices had been rising more rapidly than those of Britain's competitors, the British share of the world export market was declining, and its payments deficit was large. Many observers felt that the Labour government should have devalued immediately on coming to power in October 1964, for at that time the need for devaluation could have been blamed on the outgoing Conservatives. But the Labour Party was reluctant to take advantage of its opportunity. Labour governments had been in power before when sterling was devalued – in 1931 and again in 1949 – and party leaders were fearful of being tagged the 'Devaluation Party.' For at least three years, Britain's economic policies, as well as its international and domestic security policies, were constrained by the need to defend an overvalued currency.

By November 1967 nearly everyone except Prime Minister Harold Wilson was willing to admit that the pound would have to be devalued. While the size of the required devaluation could not be determined exactly, it was almost certain to be greater than 10 percent, since a smaller change would not have seemed worthwhile. And it was almost certain to be smaller than 20 percent, since a larger change would almost surely have resulted in retaliatory devaluations by other

European countries whose trade positions would have been excessively threatened.

Eventually, in November 1967, the pound was devalued, because the British authorities could no longer maintain the parity; their holdings of international money were exhausted and it was virtually impossible to borrow. Great Britain had already borrowed the maximum amount possible from the IMF and large loans were being negotiated with other countries. But the conditions on British domestic policy attached to these loans, especially by France, were deemed too onerous.

The French franc, 1969

The devaluation of the French franc in August 1969 was similarly influenced by political factors. To restore the domestic peace and harmony that had been threatened by the student riots of May 1968, General de Gaulle's government approved nationwide wage increases of 15 percent. Price increases were inevitable, otherwise firms could not afford to pay the higher wages. The prospect of a one-shot increase in the price level of 10–15 percent meant that the French franc would have to be devalued. The anticipated price increases and the political uncertainty associated with the riots triggered a sharp speculative attack against the franc.

Yet the necessary change in the parity was delayed for political reasons. President de Gaulle would not devalue the franc; after all, he had given France 10 years of price stability (1959–1968) following 50 years of inflation. To maintain that stability, payments abroad were restricted, and price and wage ceilings were adopted: the franc was being devalued by the 'back door'. Only the date of the 'front door' devaluation and the amount of the change remained uncertain. Less than four months after de Gaulle resigned, the franc was formally devalued.

The German mark, 1969

The way election results can influence an exchange parity was dramatically shown by the revaluation of the German mark in October 1969. The Christian Democrats wanted to maintain the existing parity until the German parliamentary elections in September. The business community, an important supporter of the Christian Democratic Party, favored retaining the existing parity with the dollar, since a revaluation of the mark would mean that the prices of German goods in the US and other foreign markets would rise relative to the prices of US goods, and that German export sales and German profits would decline. Revaluation of the mark would also lead Germans to buy more foreign goods, since they would then decline in price relative to German

---

Box 4.2   The Brussels Caper

In the mid-1960s, a foreign exchange trader in the Brussels branch of a major New York bank fell in love with the British pound. The Gnomes were bearish on sterling; they anticipated a devaluation. The forward pound was at a substantial discount – when spot sterling was at $2.79, forward pound was cheaper. Moreover, the discounts on 12-month-forward contracts were substantially larger than on one-month-forward contracts. So the trader bought the long pound contracts, which were cheap, and sold one-month forward pound contracts, which were more expensive. Thus, his position in pound was more or less even, at least for one month; from the beginning of the second month until the end of the twelfth, he was long the pound. And he had a potential profit, which was the difference between the cheap pound he had bought and the dear sterling he had sold.

A month later, he again bought the one-month pound forward to offset his position in the long forward contract, which had 11 months to run until maturity. At the same time, he bought more long pound contracts and sold an equal amount of short pound contracts; his long and short positions were offsetting, and he still had a nice potential profit. A month later he repeated the process; he repeated it for several more months. The potential profit kept increasing.

When the bank learned of its extremely large position in long pound contracts, the position was closed, at a loss of $8 million.

---

goods. Thus, the mark prices of Germans goods competing with imports would have to fall, and the profits of German firms producing these goods would decline.

The major constituency of the Social Democrats was – and is – the workers, who are interested in higher incomes and lower prices, not in business profits. A revaluation would thus benefit the Social Democrats, and a revaluation was widely expected – if the Social Democrats won the election. Had the Christian Democrats won, the outcome would have been more uncertain, for their constituency and the economic realities were pulling in opposite directions.

As soon as preliminary election results indicated that the voters preferred the Social Democrats, the speculative demand for the mark soared. On September 29 the Bundesbank ceased pegging the mark at the parity of 4 marks to the dollar, and the mark floated upward until October 24, when it was pegged at 3.67 marks by the newly installed Social Democratic government.

The Canadian dollar, 1950–70

On two occasions in 20 years, once in 1950 and again in 1970, the Canadian government shifted from a pegged to a floating rate. In both instances, the cause was the same: Canada wanted to minimize the increase in the Canadian price level resulting from inflation in the United States. The dominant factor in Canada's exchange rate policy is the very tight economic fit of the Canadian with the US economy. The close economic and geographic relationship with the United States means that Canada has an automatic tendency to import US problems. Moreover, because raw materials are such a large part of Canadian exports to the United States, US economic developments have an exaggerated impact on Canada. When the US economy has a little boom, US imports of raw materials soar, and the Canadian economy has a big boom. Both in 1950 and again in the late 1960s, as a result of the US booms, Canadian exports surged and large payments surpluses brought about large increases in Canada's money supply.

The Canadian government sought greater control over its price level by shifting to a floating exchange rate. Thus, in June 1950, the Canadian dollar (which had been pegged at the rate of $1.10 Canadian to $1.00 US) was permitted to float, and shortly appreciated by 10 percent. Similarly, when in June 1970 the Canadian authorities again freed their dollar from a parity of $1.08 Canadian to $1.00 US, it appreciated by 8 percent.

Canada wants more independence from the United States. Since Canada cannot readily move to Europe or to the Far East, it has sought financial mechanisms that would disengage its economy from the US one. Both in 1950 and in 1970, the Canadians hoped that a floating currency would provide increased insulation from US inflation. In contrast, in 1962 both the US and Canadian economies were in recessions and the Canadian government returned to a pegged exchange rate to stimulate its economy; the Canadian dollar was pegged at a rate below the market level to increase Canadian exports.

Until 1971 most exchange crises involved only one currency; there was no systematic relation between the problems of the British pound, the Canadian dollar, and the French franc. But the exchange rate changes of May 1971 and of February 1973 – both those that did occur and those that should have occurred but did not – involved more than 10 currencies. The US payments deficit associated with the Vietnam

War led foreign central banks to acquire more dollars than they wished. As a result, their domestic money supplies were growing rapidly: they were importing the US inflation. One of the few options open to foreign central banks was to use the dollars to buy gold from the US Treasury and hope that the gold losses would force US authorities to take measures to reduce the payments imbalances. Another option was to revalue their currencies and incur costs in terms of their own constituencies.

Murphy's Law – anything that can go wrong will go wrong – went to work. The other industrial countries imported the US inflation and then they revalued. Their price levels increased about as rapidly as the US price level, because the revaluation was too long delayed.

The search for flexibility: floating rates and sliding parities

Since 1960, more than 30 countries have devalued their currencies. A few – including West Germany, Austria, the Netherlands, Switzerland, Japan, Canada, France, Italy, and Great Britain – have revalued. Small wonder that speculators appear increasingly sensitive to the possibility of changes in exchange parities. Whenever it has appeared likely that a parity might be changed, the volume of funds shifted in anticipation of such a change has increased greatly year after year: the odds in the game have increasingly favored the speculators.

Inevitably, the central bankers have been forced to deny they would change their parities: not to deny is to admit. But the sequence of a succession of denials followed by a succession of parity changes quickly reduced the value of their denials. Central bankers' public statements about the exchange rate have lost credibility, and speculation about changes in exchange parities has come to resemble a game of wits between government authorities and private parties. The participants in the exchange market must constantly decide how much importance to attach to those official denials.

The inconsistency between national monetary policies and the exchange rate system – and the resulting speculation – might be reduced by a return to a gold standard monetary policy – that is, a return to dependent national monetary policies. For many countries, however, monetary independence is the essence of sovereignty. In the 'Me Generation' each country wants to do its own thing.

Independence and floating rates

Given each nation's desire for monetary independence, greater flexibility is obtained through floating exchange rates, or with more frequent changes in the parity so as to reduce the scope for speculative profits. Under a floating exchange rate system, the exchange rate varies in response to changes in supply and demand, just like any other price. Central banks are not required to support their currencies in the exchange market, although they may intervene to smooth movements in the exchange rate to accommodate the needs of traders and investors. Changes in the exchange rate are supposed to be less sudden than under the pegged system. New information about future events – and hence about future exchange rates – is supposed to be immediately reflected in the exchange rate. Thus, as the domestic price level increases or the foreign demand for domestic products declines, the price of foreign exchange increases. Investors can still speculate on changes in the exchange rate, but they no longer have the relatively riskless, one-way option available under the pegged exchange rate system. For one thing, the amount of the change in the rate is usually smaller, since the rate is adjusted continuously. And the costs of being wrong can be much greater, since the currency may appreciate by a larger amount if speculators are wrong. The need to apply controls and restrictions to limit purchases of foreign exchange should disappear, and so should currency black markets.

Academic economists – perhaps a majority of them – favor floating exchange rates. Some – those who advocate a fixed money supply growth rule for a particular country of 5, 6, or 10 percent a year – favor independent monetary policies; they abhor the idea that the growth of the money supply within a country should be affected by whether the country has a payments surplus or deficit. And economists who do not accept a fixed monetary growth rule want to eliminate both the external constraint on the choice of domestic policies and the need to balance international payments and receipts at one particular exchange rate. Most economists believe that the variations in exchange controls that would have been needed to maintain national parities indicated either that the pegged-rate system was badly managed – and that even the best and the brightest of central bankers could not make it work effectively.

Yet floating exchange rates were criticized extensively by men of affairs, especially during the pegged-rate period. Their reasons differed. Some believed that daily, weekly, and monthly movements in the exchange rate would retard the growth of international trade and investment because the increased uncertainty about future exchange rates would deter some individuals and firms from undertaking international transactions.

Choosing between pegged and floating rates

The rationale for pegged exchange rates is that central bankers are more astute in setting the price of foreign exchange – speculating in the exchange market – than are private investors. Central banks are government-owned public utilities, and they are supposed to provide public services – if necessary, at a loss. Their transactions in the exchange market are supposed to reduce uncertainty about future exchange rates. Exporters and importers benefit from the reduction of uncertainty. And since their costs decline, the benefits are passed on both to those who produce export goods (and would thus have a larger foreign market) and to those who consume imports.

The rationale for floating exchange rates, on the other hand, is that changes in the exchange rate should be depoliticized. Even if the foreign exchange traders in the central banks are more skillful than their private-sector counterparts, they cannot alter the exchange peg on their own; these changes reflect political decisions. Necessary changes in parities almost always are long delayed. Thus, in most periods, any reduction in exchange market uncertainty stemming from central bank intervention may be offset by the sharp rise in uncertainty whenever expectations develop that the exchange parity will be altered – and while politicians are mustering the political will to make the change.

In general, proponents of floating exchange rates emphasize the ease with which the market rate changes over time. Exchange rate movements are supposed to be continuous and gradual rather than sudden and sharp. Moreover, the changes in the market exchange rate would more or less track the differences in national inflation rates, so that there would be far less likelihood that currencies would become overvalued or undervalued as they had under the pegged exchange rate arrangements. In contrast, the critics of floating exchange rates are worried that movements in exchange rates will be extensive.

In choosing between pegged and floating exchange rates, one of the major questions concerns the impact of uncertainty on trade and investment. Ideally, the effects and relative costs of uncertainty under the two systems might be measured and compared. Yet until 1973 the opportunities for comparison were infrequent. Floating exchange rate systems did not work well in the 1920s, but the relevance of this experience is questionable, as is the failure of the pegged-rate system during the 1930s. The 12-year Canadian experience with floating exchange rates between 1950 and 1962 was generally acknowledged a success – but the shocks were small. Lebanon has used a floating exchange rate since 1950, and the system has worked well despite wars, revolutions, and other sources of political uncertainty in the Middle East. But Lebanon has not followed an independent monetary policy. In addition, experience with pegged rates has been biased. Since most countries have been on pegged rates during the postwar period, the problems of this system have been most evident. Thus, however dramatic the exchange crises have been, their economic cost may not have been so great. In any case, the cost derived both from delays in changing the exchange rate and from changing the effective rate by administrative controls – in effect, from the way the system had been managed rather than from the system itself. Perhaps, however, it is inevitable that a pegged system would be poorly managed.

Another issue in choosing between these two exchange rate systems concerns the likelihood that a floating exchange rate will be manipulated by governments. The fear is that some countries might manipulate their exchange rates to enhance their national advantage. The Japanese favor a low foreign exchange value for the yen as a way to stimulate exports. Without established parities, governments cannot be prevented from manipulating the foreign exchange price of their currency. Perhaps international rules could be developed that would define acceptable and unacceptable forms of central bank intervention under a system of floating exchange rates. Perhaps – but the likelihood that such rules would be adopted seems low. And the likelihood that they would be followed, if adopted, is lower still.

The academic arguments between the proponents of pegged rates and the proponents of floating rates usually ignore the success of the Bretton Woods system in the 1950–1965 period, and concentrate instead on the exchange crises in the late 1960s and early 1970s. A pegged-rate system will work well whenever there is reasonable price stability in the major countries; crises will be infrequent because the need to change parities will also be infrequent. Floating rates would also work well in this monetary environment. As price stability begins to erode, the need to change parities will become increasingly frequent, and ultimately the authorities will permit their currencies to float.

The search for flexibility

Strong resistance to floating rates stimulated the search for greater flexibility within the pegged-rate system. The widening of the support limits around parities to 2.25 percent in 1971 was a response to this search. The advantage of a wider spread is that it tends to increase the risks associated with shifts of funds between assets denominated in various currencies, since the possible exchange losses are greater.

Investors have less of a one-way option. Whether 2.25 percent is sufficient is not yet clear – a somewhat wider spread, perhaps 4 or 5 percent, might be preferable.

Even with wider spreads between exchange rate support limits, exchange crises might still arise because independent monetary policies tend to make established parities obsolete. Unless authorities manage to change their parities before they are forced to do so by speculative pressure, crises are inevitable. And the authorities have rarely changed their parities on a timely basis.

Another approach toward greater flexibility involves various mechanisms that would make it easier to change parities. Such devices, called sliding parities, crawling pegs, or gliding rates, are all minor variations on a single theme: when a country begins to move into a position of persistent payments surplus or deficit, the parity should be changed quickly. Small, frequent changes in a parity then replace large, infrequent ones. These changes might be triggered automatically by changes in a country's holdings of international money, or by the decision of the authorities, since a formula-approach might circumvent the reluctance of the authorities to change their parities. But then the speculators would begin to 'game' the formula, and attempt to forecast the changes in the parities by developing their own versions of the formula.

Brazil used a floating peg approach for more than a decade; every three or four weeks the authorities devalued the cruzeiro by 2 or 3 percent. The amount of the change was so small, and its exact timing so uncertain, that investors did not find it worthwhile to seek to profit from the predictably small change in the peg. But most governments are skeptical of using a formula to determine the amount and timing of changes in the foreign exchange values of their currencies; the domestic political consequences might be too severe. And many governments have shown an unusual reluctance to use any variant of the sliding parity approach.

Loss of credibility of pegged rates

That the Bretton Woods system would break down was inevitable; the system was fast becoming obsolete in a world of independent monetary policies and accelerating inflation. It became too easy for investors to profit from changes in parities. Central bankers continued to play by the Bretton Woods rules even while they sought to negotiate modifications. Changes in institutional arrangements occur slowly, especially when the number of national participants is large and their interests diverse. The negotiations proved unsuccessful; currencies were allowed to float because agreement could not be reached on any other exchange rate regime.

The move to floating rates in 1973 did not occur because the proponents of floating rates won the arguments; rather, pegged rates were simply no longer credible in a period when inflation rates began to exceed 10 percent. Eventually, it was realized that authorities had only modest freedom to change the exchange rate once they had selected a monetary policy. In a period of monetary stability, the differences between the two exchange rate systems were of the Tweedledee–Tweedledum variety. And, given the monetary background of the 1970s, the concerns of the critics of floating rates have been substantiated. Exchange rates have moved very sharply, not gradually, much more than is warranted by differential changes in national price levels. Governments have intervened extensively to advance their own interests without the constraint of rules. The criticism, however, should be directed at monetary instability, and not at the exchange rate system.

Floating rates – arguments and experience

The years since February 1973 provide the first extensive experience since the 1920s for evaluating the arguments for floating rates. Most currencies remain pegged; the floating currencies are almost exclusively those of the industrial countries, and there have been wide differences in the scope for changes in exchange rates, for most central banks have intervened extensively in the exchange market to dampen movements in the foreign exchange values of their currencies.

Government responses

For a while, the Bank of Canada took a 'hands-off' approach to the exchange rate, until the Canadian dollar weakened. The Bank of Japan has traditionally smoothed the daily movements in the rate and has sought to moderate the tendency toward sharp cyclical swings. The British pound has been another managed floating currency; the British authorities have decided on the range within which they want the pound to trade and have bought and sold dollars to achieve their objective. In both the Japanese and British cases, floating has largely meant the absence of a commitment to a particular parity.

The continental European countries have participated in a joint currency float as an initial step toward the eventual unification of their currencies. In effect, countries participating in the joint float peg their currencies to each other, and these currencies appreciate and depreciate together in terms of the dollar; the more or less parallel movements is called 'the snake.' The percentage changes from peak to trough and from trough to peak are sharp in terms of the dollar, as much as 15–20 percent in a relatively short interval. Moreover, these currencies also float relative to each other within a range of little more than 2 percent.

One advantage of floating rates is that the movements of the rates are no longer the occasion for great crises; the monetary authorities are no longer subject to the political embarrassment associated with changes in parities. But the quieter life for the authorities is not a free lunch for everyone: business firms and investors are concerned with the impact of exchange rate movements on their competitive position and on their profits. While international trade and investment have not declined, their rates of growth appear smaller than they would have been had currencies remained pegged.

Another major argument for floating rates has been that countries would be able to pursue independent monetary policies. Perhaps they tried. Yet one remarkable feature of the period since 1973 has been the similarity of movements of price levels and incomes among the major European countries. Intervention practices have, for example, led to the evolution of a German mark currency area.

Market rate responses

One obvious feature of floating rates is that investors have caused market exchange rates to deviate sharply from the levels suggested by changes in national price levels. The stronger currencies have tended to appreciate sharply, the weaker currencies to depreciate sharply. For example, in the decades since floating began, the US dollar price of the German mark has varied from \$.175 to \$.260. The US dollar has been on a seesaw, moving quickly from undervaluation to overvaluation. As the experience with floating rates has accumulated, the analogies with the 1920s seem stronger and stronger. In both cases, currencies became even more extensively overvalued or undervalued than under the pegged-rate system.

In the late 1970s the US dollar depreciated sharply in the foreign exchange market, much more extensively than would have been predicted on the basis of the excess of the US inflation rate over those in Germany and Japan. Then at the end of 1979, the US dollar began to appreciate, and by the mid-1980s the value of the US dollar was 60 percent higher than at the beginning of this period of appreciation – and yet throughout the US inflation rate remained higher than those in Germany and Japan. Then the US dollar began to depreciate, and again more rapidly than the difference in the inflation rates would have suggested.

Box 4.3   Playing the Exchanges

The move to floating exchange rates signaled a boom for foreign exchange traders. The demand for their services skyrocketed – and so did their salaries. Success was measured by advancement, and advancement by profits earned for their employers. The foreign exchange departments of some banks made the major contribution to their profits.

These profits arose from two sources. First, banks could buy currencies at one price and sell them at a slightly higher price. Even when the bid–ask spread is small, the sums mount if the volume of business is large. The second source of profits comes from holding long positions in currencies that appreciate and short positions in currencies that depreciate.

In the spring of 1974, traders in a number of banks believed the dollar would appreciate, so they bought dollars forward. The dollar depreciated; they incurred losses. Rather than take these losses, they bought more dollars; in effect, it was the exchange market equivalent of double-or-nothing. The dollar depreciated further, so they doubled up again. The greater their losses, the more they increased their positions. Eventually, a few banks reported losses in the tens of millions of dollars.

Exactly how many foreign exchange traders – and how many banks – played the same game, incurred unrealized losses, yet managed to break even before their losses became so large that they had to be revealed is an unsettled question. The extent to which the managements of these banks were aware of the activities of their traders – and, if so, how they could have believed that such large profits came from the bid–ask spread – is also unresolved.

Or consider the Japanese yen, which had appreciated to 80 yen to the US dollar – about its highest value ever. Then the yen began to depreciate, and by the mid-1998 was trading in the range of 140–150 yen per US dollar. Yet during this three-year period the inflation rate in Japan was several percentage points below the US rate.

So the observations belied the major claim of the proponents of floating exchange rates that the changes in the exchange rates would be gradual, and that these changes would track the differential in national inflation rates. One analyst coined the term 'destabilizing speculation' to describe these sharp changes in exchange rates; another used the term 'vicious and virtuous circle'; a third descriptive is 'overshooting' and 'undershooting.'

Investor responses

The descriptive terms differ, but the phenomenon is the same. The deviations between the observed changes in exchange rates and the changes in the exchange rate that would have been predicted on the basis of the difference in national inflation rates reflects that investors often seek to change the currency composition of the securities in their portfolios. For example, in the late 1970s, investors as a group wanted to reduce the share of US dollar securities in their portfolios, in large part because they were concerned that the US inflation rate was accelerating. If these investors wanted to move into German mark securities, they had first to induce someone to sell them the marks. So their purchases of marks induced a much sharper depreciation of the US dollar than would have been predicted on the basis of the difference between US and German inflation rates. Because of the sharp depreciation of the US dollar, the United States developed a larger trade surplus. The marks earned by US exporters were sold to the investors that wanted to increase the share of German mark securities – or, which is the same thing, reduce the share of US dollar securities – in their portfolios.

By the early 1980s, investors had sharply reduced their estimates of the US inflation rate; they decided to increase the share of securities denominated in the US dollar in their portfolios. Before they could buy these securities, they had first to buy US dollars in the foreign exchange market. So the price of the US dollar in the foreign exchange market increased by more – much more – than would have been predicted from the difference in US and foreign inflation rates; indeed, as noted earlier, the US inflation rate was higher than the inflation rates in Germany and Japan. Because of the appreciation of the US dollar, the United States developed a trade deficit. The excess of US dollar payments for the purchase of imports over US dollar receipts from the sale of exports was the source of the dollars for those investors that wanted to increased the share of US dollar securities in their portfolios.

Some generalizations

The generalization from these illustrative episodes is that whenever investors wish to alter the currency composition of the securities in their portfolios, the change in the market exchange rate will differ from the change that would have been inferred from the difference in domestic and foreign inflation rates. Hence the variability in cross-border capital flows challenges the view of the proponents of floating exchange rates that the market exchange rate will track the difference in the two inflation rates. The larger and more sudden the change in the pattern of these capital flows, the larger the deviations between the market exchange rate and the exchange rate that would have been inferred from the difference in the two inflation rates.

That the deviations between the market exchange rate and the exchange rate inferred from the difference between the domestic and foreign inflation rates may be larger when currencies float than when they are pegged reflects a combination of two factors – one is that the variability of cross-border capital flows have been much larger when currencies have been floating than when they have been pegged, in part because currencies are much more likely to be floating when changes in the anticipated inflation rates are large. The other is that the variability of the cross-border capital flows does not affect the exchange rate – by definition – when currencies are pegged.

The data suggest that the more variable the market exchange rate, the larger the revenues of the banks that trade foreign exchange. The income of these banks comes primarily from the transactions of their 'day-traders' who make their money from following the daily trends. The traders are capturing part of the income from the long swings in the exchange rates. These long swings transfer income from producers and consumers in one country to producers and consumers in another. For example, when the US dollar was appreciating in the early 1980s, income was being transferred to Americans from the residents of the countries whose currencies were depreciating; this income transfer reflected the fact that foreign goods were becoming cheaper to Americans and US goods were becoming more expensive to foreigners. The source of the foreign exchange trading income from the banks is that they were able to extract some of the income that was being transferred from the residents of one country to the residents of the others.

Frequently, the choice of exchange rate systems seems much like the choice among automobiles or brands of soap – any of the available brands might do. But the analogy is misleading, since floating rates were inevitable given the worldwide inflation of the 1970s. The historical record suggests that countries move to floating rates whenever rates of price change – or intended price changes – deviate sharply. The British pound floated in terms of gold from 1803 to 1815 during the Napoleonic Wars. The US dollar floated from 1862 to 1878 because Civil War finance was highly inflationary and the dollar remained overvalued for a substantial period after the war ended. That most European currencies were floating in the early 1920s was not an accident; floating rates were necessary as long as countries sought to deflate their price levels relative to US price level as a prelude to pegging their currencies to gold at the 1913 parities.

As long as the world economy continues to be subject to the disruptions of inflationary booms and sharp recessions, floating rates are likely to be retained. The major uncertainties then revolve around the extent of central bank intervention in the exchange market and the possibility that some countries might adopt exchange controls to limit abrupt changes in the foreign exchange values of their currencies.

Which way after floating?

The historical experience suggests that floating rates are inevitable in an era of double-digit inflation and worldwide recession. The record also suggests that countries will move back toward some form of pegged rates once the monetary environment is more stable. Individual countries will decide on their own when the time is appropriate to peg their currencies. Such a move might follow an international conference or agreement which recognizes that a move toward pegged rates is desirable; alternatively, individual countries might unilaterally peg their currencies to that of a major trading partner after they have achieved monetary stability.

Ultimately, a new agreement might be reached on pegged rates. Such an agreement would differ from the Bretton Woods system in several important ways. The support limits are likely to be wider, probably even wider than the 2.25 percent limits of the Smithsonian Agreement. The rules concerning parity changes would place greater emphasis on the need to change rates that are inappropriate. And the rules are likely to be more permissive, so that some countries might permit their currencies to float while others might peg their currencies.

Just as it is predictable that there will be a move back to pegged rates and a new exchange rate arrangements, so it is inevitable that this agreement, too, will eventually become outdated and will be shelved with the gold standard and the Bretton Woods system in the monetary counterpart of the Smithsonian Institution. Monetary agreements are matters of convenience which last for a decade or two; as the economic conditions which made the agreement feasible change, the agreement becomes obsolete.

5
Gold – How Much is a 'Barbarous Relic' Worth?

President John F. Kennedy once observed that the US balance-of-payments problem was the second most complex issues he had to deal with; the first was avoiding a nuclear war. His concern was that he might have to increase the US dollar price of gold. Yet when President Richard Nixon suspended gold sales by the US Treasury in August 1971, and then agreed to increase the dollar price of gold to $38 (and to $42 slightly more than a year later), the domestic political fallout was mild.

Actually Nixon's decision were ironic. In his 1960 bid for the presidency, Nixon had suggested that the US dollar would be devalued if Kennedy were elected President. Nixon was right – Kennedy was elected President and the US dollar was devalued! Kennedy's estimates of the political costs of devaluation, domestic and foreign, proved much too high. A number of US decisions have proved more costly, including Nixon's temporary 10 percent tariff surcharge on US imports that he adopted in August 1971 and the invasion of Cambodia.

Gold's role as an international money

Gold's role in monetary affairs often has been subject to such ironic twists. John Maynard Keynes called gold a 'barbarous relic.' Charles de Gaulle said only gold could be the cornerstone of a new international monetary system. Both may have been right.

Demonetize or double the price?

The US government's suspension of gold transactions with foreign central banks in 1971 raised the question of whether gold could continue as an international money. Demonetizing gold would have

86

greatly reduced the supply of international money, since gold then was the second largest component of international reserve assets. Indefinite suspension of the US Treasury's gold transactions would have amounted to effective demonetization of gold.

One proposed solution for the gold shortage of the mid-1960s was to double the price of gold in terms of each national currency; the US gold parity would be increased to $70. Similarly the price of gold in terms of the German mark, the Japanese yen, the British pound, and the currencies of other countries also would be doubled. The rationale for increasing the price of gold was that the world commodity price level had more or less doubled since the monetary price of gold was last increased in the mid-1930s. If the price of gold in terms of each national currency were also doubled, then the relation between the world price level and the monetary price of gold would be more or less unchanged. Then, as world inflation increased in the late 1960s, the goldbugs began to talk about a US dollar parity for gold of $100 an ounce.

In 1973 and 1974, when the price of gold in the private market began to rise, first to $100 and then to $150, the most frequent explanation in the newspaper columns was that investors around the world were losing confidence in paper monies. Perhaps. But an alternative explanation was that they were betting that the monetary price of gold would increase. Why would an investor pay $100 an ounce for gold? The primary – almost the only – reason is that the investor anticipates being able to sell gold at $125 or $150 an ounce at some future date. Indeed the calculating investor would acquire gold only in the belief that the price of gold would be higher in the future, and that the rate of increase in the price of gold would be higher than the interest rate that might be earned on a low-risk government security.

In January 1980, the gold price reached $970 an ounce – briefly. And during the first half of the 1980s decade, the price of gold price generally exceeded $600. In the second half of the decade, gold fluctuated in the range of $300–$450 an ounce. In the first half of the 1990s, the price of gold varied within the range of $325–$425 an ounce; most recently, gold has traded as low as $280 an ounce – but still about eight times its price in the 1960s.

1982 Gold Commission

In 1982, the US government set up a Gold Commission to analyze and evaluate gold's future role in both the domestic and the international monetary systems. The establishment of the commission was in response to several factors, including a statement in the Republican Party's 1980 campaign platform that urged that the United States return to the gold standard. The Reagan administration loaded the membership of the commission with individuals who were not sympathetic to a monetary role for gold. So most of the commission's report was predictable, the only positive recommendation was that the US Treasury mint a new gold coin – one that would not have any fixed monetary value. The commission also recommended that the US Treasury keep its gold, because such holdings might be valuable in future international monetary negotiations.

A market price of gold of $300 or $400 is viable only if central banks continued to consider gold an attractive international money. If gold were to be demonetized, the market price of gold would tumble, as individual central banks sold gold and took their profits. In the mid-1990s central banks in Canada, the Netherlands, and Australia sold gold in the market, and reduced the share of gold in their international reserve assets. In 1999, the Bank of England began to sell a significant share of its gold holdings. For better or worse, investors have already bet that the probability of the demonetization of gold is very low – otherwise they would have sold gold and its price would be significantly lower.

Before gold was a 'barbarous relic'

The use of gold as money predates written history. How did gold develop its monetary role? To answer this question, two more questions are relevant. Why was a money necessary? And why did gold satisfy this need better than any other commodity?

Intermediate goods

Without money, goods were exchanged through barter, a time-consuming process. First, an individual who wished to sell a good had to find someone with a desirable product to exchange and this party in turn had to like the good being offered. Next, buyer and seller had to agree on a price for the exchange. Finally, the values of the goods offered by both parties to the transaction had to approximate each other – if the buyer and the seller agreed that the fair price for one horse was three cows, the seller of the horse might acquire one or two more cows than he wished or needed.

Someone realized that an *intermediate good* would lead to less costly transactions, especially if the intermediate good were both readily divisible into small units and a good store of value. Producers of individual goods could exchange their output for the intermediate good, so that they need not spend the time searching for a good to buy at the same time they wanted to sell. Prices of many goods might be expressed in terms of the number of units of this intermediate good. Because this intermediate good was divisible readily into small units, the amount of the payment in each transaction could be matched to the price. Because the intermediate good could be used as a unit of account and a store of value, this intermediate good would also be used as a medium of payment – the functions of money.

Gold and silver as intermediate goods

Gold had several attributes that made it an attractive intermediate good. Gold was durable; it did not 'wear out.' Gold was homogeneous – one ounce of gold was virtually identical with another ounce. Gold had a high value relative to its weight, so the costs of transporting gold in payments and of storing gold were low – significantly below the costs of using some other commodity in payments. Gold could be minted into large coins and small coins. Moreover, and perhaps most importantly, because of the high costs of mining the supply of gold did not increase rapidly – which meant that the price of a market basket of commodities was likely to be more stable in terms of a unit of gold than in terms of other commodities whose supplies would be likely to increase more rapidly. So gold evolved into a commodity money because of its physical attributes.

Other commodities with an attractive set of attributes have also been used as money. Silver has had a somewhat lower value-to-weight ratio than gold, so silver coins proved more useful for transactions of lower value. The costs of transporting and storing silver were much higher than the costs of transporting gold of equal value because of its lower value-to-weight ratio. When both gold coins and silver coins were used in a country at the same time, sellers of various goods would have to quote a price for each good in terms of gold coin and in terms of silver coin – unless there was a fixed price of gold coins in terms of silver coins. A fixed price between gold and silver would not simply happen: government policies were necessary to peg the price of one unit of gold in terms of a given number of units of silver. At one time in the middle of the nineteenth century, the US government set the price ratio of 15:1 (15 ounces of silver had the same US dollar value as one ounce of gold). But this ratio proved unsatisfactory because new silver discoveries led to a more rapid increase in the supply of silver than in the supply of gold, which tended to cause a decline in the price of silver. Gold was becoming more valuable because it was becoming scarcer, so individuals began to hoard gold; pressures developed to change the silver–gold price ratio to 15.5:1 and to 16:1. It proved impossible to find a price of gold in terms of silver that would work forever, so the idea of having two commodity monies was discarded. Gold eventually dominated silver as the paramount commodity money.

Paper monies

Over the last several hundred years, the authorities in virtually every country have supplemented gold's domestic role with paper monies – currency note issues and bank deposits. Paper monies are easier to use in making payments than gold, for their storage and transportation costs are much lower. Initially, individuals were dubious about the value of paper monies. One concern was that excessive production of paper monies would lead to increases in the commodity price levels and a reduction in the value of these monies – and there have been many historical episodes (especially during wars) when paper monies have lost value. So governments required that the producers of paper monies convert these monies into gold at a fixed price; this convertibility requirement was supposed to reduce the likelihood that the amount of paper money produced would prove excessively large and lead to increases in the commodity price level.

The requirement that paper monies be convertible into gold constrained the monetary authorities in their attempts to follow independent monetary policies, and so from time to time governments suspended this requirement, as the British government did during the Napoleonic Wars at the beginning of the nineteenth century. Abe Lincoln suspended this requirement during the Civil War; it was not until 1879 that the requirement was again imposed on US banks. The British government and the other belligerents in Europe suspended their gold convertibility requirements at the beginning of the First World War.

Circularity

When the constraints on the choice of monetary policies became too severe, the monetary authorities began to reduce the role of gold in their domestic monetary systems and central banks stopped converting their domestic monies into gold. In September 1931 the Bank of

England stopped buying and selling gold at a fixed price; the British authorities wanted the freedom to pursue a more expansive monetary policy to cope with an unemployment rate of 20+ percent. In 1933 the US government required all US residents to sell their gold to the US Treasury, which effectively meant that US commercial banks would no longer be required to sell gold at a fixed price.

Central banks have held gold as an international money because they believed it would be a better store of value than other international monies. Each central bank bought gold in the belief that at some future date it would be able to sell the gold to the monetary authorities in other countries, or in the commodity market. Obviously the argument was circular – central banks bought gold because they believed other central banks would buy gold when and if they wanted to sell gold. This circularity is what confidence in any money, including the various paper monies (such as US Treasury currency notes) is all about. The reason that central banks hold gold is that they have less than complete confidence that other central banks will keep their promises about paper monies – and they can always sell gold in the commodity markets to obtain US dollars or some other attractive national money.

The decline of gold

Gold's domestic monetary functions have declined throughout the twentieth century. Today, private parties rarely use gold as a medium of payment and almost never as a unit of account. Many individuals hold gold as a store of value – as an investment, either as a hedge against inflation, or as a precaution against a political crisis that might reduce the usefulness of various national monies. This change in gold's role is a response to the demand for a reduction in the cost of payments rather than a result of planning or government decree; it is much more efficient to use various national monies than gold as a medium of payment.

Similarly, gold's role as an international money has gradually declined, so that it is now used almost exclusively as a store of value. Gold is no longer used as a unit of account for central banks; to the extent that countries have parities for their currencies, these parities almost always are stated in terms of some other national money. Central banks rarely use gold as a means of payment; instead payments imbalances are financed by transfers of deposits denominated in the US dollar or in the German mark or in the Japanese yen.

That some central banks still prefer gold to US dollars or other international money as a store of value may seem irrational, for gold earns no interest, while securities denominated in the US dollar and the German mark do. One explanation often given for this preference is tradition; central banks got used to holding gold during the nineteenth century, and their preferences remain unchanged. But this explanation is not convincing. What needs to be explained is why central banks continue to hold $400 billion of gold and forgo the opportunity to earn interest by holding their international money in the form of US dollar securities, or German mark securities, or Japanese yen securities. One advantage of gold has been greater acceptability: gold may be acceptable as money by other central banks when US dollars or German marks are not. Another advantage is gold's underlying value as a commodity; gold has retained its value despite wars, revolutions, and spendthrift sovereigns.

In the short run, holding wealth in the form of gold has been inferior to holding wealth in the form of US Treasury securities, or German mark securities, or Japanese yen securities. But gold has remained, while numerous national monies have come and gone. The continuing demand for gold reflects confidence in its future value and the belief that no sovereign can diminish this value significantly. Moreover the real rate of return on gold from the periodic increases in its price has been about as high as the real rate of return on US Treasury bills.

A new gold standard?

For most observers, the idea that gold should again play a central role in the system seems bizarre. Yet the century of the gold standard (1815–1914) was one in which there was modest secular inflation; years of increases in commodity price levels were followed by years of declines in the commodity price levels. Moreover, the year-to-year changes in the consumer price level were modest, usually less than 2 percent a year, much less than in the 1970s and the 1980s and even the early 1990s. The gold standard delivered price-level stability, more so than the discretionary monetary management of the last 100 years (Box 5.1).

One reason the gold standard delivered long-run price level stability in the nineteenth century is that the price level fell briefly and sharply in a series of financial crises. These crises frequently reflected failures of large numbers of banks. The triggers for these crises differed – in some cases, large agricultural surpluses led to sharp declines in prices of corn and wheat so that farmers could not repay their bank loans with the result that many banks in agricultural areas failed. At other times, banks failed because stock prices collapsed. Whether the long-run price

Box 5.1   Gold as an Investment

The market price of gold increased so sharply in the 1970s that the rate of return attached to ownership of gold has exceeded that available on nearly every other widely held asset. During the 1970s, when the gold price went from $35 to $800, the average annual return was 36 percent. With the mid-1980s gold price of $350, the average annual return was 22 percent. In any short-term period, the rate of return from holding gold has been high if the prices rose sharply. But over the long run, the rate of return from holding gold has been below that from holding other types of financial assets.

level stability was inherent in the system or an accident remains a matter of debate.

The criticism that the gold standard would not work in the twenty-first century might be a statement about economics or a statement about politics: it is important to keep the distinction clear. There appear no inherent reasons why the gold standard would not work, what is at issue would be the costs, compared with the costs of recent national monetary policies. The dominant objections are political; the authorities in the United States and other large industrial countries are unlikely to be willing to give up the power to manage the rates of growth of national money supplies. The implication is that the public will continue to sacrifice its own interests to the promise of discretionary monetary management, while neglecting the costs of such policies.

The persistent gold shortage

The suspension of gold transactions by the US Treasury in 1971 was a response to a shortage of monetary gold that had persisted for most of the previous 60 years. The supply of gold available to central banks was smaller than desired because the private demand for gold as a commodity – for use in jewelry and industry and especially for hoarding and even speculation – had increased rapidly while the supply of gold had increased slowly. The monetary demand for gold and the private demand for gold compete with each other: when more gold is demanded for jewelry and other commodity uses, the amount of gold available for the monetary uses declines. Similarly, when the central bank demand for gold increases – that is, when central banks agreed to pay a higher price for gold – it bids gold away from private users.

1920s–1930s

The shortage of monetary gold in the decades after the First World War reflected the fact that the world commodity price level increased more rapidly than the price of gold in terms of the US dollar, the British pound, and other national currencies. Between 1914 and 1950 the US wholesale price index increased by 125 percent and the monetary price of gold by 70 percent. From 1950 to 1970 the wholesale price level increased by 35 percent; the monetary price of gold remained unchanged. From the Second World War until the early 1970s, gold producers were squeezed between significant increases in their production costs relative to their selling price (Box 5.2).

The gold shortage first became apparent immediately after the First World War, and persisted until the early 1930s. The increase in the dollar price of gold in 1934 was intended to stimulate the US economy by reversing the 30 percent decline in the US commodity price level that had occurred in the previous three years rather than to resolve the shortage of gold. As it turned out, the increase in the gold price to $35 an ounce led to a gold glut, for the amount of gold produced exceeded the amount demanded by private parties and foreign central banks. Excess gold flowed to monetary authorities and especially to those in the United States, which was subject to a 'Golden Avalanche': US gold holdings increased from $7 billion in 1934 to $20 billion in 1939. The wholesale commodity price level doubled during the 1940s and the gold glut disappeared. The possibility of a gold shortage such as the one in the 1920s reappeared because gold mining firms were again squeezed since their production costs were increasing while the price at which they could sell gold remained fixed. The private demand for gold increased, since gold was becoming progressively cheaper in terms of other commodities.

1950s–1970s

The concern about a possible gold shortage first became acute in the late 1950s. US gold holdings peaked at $24 billion in 1949 and then declined by $5 billion in the 1950s and $8 billion in the 1960s. The sale of gold by the US Treasury to foreign central banks was viewed as necessary to provide the financial basis for the postwar growth in world trade. But by 1960 there was growing recognition that the total supply of gold available for central banks as a group was smaller than the demand.

Box 5.2 $35 an Ounce and 3.1416 are not the Same Kind of Numbers

The choice of $35 as the parity for the dollar in January 1934 was a historical accident; the price might have been $30 or $40. President Roosevelt had been convinced that the way to move the US economy out of the Great Depression was to greatly increase the gold price. Gold production would be stimulated. More gold would be sold to the US monetary authorities. The US money supply would increase, and so would commodity prices. As a result, business firms would no longer incur losses because of declines in the value of their inventories, and banks would no longer be threatened with insolvency because of the declining value of their assets.

To increase the dollar price of gold, a subsidiary of the government-owned Reconstruction Finance Corporation bought gold in New York. The price of gold in the United States then tended to exceed the price, at the prevailing exchange rates, in London. Arbitragers had an incentive to buy gold in London for sale in the United States. But they had to buy sterling first; and their purchases caused the price of sterling to rise in terms of the dollar and numerous other currencies, weakening the competitive position of British firms in the world market. The British objected. The US authorities stabilized the dollar price of gold when the free market price was near $35. Had the British objection been delayed until the free market price was $40, the US gold parity would have been $40.

The impending gold shortage was an issue during the 1960 presidential election campaign. Nixon tagged Kennedy as an inflationary spender – higher prices were around the corner. The first sharp threat of a gold shortage appeared in 1960 when purchases of gold in the London market surged. Under such circumstances, the Bank of England would normally have sold gold from its holdings to keep the London price from rising above $35; the Bank would then have used its dollar receipts from the sale of gold in London to buy gold from the US Treasury. Some British officials began to doubt that the Bank of England could buy gold from the US Treasury to replenish its gold holdings after selling gold to private parties in the London market, so the Bank of England stopped selling gold in the London market. A combination of a nervous demand and the absence of a steadying supply induced an increase in the gold price to $40, which seemed extremely sharp at the time – and trivial when compared with price increases in the 1970s. Eventually, the Bank of England supplied gold to the market and the price fell to $35. Still, the first signal of an impending gold shortage had appeared.

Two kinds of measures might have resolved the shortage of gold: either the private demand for gold might have declined if the world commodity price level fell, or the supply of gold might have been increased if the monetary price of gold had been raised. The scope for reducing the private demand for gold was small, for governments had neither the will nor the incentive to pursue financial policies that would lead to declines in commodity price levels; the costs were judged too high in terms of unemployment, business failures, and lost elections. US gold regulations were changed to prohibit American citizens from buying or holding gold outside the United States (they had been prohibited from holding gold domestically since 1933). Efforts to induce foreign governments to apply similar measures to their residents were rebuffed.

By 1965 the private demand for gold had increased above the level of new gold production; central banks sold $50 million of gold from their reserves to hold the price at $35. Uncertainties about the future parity for the British pound led to another surge in the private demand for gold. In 1967 central banks sold $1.6 billion of gold to private parties to prevent the price from rising above $35, and in the first 10 weeks of 1968, sales to private parties reached $700 million.

Central bankers were alarmed lest the experience of the 1930s be repeated: they were concerned that once the British pound was devalued, investors would conclude that other currencies would be devalued – that once again the dominoes would fall. They believed that, at a minimum, the US dollar price of gold would be doubled, so the potential profit from an increase in the gold price was attractive. Altogether, private parties bought more than $3 billion of gold from central banks in the 1965–8 period. Much of this demand was supplied, indirectly, from the US Treasury.

Then in March 1968 the monetary authorities in Europe and the United States agreed to separate the private gold market from the market in which central banks buy and sell gold to each other. Under this two-tier arrangement, non-monetary and monetary gold became 'separate' commodities; the link between the private market and the official market was severed. Most newly produced gold was to be sold in the private market to satisfy industrial, artistic, and hoarding demands. Initially, central banks continued to deal in gold with each other at the $35 price. In the private market, the gold price might rise above $35 – or, conceivably, fall below $35.

The adoption of the two-tier system raised two problems – one involved how South Africa's $1 billion annual gold output would be sold. Obviously South Africa wanted the highest price; it wanted to sell between one-half and two-thirds of its gold output to private parties, at prices of perhaps $38 or $40 or more, and the rest to official institutions at the $35 price. The European central banks liked the South African proposal, since they would be able to add to their gold holdings. At the same time, their gold holdings would be more valuable if the price in the private market climbed above $35.

The US authorities, in contrast, wanted South Africa to sell all its gold in the private market in the belief that the price of gold would then fall, perhaps to $30 or $32. According to the US scenario, central banks' confidence in the future of gold as international money would be shaken. At the same time, their demand for other types of international money (including US dollar securities) would increase, and countries would become more receptive to the need for a new international money.

Eventually, a compromise was reached. South Africa would be permitted to sell limited amounts of gold at $35 to central banks; the rest would be sold in private markets. But this compromise became irrelevant almost as soon as it was concluded, for the increase in the private demand for gold in response to worldwide inflation meant that nearly all of South Africa's output could be sold to private parties at $40 – or even higher prices.

Once the price of gold in the private market began to exceed the official price, the second problem became apparent – central banks were reluctant to buy and sell gold with each other at the $35 parity if the market price was higher. So the irony was that the increase in the market price of gold above the official price reduced the liquidity of official gold holdings.

Turbulence in the gold market

One of the oldest clichés in monetary economics is that 'gold is a good inflation hedge.' The meaning is clear: if the commodity price level increases, the price of gold will also increase. So a unit of gold will maintain its purchasing power over a bundle of goods better than currency notes or bank deposits denominated in the US dollar, or the German mark, or the Japanese yen, or the British pound.

Return on gold investments

There is much evidence in support of this view – as a long-run proposition. Assume comparable investments in gold, US dollar securities, German mark securities, Japanese yen securities, and British pound securities. The value of the investments in each of these national securities compounds with the money market interest rates in each country. The value of the investment in gold changes as the US dollar price of gold changes – first by 70 percent in 1933–4, and then with the change in the market price of gold after the 1970s. In 1999 the value of the investment in gold was 15 times the value in 1900. The value of a comparable investment in the US bonds was 65 times higher in 1999 than 1900.

Now contrast the returns on the investment in gold in the 1970s and the 1980s. In the 1970s the US price level increased by a factor of four; the US dollar price of gold increased by a factor of 20. In the 1980s, in contrast, the US price level increased by about 50 percent; the US dollar price of gold fell by one-third.

The market price of gold since the mid-1960s is shown in Figure 5.1. Earlier, from the 1930s to the mid-1960s, the price of gold remained unchanged, and even after the move to the two-tier gold market in 1968 the price increases remained relatively stable. Then, in 1973 and 1974, the price began to increase. The gold price fell to just over $100 in 1976 before beginning to increase again, initially modestly, then sharply.

The pattern is that when the world inflation rate increased, the market price of gold increased more rapidly; and when the inflation rate declined, the price of gold declined.

Assume you've won the lottery; should you buy gold or should you instead invest your wealth in bonds or equities or real estate? The choice will depend in large part on your estimates of the rates of return. The rate of return attached to holding gold depends on the difference between the price you pay for gold today, and the estimate of the price at which the gold might be sold in six month's or a year's time.

The estimate of the price of gold a year from now will depend on the estimates of the price two years from now, which in turn will depend on estimates of the price of gold three years from now, which in turn, etc. *Time consistency* is the name of the game. So the market price of gold increases whenever the price is low relative to the anticipated price and the interest rate used to discount this anticipated price.

The price of gold increased in the 1970s because the inflation rate was increasing relative to the interest rate. And the price of gold fell in

Figure 5.1 Market price of gold, 1965–2000

the 1980s because the inflation rate was declining and the interest rate was rising.

The US game plan

The objective of the US game plan for gold in the 1960s was to avoid an increase in the US dollar price of gold, largely for political reasons. Successive US presidents following Eisenhower – Kennedy, Johnson, and then Nixon – had said that the dollar price of gold would be fixed forever. The retention of the $35 gold parity was a US commitment like the Monroe Doctrine. The party line was that altering one US commitment would undermine the credibility of every other. The adoption of a $38 parity and then a $42 parity by the Nixon administration helped resolve the impasse over exchange rate structure, but it made no dent in the gold problem. Yet this minor change led to an important insight; it demonstrated that while a few economists and government officials were vitally interested in the gold price, the American public was bored. The price of gold was not a domino; increasing the US dollar price of gold had no significant adverse reaction, at home or abroad.

The US government's response to the gold shortage was that gold should be gradually phased out of the international monetary system; if gold were demonetized, it would not appear as if the United States had altered its parity. After the US dollar price of gold was increased, first in the Smithsonian Agreement and again in February 1972, the government's commitment to phasing out gold as an international reserve asset was retained, even though the costs of altering the $35 parity had already been incurred.

The choices now available

One of the alternatives to the US response is a return to the gold market arrangements of the 1940s and 1950s, only at a monetary price related to the market price of gold. In the late 1990s, this price might be $350 or $400 an ounce. Because the increase in the price of gold would be about 10 times the $35 parity of the 1950s and the 1960s, while the world price level has increased by a factor of four to five, there would be stimulus to gold production. At the higher gold price, the supply of newly produced gold would be larger, while the private demand would be smaller. The other basic option involves continued and probably sporadic sales of gold by central banks from their monetary stocks.

Now that the price of gold has been increased and the political costs of this change have been incurred (and almost certainly long forgotten), the costs and benefits of retaining gold as a monetary asset or of keeping gold in limbo can be evaluated. Nearly every country has a vested interest in the monetary price of gold. An increase in the gold price – or gold demonetization – would make some countries better off, some more so than others. The big gainers would be the countries that produce a great deal of gold, primarily South Africa and Russia, and the countries that hold significant part of gold in their reserves, particularly the United States, France, Germany, Italy, and Switzerland. And the individuals who own gold would be richer.

Officials in other countries might feel worse off because they would not share in these gains. And many of them would blame the United States, since the change in the price would be seen as a result of US policy. Since the United States produces and consumes minimal amounts of gold, direct US economic interests are trivial. The central US interest in the monetary role for gold is the functioning of the international monetary system and, to a much lesser extent, its consequences for US foreign relations.

Changes in the gold price have an impact on gold producers – on the owners of gold mines and their labor force – and on the producers of competitive monies and commodities. When gold is valued at $400 an ounce, investors' holdings may approach $100 billion. Should the monetary price of gold rise, the producers of competitive monies would lose. If, on the other hand, gold is demonetized, the pattern of winners and losers is reversed.

Several questions remain. One is: what will happen to the market price of gold if gold is demonetized? A second involves the monetary price, should gold be retained as an international money?

Costs and consequences of demonetizing gold

Demonetization would probably result after the gradual realization by central banks that their holdings of gold would be of greater value and utility if they sold it in the commodity markets. Central bank gold sales in the commodity markets might sharply depress the price because the stock of gold held by central banks, 37 000 metric tons, is large relative to the annual production of gold, which is about 1000 metric tons. Sales that seem small relative to central bank holdings would be quite large relative to the new supply from each year's production. Once the price began to fall, numerous private holders of gold would sell to take their profits or cut their losses, and the gold price would fall sharply; how rapidly and how far would depend on the size of central bank sales – and on investor anticipations of central bank sales. Almost immediately the six or eight central banks that are the major holders of gold would seek to establish an agreement limiting their sales in the commodity market.

What would be the international consequences of demonetizing gold? Gold producing countries and those European countries which hold large amounts of gold as international money would lose, since the value of their holdings would decline. South Africa would lose since the price of its major export would decline. Russia would lose. The gainers would include industrial users of gold, since the commodity price would fall. Your dentist – and mine – would be better off. But this gain would have to be balanced against the cost of having a smaller supply of international money than was formerly deemed optimal.

Costs and consequences of retaining gold

Assume, on the other hand, that a decision is made to retain gold as an international money; then the price at which gold would be traded among central banks would have to be set. This price must be somewhat above the recent market price. If this price is substantially above the price at which gold had been trading, some private investors might realize their gains; they would sell gold and so monetary gold holdings would increase. The authorities would be concerned with a gold glut, much as in the 1930s.

Setting the 'right' monetary price for gold, which is sometimes called the 're-entry problem,' would be especially difficult. As long as investors anticipated that the US price level would continue to increase by more than 2 or 3 percent a year, their demand for gold would remain strong. If the US inflation rate remained low, then the US dollar price of gold might remain in a trading range of $250–$350 an ounce

A move to a higher monetary price seems unlikely to occur as a result of a formal international agreement. Rather, the US government may gradually come to recognize that an important US national interest would be served by retaining gold as an important component of international monetary arrangements. The elements in this decision would include the usefulness of having an international money in the system in addition to the US dollar and other national currencies, and the difficulties in having this money produced by an international institution.

The US Treasury would then have to calculate the appropriate price for gold, but it would recognize the chanciness of trying to determine the right price. If the new parity is $400 an ounce, the monetary gold holdings of central banks as a group would be worth $450 billion and the monetary value of *current* annual output would be $8 billion. A higher market price for gold would stimulate production, so new output might reach $10 billion annually. If private expenditures on gold remained unchanged – the percentage decline in the number of ounces purchased approximating the increase in the market price – monetary gold stocks might increase by $5 or $6 billion annually.

These are rough estimates, not definite projections. There is a US dollar price of gold which would enable both official and private demands to be satisfied adequately, at least for a few years, unless world inflation increases sharply. The monetary price of gold might be initially set at a level at which the amount supplied exceeded the amount demanded. In that case – if the gold supply were initially excessive – gold would flow into the US Treasury, as in the late 1930s. Because of the higher value of the gold output, other countries could satisfy their gold needs without forcing the United States to sell gold.

Some economists have argued that an increase in the gold price would be inflationary: private parties would spend more as a result of their revaluation gains. This concern might be valid if gold were still used as a domestic money; it has much less force now, with gold's monetary role limited to transactions among central banks, and since private gold holdings are such a small fraction of total private wealth. Some central banks might follow a somewhat more expansive monetary policy as a result of their revaluation gains. Any increase in commodity price levels from an increase in the monetary price of gold would be extremely small relative to increases resulting from other factors such as financing government deficits or sharp increases in stock prices.

Political and international generalizations

When Keynes called gold a 'barbarous relic,' he meant that mining gold to produce an international money is unnecessarily expensive. Producing $6 billion of gold uses labor and machinery that might produce $6 billion of other goods. If the IMF or some other international institution produces $6 billion of paper gold, the costs are minimal – the time of some government negotiators and a few clerks to record which central banks owe how much money to whom. And the labor and machinery otherwise used to mine gold for monetary purposes could then be diverted to producing dams, schools, hospitals.

The cost of producing $6 billion or $8 billion of gold falls on those countries which prefer to hold gold in their reserves when they might otherwise hold IMF-produced money or US dollar securities, since these countries must earn the gold by exporting goods and services, in effect to the gold mining countries. The European countries with a strong demand for gold would acquire most of the newly produced gold. They would also bear most of these costs.

What about the political consequences of changing the gold price? At one time, it was feared that raising the gold price would give substantial windfall gains to the Soviet Union and South Africa; and that is bad, the argument went, because the former was part of the Sino–Soviet communist conspiracy and the latter practiced apartheid. So reducing the gold price inflicts losses on the Soviet Union and South Africa, and that is good.

Much has happened since the first editions of this book. The Sino–Soviet conspiracy to take over the world has disappeared; the Soviet Union has fragmented into a confederation of republics, and the

United States and other industrial countries are providing loans and grants to these countries. And apartheid is dead in South Africa; South Africa has moved to majority rule. If gold is valued at $400 an ounce, South Africa's gold production would account for 15 percent of its GNP and 50 percent of its exports. At this gold price, the blacks gain in economic welfare. If gold is demonetized, South Africa would take a big hit.

If gold is demonetized, then the credibility of the commitments to satisfy the world's demand for international money by producing paper gold would be low. Raising the gold price would also be more nearly consistent with the structure of the IMF and its Articles of Agreement than would gold demonetization – but the IMF is almost certainly against a larger role for gold because it implies a smaller role for the Fund as an institution. Gold demonetization would impose substantial losses on those now holding gold, whereas retaining gold by increasing the monetary price imposes losses on no one, although those central banks that hold US dollars and other reserve assets might be upset because they would not share in the revaluation gains.

The move toward increasing the gold price might occur after exchange rates were again pegged, or even before. If exchange rates were again pegged, the United States would again need to concern itself with its payments position. Both the demonetization of gold and a gold price increase would help reduce any US payments deficit. Demonetization would work because the US authorities would no longer have to worry about a US payments deficit, since foreign official institutions could no longer require the US Treasury to sell gold. And the gold price increase would work because the annual increase in the gold supply could be large enough to enable other countries to satisfy their demand for international money without forcing the United States to incur payments deficits and sell gold. Indeed, because of the increase in the value of the annual gold production, every country might add to its gold holdings at the same time.

It is true that reliance on gold is an inefficient way to meet the demand for international money; there are less costly alternatives. The problem, however, is not with gold, but rather with the attitudes and preferences of central banks around the world – and their experience with the credibility of commitments made by their counterparts in foreign governments. The European preference for gold may seem archaic. But it is their preference – and they pay the costs of retaining gold in the system.

Ultimately, the role of gold in international monetary arrangements is, as de Gaulle knew, a US choice. The United States must decide whether the international financial arrangements will function more smoothly and US interests will be better served if the European preferences are satisfied or frustrated. For at least three decades, US authorities focused on trying to wean the European central banks away from their preference for gold; the effort was not notably successful. At some stage, US officials may still seek to build a system around these preferences.

In monetary affairs, the authorities cannot afford to be ambiguous; to do so would point toward profit opportunities open to private investors. So they can never hint that they will change a parity, shift from pegged to floating rates, or favor a change in the monetary gold price. When the timing seems appropriate, however, they can suddenly reverse their policies.

6

The Dollar and Coca-Cola are Both Brand Names

The money-producing industry

The money-producing industry is like the soda pop industry; a large number of firms make a similar product. Soda pop is basically carbonated colored water. One brand of pop is a good substitute for another; Coke and Pepsi compete vigorously for the same customers. Each pop-producing firm strives to make its brands attractive; the product is available in large, small, and medium-sized packages, and in bottles and cans. The packages are attractively designed. Once a product is successful, variants or extensions are developed – Coke begat Diet Coke, and then Caffeine Free Coke, and then Diet Caffeine Free, and then Classic Coke.

Coca-Cola has been so successful in its marketing strategy that a gallon of Coke – caramel-colored fizzy water – sells for more than $1, or more than twice the pretax price of a gallon of gasoline. High pre-tax profits automatically attract competitive imitators who frequently choose a similar name and try in other ways to infringe on the market position of the brand leader. The market leaders strive to distinguish themselves from their competitors; they protect their brand names by copyright.

Brands of money

So it is with money. Each national central bank produces its own brand of money. Each of these national monies serves an identical set of functions – as a medium of payment, a store of value, and a unit of account – but in a different political jurisdiction. Each national money is as a minimum slightly differentiated from every other national money, and some national monies are extremely poor substitutes for other national monies. Thus the US dollar and the Canadian dollar are not perfect substitutes for each other; similarly the French franc is an imperfect substitute for the Swiss franc. Some national monies have proven much better than others as a store of value. The Swiss franc has a remarkable track record as a store of value, even more impressive than the US dollar. And the Dutch guilder also has performed admirably.

The analogy between the soda pop industry and the money industry may seem invalid within the United States, for while the supermarkets carry numerous brands of pop, the banks carry only one brand of money. Nearly all transactions in the United States are settled by payments in US dollars. But some US firms and some US residents hold large amounts of money in London, the Bahamas, Zurich, and elsewhere for business convenience, or to avoid US monetary and fiscal regulations (see Chapter 7 on the Eurodollar market and Chapter 15 on tax avoidance). More importantly, foreign residents have had a much greater incentive to hold US dollar securities because of the brand leadership position of the US dollar in the money production industry. Russian citizens, for example, mistrust their national money, and their holdings of US dollars are as large as their holdings of roubles.

During the 1950s and the 1960s, the US dollar was the leading brand name in the money industry. Immediately after the Second World War, US currency notes circulated extensively in Europe; the US dollar was viewed as a better store of value than most of the European currencies. In Latin America, Europe, and Asia, many firms and individuals held a substantial portion of their wealth in the form of US dollar securities. There may be more $100 bills in circulation in Moscow than in Washington and New York City combined. Some business firms in Europe and Asia with substantial international business interests kept their books in dollars – even though they met their payrolls in their national currencies.

Some central banks have changed the brand name of their own product to 'dollar' to increase its attractiveness; this name change is sometimes accompanied by changes in packaging. When Australia, Jamaica, and Malaysia changed from the traditional British system of pounds, shillings, and pence to a decimal-based systems, they named their standard currency unit the dollar, a tribute to the preeminent standing of the US dollar. But there is only one US dollar; the other central banks were seeking to establish a kinship relation with the established market position of the US producer.

Another favored brand of money, one that appeals to a specialized and small segment of the market (like the Ferrari in automobiles or

Glenlivet in Scotch whisky, or Perrier in the bottled water industry) is the Swiss franc. In the 1970s and the 1980s the German mark became increasingly attractive because of Germany's success in achieving a low inflation rate.

Selling the brand

Central banks, like the soda pop-producing firms, sell their product. The public 'pays' for the money produced by the central bank by supplying goods and services to the government. When the Federal Reserve produces more dollars, Americans acquire these dollars by selling goods, services, and securities to the Fed's owner, the US government. The larger the public's demand for money in the form of US dollar currency notes, the larger the volume of goods and services that the US government can acquire without having to raise taxes. Each central bank, like each firm in the soda pop industry, has a vested interest in increasing the demand for its brand of money as a way to reduce the interest rates that must be paid to induce investors to hold securities denominated in the national currency.

The production of commemorative postage stamps provides a good analogy to the production of money. Like money, these stamps can be produced at very low cost; the major expense in producing stamps is developing both designs and paper that are costly to imitate. The producers of these bits of colored engraved paper want the public to hold more and more of their stamps; they much prefer to have these stamps pasted into collectors' books than onto letters. Liechtenstein would go broke if most of the postage stamps it sells were used to mail letters.

Similarly, the producers of traveler's checks profit handsomely from their sale, for the receipts from the sale of these non-interest-bearing checks are used to buy interest-earning assets. Travelers' checks are close substitutes for currency and are almost equally profitable. So more and more banks and travel companies have begun to produce traveler's checks with their own names, hoping to cash in on the profits of the market leaders in the industry.

Each central bank has a marketing strategy to strengthen the demand for its particular brand of money. Just as each of the soda pop firms wants the public to buy more of its pop and less of its competitors', each central bank wants the public to buy and hold more of its money. The greater the demand the more readily the product – the national money – can be sold, and the smaller the need to sell interest-bearing bonds or to raise taxes to pay for the government's expenditures.

Packaging is one element in the marketing strategy – two or three colors are used in printing the money. In the United States, most of the currency notes carry the portraits of presidents (although Alexander Hamilton, the first US Secretary of the Treasury is on the $10 bill and Benjamin Franklin is on the $100 bill); in Great Britain, the reigning king or queen; in Austria, the composers. Frequently, a central bank provides a money-back guarantee, and offers to repurchase its own money in exchange for a leading foreign money at a guaranteed price, the exchange parity for its currency.

In 1997 the US Treasury introduced a new $100 bank note; the motive was to develop a currency note that would be more difficult to counterfeit. The Russians are estimated to hold $40 billion of these notes. If the Russians had not bought these US notes so that the US Treasury had instead sold new bonds that paid 5.5 percent interest, the US Treasury's annual interest payments would have been $2.2 billion higher.

The packaging arrangements in the soda pop industry are a component of pricing policy: the more attractive the package, the higher the price. Brand name products sell at substantially higher prices than virtually identical unbranded generic goods. In some cases, the firm sells a way of life or a self-image rather than a product.* In much the same way, the packaging arrangements in the money-producing industry are designed to enhance the attractiveness of brand names, so interest rates on securities denominated in its currency are lower. Finance ministers and treasury secretaries want low interest rates to minimize their government's borrowing costs. In Great Britain, holders of certain treasury securities can participate in a special lottery; the British Treasury sells these securities at a lower interest rate. The lottery prizes cost the government less than the savings in interest payments. Similarly, holders of some US Treasury securities receive special tax advantages that are intended to reduce the interest rates necessary to attract investors to buy these securities. From the US Treasury's point of view, the cost of the tax advantages is smaller than the reduction in interest payments. Some countries link the interest rates on domestic securities to the price of gold or to the foreign exchange price of the US dollar to increase the attractiveness of these securities. All such devices are marketing gimmicks designed to create investor interest in particular money brands – the central bank's counterpart of commemorative postage stamps and baseball cards.

---

* This technique conforms to Michael Aliber's First Theorem: 'When you buy baseball cards, you get the gum free.'

Overproduction

In the money industry, just as in the soda pop industry, overproduction occurs. In the soda pop industry, any firm that increases its output very rapidly may have to cut the price or else its cans and bottles will pile up on supermarket shelves. When too much money is produced, people may shift from domestic money to goods – and to other brands of money. Central banks can produce more money, but individuals cannot be forced to hold more money than they wish. So individuals sell this money for other monies, and its value in the foreign exchange market falls, until investors can be attracted to acquire and hold this money.

Enhancing demand

Authorities frequently take direct measures to enhance investor demand for the national brand of money. Most governments stipulate that only the national money is legal tender within their boundaries; tax collectors refuse to accept payment in foreign monies. Ministers of finance and secretaries of the treasury continually 'talk up' the national brand by wrapping their policies in the flag. When the voluntary approach proves inadequate, compulsory measures are often used, and purchases of monies and securities denominated in foreign currencies may be taxed or licensed.

The market position of currency brands

Own-brands of money

The contrast between the number of brand names in money – and the number of brand names in automobiles and jet aircraft – is strong. While every country except the very small ones – the Panamas and the Luxembourgs and the Liechtensteins – has its own currency brand, most countries import their jet aircraft and automobiles from foreign firms. Thus Japan Airlines and AeroMexico buy US-produced jet aircraft because they are cheaper than domestically produced jets would be. Their national airlines – which compete with United, American, and Delta and other foreign airlines in the search for customers and for profits – are reluctant to incur the additional cost of buying higher-priced, domestically produced aircraft, for they would then be at a competitive disadvantage in the world market.

One reason nearly every country insists on producing its own money is that there seems to be *no cost to having a national money* – at least, the costs are not obvious. But for most countries, the decision to have a national money means that the interest rates on its loans and securities are higher than they would be if its currency were merged with that of a major country with a stable currency. If Canada, for example, were to give up its own money and adopt the US brand, the interest rates to borrowers in Canada would inevitably decline to level of interest rates on US dollar loans. Having a national currency has meant that borrowers in Canada have been at a cost disadvantage in the international marketplace because they have had a higher cost of capital.

Indeed, many Canadian firms, as well as the provincial governments like those in British Columbia and Quebec, come to New York and issue US dollar-denominated securities to reduce their interest costs below the rates they would pay if they borrowed in Canada. To the extent that the higher interest rates charged Canadian borrowers are a result of having a national money, there is a real cost to Canada, for some investment projects which might be undertaken if interest rates were lower are never launched.

Yet governments continue to retain national monies despite the costs; relatively few have decided to abandon their national brands – although 11 of the 15 members of the European Union have agreed to adopt the Euro as their currency and to give up on their national brand. One reason that some countries retain their national currency is that they want the prestige of a national money. Moreover, a country can have a monetary policy only if it has a national money. And kings and presidents want their constituents to be proud of their heritage: the prouder they are, the less reluctant they will be, in theory, to pay taxes.

Each government profits from having a national money, for the cost of producing it – printing the bank notes or issuing the deposits – is less than the purchasing power of the money in terms of goods and services. These profits are an indirect form of taxation. Indeed, issuing money is often a less costly way of taxing the public, especially if the fiscal apparatus for collecting taxes is inadequate, or corrupt, or cumbersome. Being able to produce money enables government leaders to circumvent parliamentary opposition to higher tax rates.

Brand attractiveness

In market economies, the prices of financial securities – or the prices of most of them – vary continuously in response to changes in the supply and demand. Prices adjust to find buyers. If prices are sufficiently low, buyers can be found even for such risky securities as the bond issues of Penn Central in 1976 and the Czar Bonds of 1912. Within a country, investors continually shuffle the ownership of short-term securities, long-term securities, growth stocks, and public utility stocks as their assessments of the future change. Similarly investors continually compare the attractiveness of monies with different brand names.

All financial securities – bank notes, demand deposits, government bonds, corporate bonds – must have a brand name. The buyers of securities can choose among 12 kinds of dollars, eight kinds of francs, a variety of pesos (Spain, Mexico, Argentina, Uruguay), several different yen (the Chinese yuen, the Korean won, the Japanese yen) the real, several baht, the ringgit, and numerous other national currency brands. Investors must calculate whether the currency brands that currently are most attractive will remain so. Possible changes in the market position of the various brand names – and hence in the foreign exchange values of their currencies – are closely examined.

In the 1980s, interest rates on securities denominated in Danish kroner were higher than interest rates on comparable securities denominated in Swedish kroner because investors were concerned that the Danish currency might depreciate; they wanted the additional interest income to offset the possible loss from holding depreciating Danish kroner securities. If there were complete confidence in the predictability of future changes in exchange rates, then investors would shift funds between Danish securities and Swedish securities until the difference between interest rates on the securities denominated in these currencies reflected the anticipated change in the Danish kronor price of the Swedish kroner. If they anticipated that the Danish kroner would depreciate by 1 percent a year relative to the Swedish kroner, they would buy Swedish securities and sell Danish securities until interest rates on Danish securities were 1 percent a year higher than on comparable Swedish securities. In all likelihood, if the Swedish securities were preferred, then the interest rates on Danish securities would exceed those on comparable Swedish securities by somewhat more than 1 percent a year – a reflection of a currency preference.

Currency brands can be ranked like songs on a hit parade, with the standings based on the interest rates on securities that are similar except for currency of denomination. Investor preferences for currency and checking account money – securities which usually carry no explicit market yield – can be inferred from their preferences for long term, interest-bearing securities denominated in the same currencies. For example, if the interest rates on long-term US dollar securities are below those on long-term British pound securities, then the US dollar stands above the British pound on the currency hit parade. Investors would hold securities denominated in the British pound only if interest rates on these securities were sufficiently high to compensate for the probable fall in the value of the British pound relative to the US dollar. Higher interest rates are necessary to find buyers for money and other financial securities denominated in the pound – that is, to adjust for overproduction of British pounds. Higher interest rates are the international money market's counterpart to price-cutting in the soda pop market.

Some investors seemingly ignore the brand name problem when buying securities, as do many borrowers when they issue new liabilities. Most investors deal in securities denominated in the national brand, the currency of the country in which they live. Similarly, most individuals vote for the same party in election after election. Candidates for office pitch their campaigns at the 10–20 percent of the electorate whose changing preferences swing the election results.

Brand loyalty is – or once was – strong in cigarettes and beer. Producers within such industries – money, politics, and tobacco – market their products toward swing voters and swing buyers. Convenience, ignorance, uncertainty about exchange rates, and exchange controls explain the preference for the domestic brand of money. Still, an increasing number of investors calculate – or at least attempt to calculate – the advantages of acquiring securities denominated in one of several foreign currencies. The smaller the country, the more likely that its residents will compare foreign alternatives to domestic monies and securities. Dutch and Swiss investors, for example, are much more aware of securities denominated in foreign currencies than US investors are; many US dollar securities are listed on the stock exchanges in Amsterdam and Zurich.

Throughout the nineteenth century and until the First World War, the British pound was at the top of the currency hit parade, in part because London was the world's principal financial center. At that time firms and governments headquartered in the United States, Argentina, and Canada found it cheaper to issue securities denominated in the British pound in London than to issue comparable securities in their own currency in their domestic market.

The US dollar displaced the British pound as a result of the financial events associated with the First World War. Great Britain had adopted exchange controls that prevented foreign borrowers from selling new securities in London. Moreover during the war the US price level had increased by significantly less than the British price level and interest rates on US dollar securities had declined below interest rates on comparable British pound securities.

For most of the period between 1920 and 1980, securities denominated in the US dollar were at the top of the brand name hit parade. In contrast, currencies that had been more or less subject to continuous devaluation had lower ranking, evidenced by the higher yields on securities denominated in these currencies. Thus, interest rates on securities denominated in the British pound, the Canadian dollar, the Japanese yen, and even the German mark were higher than interest rates on securities denominated in the US dollar because investors believed that securities denominated in these currencies were riskier.

The Swiss franc has had a special place on the hit parade; interest rates on securities denominated in the franc have been lower than those on securities denominated in the US dollar. Switzerland is attractive to investors for a variety of reasons – one is political stability and another is financial stability and a record in achieving price-level stability. The Swiss franc has been a very strong currency. And the tax rates on interest income on Swiss franc securities have been low. The Swiss authorities are not especially curious about the sources of the suitcase money carried over the Alps to Lugano, or flown in from New York or Cali, Columbia. The Swiss have provided a laundry for money – at a price, because investors were willing to accept a low interest rate on their holdings of securities denominated in the Swiss franc because of these other advantages.

The US dollar was the only major currency that remained pegged to gold during the First World War. Moreover, during the war the US price level had risen much less than the British price level (Table 6.1). US financial markets offered investors a wide range of securities, and the United States took on a dominant role in the international economy. Central banks in Europe and elsewhere began to acquire US dollar securities as part of their holdings of international money.

The question today is whether the depreciation of the US dollar in terms of the German mark, the Japanese yen, and the Swiss franc may lead to a displacement of the dollar from the top rank, much as the British pound was displaced earlier.

Table 6.1 Interest rates nominal and real: 1965–98 (percent)

	1965	1970	1975	1980	1985	1990	1995	1996	1997	1998
United States										
Interest rate	4.3	6.9	8.2	11.4	10.6	8.6	6.6	6.4	6.6	5.3
Inflation rate	1.3	4.2	6.8	8.9	3.6	5.4	2.8	2.9	2.3	1.6
Real interest rate	3.0	2.7	1.4	2.5	8.0	3.2	3.8	3.5	4.1	3.7
Germany										
Interest rate	7.1	8.3	8.5	8.5	6.9	8.9	6.5	5.6	5.1	4.4
Inflation rate	3.2	3.4	5.9	5.4	2.2	2.7	1.8	1.5	1.8	1.0
Real interest rate	3.9	4.9	2.6	3.1	4.7	6.2	4.7	4.1	3.3	3.4
Japan										
Interest rate	NA	7.2	9.2	9.2	6.3	7.4	2.5	2.2	1.7	1.1
Inflation rate	6.7	7.6	11.8	7.8	2.0	3.1	-0.1	0.1	1.7	0.6
Real interest rate	NA	-0.4	-2.6	1.4	4.3	4.3	2.6	2.1	0.0	0.5
Great Britain										
Interest rate	7.1	8.3	8.5	8.5	10.6	11.1	8.3	8.1	7.1	5.5
Inflation rate	2.7	2.4	6.1	4.1	6.1	9.5	3.4	2.4	3.1	3.4
Real interest rate	4.4	5.9	2.4	4.4	4.5	1.6	4.9	5.2	4.0	2.1
France										
Interest rate	5.3	8.1	9.5	13.0	10.9	9.9	7.6	6.9	5.6	4.7
Inflation rate	3.7	4.4	8.9	10.4	5.8	3.4	1.8	2.0	1.2	1.7
Real interest rate	1.6	3.7	0.6	2.6	5.1	6.5	5.8	4.4	4.4	3.0

Table 6.1 continued

	1965	1970	1975	1980	1985	1990	1995	1996	1997	1998
Switzerland										
Interest rate	4.0	5.8	6.4	4.8	4.8	6.7	3.7	3.6	3.1	2.4
Inflation rate	3.2	3.5	7.7	5.9	3.4	5.4	1.8	0.8	0.5	0.1
Real interest rate	0.8	2.3	-1.3	-1.1	1.4	1.3	1.9	2.8	2.6	2.3
Canada										
Interest rate	5.2	7.9	9.0	12.5	11.0	10.9	8.3	7.5	6.4	5.5
Inflation rate	1.6	3.9	7.3	8.7	4.0	4.8	2.2	1.6	1.6	1.0
Real interest rate	3.6	4.0	1.7	3.8	7.0	6.1	6.1	5.9	4.8	4.5

A dollar standard world?

Gold and dollar standards

The US dollar has been a workhorse currency during the second half of the twentieth century, the currency used by most central banks when they have intervened in the foreign exchange market. Holdings of US dollar securities have been the largest component of central bank reserves since 1970. International firms and investors have used the US dollar as a vehicle currency: more international trade transactions are denominated in the dollar than in any other currency.

These multiple roles reflect the dominant size of the United States in the world economy: economic changes in the United States have a substantial impact on economic events abroad. Changes in the US money supply have a major impact on changes in the world money supply, and changes in US interest rates have a major impact on interest rates in other countries. Changes in the US price level necessarily have a major direct impact on the world price level, and extensive indirect impacts. A change in the US price level has a greater effect on the world price level that is suggested by the US share of world GNP.

Because of the central importance of the United States, the dollar is frequently the numeraire currency, or the unit of account on transactions that do not involve Americans. Thus international airlines fares are stated in terms of dollars; the price of a London – New York ticket in London is the product of the US dollar price and the British pound – US dollar exchange rate. The prices of many international commodities – gold in Zurich, petroleum in the Gulf – are stated in terms of dollars. So it seems that the world is on a dollar standard, much as the world was once on the gold standard.

The meaning of the term 'gold standard' is unambiguous – central banks stated parities for their currencies in terms of gold, gold was the largest component of the assets held by central banks, and changes in the money supply in each country resulted from gold inflows and gold outflows. The term dollar standard is more ambiguous. One meaning of the term is that the rest of the world holds US dollar securities for a variety of purposes. The large amounts of US dollar securities owned by different groups of investors resident in various foreign countries highlights the unique US role as a producer of international money. The United States exports dollar securities to satisfy the needs of foreigners, just as Germany exports Volkswagens, Ecuador exports bananas, and South Africa exports gold. As long as investors retain confidence in the brand name of the US dollar, the use of the term 'deficit' to describe intended and voluntary increases in the dollar holdings of foreigners is misleading. During the late 1960s, the late 1970s and the later 1980s, some foreign central banks acquired more US dollars than they would have preferred; their dominant motivation for buying the dollar in the foreign exchange market was to limit the appreciation of their currencies.

(Of course, separating the intended from the unintended increases in foreign holdings of dollars would be difficult. But the errors that might arise in making this distinction operational are likely to be smaller than those resulting from a following misleading concept.)

One of the paradoxes of the late 1960s was that just as the US payments deficit began to increase, some analysts asserted that the world was on the dollar standard. The meaning of the term was vague; the implication was that changes in the US dollar money supply, like changes in the monetary gold supply 60 and 70 years earlier, determined the world price level. True, the US government's policies for financing the Vietnam War led to sharp increases both in the US price level and in the US payments deficit, and the parallel increases in the payments surpluses of other countries meant that their own money supplies increased sharply, so that their price levels rose as rapidly as the US price level. The United States was exporting inflation. But the logical implication of the phrase 'the world is on the dollar standard' was that foreign central banks had shifted to dependent monetary policies and were unwilling to revalue their currencies relative to the US dollar.

This dollar standard view of the world was shattered by the decisions of Canada, Germany, and the Netherlands to permit their currencies to float in 1970 and 1971, and by subsequent appreciation of various European currencies and the Japanese yen relative to the US dollar.

Superdollars

Does the depreciation of the US dollar in the late 1970s and again in the late 1980s mean it is 'Afternoon on the Potomac' for the US currency? The answer involves disentangling two overlapping but distinct relationships. The first concerns the market position of all national currencies – the US dollar, the British pound, the Swiss franc, the German mark, the Japanese yen – relative to gold. The second concerns the position of the US dollar relative to the German mark, the Japanese yen, and to other currencies on the hit parade.

Both relationships can be analyzed in terms of interest rate structures. Interest rates on securities denominated in the US dollar, the

German mark, the Japanese yen and most other currencies increased substantially in the 1970s and were much higher in the 1980s than in most previous decades. The market position of all national currencies as a group declined relative to that of gold, which was evident from the increases in the price of gold.

The combination of US gold sales and the increase in foreign-owned dollars led many observers to conclude that the US dollar was overvalued in relation to the German mark, the Japanese yen, and the currencies of the other countries with payments surpluses. If a currency which serves as international money is overvalued, then the currencies of some other large countries – perhaps Germany, Japan, and France – must have been undervalued; that is, either the international money holdings of these countries were too large, or they were increasing at too rapid a rate. One test of whether the US dollar was overvalued is to ask: what would have happened if the dollar had been devalued in terms of gold by 10 or 15 percent? How many countries would have maintained their exchange rates relative to the US dollar (thus also devaluing their currencies in terms of gold), and how many would have allowed their currencies to appreciate in terms of the US dollar?

The answer depends on when the question was asked. During the early 1960s nearly every country, with the possible exception of Germany, the Netherlands, and Switzerland, would have maintained its exchange rate parity against the dollar. In contrast, if the currency of a small country, say Denmark, had been devalued, few if any other countries would have devalued their currencies. Most would have permitted their currencies to appreciate relative to the Danish krona.

Until 1968 or 1969, the international payment imbalances could more easily be explained in terms of the demand of foreign central banks for international money and the undervaluation of several currencies – primarily the mark – than in terms of an overvalued US dollar. The statement that the US dollar was overvalued was wrong in the early and mid-1960s. The statement became correct in the late 1960s as the increase in the US inflation rate led to a larger US payments deficit. The surge in the US dollar holdings of foreign central banks in the early 1970s led to great concern about the stability of the international monetary system. Several questions arose. One involved determining how much of the total reserve holdings of foreign central banks were excessive. A second was how much of their dollar holdings were excessive.

The increase in foreign holdings of US dollar assets in the 1970s proved extremely large relative to the increase in the 1960s. Until the various currencies began to float in 1973, part of the increase in foreign dollar holdings reflected the weakness of the US dollar; foreign monetary authorities were reluctant to take the initiative and revalue their currencies. In the late 1970s, when the US inflation rate was accelerating, foreign monetary authorities acquired dollar assets to limit the rate at which their own currencies appreciated. The paradox is that they apparently acquired assets denominated in a currency deemed weak – to limit the rate at which it would become weaker. But in the early 1980s, the combination of higher interest rates on US dollar assets and a decline in the anticipated US inflation rate led to a surge in the foreign exchange value of the US dollar. The result was the 'Superdollar.' Foreign holdings of US dollar assets were increasing rapidly; the US dollar was greatly overvalued, evident in the large US trade deficits. The paradox was that foreigners were large buyers of US dollar securities when the dollar was weak in the foreign exchange market, and yet they were large buyers of US dollar securities when the dollar was strong in the foreign exchange market.

The dollar on the hit parade

Demise of the pound

The demise of the British pound as the world's pre-eminent currency suggests one possible future scenario for the US dollar. When Great Britain entered the First World War, the Bank of England immediately withdrew its money-back guarantee on the British pound by its decision to suspend the convertibility of the pound into gold at the historic parity. Exchange controls limited imports of foreign securities. British prices rose rapidly as a result of an inflationary monetary policy.

At the end of the war, official sentiment in London was strongly in favor of a return to the gold standard at the prewar parity. But the pound then was overvalued by at least 10 or 15 percent. Throughout the early 1920s, British economic policy was geared to re-attaining the 1913 gold parity. This target was reached in 1925; then the problem was to maintain the parity, since the pound still remained overvalued. Investors were increasingly apprehensive that a change in British policy would lead to a depreciation of the pound relative to the dollar and gold. But these factors were the result of overproduction of the pound during the war. They should be distinguished from the real factors: the sharp decline in British foreign investments and the sluggish British industrial performance.

The error of the British authorities was that they confused a pegged exchange rate for the pound with a particular rate at which the pound should be pegged. When Britain deemed the time appropriate for again pegging the pound to gold, it should have chosen a parity that left the dollar – pound exchange rate at \$4.00 or \$4.20. Interest rates on securities denominated in the British pound would then have been lower, since there would have been lesser need to pay a high interest rate to investors concerned about the risk that the pound might be devalued. Business in Britain would have boomed, and foreign capital again would have flowed to London.

Whether the pound could have retained its brand leader position with even the most sensible of policies is doubtful; as we have seen, the war hastened a move of the US dollar to the top of the hit parade which seemed inevitable in any case. The US economy was growing very rapidly, and financial markets in New York were developing 'depth, breadth, and resiliency.' Investments in Europe seemed riskier than investments in the United States, partly for political reasons.

Demise of the dollar

Just as the British pound was displaced by the US dollar, so the US dollar might be displaced from its dominant position by another currency brand. In the past, every country whose currency has been at the top has had attractive financial markets, an economy open to international trade and investment, relative price stability, and has been the dominant international economic power. Today no country appears to satisfy all these criteria. Switzerland is too small and lacks adequate financial markets. Japan is too peripheral and its economy is still too closed to foreigners. Germany's long-run record for monetary stability and political stability is poor; its remarkable performance in the 1960s and 1970s follows two hyperinflations earlier in the century. No country other than the United States appears to combine economic size and a record for financial stability. But as the US scorecard on financial stability declines, investors will explore the alternatives.

The newspaper chatter highlights the roles of New York, London, and Tokyo as the major financial centers. Tokyo is much the junior member of this group of three; its big advantages are a massive pool of savings available for foreign investment and low interest rates. But Tokyo has significant disadvantages – for a long time, regulations and controls limited the participation of foreign firms in the financial markets, and recently there have been a remarkable series of stories about corruption and favoritism in the financial markets.

In some ways London is the mirror image of Tokyo. The pool of domestic savings is trivially small. There is a strong tradition of a 'hands-off' approach to the regulation of the financial transactions, especially when the transactions involve currencies other than the British pound. Indeed London's primary role is as an offshore financial center – more transactions in London are denominated in the US dollar than in the British pound. London's principal advantage over New York is its daily five-hour head start; if by some magic London and New York were open during the same hours, London's role as a financial center would shrink, and probably dramatically. London's primary role is as a center that enables Europeans to trade US dollar securities when the markets in New York are closed.

The euro's challenge to the dollar

The central question now is whether the euro – the planned new currency of the members of the European Union – might impinge on or even displace the US dollar as the dominant international currency at the top of the hit parade. The new Europe would still be smaller in economic size than the United States, and its financial markets, even if integrated, would be considerably smaller than the US market. The European countries must first succeed with the plan to merge their currencies – that is they must give up monetary sovereignty. Then the new currency will have to establish a record for monetary stability.

Already, long before the new European currency appears, investors are already beginning to acquire relatively more securities denominated in the German mark. Some central banks outside Europe have acquired reserves denominated in the German mark and the Swiss franc. Firms within Europe – in Scandinavia, the Low Countries, and the Mediterranean countries – are increasing the share of German marks in their working balances; the variations in the price of the mark are substantially smaller than those of the dollar in terms of their own currency.

One of the major advantages of the US dollar that is so attractive to investors is the liquidity of the financial market in New York. A transaction of hundreds of millions of dollars in US government securities has a trivial impact on the price. In contrast there is no European counterpart to US dollar securities, since there is as yet no European Union security that is 'backed' by the ability of its government to collect taxes.

The position of the US dollar on the hit parade has been enhanced by US success in reducing its inflation rate, by changes in the foreign exchange value of the US dollar, and by changes in the monetary role of gold. In the early 1980s, the US dollar appreciated sharply in response to the contractive US monetary policies. If the US inflation rate continues to remain below 2 percent, then the likelihood of any significant trend movement in the exchange rate will be low, and the US dollar will remain at the top of the hit parade.

The future attractiveness of the US dollar will be directly affected by decisions about the future role of gold. A decision that gold would again be a reserve asset would remove the uncertainty about the future of gold as an international money. The US international monetary position would be stronger, since US gold holdings would increase greatly in relation to foreign holdings of US dollar securities. The US Treasury would be able to sell gold in exchange for any excess dollar holdings of foreign monetary authorities. And for some time thereafter, the United States would no longer need to produce international money in large amounts to satisfy the demands of other countries.

One lesson that can be learned from experience is that decisive action may be preferable to continued piddling with minor changes in financial arrangements. The British paid an extremely high price for attempting to avoid or delay inevitable changes in the parity for the pound. Throughout the 1960s, US authorities followed a similar strategy of trying to avoid what proved inevitable – initially a change in the monetary price of gold, then a change in the exchange rate structure. Fortunately, the US authorities are no longer hung up on the need to hold the dollar to a fixed value. But they have no clear view of the unique role of the dollar in international financial arrangements.

The real factors – the size and wealth of the US economy – suggest that the dollar will continue at the top of the hit parade. The monetary factors are uncertain, however. Economic mismanagement in the future could tarnish the dollar's attractiveness to investors.

7

Radio Luxembourg and the Eurodollar Market are both Offshore Stations

Externalized activities

Radio Luxembourg developed as a commercial broadcasting station whose programs were beamed primarily to the hundred million potential listeners in two foreign markets, Britain and France rather than to the several hundred thousand locals. A few years ago, neither country permitted commercial broadcasting; each relied solely on government-owned stations. Programs within each country reflected what the producers – the bureaucrats of the British Broadcasting Corporation (BBC) and Radiodiffusion Française – felt the public should have. Perhaps these government officials had correctly gauged their public's wants and needs. Perhaps, but unlikely. If they had, they would not have needed their monopoly power to limit the public's choice of programs.

Radio Luxembourg found a market niche by producing consumer-oriented programs as a way of selling commercials – and the sale of commercials was a way to generate profits. (Initially Radio Luxembourg was also a monopolist, but its success attracted a number of imitative competitors.) Although the radio signals were produced in Luxembourg, they were 'consumed' in Britain and in France; neither country, however, was willing to raise 'tariffs' or other barriers to the imports of foreign commercial broadcasts. (At the time only the Russians and the Albanians then 'jammed' airwaves.) Transport costs for radio waves are extremely low. Radio Luxembourg prospered. Predictably, numerous competitive stations were established. Radio Caroline, for example, parked its transmission facilities on a tugboat just outside the three-mile limit of British jurisdiction.

Radio Luxembourg is a classic example of an externalized activity – that is, a good or service produced in one legal jurisdiction and consumed in another. Another example is the sale of alcohol and tobacco products at duty-free airport shops: the buyers pay no tax since the products will be consumed abroad. The traveler does not pay transport costs or customs duty on imports. Washington, DC is 'a duty-free shop' because taxes on purchases of alcohol and tobacco products are much lower than the taxes on sales of comparable products in Maryland and Virginia. So residents of both states buy their booze in Washington. (These 'export' sales are one of the two reasons liquor consumption is so high in the nation's capital.) Imports of these untaxed products into Maryland and Virginia are illegal, but are not significantly regulated. Once or twice a year the local revenue agent may nab someone for the newspaper exposure.

Externalized activities occur because governments – national, state, and even local – often regulate the same transaction or activity in different ways. Production will thus often occur in jurisdictions with low taxes or minimal regulation to satisfy the demands of individuals resident in jurisdictions with higher taxes and more severe regulation. Americans travel to Mexico and to Canada to buy pharmaceutical drugs not available in the United States. The British buy their autos in Belgian to secure lower prices. Residents of Vermont and Massachusetts shop in New Hampshire to avoid the sales taxes in their home states.

Differential regulation is necessary for an externalized activity, but these activities occur only if both the costs of transporting the goods or services from the production area to the consumption area and the barriers to these movements are low.

The external currency market

Today, the largest external transactions involve the production of US dollar deposits in London, Zurich, and other centers outside the United States and of German mark deposits in Luxembourg and other centers outside Germany. The generic term for all these transactions is the 'external currency market'; the popular terms are the 'Eurodollar' or 'Eurocurrency' market. The unique feature of this market is that banks produce deposits denominated in a currency other than the currency of the country in which the banks are located. Hence any deposits denominated in a currency other than the British pound and produced in London can be considered a Eurodollar deposit.

Eurobanks and Eurobanking

The banks that produce external currency deposits are known as Eurobanks. Banks in London become Eurobanks whenever they sell deposits denominated in the US dollar or the German mark – or indeed, in any currency other than the British pound. Similarly, banks in Zurich are Eurobanks whenever they sell a deposit denominated in a currency other than the Swiss franc. Eurobanks need not be located in Europe. Singapore, for example, is a thriving center for the Asian branch of the Eurodollar market, while Panama City performs the same function in Latin America.

Eurobanking is only one activity of a commercial bank. A bank in London that sells US dollar deposits will also sell British pound deposits. Altogether, there are more than 500 Eurobanks; for most, these Eurotransactions are a sideline to their activities as domestic banks. And their reputation and credit-rating as domestic banks determines how competitive they will be when they want to sell US dollar deposits and German mark deposits and Swiss franc deposits in London – the higher their credit rating, the lower the interest rates they pay when they sell deposits that carry one of these brand names.

Some of the leading Eurobanks are branches of Citibank, the Bank of America, JP Morgan, and other US-based banks in London, Luxembourg, Frankfurt and other major European financial centers. Participation in the Eurodollar market is the primary activity of most of the London branches of US banks. In the absence of the ability to sell US dollar deposits in London, most of these banks would not have established London branches.

That banks in London conduct some of their business in US dollars, German marks, Swiss francs, Dutch guilders, and Japanese yen, may seem strange. It seems natural that the banks in each country would sell deposits and make loans denominated in their domestic currency. Thus banks in Zurich would deal in Swiss francs and banks in Amsterdam would deal in Dutch guilders. But dealing only in the domestic currency is a traditional bank practice rather than a legal necessity.

Banks outside the United States sell US dollar deposits because investors have a strong demand for these deposits. The US dollar is a unit of account – one of the yardsticks of the world of money, a measure comparable to the gallon or meter. The 'real' meter – the piece of metal about 39+ inches long, which is one ten-millionth of the distance between the equator and the North Pole – remains in the International Bureau of Weights and Measures near Paris. The French could not prevent Americans or Swiss from using the meter as a measurement even if they wished. Similarly, the US government cannot prevent banks in London and Zurich and other financial centers from selling deposits denominated in the US dollar, since these banks are outside US legal jurisdiction. There are London dollar deposits and Zurich dollar deposits, and perhaps one day there will even be Beijing dollar deposits. The adjective is important, for US dollar deposits in London are subject to British regulation, and US dollar deposits in Zurich are subject to Swiss regulation.

The British authorities have no incentive to regulate US dollar transactions in London; if they did, banks would incur higher costs, and hence would only pay lower interest rates on their deposits. And if the interest rates paid on these deposits declined, then investors might go to Zurich or Luxembourg or some other financial center in search of higher interest rates on US dollar deposits.

Banking readily satisfies the requirements for an externalized activity. The transportation costs for money from one country to another are extremely low. 10 million dollars, or a billion dollars, can be moved across the Atlantic at the cost of a phone call. Bank regulations differ widely among countries; regulation of banks in the United States, for example, has been more restrictive than in Great Britain and in most other countries. In most countries, moreover, deposits denominated in foreign currencies are less extensively regulated than deposits denominated in the domestic currency. In London, for example, US dollar deposits are not subject to the regulations applied to British pound deposits. Similarly in Zurich and other major centers for external currency transactions, the interest rate ceilings and the regulations that are applied to deposits denominated in the domestic currency are not applied to deposits denominated in a foreign currency.

Thus, borrowing and lending activities are externalized in the Eurodollar market – investors shift funds from regulated US dollar deposits in New York and Chicago to the less severely regulated foreign centers like London and Zurich, primarily for higher interest income. US banks and Japanese banks and German banks set up branches in London and Zurich to 'intermediate' – to bring borrowers and lenders together – because they are able to circumvent government regulations on geographic expansion of branches domestically.

Where Eurodollars come from

By the end of 1998, bank deposits denominated in external currencies totaled $7000 billion compared to $1 billion in 1961. About 70 percent of offshore deposits are denominated in the US dollar and about 10 percent are denominated in the German mark. The proportion of US dollar-denominated deposits to total external deposits has declined modestly. Offshore deposits have grown at an average annual rate of 30 percent, much more rapidly than domestic deposits. London is the principal financial center for Eurodollar transactions. The volume of foreign currency deposits in the United States is small, not because they are prohibited but because US regulations make such transactions financially unattractive to US investors since such deposits would be subject to reserve requirements.

For a long time a mystery seemed attached to Eurodollars; no one could figure out where they came from. Consider the following analogy – an individual with a deposit in a bank on the west side of Fifth Avenue in New York City (the West Side bank) transfers funds to a bank on the east side of Fifth Avenue (the East Side bank). So the deposits produced by the East Side bank have increased – and for a brief period, the deposits of the East Side bank in the West Side bank increase. The only difference is that the Eurobank is in London rather than on the East side of Fifth Avenue. If an investor with a dollar deposit in New York decides to shift funds to the London branch of the same bank, the London branch produces an offshore dollar deposit. The investor now owns a US dollar deposit in a bank in London rather than in a bank in New York. The London branch deposits this check in its account in a bank in New York. The total deposits of the banks in the United States are unchanged; however, individual investors hold smaller deposits in the United States, and larger deposits in London and a US bank branch in London has a larger deposit in New York. The volume of US dollar deposits in London has increased and so has the total US dollar deposits worldwide.

In the domestic economy, the capacity of banks as a group to expand their deposits is limited by the monetary authorities, which determine both the reserve base of the banking system (the supply of high-powered money) and reserve requirements. In the external currency market, in contrast, there are no reserve requirements. Eurobanks sell additional deposits whenever the interest rates they are willing to pay are high enough to attract investors in search of higher returns.

But the absence of reserve requirements on offshore deposits does not mean that there is the potential for an infinite expansion of deposits and credit. The growth of offshore deposits is limited by the willingness of investors to acquire such deposits in competition with domestic deposits; this comparison involves the risk and return on offshore deposits with the risk and return on domestic deposits. The markets in US dollar deposits in London and in Zurich are an extension of the domestic dollar banking system into unregulated offshore jurisdictions. There are no important Eurobanks that are not branches of the major international banks.

One explanation why US banks were eager to set up branches in London in the 1960s and the 1970s is that they wished to grow, and branch expansion abroad was easier than in the United States. Another is that if they did not expand abroad, they might have lost dollar deposits to foreign banks and to domestic competitiors who had offshore branches, so there was a 'follow-the-leader' tendency. A third is that even though the interest rates paid on US dollar deposits in London were higher than the interest rates paid on dollar deposits in New York, the other costs were lower. US domestic banks were required to hold reserves in the form of a non-interest-bearing deposits at the Federal Reserve. This requirement is a 'tax' on their earnings, since otherwise the bank would have invested nearly all these funds in income-earning assets. Eurobanks – including the London and Zurich branches of US banks – are not subject to reserve requirements and hence do not pay this tax. Similarly Eurobanks were not required to pay deposit insurance premiums as were US domestic banks. Moreover, the costs of Eurobanks are low because the market is a wholesale market; the minimum deposit size is $50,000, and the average deposit is much larger. Thus, offshore banks can afford to pay higher interest rates on US dollar deposits than domestic banks can because of savings in other costs.

What remains to be explained is why some US investors continue to hold domestic US dollar deposits when, with minimal effort, they could earn higher interest rates on external dollar deposits. One answer is the owners of US dollar deposits are not knowledgeable about the higher yields available on US dollar deposits in London. This answer might have been plausible 10 or 15 years ago; it now no longer seems so. Another answer is that US dollar deposits in London are believed to be subject to risks not encountered on domestic deposits, and these risks deter some depositors from buying offshore deposits. For example, the British authorities might restrict banks in London from fulfilling their commitments on foreign currency deposits; they might be told that depositors could withdraw deposits only if they satisfied conditions *X*, *Y*, and *Z*. Or they might require the external deposits be sold to the Bank of England in exchange for deposits denominated in the British pound. Or the investors might be concerned that US authorities would penalize the repatriation of dollar funds from foreign countries. These risks are very low. And yet the additional interest income on offshore deposits relative to domestic deposits also is small. The growth of money market funds in the United States is the domestic equivalent of the growth of the offshore money market. Those who own these funds can write checks on these accounts (usually the checks must be larger than $100) and at the same time, earn interest on their balances. But money market funds are not 'guaranteed' against loss by the US government. London dollar deposits differ from New York dollar deposits in terms of political risk: they are subject to the whims of a different set of government authorities. Investors who hold dollar deposits in New York despite the higher returns on US dollar deposits in London believe that London dollar deposits are riskier than comparable deposits available in New York. Moreover, the additional risk dominates the additional interest income they might earn if they shifted their funds to London. The continued growth in offshore deposits during the 1960s and the 1970s and the 1980s reflected that interest rates on offshore deposits were increasing relative to interest rates on US dollar deposits, and that perceived risk attached to offshore deposits was low and declining.

External currency transactions probably go back to the seventeenth century, when one sovereign would counterfeit the gold coins of another. One popular explanation for the growth of the external market in the 1950s is that during the early years of the Cold War, the Russians wanted to hold US dollar deposits because the dollar was the most useful currency for financing their international transactions. But the Russians were reluctant to hold these deposits in New York because of the threat that the US authorities might 'freeze' their deposits. In effect, the Russians believed that the political risk of London dollar deposits was lower than New York dollar deposits.

The rapid growth of offshore deposits in the 1960s and the 1970s reflects three factors: the steep climb in interest rates on US dollar deposits, which made it increasingly profitable to escape Washington's regulations, the expansion of multinational firms, and the desire of banks headquartered in the United States and most other industrial countries to become larger. Depositors contemplating a shift of funds to the external market must decide whether to acquire offshore deposits in London, Zurich, Paris, or some other center. Depositors choose among centers on the basis of their estimates of political risk. Moscow and São Paulo seem risky – the heavy hand of bureaucratic regulation is all too evident. Even though there is undoubtedly an interest rate that would induce lenders to acquire Moscow dollar deposits, banks issuing these deposits do not have the investment opportunities to justify paying such high interest rates.

Links between external deposits in different currencies

External deposits denominated in the US dollar, the German mark, and other currencies are closely linked by *interest arbitrage*. A bank in London offers to sell deposits in any of eight or 10 currencies: in general, the bank would offer a different interest rate on each of these currencies. For example, a bank in London might sell a Swiss franc deposit. Rather than buy a Swiss franc security, the bank might sell the Swiss francs for German marks in the spot exchange market and buy a loan denominated in the German mark. To protect itself against the loss from a depreciation of the Swiss franc, the bank would buy Swiss francs in the forward exchange market at the same time that it sold Swiss francs in the spot exchange market. Hence the bank might incur a loss on these two foreign exchange transactions because the Swiss franc would be more expensive in the forward exchange market than in the spot exchange market. This loss is a cost that the banks incur in this interest arbitrage activity; as a result, the interest rates banks offer on deposits in various currencies differ by the cost of hedging their foreign exchange exposure – the interest equivalent of the difference between the forward exchange rate and the spot exchange rate.

The external currency market links the national money markets. Funds flow continuously between the domestic and external markets in response to changes both in interest rate differentials and in investor estimates of the risk of offshore deposits. By increasing the links between national money markets, the growth of the external currency market has further reduced the scope for independence of individual national central banks.

Internationalizing regulation

The 'house of cards'

Central bankers lie awake at night worrying about the wheelers and dealers trafficking in their currencies in jurisdictions outside their direct control. US dollar deposits in London seem outside US control because they are in London, and outside British concern because they are denominated in the US dollar. The authorities are worried that much of the growth in Eurodollars has resulted in an expansion of credit, arranged in an inverted pyramid, and the pyramid might collapse. Thus, each transfer of $1 million from New York to bank *A* in London may lead to a large increase in Eurodollar deposits, for bank *B* in London might borrow dollars from investor *A* to lend to bank *C*, and so on. The borrower from one Eurobank may deposit the proceeds in another Eurobank – or buy goods, services, or securities from a seller who deposits his proceeds in a Eurobank. As a result, total London dollar deposits might increase by much more than the initial transfer of dollar deposits from New York to London. The central bankers worry that a shock to the base of the pyramid could have a disastrous impact, bringing the whole credit pyramid down with a crash – and wrecking their own careers. The metaphor is a 'house of cards'. The concern increases when the authorities remember that offshore deposits are not subject to reserve requirements – and, even worse, that the offshore banks hold no significant reserves.

Assume that bank *A* decides to ask bank *B* to repay its loan. Where will *B* get the money? Perhaps from bank *C*. Ultimately, some bank in the system must reduce loans to non-bank borrowers to get the cash to repay maturing loans. If the borrowers cannot repay, then bank *C* may not have the cash to repay bank *B*. And if bank *B* can't collect from bank *C*, then bank *B* may not be able to repay bank *A*.

In 1974, the pyramid began to shake when two banks, Herstatt in Frankfurt and Franklin National in New York City closed because of their losses in foreign exchange speculation. Both banks had borrowed extensively from Eurobanks. The fear was that some of these Eurobanks would be unable to repay their depositors; then a run on the Eurobanking system would begin, and Eurobanks would have to call their loans to get the funds to repay their scared depositors. The house of cards would tumble.

The worry is needless; a collapse of the offshore system is no more likely than the collapse of the domestic banking system. All Eurobanks are branches of US, Swiss, German, and other major banks and as long as the domestic branches remain open, the offshore branches cannot close. A central bank would be likely to provide funds to forestall closing of an offshore branch of a domestic bank. Nevertheless, central banks might delay their assistance, since they might feel less than completely responsible for the survival of banks whose raison *d'être* has been the avoidance of regulation.

The authorities are also concerned that access to the Eurodollar market enables borrowers, lenders, and intermediaries to circumvent domestic monetary control, thus reducing the effectiveness of Eurodollar regulation and creating inequities between banks that participate in market and banks that do not. Someday a clever entrepreneur might establish a Eurobank on a tugboat 5 or 10 miles from New York City in the Atlantic Ocean; this would be the monetary equivalent of Radio Caroline. US residents would shift funds to the Tugboat Bank because it would offer higher interest rates on its deposits than those available on deposits in New York and in Chicago; borrowers would seek loans from the Tugboat Bank rather than from banks in New York. The Tugboat Bank would be in a favored competitive position since it would be beyond the scope of US regulation, and avoid the costs of this regulation.

Regulation in action

So, increasingly and inevitably, the long arm of regulation must reach out to Eurobanks and to external currency transactions. The Bank of England and the Bundesbank control the foreign currency activities of banks within their legal jurisdictions, although the British do so in a relaxed way. US authorities apply a reserve regulation to funds received by US banks from their foreign branches. These controls have usually been applied only to commercial banks, for only these entities are within the functional jurisdiction of the central banks. Since regulations reduce the profitability of Eurobanking in London and Zurich, the inevitable next step is that the offshore banking activity would move to less extensively regulated jurisdictions.

Just as Radio Luxembourg can satisfy its customers because of official reluctance to disrupt its signals, so Eurobanks can flourish in Luxembourg and Nassau as long as depositors and borrowers are free to do business there. The Eurobanks will flourish as long as US authorities permit the offshore branches of US banks to operate with lower reserve requirements than the domestic offices of these banks. If the US authorities were to begin to unify reserve requirements, raising them on offshore branches of US banks, and reducing them on domestic deposits, the offshore offices of US banks would be in a disadvantageous competitive position relative to non-US banks.

The belated US policy response to the growth of offshore deposits has been to enable banks in the United States to establish International Banking Facilities (IBFs) – deposits in these facilities in New York, Chicago, and Los Angeles are not subject to reserve requirements. Thus far only foreigners are eligible to acquire such deposits – the irony is that foreigners can get higher interest rates on US dollar deposits in these international banking facilities in the major US cities than US residents can. The US authorities are discriminating against US taxpayers!

One day, perhaps, countries will unify their regulations both for radio broadcasting and for commercial banking. Radio Luxembourg will fade away, and the Eurobanks will diminish as a group and many will completely disappear. That day, however, does not seem imminent. The central bank authorities have had the choice of harmonizing their regulations to reduce the incentives for Eurocurrency transactions or of attempting to regulate these transactions. They have done both. As long, however, as the cost of regulation exceeds the costs of circumventing regulations, then the regulations will be circumvented. Reductions in the cost of communication mean that the cost of circumventing regulation will decline relative to the cost of regulation. Increasingly the volume of regulated transactions and the scope of regulation will decline.

8
They Invented Money so They Could Have Inflation

The value of money

100 years ago, a mile was a mile, a dollar was a dollar, and a liter of water weighed a kilo. The 1999 kilo is identical to the 1899 kilo. The 1999 dollar is only a pale shadow of the 1899 dollar and of the 1969 dollar. All the national monies in 1999 measure less than they did in 1989, and they were less valuable in 1988 than in 1978.

100 years from now, the mile and the kilo will be unchanged as units of distance and weight (although the mile almost certainly then will be an obsolete measure). It is equally certain that the US dollar will have a smaller value, and so will the Swiss franc and the Japanese yen. While the measurement of the value of money may be less scientific than the measurement of the speed of light or the distance to the moon, the error in the measurement is not in question – the orbit of the earth around the sun also varies within a range. Rather, the question is why, of all the units of account in the world, money is the only one which shrinks in value – gradually at some times and rapidly at others but inevitably. True, there are a few periods when the value of a money increased – but probably less than one-half of 1 percent of yearly episodes of annual changes in the price level.

Inflation in the twentieth century

From time to time, the monetary authorities in various countries acknowledge the debasing tendencies of their predecessors – they knock three zeros off the monetary units, usually after the bills become too large, and the token coins have been melted because their value as commodities has begun to exceed their value as money. In 1959, General de Gaulle adopted the 'heavy franc': 100 old francs would buy one new franc. In 1983, Argentina adopted a new peso, equal to 1000 old pesos, and they repeated the exercise in 1985 when 1000 pesos were set equal to one Austral. The Brazilians knocked 3 zeros off the cruzerio in 1993; the new money became known as the cruzerio real. The Russians dropped three zeros at the beginning of 1998.

The periods of inflation have been so pervasive in the last several decades that previous episodes of sharp declines in price levels have been forgotten. The US wholesale price index declined by 50 percent in 1920–1; during the same period, the consumer price index fell by more than one-third. The US price level also declined sharply during the Great Depression of the 1930s. The nineteenth century was one of the relative price stability; if the US wholesale price index is set at 100 in 1800, the 1900 price index is 64 – an annual average decline of 0.4 percent a year. The opening of new lands – the American West, Canada, Australia, and the Argentine – led to declines in food prices, which then were a more important component of the price indexes.

Two factors distinguish the inflationary record in the twentieth century. One is that the wartime episodes have been more frequent than in the nineteenth century. And the wars are bigger and much more expensive. The First World War, the Second World War, Korea, even Vietnam. The second is that price levels have not declined for nearly 50 years. The anticipated depression after the Second World War has not occurred – yet.

Traditionally, shrinkage in the value of money is associated with finance during wartime; the sovereign prints money to pay the army and buy guns – better inflation than defeat. The US consumer price level nearly doubled during the 1915–20 period identified with the First World War; the annual rate of increase averaged 15 percent, about as high as during the Civil War period. From 1940 to 1948, the annual rate of price increase averaged 7 percent; price controls in the Second World War limited the increase in the price level, and much of the increase occurred when ceilings were lifted after the end of the war. During the Korean War the rate of price increase averaged 5 percent for about two years. From the beginning of major US involvement in Vietnam in 1965 to the climax in 1970, the annual increase in the US consumer price index (CPI) averaged 4 percent; however the US inflation rate peaked at nearly 7 percent in 1970.

The progressive decline in the annual rate of price increase over these four wartime episodes suggests that the US government has slowly become more successful in putting wars on a pay-as-you-go basis.

However, increased confidence in the ability of governments to control inflation was shattered by the increase in the price levels in the

1970s. A new term, 'double-digit inflation,' hit the newspaper head-lines. The US price level was increasing nearly as rapidly in peacetime as it had in most previous wartime periods. By almost any peacetime standard, inflation during the four-year interval 1972–5 was unprecedented: the US consumer price level increased by 36 percent, or nearly 10 percent a year, more rapidly than during the Second World War. Yet the inflation rate in the late 1970s was even more rapid than in the first half of the decade. In 1980, the inflation rate peaked at 13 percent.

The world inflation of the 1970s should be distinguished from the Vietnam inflation of the late 1960s. A tight money policy in 1969 pushed the US economy into recession. The US commitments in Vietnam and the US inflation rate were winding down together. Whereas during the late 1960s the US price level increased more rapidly than the price levels in other industrialized countries, the 1970s inflation was a worldwide phenomenon Price levels in most foreign countries were increasing as rapidly as the US price level – or more rapidly; only in Germany and Switzerland did the price levels increase somewhat less rapidly than in the United States.

Is inflation inevitable?

While inflation has been around as long as money, there remain sharp disagreements about its causes. Is the cause economic, sociological, or psychological? If the cause is economic, do the price level increases result from supply shortages of a natural or of artificial kind, or from the sudden expansion of demand? The worldwide inflation of the 1970s has been attributed to the growth of the Eurodollar market, to the move to the floating exchange rate system, to the loss of confidence in money, and to the sharp increases in the price of oil. Indeed, some experts suggested that 2 percentage points of the increase in the US price level resulted from the increase in oil prices, 4 percentage points from the devaluation of the US dollar, and so forth. Some of the chatter in London highlighted a sociological theory of British inflation: strong unions – the railway workers, miners, electrical workers, and other public-sector employees – secured large increases in wages after striking or threatening to strike and firms then had to raise prices to cover their higher labor costs.

Some Americans wonder whether inflation is inevitable in a democracy. Competition among politicians for votes compels them to promise more free lunches – government services will be expanded while taxes will be reduced. When the bills come in, the government prints money so its checks will not bounce.

Box 8.1   Does the Fed Cause Bank Failures?

Bank failures were commonplace in the nineteenth century. Banks closed their doors when their deposit liabilities exceeded the value of loans, mortgages, and other assets. Once the word got out that a bank might be in difficulty, the depositors rushed to get their money, much more rapidly than if they were to sell a currency about to be devalued. If the bank closed, the depositors might receive 30 or 40 cents on the dollar, depending on how badly the bank had been managed.

In some cases, the run on the bank caused an otherwise good bank to fail. Banks were forced to sell assets to meet their depositors' demand for money. Such sales further weakened the banks' position, for inevitably the best assets were sold first. The failure of one bank had a domino effect on the stability of others; bankruptcy became contagious. Credit systems collapsed when the public lost confidence in the banks. Bank failures also meant that the money supply fell, so recessions resulted.

Several institutional innovations were adopted to minimize failure. The National Banking Act of 1863 provided for a comptroller of the currency to protect banks and depositors by ensuring that the assets held by banks were good. Yet there were substantial bank failures in 1883, 1896, and 1907. The Federal Reserve was set up in 1913 to act as a lender of last resort, supplying funds – newly printed money – to banks in distress so they could pay depositors who sought to reduce or close their accounts. Nevertheless, nearly 6000 banks failed in the 1920s, 1352 in 1930s, 2294 in 1931, 1456 in 1932, and 4000 in 1933. To dampen the snowball effect of deposit withdrawal, the US government in 1933 set up the Federal Deposit Insurance Corporation (FDIC). Initially, individual deposits were insured to $10,000, then $20,000; in 1975 the ceiling was raised to $40,000, and in April 1980 to $100,000. Banks pay an insurance premium to the FDIC, and it has built up reserves over the years. At the end of 1977, capital accumulated by the FDIC from these insurance premiums totaled $9 billion; the FDIC supposedly has an open credit line at the Treasury if its losses should be larger.

A few banks have failed recently, despite these institutional safeguards. US National Bank in San Diego failed because its managers

Box 8.1   continued

made high-risk loans to captive firms. The Franklin National Bank went under in 1974 because of foreign exchange losses. The Security National Bank of Long Island was closed because it had made too many non-secured loans. The Penn Square Bank of Oklahoma City closed its doors in 1982 because many of its loans to firms involved in oil exploration went sour when the price of oil fell; many of these loans appeared to have been made in the belief that the oil price would go to $50 or $60 a barrel.

The key question is whether a significant number of banks might fail again, and how adequate the safeguards will be. In 1974 and 1975, newspaper reports suggested that the Treasury and the Fed were keeping a close watch on several hundred banks. Some of the business and real estate loans made by these banks went sour during the recession. And the market value of their assets was less than that of their liabilities. The losses dwarfed the accumulated reserves of the FDIC.

The Fed faced a dilemma. Its tight-money policy had caused the value of bank assets to decline and had forced the banks into technical bankruptcy. The rationale for setting up the Fed was to prevent the failure of banks. But the desire to break double-digit inflation had driven the banks to the brink of failure. To prevent bank failure, the Fed was obliged to expand the economy – to float off the credit crises. Monetary expansion could lead to inflation, which would lead to tight money, which would lead to increased bank failures. And so it goes.

Still, inflation rates in the 1980s averaged significantly lower than in the 1970s – the 1980s was a decade of declining inflation rates while the 1970s had been a decade of increasing inflation rates. And by the end of the 1990s the inflation rates in the United States and in France and in Great Britain were below 2 percent a year – more or less where they had been in the 1950s and the early 1960s.

Where inflation comes from

Many events occur at about the same time in the worlds of business and money. Distinctions must be made between causes and consequences, between causes and associations, between causes and definitions. A frequent pairing of two events sometimes leads to a 'scientific truth' or rule, as if causation could be inferred from association. An exception to a general tendency leads to the statement, 'This is the exception that proves the rule' – a statement that should read, 'This is the exception that proves the rule *wrong.*' It is a fact that the money supply increases with great statistical regularity toward the end of the year, but it would be risky to suggest that increases in the money supply cause Christmas. Casual observation suggests that fire trucks are frequently found near fires, but only a fool would suggest that fire trucks cause fires, or that the fires caused the fire trucks.

To say that inflation is caused by rising prices is like saying that all deaths are caused by heart failure; while all deaths are associated with the stoppage of heart movement, heart failure has not put cancer, strokes, and auto accidents out of business. A definition is not a statement about causation. Brain stoppage measures death, just as rising price levels measure inflation; the questions that need to be answered are why the brain stops functioning and why the price levels increase.

Whether an alleged example of economic cause and effect is in fact another example of argument by association can sometimes be determined by asking whether the relationship holds over a number of years. While the five-fold increase in the price of oil in the fall of 1973 led to a more rapid increase in the world price level, oil market events do not explain the rapid increases in price levels that had previously occurred. Nor do oil market events explain why the prices of sugar, copper, groundnuts, and virtually every other primary product also increased by 200 percent and in some cases by 300 or even 400 percent in the early 1970s. Across-the-board increases in the prices of a wide range of commodities are typical of world booms.

The move to floating exchange rates in the early 1970s may explain why price levels increased more rapidly in some countries than in others – yet this move almost certainly would not have been necessary if the US price level had not already been increasing more rapidly than the German price level. The move to floating exchange rates was the result of a difference between the US inflation rate and the German inflation rate of nearly 5 percent a year. While the growth of the Eurodollar market may have had inflationary consequences, the market grew no more rapidly in 1973 and 1974 than it had in earlier years, when the rate of inflation was much lower.

In the long run, inflation will not occur without an increase in the money supply. But an increase in the commodity price level may occur in response to shortages of individual commodities, even if the money supply is constant. A failure in the corn crop almost certainly will lead to an increase in the price of corn, for the higher price of corn 'rations' the reduced supply of corn among competing buyers. The theory is that if individuals spend a larger share of their income on corn, they will have less money to spend on other products, and so the prices of these other products should decline, with the result that the consumer price level will tend to remain unchanged. Still increases in the prices of a few products may induce households to become increasingly sensitive to the prospect of a more rapid increase in the price level – and they may go on a spending spree and reduce their holdings of money to avoid declines in their wealth. Nevertheless, these factors lead to one-shot (or perhaps two-shot) increases in the price level rather than continuing increases.

The question is not what was happening in 1973 and 1974, and again in 1979 and 1980, but rather what happened in these years that had not happened before. A second question is why the rates of increase in the price levels differed so sharply among countries. A third question involves the relation between the severity of the inflation and the severity of the recession that follows.

Watergate economics

In the United States, the year immediately preceding presidential elections is likely to be one of expansive financial policies. The party in power wants the economy prosperous when the voters go to the polls. If the economy is sluggish, those in power may soon be the outs. If inflation is soaring, the government may also be in trouble. So the government wants to 'fine tune' the economy and somehow achieve full employment and a stable price level in the months prior to the election.

Assume the economy is in recession. Initially, measures taken to expand the economy are likely to lead to higher output and employment rather than to increases in prices and costs, as long as there remains substantial spare capacity. As the economy expands, it will bump against more and more supply constraints, and prices will rise to ration those goods that are increasingly scarce. At first, price increases will be selective, as scarcities develop in particular goods; then the price increases will become more general as scarcities become more pervasive. Fine tuning suggests that the authorities will try to time the expansion so that the maximum employment effects are felt in the two or three months before the election; someone else can worry about subsequent price increases after the election.

In 1959 the prospects for a recession in the US economy by November 1960 seemed strong. Arthur F. Burns, formerly chairman of the Council of Economic Advisers and an informal adviser to then Vice-President Nixon, recommended an expansion of the economy to set the stage for a Nixon victory in the 1960 election. Supposedly, President Eisenhower refused to pass on the advice to William McChesney Martin, then chairman of the Federal Reserve Board. Kennedy won the election on the promise of 'Getting the Economy Moving Again.' Nixon moved to California.

In 1969, President Nixon appointed Arthur F. Burns as a White House adviser; a year later Burns became chairman of the Federal Reserve. After continuing a monetary crunch designed to wring the inflationary excesses out of the US economy in 1970, in the spring of 1971 the Fed began to expand the rate of money supply growth to stimulate the US economy. In August 1971, one element in Nixon's New Economic Policy was price and wage ceilings, which tilted the impacts of increased expenditures from the increase in the growth rate of the money supply toward increases in output and employment rather than to increases in prices. The US economy began to boom – industrial production, employment, worker-hours per week, and the stock market all went up.

As a recession year, 1971 was unusual. The unemployment rate peaked at about 6 percent, but the consumer price level was still increasing at an annual rate of 3 percent. In previous recessions, in contrast, the price level usually increased by no more than 1 percent when unemployment peaked.

One interpretation is that the structure of the US economy had changed: an increase in the unemployment rate to perhaps 7 or 8 percent for several years would have been necessary before the inflation rate declined to 1 percent. A second interpretation is that if monetary expansion had not begun in mid-1971, the economy would not have been booming in November 1972. Nixon's margin of votes in the 1972 election was the largest ever.

The 1972 inflation began at a time when the price level already was increasing at a rate of 3 percent a year rather than at the 1 percent rate in the recession years of the 1950s and early 1960s. In 1972 the American public had seen the purchasing power of the US dollar shrink by 30 percent in the previous five years – an unprecedented peacetime event. So when the price level resumed its rapid increase, the public began to anticipate that the inflation rate might increase; rather than risk holding money while its value declined, the public began to reduce its money balances to avoid further losses in wealth from further increases in the price level. The public spent money more rapidly (and the price level increased more rapidly than would have been predicted from the increase in the money supply alone) but the increase in the spending rate transferred money to someone else.

Increases in price levels were inevitable after the election when the price ceilings on wages and prices would be lifted; the uncertainty was the timing. The price ceilings of phase 1, phase 2, and phase N in Nixon's economic policy delayed the upward movements in prices. Nixon and Burns had a tiger by the tail, and they could not afford to let go – at least not until after the election.

Upward pressures on US prices also resulted from the devaluation of the US dollar at the end of 1971 and again in early 1973. In the late 1960s, US consumption increased more rapidly than exports. As long as foreign central banks were willing to add to their holdings of US dollar securities, it was not necessary for the US dollar to be devalued, and the increase in US imports relative to US exports dampened upward pressure on the US price level. The combination of the delay in the devaluation of the US dollar and price ceilings meant that the price increases, which would have occurred in 1971 and 1972, were instead bunched in a much shorter interval in 1973. After the devaluation, the incomes of US consumers increased more rapidly than the supply of available goods, so price increases were needed to ration the available supply. Prior to the devaluation, the increase in imports relative to exports meant that domestic prices increased less rapidly than they might otherwise have done given the growth in the US money supply; after the devaluation, the prices of imported goods increased more rapidly than prices of domestic goods. Following the devaluation of the US dollar in 1973, the price of US goods to consumers in other industrial countries declined; US exports soared, and US consumers shifted to domestic from more expensive foreign goods. The reduction in the supply of goods because of the decline in the US trade deficit, together with the higher domestic price of US imports, reinforced the upward pressure on the US price level caused by the Fed's monetary expansion. The price ceilings delayed the increases in the price level, but these ceilings were removed early in 1973 – soon after the 1972 election, long before the 1976 election.

Governments rarely admit their mistakes. If their policies backfire, the problem is that unforeseen – and unforeseeable – events occurred. So the US inflation of the mid-1970s was attributed to supply shortages. The anchovies disappeared from the west coasts of Peru and

Ecuador, so there was a deficiency in the world supply of protein. The Russians had a bad wheat crop, and so the world price of wheat soared. These supply shortages contributed to the increase in the price level. But the prices of most other commodities were also increasing. In the absence of a demand boom, the supply shortfalls would have had a much less severe impact on the price level. The Federal Reserve had sailed too close to the wind; these supply shortfalls would have been far less troublesome if the government had followed a less expansive monetary policy in the months prior to the 1972 election.

Watergate was an exercise in overkill: Nixon would have won the 1972 election even without any possible information that might have been gathered illegally from Democratic national headquarters. Similarly, Nixon would have won in 1972 even without the rapid monetary expansion of 1971. The Nixon group chose not to take the risks. These costs fell on the American public, and the costs were immense.

Carter economics

Traditionally, Democrats place more emphasis on jobs and less on price stability than the Republicans. Jimmy Carter stuck with tradition. When Carter took the oath as President in January 1977, the unemployment rate was 7.4 percent, and the price level was increasing at a rate of 5 percent a year. When Carter returned to Plains, Georgia four years later, the unemployment rate was 7.4 percent, and the US price level was increasing at an annual rate of 12 percent. Carter's tax and monetary policies clearly got the economy moving again, and the expansion of demand led to a doubling of the US inflation rate.

Political leaders – at least US political leaders – frequently suggest that if things are not quite perfect at home, at least they are much worse abroad. Nixon was fond of comparing the rate of US inflation with the inflation rates in other countries – as long as the US inflation rate was lower. One of the factors – the Fed's expansive monetary policies – which put upward pressure on US prices during the early 1970s did not directly affect other countries; the Europeans and the Japanese could not vote in the 1972 election. Moreover, if the devaluation of the US dollar was supposed to have led to a more rapid increase in the US price level, the converse – the mirror-image appreciation of the German mark, the Swiss franc, and the Japanese yen – should have dampened upward pressure on price levels in these countries. For both reasons, price levels abroad should have increased less rapidly than in the United States. But in fact, prices in most foreign countries including those with the appreciating currencies increased more rapidly than in the United States. See the inflation rates in Table 6.1 (p. 115).

Differences in inflation rates

One simple explanation for the differential movements in national price levels is that the market baskets of goods used in the comparison are not identical. The British price level might be heavily weighted with fish and chips, the American with Big Macs and French fries. The implication is that if the components of the indexes are more or less the same, then the indexes should tend to move together. But this explanation is too simple, for while the indexes with similar components may tend to move together, they may not move by the same amount. Within the United States, the price of a particular market basket of goods is almost always higher in New York and San Francisco than in Chicago and Denver. While the goods markets in the various cities are linked by arbitrage, there are enough frictions so that the price levels in some cities increase more rapidly than in others. The US Department of State and the United Nations have calculated the cost of living in various national capitals; if New York is 100, then Tokyo might be 160, Rome 180, and Katamandu 75.

The rate of inflation in each country is best measured by the increase in the *consumer price level*, although the GDP deflator and even whole-sale price levels are sometimes used. The wholesale price levels in various countries are more nearly similar to each other than the con-sumer price levels are, because relatively more of the goods included in the wholesale level have their prices set in competitive markets. The movements in the consumer price levels in several countries are less similar than the movements in the wholesale price levels because the consumer price levels include non-traded services.

Two different approaches can be used to explain the national differ-ences in inflation rates. The simplest is that prices increase most rapidly in countries that follow the most expansive monetary policies. For years, price levels in Argentina and Brazil increased more rapidly than the price levels in most other countries, and as a result Argentina and Brazil were obliged to devalue their currencies; the increases in their price levels and the depreciation of their currencies should be largely offsetting, or else their goods would become increasingly over-valued. The growth in the money supplies in Germany and Japan in the early 1970s was more rapid than in the United States, in part because their very large payments surpluses in 1971 led to sharp increases in the rates of money supply growth. Japan had money supply increases of 30 percent in 1971 and 25 percent in 1972; the money supply growth rates in Germany were 13 percent and 14 percent, marginally below those in other European countries. Their reluctance to revalue in 1971 had belated consequences for their price levels – in effect, they were importing inflation because of their large payments surpluses.

Changes in the foreign exchange values of national currencies generally follow changes in the relationship between national price levels, at least in the long if not in the short run. Thus the currencies of the countries with more rapid price level increases have tended to depreciate while the currencies of the countries with the less rapid price level increases have tended to appreciate. The relationship is reciprocal: if a country devalues its currency, its price level is likely to rise, because the domestic prices of both imports and exports increases, and the trade deficit is likely to decline. If instead the country revalues its currency or if its currency appreciates, its price level should increase less rapidly, because imports now cost less, and so there is one less source of upward pressure on the price level; moreover the trade deficit may increase.

The way out of the inflationary spiral is straightforward – although the political costs of the necessary measures may not be low. The authorities need to secure a sharp downward revision in the anticipated inflation rate – which usually means that they must adopt a contractive monetary policy.

Throughout the 1970s and the 1980s, Germany, for example, generally followed a more contractive monetary policy than the United States, although this is was not always evident in the differences in money supply growth rates. High German interest rates led investors to acquire securities denominated in the German mark, and the mark tended to appreciate. Because the mark appreciated, commodity prices in Germany increased less rapidly than in the United States. Eventually, because commodity prices were rising less rapidly, investors held German monetary securities at interest rates substantially below the interest rates on comparable securities denominated in the US dollar.

Reaganomics

When Ronald Reagan entered the White House in January 1991, the US inflation rate was nearly 15 percent, and the US government's debt was $1,000 billion. When Reagan left the White House, the US inflation rate was 3 percent, and the debt $3,000 billion. The US Treasury's debt increased by another $1,000 billion during the four years that George Bush was President.

The decline in the US inflation rate was attributable to the tough contractive monetary adopted by the Federal Reserve in October 1979. Two months earlier, President Carter had appointed Paul Volcker, then President of the Federal Reserve Bank of New York, as Chairman of the Federal Reserve Board, and charged him to get the inflation rate down. The Fed adopted a new set of operating procedures – rather than seek to minimize changes in interest rates, the Fed would instead seek to stabilize the rate of growth of the money supply. The rate of growth of the money supply declined, and interest rates on US dollar securities soared, because the limits to the rate of money supply growth meant a significant reduction in the rate at which banks could make loans.

For the first time in more than a decade, the increase in US interest rates was larger than the increase in the US inflation rate. As a result, real interest rates – which are calculated as the nominal interest rate adjusted by the inflation rate – surged to the highest level since the Great Depression. Throughout the 1970s, real interest rates on US dollar securities had been trending down; by the late 1970s, real interest rates were negative. The surge in nominal interest rates led to an almost comparably large surge in real interest rates.

The immediate result of the sharp increase in real interest rates was that spending declined – the United States moved quickly into a recession. Investors were attracted to US dollar securities by the combination of the high interest rates on US dollar securities and the reduction in the anticipated US inflation rate. Before these investors could buy US dollar securities, they had first to buy US dollars in the foreign exchange market, which induced an appreciation of the US dollar. In turn, the stronger dollar led to a sharp increase in US imports, which reduced the US inflation rate – both because the supply of goods available to Americans increased and because US producers were less able to increase their prices.

The waves rule Britannia

In the 1970s Great Britain appeared to be extreme case of graceless economic aging. In the nineteenth century Britain was the first country to industrialize, and the resulting increases in income provided the economic base for the expansion of the British empire. Britannia ruled the waves. London was the world's financial center.

Empires have their own built-in self-destruct systems; they become too large and too rigid to adjust to change. Rome flourished for centuries. In 1914 the sun was never supposed to set on the British Empire. In 1975 the sun never appeared to shine on British economic performance. In 1950, British *per capita* income was twice that in West Germany; by 1975, *per capita* income in Germany was twice than in Britain. Moreover, the British price level increased more rapidly than the price levels in any other industrial country.

Sociology and inflation

The British self-analysis was in terms of the sociological theory of inflation. The workers expected – and demanded – continual increase in their real standard of living. They expected that their demands could be met by taxing – or soaking – the rich, or from redistribution rather than from productivity gains. And by raising the price at which they sold their labor services, they obtained higher money incomes. For the most part, the increase in wage costs were passed on to consumers in the form of higher prices – otherwise the firms would have gone out of business because their costs would have exceeded their revenues. So taxes were raised, especially on the middle and upper classes, and extensive subsidies were given to the population at large. The cost of medical services was financed by the government, although patients paid token amounts for spectacles and drugs. Universities were free. Since many services produced in the government sector had been priced below their production costs, their losses must somehow be financed – which meant a higher level of taxes. Moreover, as wage costs increased in the automobile industry, the British-owned private companies went bankrupt.

But because there were so few rich, high taxes on their incomes and wealth had only a modest impact in lifting the living standards of others. The time has long since passed when the living standards of the workers could be significantly raised by further taxing the rich; the rich may be conspicuous in their spending habits, but there just aren't enough of them to go around as a lucrative tax base. Moreover, a thriving cash economy had developed alongside the taxed economy as plumbers and mechanics moved into a cash economy to get tax-free income, and so the tax base increased slowly. So Great Britain borrowed abroad to finance the consumption of its workers. As the ability to borrow abroad declined, the demands of workers could be satisfied only as some workers – or retired workers – accepted a decline in their real incomes.

The government and its sympathetic supporters suggested that the source of the problem was the aggressive behavior of the unions rather than the financial policies of the British government. Most sellers recognized that if they increased their prices, demand would fall and eventually they would be left with unsold goods and idle labor. If the government pursued a tight money policy, then the sellers would be cautious about increasing their prices, least their goods remain unsold. In contrast, if the government was concerned that no resources be unemployed, then it in effect surrendered control of the price level to the aggressive unions.

When prices and wages increase by 10 or 15 percent a year, it is hard to determine whether wages are pushing up prices or prices are pulling up wages. For regardless of the initial cause, the government is unwilling to bear the costs associated with measures that would lead to a significant decline in the inflation rate. By exaggerating these costs, the government provided a rationale for doing nothing.

The rate of inflation in Britain was 7 percent in 1972, 9 percent in 1973, 16 percent in 1974, and 25 percent in 1975. In 1975, and to a greater extent in 1976, investors sold British pounds in the foreign exchange market, and the pound depreciated much more sharply than was suggested by the increases in British prices relative to world prices. British goods became increasingly undervalued. The Parisians trouped to London on Saturdays for their weekend shopping. The rapid depreciation of the pound was in anticipation of continued inflation; the depreciation intensified the increases in the British price level.

Overvaluation

Then, a combination of events – the decline in the world inflation rate in 1975 and 1976, government success in getting the unions to limit wage demands, and the rapid increase in North Sea oil production – facilitated a reduction in inflation to 15 percent in 1976 and 1977 and to 10 percent in 1978. Few had predicted that the inflation rate could drop so sharply. As the anticipated inflation rate declined, the British pound began to appreciate in the foreign exchange market; in a few months, the pound went from $1.55 to nearly $2.00. As the pound appreciated, the cost of imports fell, which contributed to a reduction in the inflation rate. British goods were becoming too expensive, and the French found shopping in London far less worthwhile.

By late 1980, sterling was back at $2.40, a result of three factors – the turnabout in Britain's position from being an oil importer to an oil exporter, the surge in the oil price, and the contractive monetary policy associated with the Conservative government of Margaret Thatcher. At $2.40 = £1, the British pound was overvalued, at least by 10 percent, and probably by 20 percent. As a result of overvaluation, exports of industrial products declined while imports increased; the unemployment rate reached 12–13 percent. It almost seemed as if the revenues the British government collected from taxes on the profits of North Sea oil production were absorbed in the unemployment compensation payments to those who had lost their jobs as a result of the overvalued British pound. Mrs Thatcher's standing with the British voters plummeted – until the Argentineans grabbed the Falkland Islands. But the war in the South Atlantic did not make a significant dent in the unemployment rate.

The tunnel at the end of the light

What will be the US price level at the beginning of the second millenium? One inference from monetary history is that inflationary episodes are followed by periods of relative price stability. The US inflation rate peaked in 1980; since then the US inflation rate has fallen sharply and in the mid-1980s averaged 3–4 percent a year. Moreover the US inflation rate did not increase measurably from the lows of the recession of 1982, despite the rapid and protracted business expansion throughout the 1980s and again in the 1990s. A number of seers have been looking for a return to inflation, in part because there was so much inflation in the 1970s.

Continuation of a succession of rounds of price increases interspersed with periods of price stability means that the value of money will decline, although not at a stable rate. Indeed, the record of the 1965–75 decade suggests that inflation may get worse before it gets better. Contrast three episodes. In 1965 the economy began to expand after a period of price stability going back to 1959; during the 1959–64 period the unemployment rate was in the range of 4–5 percent. Expansion occurred when the rate of price increase was still around 3 percent and the unemployment rate had reached 6 percent. A move to monetary contraction had substantial business casualties – Penn Central failed, Lockheed teetered on the brink, and many long-established stock brokerage firms (Walston, Glore Forgan, Frances I. Dupont) went out of business.

When the authorities began to expand the money supply again in 1971, the economy boomed; then the 1965–9 scenario was advanced to 1971–5. The monetary contraction of 1974 was much more severe than that of 1970; business failures were more acute. Franklin National Bank and Security National Bank were closed, W. T. Grant failed, Pan Am, TWA, and Eastern Airlines were all on the ropes, and numerous real estate investment trusts fell far behind in making scheduled payments to their bankers. The years of inflation had weakened the capital structure of numerous firms. The unemployment rate mounted; the automobile industry was shocked by the sharp decline in sales and large increase in imports.

Then, in late 1974, the monetary reins were relaxed and expansion resumed. In 1971 the monetary expansion began when the price level was increasing at the rate of 3 percent a year; the 1975 expansion began when it was increasing at nearly 6 percent a year. While the economic expansion tended to have an upward impact on the price level, the combination of excess industrial capacity and good crops led to downward price pressures. By 1978, as excess capacity diminished, prices began to inch upward at a more rapid rate.

Double-digit inflation returned in 1980, and the rate reached 13 percent at the peak. By 1981 the inflation rate was down to 8 percent, by 1982, to 6 percent. Yet the unemployment rate was climbing almost as rapidly as the rate of inflation was falling. At some stage, the unemployment rate would begin to fall – and the key question was what the subsequent change in the price level would be. One group of seers had the US economy on a roller coaster of accelerating inflation – there may be dips, but the trend is up. The competing story is that politicians eventually respond to the demands of the public, and the public had become tired of inflation.

By the end of the 1990s, inflation rates were less than 2 percent a year in most of the industrial world. The United States had experienced an unprecedented economic expansion that had continued for more than seven years and the inflation rate at the end of this period was much below the rate at the beginning of the expansion, even though the unemployment rate had declined below 5 percent. In retrospect, the inflation genie had escaped from the bottle in the late 1960s and then increased for nearly 15 years. It then took another 15 years to reduce the inflation rate to below 2 percent a year.

The inflation genie is firmly back in the bottle – and likely to stay there for an extended period.

9
Oil and the OPEC Roller Coaster

OPEC to rule the world?

The quadrupling of the price of crude petroleum in late 1973 from $2.75 a barrel to $12.50 a barrel led to visions of financial disaster for the industrial countries and for many developing countries such as Brazil and India. The World Bank, headed by Robert McNamara, remembered at Ford for the Edsel and at the Pentagon for the McNamara Line in Vietnam, projected that the financial wealth of oil-producing countries would climb to $300 billion by 1980 and $650 billion by 1985. The specter was that much of the money and the wealth in the West would be transferred to Saudi Arabia, Kuwait, Venezuela, Nigeria, and other OPEC countries, who would stuff dollars into the wells almost as fast as they pumped the oil out. Since OPEC wealth would increase more rapidly than world wealth, it seemed only a matter of time before OPEC would own the world. The Western industrial countries seemed squeezed; the OPEC countries sat on their lifeline. Inflation rates were higher and employment levels lower in both the industrial countries and in the developing countries as a result of the four-fold price hike in oil.

International impacts

The sharp increase in the price of oil did not cause the inflation of the early 1970s – indeed, the OPEC countries probably could not have increased the oil price in the absence of a world boom and inflation. Yet inflation rates in the Western industrial countries in 1974 were several percentage points higher because of the increase in energy prices. While the OPEC action did not cause the recession in the industrial countries, it intensified unemployment, especially in the firms that produced automobiles – and particularly those that produced large automobiles.

The financial collapse of the West seemed imminent. Italy seemed about to go bankrupt, with the rise in oil prices the straw that tripped the boot. Japan imported all of its petroleum and most of its energy and seemed particularly vulnerable and defenseless. Great Britain seemed threatened because OPEC members would eventually shift from holding British pound deposits in London to US dollar deposits in New York and Swiss franc deposits in Zurich. Western capitalism was said to be in serious danger, for the OPEC members would buy up the shares of the major industrial companies in the United States and Europe and then run these firms to suit their own political aspirations.

Newspaper headlines gave content to the threat. Iran bought 25 percent of Krupp, the major German conglomerate. Kuwait bought a large bloc of shares of Daimler Benz, one of the most prestigious car firms in the world. Libya bought into Fiat, the major Italian auto firm. The Iranians showed interest in buying Pan Am Airlines and offered to become bankers for Grumman Aircraft. All the major symbols of Western industrial success seemed to be up for auction. One unidentified group of Middle East investors tried to buy a small town in northwestern United States – George, Washington.

Economic checks and balances

The view that the OPEC members would eventually own the world was based on extrapolation – the $12.50 a barrel price of crude petroleum was multiplied by 30 million barrels a day of OPEC production and exports to project the total daily revenues of the OPEC countries, their receipts were then forecast on the basis of a $20 per barrel price. Determining long-term trends by extrapolating from a few short-term observations can be risky – as many bankers and oil firm executives learned.

The analysts had forgotten that OPEC wealth could grow more rapidly than world wealth for a short interval, but thereafter OPEC wealth could grow no more rapidly than world wealth (Box 9.1, p. 156. An economic system has its checks and balances, even if it does not have a written constitution. One possible check to the growth in OPEC wealth was that the OPEC countries might become increasingly reluctant lenders as the oil price increased. Or the check to the growth of OPEC wealth might have arisen because the oil-importing countries proved unwilling to increase their debts as rapidly as McNamara suggested they would. Or the check might arise because the OPEC countries would increase their spending on imports of consumption and investment goods more rapidly than predicted. Finally, the check might occur because the very high real price would have induced both an increase in the supply of energy from non-OPEC sources and a reduction in the demand for energy.

All countries want the highest possible price for their production and their exports. The OPEC members were no exception; they wanted the highest possible price for their oil. If there had not been a Yom Kippur War, they might have invented a reason to raise the price whenever they believed that market conditions would sustain a new and higher level. Nevertheless, most OPEC members faced a dilemma. They knew that sharp increases in the price of oil both encouraged conservation and reduced demand, and increased energy supplies by both stimulating exploration for oil and encouraging substitution of other energy sources, including coal and nuclear power, for oil.

By 1978, the imports of OPEC countries had increased so rapidly that OPEC countries as a group were spending their export earnings about as fast as the funds were received; they had ceased adding to their foreign exchange reserves. Some OPEC members were spending more than their export earnings and they financed the difference both by spending part of their foreign exchange reserves and by borrowing abroad.

In 1979 the price of oil increased to $18 a barrel, because oil production declined following the departure of the Shah from Iran and sharp reduction in Iranian oil exports (Table 9.1). A further increase in the oil price occurred when exports of oil from the Middle East declined after Iraq invaded Iran. By early 1981, the oil price was $34 a barrel. Projections of the OPEC payments surplus for 1981 reached $120–$150 billion. Once again, the seers forecast that these OPEC payments surpluses would persist, a permanent feature of the economic scene. Yet by 1982, OPEC countries as a group were in a payments deficit. The check to the growth in their wealth arose this time from the combination of an increase in their imports and a reduction in export earnings as both export volume and price per barrel of oil declined.

The skeptics were proved correct. By 1978 OPEC wealth had grown far less rapidly than had been anticipated in 1974. Moreover, the $180 billion in financial assets of OPEC countries was worth only about $120 billion in 1974 prices, much below the earlier forecasts. And by January 1986, the OPEC countries were in a desperate situa-

Table 9.1   The price of oil, nominal and real, 1950–98

Year	Nominal price (Dollars/Barrel)	Price level (1990 = 100)	Real price (1950 = 100)
1950	1.71	12.1	1.71
1960	1.50	16.7	1.09
1970	1.30	25.7	.61
1975	10.60	38.7	3.31
1980	28.67	60.6	5.71
1985	29.69	83.0	4.32
1990	22.05	100.0	2.31
1995	17.20	116.2	1.55
1996	20.37	118.8	1.80
1997	19.27	121.2	1.67
1998	13.07	122.9	1.12

tion, for the price of oil had fallen to $12 a barrel – and appeared headed south.

The oil price rose to $40 after Iraq invaded Kuwait in August 1990; both Kuwait and Iraq were no longer sources of supply for other countries. When the war started, the price declined as sharply as it had increased. After the brief war and an extended period to clean up the destruction, Kuwait returned as an oil exporter. In contrast Iraqi exports of petroleum were halted as a result of an embargo, although subsequently some exports were permitted so the country might obtain the foreign exchange to use to pay for imports of medicines and foods.

In the late 1990s oil was trading in the range of $12–$15 a barrel, modestly higher than where it had traded after the first sharp oil price increase in the early 1970s. But there was a significant difference, because the world price level in 1998 was more than twice as high as in 1973, so the real price of oil was one half the real price in the earlier period. Eventually Iraq will again produce, and export nearly 2 million barrels a day.

Recycling money

If the OPEC members spend less than their export earnings on imports of goods, their financial wealth accumulates in the United States and other industrial countries. While they might be able to bury the checkbooks in the desert sands, they cannot bury the money: it remains

Box 9.1   A Little Forecasting Experiment

Assume the year is 1950. You're employed in a petroleum company – or perhaps as a consultant to a petroleum company. You've been asked to develop a forecast of the price of petroleum in the year 1960 – 10 years into the future. To make this assignment easier, assume there is no inflation – or, alternatively, that you have been asked to make the forecast after adjustment for any increase in the consumer price level.

This forecasting assignment is typical of many. The profitability of current investments in exploration and development of various oil fields will depend on the price of oil in the distant future. Once oil is discovered, 8 or 10 years may elapse before the oil is produced, and then a well may produce for 10 or 15 years.

One cautious approach to your assignment is to assume that the price of oil remains unchanged – or, which is the same thing, that the price of oil increases about as rapidly as the consumer price level. In this case, the cliche that 'gold is a good inflation hedge' could be extended to petroleum, – 'oil is a good inflation hedge.' The rationale for this approach is that the price of oil had not changed significantly from 1900 to 1950, although there had been significant changes in the real price within this extended period.

An alternative approach is that the price of oil might increase at the interest rate. The assumption implicit in this view is that if the price of oil were expected to increase at a rate more rapidly than the interest rate, investors would have an incentive to buy oil and hold the oil in inventory; the oil would then be sold at the higher price in the future.

The price of oil was $1.71 a barrel in 1950, which is your 1950 forecast for the price in 1960. The actual price of oil in 1960 was $1.50.

Your 1950 forecast didn't do very well. You missed the price decline in the 1950s.

So you're asked in 1960 to once again make a forecast for the price of oil ten years into the future. You might repeat your 1950 forecast in 1960, either that the real price would remain unchanged at $1.50 in 1970. The price of oil in 1970 turned out to be $1.30.

So now you're asked a third time, now in 1970, to make a forecast of the price of oil in the year 1980. You might repeat the same process; your forecast in 1970 for the price in 1980 is $1.50.

Box 9.1 continued

A massive error. In 1980 you might continue your forecast for the year 1990.

So in 1980 your forecast is more or less like all the other forecasts – the oil price will continue to increase, perhaps to $60 in 1990. Most of the banks and the oil companies shared the view that there would be sharp price increases.

So move forward to 1990. The oil price is $20 a barrel – although it soared briefly after Iraq invaded Kuwait. You missed the sharp decline in the price of oil in the 1980s.

By now, of course you're likely to be sensitive to the errors that you've made in your previous forecast, and the source of the errors. In 1950, 1960, and 1980, your estimate of the market price of oil 10 years late proved high relative to the market price of oil on the terminal date of the forecast 10 years later. In contrast in 1970, your estimate of the market price of oil proved low relative to the market price of oil in 1980; you failed to foresee the world economic boom and inflation and price consequences of the Iraqi invasion of Iran.

You might conclude from an analysis of these forecast errors that your forecast of the price will be low relative to the actual price if the OPEC cartel becomes more powerful or if there is a war; otherwise your forecast of the price in the future will prove higher than the price of oil in the year that the forecast 'matures'. In the absence of political shocks, competitive forces in the market-place will lead to a more rapid decline in the price of oil than you had forecast.

Consider one more forecast. The year is 1970. You're asked to develop a forecast for the price of oil in the year 2000. The conservative forecast is that the real price of oil will not change. So you buy into this forecast. By 1980, the real price of oil is ten times higher than the 1970 real price. So how do you revise your forecast for the year 2000 on the basis of the new information? Most forecasters extrapolated from the price increases in the 1970s to predict that prices would continue to increase in the 1980s and 1990s. This was an extremely expensive error, for they based their investment activities on the forecast. They ignored or underestimated that the surge in the real price would induce tremendous initiatives toward the conservation of energy. And they underestimated that the surge in the real price would induce significant increases in the production of petroleum from non-OPEC countries, and significant shifts from petroleum to non-petroleum energy sources.

either as deposit balances in the banks of petroleum-importing countries (hereafter PICs), or in the form of securities purchased with these balances. The early view was that the money paid the sheiks for oil had to be recycled, or it would somehow disappear from the system. But this view was incorrect: money paid to individual OPEC countries for oil was recycled automatically. The OPEC members are paid for oil with checks drawn on the major international banks in New York, London, Frankfurt, Zurich, and Tokyo. The OPEC countries deposited these checks in their own banks (more or less the same 50 or 60 major international banks), and their bank deposit balances increased accordingly. Then they could spend the money, give it away, or lend it, or invest it. Unless the OPEC countries spend, lend, or give the money away, the major international banks would be in a position to increase their loans – for example, to importers of oil, to developers of new energy sources, and to other borrowers.

Investing OPEC money

The rich have one problem the poor lack: they must decide how to invest their savings. OPEC members had the same problem – or at least most of them did for a while. They had to choose between securities issued by primary borrowers, such as firms and governments, and securities issued by banks and other financial intermediaries; between securities denominated in the US dollar and securities denominated in Swiss franc, the German mark, or the British pound, and many other currencies; between fixed-price securities, such as bank deposits and bonds, and variable-price real assets, such as real estate and stocks. And if they choose to buy stocks, they had to decide whether they wanted a controlling interest or a minority interest in the firms whose shares they buy.

Soon after the first increase in the oil price in 1973–4, concern developed among the PICs over whether there was a sufficient volume of the 'right securities' – securities that would appeal to OPEC members. The fear was that the rapid growth in oil wealth meant that OPEC members could quickly buy all available PIC securities. And then they would reduce their oil production.

In 1974, when OPEC wealth rose sharply, the $50 billion annual projected increase in OPEC financial wealth seemed large compared with the value of listed stocks in the United States, Great Britain, and Continental Europe. At the end of 1974, the market value of IBM – the product of the number of its shares outstanding and the price of each share – was $8 billion. The implication was that if OPEC countries wanted to buy IBM, they could buy the company – lock, stock, and barrel – with the excess cash that they would accumulate in two months. The extrapolators calculated that it would take only 10 years for OPEC to buy all US stocks, three years to buy all of British stocks, and a year to buy all of the stocks in Continental Europe.

But the extrapolators fell into a logical trap (some might say, once again), for they forgot that the prices of these stocks and all other stocks would rise as OPEC members bought more of them. The rumor that the Kuwaitis would buy IBM shares led to a 10 percent increase in the price of these shares in one day – even before the Kuwaitis had bought one share of IBM. Relatively small OPEC purchases of stocks would lead to increases in their price, so that the same dollar volume of purchases would buy fewer and fewer shares.

Long before OPEC countries could buy up IBM or Shell, the governments of their countries of origin would apply limits on these purchases; they would be concerned about loss of control. So total foreign ownership of firms in industries deemed sensitive might be limited to 25 percent – or perhaps even less. Such limits would deflect OPEC demand to other securities.

OPEC asset preferences

Matching the $50 billion annual increase in OPEC wealth with the increase in the supply of PIC stocks, or even with the total supply of stocks, is a straw-man argument; stocks are a modest part of total financial wealth in most countries. The more effective comparison is between the annual increase in OPEC financial wealth and the annual increase in wealth in the United States and other industrial countries. The increase in financial wealth covers a wide range of securities – bank deposits, stocks, bonds, mortgages, and so on. Total financial wealth in the United States at the time was about $20,000 billion, and the annual increase in US financial wealth was about $1,500 billion; the annual increase in world financial wealth was about $5,000 billion. So $50 billion of OPEC purchases would be modest compared with the annual increase of world financial wealth.

The asset preferences of OPEC members are similar to those of investors in other countries in one important respect: they like diversification. To the extent that the oil producers preferred securities denominated in a particular PIC currency, the price of this currency would increase in the foreign exchange market. The greater their demand for securities denominated in the Swiss franc, the greater the appreciation of the Swiss franc. Then, as the Swiss franc became more expensive relative to both the German mark and the US dollar, Switzerland's ability to export cheese and chocolate bars would decline. But the more expensive Swiss franc would mean that it would be cheaper for the Swiss to finance their oil imports.

An OPEC preference for securities denominated in some currencies would have meant that securities denominated in other currencies were disfavored. Some PICs were not able to borrow to finance their oil imports. Bangladesh and India were in this group, and for a while, Italy appeared likely to join them. If these countries could not borrow to finance their more expensive imports, they would have been forced to curtail their imports – if not of oil, then of other raw materials and of various consumer and producer goods. The analogy with the household is useful: if John Doe loses his job and cannot borrow to finance his consumption of cars and corn muffins, he will consume less. Charity from the Salvation Army and checks from the unemployment compensation office and the welfare department may help finance some consumption. If Doe consumes only essentials and their prices rise, then he must tighten his belt even further and consume fewer essentials. Similarly, if a country cannot borrow to finance its imports of petroleum and other essentials, its consumption will decline. And OPEC exports of petroleum will decline.

The OPEC countries might find it in their interest to extend credit to Bangladesh and India; subsidized or cheap credit is a sales supplement for high-priced oil. As long as the effective price of oil exceeds the cost of producing the oil – and it does by a factor of 50 or 100 – then such sales would enhance OPEC wealth. OPEC would be a price-discriminator. If the cost of producing a barrel of oil is 20 cents while the world price is $30 and the discounted price is $20, the profit from cutting the price for the poorer countries is $19.80 – if cutting the price leads to an increase in the volume of sales.

The difference between the $30 world price and the $20 'sales price' would be counted as OPEC foreign aid. OPEC members have sold some oil to the developing countries at reduced prices or at subsidized credit terms; these discounts and credits have been small relative to their total sales to the developing countries. If the OPEC members are not willing to lend to the least creditworthy borrowers, then the rate at which their foreign investments would increase would be smaller than McNamara's estimates.

The International Monetary Fund (IMF) developed a credit arrangement under which the fund would borrow from OPEC members and in turn lend to its poorer members. Similarly, Saudi Arabia made funds available to the World Bank. While OPEC members could lend directly to the oil importers, the international institutions provide more attractive guarantees, and they can still sell their oil at the discounted $20 price. Bangladesh may fail to repay the individual OPEC countries and not go out of business, but the IMF would always repay members.

Every surplus requires a deficit

Half the readers of this book are above average. Booms have economic significance only because there are busts. For every payments surplus there must be a payments deficit. And for every trade surplus there must be a trade deficit.

Impact of OPEC investments

The oil price increases were the biggest economic shocks to the international monetary arrangements since the Second World War. From 1974 through 1981, OPEC surpluses summed to $300 billion. Where did the money go – how did they invest the money? Most of these investments were made by government agencies. There were a few purchases of ongoing businesses – the Kuwaitis bought Santa Fe International, a US oil field service business for more than $2 billion, and 25 percent of Daimler Benz, producer of Mercedes cars and trucks. Individual investors resident in various oil-producing countries bought banks and insurance companies and hotels in the United States, Great Britain, and other industrial countries.

The oil price increase would have had impacts on the foreign exchange values of the German mark, the Japanese yen, and other foreign currencies even if the OPEC members spent their export earnings as fast as the money came in. There are two sides to these impacts – one involves the impact of the importing countries' increased oil bills on the foreign exchange value of their currencies. The OPEC members required that the buyers of oil pay in US dollars. So one question is how the oil-importing countries obtained more US dollars to pay for oil. Some countries might adopt contractive monetary and fiscal policies, which would reduce the level of income or the rate of growth of income; as a result the demand for imports would decline, and domestic firms would be more eager to export. In contrast other countries might adopt policies so their currencies would depreciate in the foreign exchange market; as a result, their exports might increase relative to their imports, so that more of their increased export earnings could be used to pay for imported oil. The second side involves how individual

OPEC countries choose to spend or invest the increase in their net export earnings. To the extent that the OPEC countries buy Swiss goods or Swiss securities, the Swiss franc will appreciate.

If OPEC members as a group had payments surpluses of $50 billion a year, then as a group the oil importing countries must have payments deficits of $50 billion a year. Some oil-importing countries that had been international lenders might have become borrowers. Unless oil-importing countries are willing to borrow $50 billion a year, OPEC cannot have surpluses of $50 billion a year.

How the $50 billion of borrowings by the oil importing countries as a group is distributed among the individual oil-importing countries will have major impacts on the changes in market exchange rates. One approach toward the distribution of $50 billion would be for each PIC to increase its annual borrowing by the increase in its oil import payments, *less* any increase in its commodity exports to OPEC members. For example, assume the oil import bills of both Germany and Japan had increased by $10 billion as a result of the higher oil price. To the extent that Japan and Germany increased their commodity exports to various OPEC members, their need to borrow to maintain the foreign exchange values of their currencies. If each PIC increased its exports to OPEC members in proportion to the increase in its oil import bill, then the foreign exchange values of the currencies of the oil importing countries would not change. The difference between the increase in each country's oil import payments and the increase in exports would be borrowed from OPEC countries or from international lenders. This approach toward distribution of PIC borrowings would not lead to a change in the pattern of exchange rates.

The alternative way to distribute the $50 billion among PICs would be for many or most PIC countries to choose to pay for oil on a pay-as-you-go basis, because of their reluctance or inability to incur the international indebtedness by the amounts implied in the standstill approach. These countries would adjust to the increase in their oil import bills by allowing their currencies to depreciate in the foreign exchange market; thus their exports would increase to help finance the increase in their oil-import payments and their non-oil imports would decline. The combination of the increase in export earnings and the reduction of non-oil import payments would equal the increase in their oil import payments.

At the extreme, the currencies of all PICs except one might depreciate in the foreign exchange market; this country – the *N*th – would incur the international indebtedness that would mirror the increase in

OPEC investments. The Nth country would be the United States. Just as the US payments deficits in the 1950s and early 1960s were determined by the reserve demands of other countries, so the post-OPEC increase in foreign holdings of US dollar securities would equal the difference between the increase in wealth of OPEC members and the increase in foreign indebtedness of all other PICs. At most, the United States would increase its foreign indebtedness by $50 billion annually as a result of the oil price shock. Germany, Japan, and other PICs would increase their exports of autos, steel, and chemicals to the United States to earn the dollars to pay for their oil imports; their levels of foreign indebtedness would remain unchanged.

Both the standstill and the pay-as-you-go approaches represent the ends of a spectrum. And so the question became where each country was on the spectrum. If countries followed the standstill approach, then they would have had to take the initiative and borrow abroad. If they were reluctant or unwilling to borrow abroad, their currencies would automatically depreciate, and they would – willy-nilly – move toward the pay-as-you-go end of the spectrum.

The more that individual PICs borrowed abroad – that is, the more they exported their securities – the less their currencies would depreciate. Increased exports of securities would be substitutes for increased exports of goods. But there is a difference – if a PIC borrowed, then at some time it must repay. To get the foreign exchange necessary to repay the loan, the country must increase its exports in the future – or else borrow in the future to repay its maturing loans.

The choice for the authorities in each PIC is not whether its currency will depreciate to pay the higher cost of imported petroleum, since the currency will depreciate – in the immediate future if the country follows the pay-as-you-go approach and in the distant future if it follows the standstill approach. If the line of least resistance is to do nothing, the automatic and instantaneous depreciation of the currency will ensure that oil imports can be paid for currently – provided the country has the ability to increase its exports.

Whenever a PIC permitted its currency to depreciate, the domestic price of oil increases and the amount spend on oil imports declined. Domestic production of coal, petroleum, and other types of energy would be encouraged. Some countries adopted a non-market measures to limit their oil imports; they placed ceilings or quotas on these imports. Others raised tariffs to reduce oil imports. Several engaged in barter deals with individual OPEC members, exchanging tanks and trucks and atomic plants for oil. Some placed a ceiling on the rate at which they allowed their foreign indebtedness to increase. Taken together, these various measures determined the upper limit of PIC borrowings – and the OPEC payments surplus. The increased oil payments by the PICs caused their currencies to depreciate. The increased PIC exports of goods and securities caused their currencies to appreciate. Both depreciation and appreciation were measured relative to the US dollar, because payments for oil traditionally have been made with it. Whether the currency of an individual PIC appreciated or depreciated depended on whether the increase in its payments for oil was smaller or larger than the increase in its exports of goods and securities.

Shortly after the oil price increased, the common view was that the Western European currencies and the Japanese yen would weaken relative to the dollar, because these countries imported much more of their oil than the United States. Subsequently, however, the European currencies and the Japanese yen appreciated, for the increase in their exports of goods, services, and securities to OPEC members dominated the increase in their oil import payments. For example, Germany's oil-import bill increased by $10 billion as a result of higher oil prices; yet in 1974 the increase in German exports was several billion dollars larger than the increase in German oil imports. And the Germans borrowed several billion dollars abroad. Similarly, the Japanese trade surplus in 1974 decreased by much less than the increase in the Japanese oil-import bill.

Thus, Germany and Japan, two of the three largest countries in the system, followed the pay-as-you-go approach. The major PIC borrowers were Great Britain, Italy and, to a lesser extent, France. More than half of the increase in OPEC financial wealth was associated with the increase in the payments deficits of the developing countries.

Initially, the countries with the weakest economies did much of the borrowing. As they reached the limit in their ability or their willingness to borrow abroad, the deficits were shuttled elsewhere in the system. If OPEC had a surplus, the United States would end up with the counterpart deficit as other countries as a group moved to the pay-as-you-go-approach.

Hawks, doves and export-earning pressures

Twice in a decade, once in 1973–4, and again in 1979–80, sharp increases in the price of OPEC oil shocked international financial arrangements. In both instances, OPEC countries achieved large payments surpluses, peaking at $60 billion in OPEC I (1973–4) and $120 billion in OPEC II (1979–80). Yet the OPEC surpluses evaporated almost as rapidly as they appeared. When the oil price went up sharply, the OPEC countries appeared to have unlimited market power. For a while, it seemed that only their benevolence toward the oil-importing countries restrained them from setting an even higher oil price. Yet by mid-1980, an oil glut had appeared and, by 1985, OPEC's share of the world oil market had fallen in half.

Each producer of oil – and each producer of every other raw material – faces the following economic decision: am I better off if I produce one more barrel of oil and put the money in the bank, or would it be more rewarding to keep the oil in the ground and profit from the subsequent increase in its price? If the interest rate that can be earned on the money in the bank is higher than the anticipated rate of increase in the market price of oil, then the producer would be better off pumping one more barrel of oil and putting the money in the bank. In contrast, if the interest rate is lower than the anticipated rate of increase in the price of oil, then the more profitable course is to reduce or delay production.

One group of OPEC countries, the Hawks, leaned toward reducing output and charging higher prices. Another group, the Doves, wanted to increase production and charge a lower price. The Hawks raised their selling prices – and for a while, they could sell all the oil they could produce. The Hawks believed that they would benefit by raising the current price even more rapidly than they did. The Doves were concerned that too-sharp increases in the current price of oil would prove counterproductive in the long run, both because producers of other types of energy – coal, gas, nuclear and hydro – would increase output, while users of energy would economize on the consumption. Countries like Algeria, Nigeria, and Venezuela, where populations are large relative to oil reserves, were among the Hawks. In contrast, Saudi Arabia and Kuwait were the principal Doves; their oil reserves will last for decades because their relatively small populations required only a limited amount of imports.

The dispute between the OPEC Hawks and the OPEC Doves became especially sharp in 1980, when the reductions in supply lead to the increase in the price to $38 or $40 a barrel, substantially above the OPEC-agreed price of $32 a barrel. The oil companies bought as much as they could of the lower-priced oil; then, to meet world demand they filled up at the higher-priced suppliers. The companies able to buy from Saudi Arabia – the former Aramco partners – had a bonanza for they were able to fill up at the low-price source and sell at the higher world price.

As demand for oil fell, the oil companies reduced the amount of oil they bought from the Hawks. The Saudis increased their output from 9 million to 10.5 million barrels a day as part of the deal to induce the US government to sell them sophisticated aircraft; more production of low-price Saudi oil meant less demand for the Hawks' oil. Subsequently the Saudis cut production to 6.5 million barrels a day to reduce excess supply.

By the spring of 1982, the demand for OPEC oil had fallen to 17 million barrels a day, only slightly more than half of the 30 million barrels that OPEC had produced in 1980. One explanation for the decline in demand was the worldwide recession; the implication was that the market power of OPEC – its ability to raise production and increase exports – would be restored when the recession ended. The other explanations for the decline in OPEC production were less favorable to the restoration of OPEC power; these centered on the substitution of non-OPEC oil – from sources such as the North Sea, the North Slope of Alaska, Mexico, and Egypt – for OPEC oil and the substitution of other types of energy such as coal and natural gas for oil. Moreover, demand for energy declined in response to the much higher price; thus the 1983 model cars were twice as efficient as the older cars being scrapped. The 1983 models, however, were designed when the oil price was $18 a barrel; the 1995 autos are much more efficient. As new cars enter the fleet and older models are scrapped, energy demand will decline further. Similarly, throughout the 1980s, new aircraft were introduced which were 50 percent more efficient in terms of passenger seat miles per gallon of fuel than older aircraft. The changeover to a more energy-efficient capital stock in housing and industry and office buildings means that total energy demanded will increase far less rapidly than national income.

The OPEC members found themselves in a quandary as their export earnings fell relative to their import bills. If they raised their selling price in an effort to generate more revenues, they might quicken both the reduction in demand for energy, and the substitution of non-OPEC for OPEC energy. If they reduced the price to maintain market share, other energy producers might follow with price cuts of their own; in this case OPEC revenues would decline further.

Moreover, OPEC's ability to sell at $20+ was strengthened by the reduction of Iranian and Iraqi oil exports. At some stage Iraq would increase its oil exports, if only to get the foreign exchange to help pay for imports necessary to rebuild its economy – and its military machines. Increased oil exports from Iraq would put sharp downward pressure on the oil price unless other OPEC members reduced their exports by about the same amount. Yet no OPEC country can reduce its production without causing its export revenues to fall significantly.

The Kuwait invasion

The oil price nearly doubled in the few days after Saddam Hussein invaded Kuwait in August 1990. In part, the surge in the price resulted from the decline in the supply of petroleum as exports of oil from both Kuwait and Iraq declined sharply. Saudi Arabia sharply increased its oil production and its exports, so the net supply of oil did not decline significantly. Still the oil price remained high, largely because the oil consumers were building their own inventories to hedge against a sharp reduction in supplies. The major concern was that the capacity or willingness of other oil-producing countries to export would decline, so that a real shortage might follow.

Russia and the republics

The Soviet Union had been one of the world's largest petroleum producers and one of the world's largest petroleum exporters. Production and exports both declined as the Soviet Union disintegrated. The prospect, however, is that both production and exports again will increase as energy prices in Russia and other republics increase to world levels – which will also reduce energy consumption. Many Western oil companies are involved in joint ventures with the oil-producing enterprises in Russia and around the Caspian Sea, in effect bringing Western technology to replace production technologies that are 20–30 years behind-the-times. Care to become involved in energy- price forecasting activity?

10
The Three Ds – Disinflation, Deflation, and Depression

All inflations end, some with a bang, some with a whimper.

Currency reform

The 'bangs' involve a currency reform – usually after the economy has been hyperinflating at rates of 600 or 800 percent a year (Box 10.1). The production and import of currency notes becomes a major growth industry. The experience from many countries suggests that once the price level triples in a year, the 'point of no return' has been passed, and the inflation rate will continue to accelerate until there is a currency reform – the old money is thrown out and a new money is introduced.

Accelerating decline in money values

Inflations accelerate when governments appear incapable of increasing their taxes in line with their expenditures – and so they borrow to meet the payroll. Because money is losing its value at an increasing rate, government borrowing also must occur at an accelerating rate if the government's checks are not to bounce. Government expenditures usually increase at the same rate as the inflation rate – tax collections frequently lag the inflation rate, and for several different reasons. One reason is that some types of taxes may be stated as a fixed amount. A second is that collecting taxes becomes more difficult – some people delay paying taxes because they wish to pay in cheaper money, and they've made the bet that tomorrow's money will be worth less than today's; indeed next week's money will be worth even less than tomorrow's. Almost always the interest rates and penalty payments on delayed tax payments are smaller than the decline in the value of money – which means that the effective tax rate is lower, the longer the delay in making the tax payment. (In effect, the delayed tax payments is a low interest rate loan from the government to the taxpayer – but a loan arranged at the taxpayer's initiative.) Others respond to the inflation by ignoring the tax collector completely – for them, there is an infinite delay.

Because of the decline in the real value of money, individuals become increasingly reluctant to hold money, and so they spend money as soon as they receive it – or even before. Some individuals borrow to buy goods and real assets or hard assets in the belief that the value of these assets will increase more rapidly than the interest rate on the loans incurred to finance these purchases. In the inflationary environment, they're likely to be more casual in their investment decisions – their rationale is that inflation will bail them out of any major errors. And so spending increases relative to the money supply.

Because the real value of money balances is declining, the government must increase its borrowing and its spending at an accelerating rate. And so it goes.

In 1985, Argentina had an inflation rate of 1000 percent before the move to a currency reform and sharp deflation and a new money.

Box10.1   A Story from the German Hyperinflation

As the inflation rate increases, individuals wish to be paid more and more frequently to minimize the losses from being owed wages and salaries while purchasing power declines. Initially individuals might have been paid monthly, then they were paid weekly, then daily, and then twice a day. And the amount of each payment was increasing. The currency notes were also getting larger. The increases in the size and denomination of the currency notes lagged the increase in the inflation rate, with the result that a larger amount of bank notes was involved in each payment; the physical size of the payment increased. The story is told of one man who was paid twice a day, and took the money home in a wheelbarrow because of the bulk of the currency notes. On the way home during his lunch hour break, he saw a traffic accident. He put the wheelbarrow down to view the accident. When he returned, the money was still there – but the wheelbarrow was gone. That's hyperinflation.

Bolivia's inflation rate in 1984 was 2000 percent; its inflation rate in 1985 was about 8000 percent – which meant the price level doubled about every 50 days. But this was only true on average, since the inflation rate took fewer days to double at the end of the year than the beginning because the inflation rate was accelerating. Tax revenues of the Bolivian government were then 15 percent of its expenditures. A large part of government expenditures were used to pay for the import of new bank notes from the printers in Great Britain and Germany – indeed, Bolivia's imports of new bank notes was the country's largest commodity import after petroleum.

As the inflation accelerates, more and more economic activity involves money-changing; less is involved with the usual productive activities. More and more transactions involve payment in a foreign currency – or barter – or some other asset that is expected to maintain its value better than money. Illegal transactions soar. Domestic money becomes less and less useful. And so individuals economize even more on their money balances, and because of the rise in the price level, the purchasing power of money balances declines at even more rapid rates than the increase in the money supply. So the government finds it harder and harder to get any benefit from inflation because the public is so reluctant to acquire any more money.

The 'cold turkey' approach to stopping inflation

At some stage, the costs of coping with the hyperinflation become so pervasive and so high that a strong man comes to power and is given – or takes – the authority to raise taxes and cut government expenditure. The government payroll is reduced. Some government projects are delayed. The public is given 48 hours to turn in its old currency notes for the new currency notes – and in some cases, there are limits on the amount of old money that each person can convert. In some currency reforms, each 1000 units of old currency may be converted into a new money on a 1000 for 1 basis. Or each resident given 10 units of the new currency, regardless of the amount of old money owned previously.

Currency reforms involve a 'cold turkey' approach to stopping the inflation. Severe limits are placed on the rate of growth of money. Because government borrowing is restrained, the government must raise its taxes and cut its expenditures. Almost immediately the inflation rate falls from triple-digit to single-digit values. Price controls may facilitate the reduction in the inflation; the spending binge that had fueled the inflation disappears. The decline in spending always causes the economy to move into a recession. Business spending on new plant and equipment declines sharply. Business failures surge. Unemployment increases. These casualties and hardships are inevitable with the move to the currency reform.

Disinflation

The 'whimper' approach to reducing inflation isn't very different in terms of its impacts – except that the decline in money supply growth occurs before hyperinflation has occurred and so a currency reform isn't necessary. Interest rates rise, investment spending declines, income falls, and bankruptcies increase. Unemployment increases.

Monetary contraction and interest rates

Inflations always redistribute wealth from savers and lenders to borrowers because interest rates just don't rise fast enough to compensate for the decline in the purchasing power of money. Business firms go on an investment binge because the real cost of borrowed funds is so low – indeed, in some periods, the money interest rate may be below the inflation rate, which means that the real interest rates are negative. And in such an environment, anyone who has access to credit can readily profit by purchasing a market basket of goods, since the increase in the price of the market basket exceeds the interest rate on the borrowed funds. Indeed, if interest rates rose fast enough to keep up with the inflation rate, there'd be no point in having the inflation. In contrast, savers and lenders get even when the disinflation (a decline in the rate of increase in the price level) or deflation (a decline in the absolute level of the price level) occurs, for then interest rates are higher than the inflation rate and often much higher, especially during the initial several years of the disinflationary period.

Investment spending is curtailed in response to the high level of interest rates and the reluctance of banks to lend, and the economy sinks. When investors recognize that increases in the prices of these commodities will no longer exceed the interest rate and other carrying costs, they unload their inventories because the interest costs associated with financing the inventory are too high. Prices of basic commodities, especially those held for speculative purposes, plummet. Disinflations inevitably follow inflations, just as outgoing follow incoming tides and waxing follow waning moons. And the reason is that the economic factors that initially led to the inflation must in turn lead to an acceleration of the inflation rate if those who benefit from the inflation are to continue to benefit. Otherwise the inflation will end automatically.

The US disinflation of the 1980s

To cope with the double-digit inflation of the late 1970s, the US Federal Reserve adopted a new doctrine – *monetarism* – in October, 1979. During the previous three decades, the Fed's operating strategy had been to limit the ups-and-downs of interest rates, primarily because large increases in interest rates meant large declines in bond prices, which complicated life for bankers and other financial institutions. The Fed's stance usually was to 'lean against the wind' – to dampen both the increases and declines in interest rates. This decline in bond prices occurred at the same time that the banks were experiencing unusually large loan losses. So the pressures on the Fed were to manage the financial economy so as to keep interest rates reasonably stable. If the Fed stabilized interest rates, then the rate of growth of the money supply was outside its control – if firms and individuals wished to borrow more from the banks, then the increase in their loan demand would lead to an increase in the money supply: in effect the Fed set the price of money when it pegged interest rates, and together private bankers and the public determined the amount of money that the system would produce. If the rate of growth of the money supply then proved too rapid, the inflation rate would accelerate; then the Fed would allow interest rates to rise and that usually put the economy into a recession. As interest rates increased, there was usually a liquidity squeeze, and the economy would move into a recession before the inflation rate reached 5 percent.

The uniqueness of the 1970s was that inflation increased more rapidly than interest rates, so that real interest rates declined – and anticipated real interest rates declined even further because the inflation rate was expected to accelerate. In the summer of 1979, borrowers were in heaven, or close to being there, in that the inflation rate was higher than the interest rate, so the real interest rate was negative, so the incentive to borrow increased the higher the anticipated inflation rate. And this comparison was even more acute on an after-tax basis, since the interest payments reduced taxable income. Many investors positioned themselves to convert ordinary income into capital gains – and capital gains were taxable at much lower rates than ordinary income.

Many investors and financial institutions made investment decisions in the 1970s in the belief that the inflation would continue. The price of crude oil was rising, and it took little imagination to extrapolate the increase in oil price from $3 a barrel in 1970 to $12 in 1974 to $18 in 1979 to $65 in 1985 and $85 in 1990. Farmland prices rose rapidly. Residential real estate prices doubled and tripled. The price of land which might contain oil was also rising sharply. These investment decisions were smart in the inflationary 1970s. Aggressive investors did very well. So did aggressive lenders, since the losses on their loan portfolios were extremely low, because rising asset values meant that the banks could sell the collateral behind any bad loans.

To break inflationary expectations, the Fed had to secure a level of interest rates higher than the anticipated inflation rate. Then investors would no longer find it worthwhile to borrow to profit from the inflation, because the carrying costs would exceed the price-level increases. After October 1979, the Fed sought to limit the rate of increase in the money supply, which was what Monetarism was all about. The consequence was that US interest rates soared, and double-digit interest rates began to chase – and then surmount – the double-digit inflation rates. US interest rates soared to the highest level in the 200 years of the American Republic. Soon after the new monetarist policies were in place, inflation anticipations were reversed. In January 1980, the market price of gold peaked at $970 an ounce. The silver price peaked several weeks later, and the most rapid monthly increase in the US inflation rate occurred in the spring of 1980.

One impact of the reversal of inflationary expectations was that the US economy went into a tailspin, and the most severe recession in the postwar period resulted. Some firms were obliged to continue to borrow to complete a number of their investment projects. Even though inflation expectations had been reversed, their demand for borrowed funds remained high. So there was the beginning of *distress borrowing* – firms continue to borrow to complete projects underway, even though these projects would be unprofitable when completed. A number of US electric utilities had started construction of nuclear generation facilities in the late 1960s or early 1970s; in the early 1980s some of these utilities needed to borrow to complete the facilities.

Many investors who had discovered how to get rich in oil, farmland, and real estate in the inflationary 1970s soon experienced how to get poor once the interest rates had risen significantly relative to the inflation rate. The value of US farmland declined sharply (see below). The US financial system was under great stress, with more bank failures than in any previous period since the Great Depression. For a while, the US savings and loans associations had a negative net worth of

$4 billion – the amount by which their liabilities exceeded their assets. Several hundred failed. Many US commercial banks probably were underwater, given the market value of their loans to the booming sectors of the 1970s – agriculture, real estate, energy, and oil tankers.

Disinflation and the valuation of farmland

US farmland prices illustrate the turn from inflation to deflation. The value of US farm real estate rose from $170 billion in 1965 to $830 billion in 1981 – or at an annual rate of 10 percent a year; in effect, farm prices were doubling about every seven years. One explanation for the increase in the price of farmland was that the prices of corn and wheat, cattle, and chicken feed were increasing. Prices received by farmers in 1982 were two-and-a-half times higher than in 1965; prices paid by farmers were three times higher than in 1965. Farm incomes, however, increased more rapidly than the prices farmers received, for farm productivity was increasing; farm output was up and there were fewer farmers.

A second explanation for buying farm real estate was the anticipated capital gains from further increases in its price. This gain averaged $40 billion a year in the 1970s; in some years these gains were $50 or $60 billion – and in 1980 the gain exceeded $100 billion. The increase in farmers' wealth from the increase in the price of farm real estate was about equal to the income that farmers were getting from raising crops – in effect many farmers found themselves in the land speculation rather than the crop production business. Not every farmer played this game, yet anyone contemplating the purchase of real estate – or even contemplating the expansion of existing real estate holdings – had to be concerned with the possible increase in the price of land. Owning farmland was one of the best investments around; the return on farmland exceeded that on most other investments. Some farmers were leveraging themselves into great riches, in that they purchased farmland with a very small down payment; modest increases in the price of farmland led to a sharp increase in their net worth; and so they doubled up, and bought more farmland.

Some non-farmers got into the act – including some Europeans who belatedly rediscovered what Christopher Columbus had discovered in 1492, namely, that land prices in the United States were a bargain compared with land prices in Europe. Foreclosures of farmland – forced sales – were infrequent, for in a period of rising prices those farmers who had difficulty meeting their interest payments could sell their land at a price above the amount of their mortgage debt.

Farm debt was increasing slightly more rapidly than the increase in the value of farm real estate. Total farm debt was only 10–15 percent of the value of farmland, so farmers' net worth went up sharply. A few of the new entrants into farming as well as those who had greatly increased their land ownership were heavily in debt; most farmers had little debt. It was too good to last – and it didn't. Once interest rates surged, the carrying costs of farm debt soared. The price of the products that farmers were receiving began to fall in the early 1980s' recession. Once the prospect of further increases in the price of farmland had disappeared, the demand for farmland declined and the price of farmland began to fall. Foreclosures increased. Willie Nelson gave a concert in 1985, and raised $160 million for 'farm-aid' relief. The value of farm real estate fell by $50 billion.

The lenders to the farmers – many small banks in Illinois, Iowa, and Nebraska – were caught in a squeeze. They were obliged to pay higher interest rates on their deposits, but some of the farmers to whom they had made loans were unable to pay the interest on a scheduled basis. Farmers that had bought their land in the late 1970s were in deep trouble; the consequence was that dozens of small banks in Iowa, Illinois, and Nebraska were also in trouble.

Residential real estate

In Los Angeles, San Francisco, San Diego, and selected other sections of the country, the price of residential real estate rose by several hundred percent. The story was the same – a little money down, home prices would increase, and individuals would sell, take their capital gains, and trade up. Real estate values increased by several hundred percent in three or four years. In some neighborhoods, the houses were too expensive to live in – or so it seemed. But the story was like that in farmland. People were buying houses because they anticipated that prices would increase. For many investors, houses and condo agreements became the principal way to hedge wealth against inflation.

Disinflation and financial institutions

Banks and savings and loan associations (S & Ls) were extremely hard hit by the move to disinflation, and for two reasons. The first was that their interest costs were higher; these institutions could either pay the higher interest rates or lose deposits to institutions that were willing to pay the higher interest rates. The second was that the losses of these institutions were large on loans to agriculture, energy, residential real estate, tankers – indeed to all the borrowers who were doing so well in the 1970s.

S & Ls

The S & Ls were especially hard hit because a large part of their loans were at relatively long maturities, frequently 20 or 30 years and at fixed interest rates. In contrast, their deposits were of much shorter maturities – indeed, most of their deposits had maturities of six months or less. And in a period of financial deregulation, the interest rates the S & Ls were obliged to pay on their deposits were increasing rapidly – much more rapidly than the interest rates that the S & Ls were receiving on their outstanding mortgages. So many S & Ls had negative income. However, several believed the way out of this bind was to seek to grow rapidly, which would mean higher interest rates on their most recent mortgages, and large fee income associated with placement of new mortgages. To maintain their growth, these institutions had to be a little less demanding in the quality of the mortgages they were buying. These institutions were on a treadmill – and in 1984 and 1985 there were substantial depositor runs on the state-guaranteed associations in Ohio and Maryland.

Banks

The US commercial banks had two big advantages relative to the S & Ls. The first was that they were generally able to raise interest rates on their loans as their own cost of deposit funds increased; they were much less likely to be caught in a squeeze because the maturities of their loans was much longer than the maturity of their deposits. The second was that the banks had a much more diversified set of loans – in addition to loans to farmers, the commercial banks had substantial loans to consumers, industry, energy companies, urban real estate developers, and the developing countries. Yet these loans were less diversified then they had thought. What the lenders learned is that loans for real estate in Houston and Denver, loans for oil in Oklahoma and Kansas, loans for tankers, and loans to Mexico and Nigeria were all affected by changes in the oil prices and changes in interest rates.

In the spring of 1984, the largest US lender to industry – Continental Illinois National Bank – was subject to a massive depositor run that exceeded $10 billion. Only a few years earlier one of the major US business magazines had described Continental Illinois as one of the best managed US financial institutions, and in the inflationary 1970s Continental Illinois had grown rapidly. One reason for its growth was that it had greatly increased its energy loans; nearly $1 billion of its energy loans had been made through loan participation with a modest-sized bank in Oklahoma, Penn Square. When the oil business went South, these loans proved to be worth much less than book value. Large uninsured depositors eventually realized that Continental Illinois' loans losses might exceed its capital, and so they took their money and ran. The US authorities responded with measures to forestall the closing of the bank – in effect, Continental Illinois became a ward of the US government. The shareholders of the bank lost their investments, the directors of the bank and the top officers lost their positions. The stock options of the senior officers became virtually worthless.

Disinflation and the government deficit

Disinflations are the inevitable aftermath of an inflation. Once the inflation is over, the disinflation begins – by definition. And one regularity of every disinflation is that real interest rates rise. And the consequence of the increase in real interest rates is that business activity falls. The Great Depression occurred as a result of high real interest rates.

The US fiscal deficit of the mid-1980s was attributable to the tax cuts of 1982. The Reagan Administration bought the supply-side rhetoric, and cut taxes by $100+ billion. The large fiscal deficits meant that US interest rates were higher than might otherwise have been the case; but fortunately for the US economy, the stimulus of the large fiscal deficit offset the depressing effect of the higher real interest rates associated with the move to disinflation. So the US economy expanded in the 1982–5 period because of the large government deficits. As the investors came to realize that the inflation was less likely to return, US interest rates began to fall – despite the persistence of the fiscal deficits.

The Asian financial crisis and the world inflation rate

It's an axiom of economics that if supply increases more rapidly than demand, prices will fall. One hallmark of the countries in Asia – Japan, China, Hong Kong, Singapore, Korea, Thailand, and Malaysia – is their very high levels of savings, especially when the savings rates in the United States and various industrial countries in Europe are used as benchmarks. High levels of saving facilitate high levels of investment in plant and equipment. So the ability of these countries to produce goods and especially goods for sale in foreign markets has increased at a rapid rate. In the mid-1990s the export capabilities of many of these countries were increasing at 30 percent a year, far greater than the rate of increase in foreign demand for these products. So it was inevitable that producers would reduce prices as the means to increase their share of foreign markets – and to protect the share against price-cutting by foreign competitors.

Throughout most of the 1990s Japan has been in the economic doldrums as a result of the collapse of real estate prices and stock prices and the decapitalization of the banks as a result of their massive losses on real estate loans. Japanese industrial firms began to increase export sales as an offset to the slow growth of domestic sales, and Japan began to develop an increasingly large trade surplus.

Throughout the 1990s Korea, Thailand, and most of the other Tigers and Dragons (Singapore and Taiwan were the major exceptions) experienced trade deficits; these countries were experiencing high rates of economic growth and so their demand for imports of both investment goods and consumption goods was high. Once the Asian financial crisis developed, the currencies of these countries depreciated sharply and their rates of growth of income fell sharply, so their demand for imports declined while the incentive to export increased. The general view was that these countries would rely on an increase in exports to stabilize their economies. The turnaround in their trade balances has been estimated to be in the range of $100 billion–$150 billion.

The counterpart of the increase in exports from Japan and the Tigers and the Dragons is an increase in the US trade deficit and perhaps a reduction in the trade surpluses of France, Italy, and the European countries as a group. Skeptics and cynics might say that the behavior of the first group of countries is reminiscent of the 'beggar-thy-neighbor' policies of some countries during the Great Depression.

One impact of the increase in US net imports will be downward pressure on the prices of similar goods produced by US firms, with the result that there will be more downward pressure on inflation rates because of declines in the prices of tradable goods. A second impact is that the profits of US firms that produce similar goods may decline – similarly the profits of US firms that produce the exports for sale in these Asian countries will decline. This decline in sales and profits is likely to lead to downward pressure on the US stock prices because of the downward impact on the profits of US firms.

11

Optimal Bankrupts – Deadbeats on an International Treadmill

Ponzi finance

Deadbeat: Someone who deliberately avoids paying his debts.

One of the most famous bankers in US history was Charlie (neé Carlos) Ponzi, who ran a small financial institution in one of the Boston suburbs in the 1920s. Charlie promised to pay his depositors or investors 30 percent interest a month. All went well for three or four months; the number of investors increased rapidly and the earlier investors received their interest payments on a timely basis. Then in the fourth or fifth month, the inflow of new funds was smaller than the interest payments on the outstanding deposits, and Charlie defaulted on his promises. Eventually Charlie went to jail.

This otherwise obscure individual is immortalized in the term, 'Ponzi Scheme.' The generic version of the Ponzi scheme is that investors on Monday receive the promised interest on Tuesday from the cash that the operator or banker has received from new depositors. These 'banks' succeed as long as the rate of growth of new deposits is larger than the interest rate promised on outstanding deposits. Once the rate of growth of new deposits declines below the interest rate on outstanding deposits, the scheme goes bankrupt, because the new cash coming in isn't enough to enable the banker to make the scheduled interest payments to the earlier depositors. Just before the scheme goes bankrupt, the operator inevitably raises the interest rate to be paid on new deposits in an attempt to forestall the collapse.

But the collapse is inevitable, often with a big bang. The losses appear enormous. The inevitable question then becomes: 'Where did the money go?' There is a two-part answer to the question. The first part is that the operator of the scheme used some of the cash for expenses and may have gone to Las Vegas or Monte Carlo or otherwise used some of the cash for fast cars and faster women. The second part is that most of the cash never existed; the buildup in the assets of the scheme reflected the powers of compound interest at interest rates of 20 or 30 percent a month. At an interest rate of 20 percent a month, $100 invested on 1 January compounds to $1200 by the end-year; at a 30 percent interest rate, the end of the year value is $2800.

During the course of the year, the 'feel good' factor is powerful; there is lots of spending on consumption and on investment – an extended period of economic euphoria. Some individuals stop working, and spend their days moving between the cafes and their brokers' offices watching their wealth multiply.

There are lots of examples of Ponzi finance. Some start as Ponzi schemes, in some cases by innocents and in others by swindlers: others move into a phase of Ponzi finance when the rate of sales declines and the operator seeks to delay the day of reckoning by any of a number of measures to attract new cash. There also are a number of examples of Ponzi finance in the world economy. The developing country debt problem of the 1980s is one example. Another is the surge in the prices of real estate and stocks in Tokyo and Osaka in the late 1980s and the subsequent implosion of these prices in the early 1990s.

Then after the remaining dormant for a several years, the Ponzi virus infected the markets for real estate in Hong Kong, Bangkok, Kuala Lumpur, and Jakarta in the mid-1990s; these economies boomed and there was lots of buzz about the 'Pacific Century'. The buzz disappeared with the collapse of stock prices and currency values. Most of the countries in Central Europe and Russia experienced Ponzi schemes as a form of the new capitalism on their move to a market economy.

The developing country debt crisis

The third edition of this chapter, published in 1979, began:

If history is a guide, then in 1984 the structure of public international credits will collapse. A number of developing countries will threaten to default on a substantial part of their debts to government agencies in the developed countries and to international institutions. New York bankers will propose an international financial conference in Paris. The World Bank will call for borrowers and lenders to sort out their problems amicably. At the end of the conference, the terms on the $400 billion owed by the governments of developing countries will be renegotiated. A new international agency, Development Refinance International, will be established to help the borrowers consolidate their debts.

Some sentences in the previous paragraph were in the right ballpark. The structure of international debt began to collapse in the summer of 1982, when the foreign loans of the developing countries as a group totaled $800 billion. The increase in the external debt of the MBA countries (Mexico, Brazil, Argentina *et al.*) in the 1970s resulted primarily from the surge in bank loans to the governments in these countries and to government-owned enterprises such as railroads and steel mills. In 1972 the foreign loans for this group of countries totaled $125 billion, so that the rate of growth of their external debt averaged 20 percent a year. The interest rates on these loans averaged about 8 percent.

But there is a built-in time bomb, because new loans cannot increase more rapidly than the interest rate for an indefinite future. When the rate of growth of new loans declines below the interest rate on the outstanding loans, the borrowers have a new problem – they no longer will be able to get all the money from new loans necessary to pay the interest on outstanding loans.

The trigger for the developing country debt crises was the decline in the oil price from $36 $29 a barrel in April 1982. Because the banks were reluctant to lend more money to borrowers in Mexico once the oil price declined, these borrowers did not have the cash to pay the interest on their foreign loans. The major international banks began to reappraise and downgrade the creditworthiness of borrowers in

---

Box 11.1 A Simple Example

Consider a simple example. At the beginning of the year, you owe $100, and you agreed to pay your lender 8 percent interest a year. The lender thinks you're a good credit risk, and agrees to lend you an additional $20 during the coming year. Note that after you pay $8 interest on the outstanding loan you're still ahead by $12 in new cash. The lesson from this example is that as long as the loans available to you are increasing at a rate in excess of the interest rate on the outstanding loans, you have a powerful incentive to pay the interest on the outstanding loans on a timely basis. Indeed your credit reputation is impeccable. And of course the lenders will not encounter any loan losses. So the borrowers and the lenders form a mutual admiration society.

particular developing countries, especially oil-exporting countries such as Mexico, Venezuela, and Nigeria. The decline in both the price of oil and the volume of oil exports meant that the export earnings of these countries were declining and would decline further; as a result, the incomes of the government and government-owned firms would decline. Hence the ability of the borrowers to pay the interest on their foreign loans would decline. And then the bankers realized that there were overextended on their loans to the MBA countries as a group, which meant that the Brazil and other oil-importing countries also could no longer borrow the money to pay the interest on their outstanding foreign loans.

By the end of the 1980s it became clear that the banks had incurred losses of $200 – $300 billion on the $800 billion of developing country loans outstanding in 1982. These losses reflected declines in the market value of these loans, write-downs in their value, and a reduction in the interest rates charged borrowers when the loans were restructured to levels significantly below those appropriate for borrowers in their risk class.

The losses would have been even greater if loans from public-sector institutions such as the World Bank had not facilitated repayment of the loans to private lenders; in effect, the cash from public-sector lenders was being used to pay part of the interest to private-sector lenders. The losses also would have been significantly larger if the US government had not in effect guarantee some of the bank loans in exchange for a write-down of the total amount of the loans. The debt crisis was the major topic at the September 1982 meetings of the International Monetary Fund (IMF) and the World Bank. Mexico threatened to delay interest payments on its external debt for three months. Argentina was falling behind on its ability to make interest and amortization payments, a result of its abortive and costly attack on the Falkland Islands – or, as they say in Buenos Aires, the Malvinas.

Domestic and international loans

Within domestic economies, bankers shy away from deadbeats. Lending money when the probability of repayment is low is an inefficient form of charity. Nevertheless, loans sometimes go sour because of unforeseen events. Businesses fail. Some borrowers are incompetent, some untruthful; a few are incompetent and untruthful. Credit bureaus develop elaborate intelligence scorecards on the habits of individual borrowers – who repays promptly, who repays slowly, who rarely repays. Lenders pay for these credit histories to reduce their loan losses; they recover the costs of their payments to the credit bureaus by scaling interest rates to the riskiness of the borrowers. In some cases, the lenders may say 'no' when an individual or a firm applies for a loan; the borrower's credit reputation may be too poor. To further protect themselves against loss, the lenders frequently require that the borrowers pledge real property – houses, land, cars, and rings – as collateral for the loans. If the borrowers do not repay according to schedule, the lenders may take title to the property – the borrower's car is repossessed, the wedding rings and the engagement rings go to the pawnshop, and the sheriff arranges a foreclosure sale on the house. The borrower's income may be garnisheed – that is, the court may direct the borrower's employer to pay a fixed amount of the borrower's salary to the lender.

The flow of credit from a lender based in one country to a borrower resident in another country is an altogether different proposition. Most loans – probably two-thirds of the loans to the developing countries – are either to governments, or to government-owned firms, or to the firms that have government guarantees.

About $250 billion of the $800 billion owed by the various borrowers in the developing countries in 1982 was to governments in the industrial countries and to multinational institutions like the IMF and the World Bank. (The Fund and the Bank are on a treadmill – if they stop providing new loans to some of the borrowers, these borrowers have a modest incentive to pay the interest on their outstanding loans.) The remaining $550 billion was owed to commercial banks and other private lenders, including exporters in the industrial countries. Some of the loans were politically inspired: the governments in the lending country wanted something from the borrower, like an air base or support in a UN vote, and were prepared to ease the usual credit standards. Credit checks on such loans are limited, for the rules and practices of international diplomacy rule out an analysis which might suggest that Upper Volta is not as good a credit risk as Finland. (Finland, after all, was the only country that repaid its first World War loans.) When Finland borrows from an international institution at an interest rate of 6.5 percent, so does Upper Volta. The income of kings cannot be readily garnisheed; kings no longer mortgage their castles – and even if they did, the US Marines are no longer used for debt collection from foreign governments, as they sometimes were before first World War.

The most important distinction between domestic and international loans is that governments may abrogate contracts with foreigners, which is what sovereignty is all about. A government cannot be sued, except with its permission. Failure to repay, a legal problem within a country, becomes a political problem internationally. Within a country, the law specifies the options open to the lender if the borrower fails to repay according to the terms of the contract. And if the borrower is overwhelmed with debt, there are established bankruptcy procedures – indeed, these procedures were developed so there would be a systematic approach to reducing the excess debt of the borrowers, and enable them to get on with their lives without stays in debtor's prisons. But no such rules have been available internationally; the procedures have been largely ad hoc.

Moreover, governments in borrowing and lending countries are usually involved in a web of other relationships – trade issues, airline landing rights, military alliances – and government lenders are reluctant to demand repayment on overdue loans because the whole fabric of the two countries' relationships would be endangered, without significantly increasing the likelihood of repayment. Thus, the US government was reluctant to be hard-nosed about Mexico or Poland's failure to repay the US banks: Mexico 'protects' the US southern flank. The US government needs the cooperation of the Mexican government in dealing with the drug problem and with illegal immigration. US firms view Mexico as a low-cost manufacturing base. Borrowers and lenders within the domestic economy are rarely involved in such a complex set of relationships with each other.

50 years ago, international credits were primarily commercial; since then, they have become increasingly governmental, with political overtones. Yet the terms of commercial credits are retained. Commercial loans are supposed to be repaid, the lenders and, to a lesser extent, the borrowers, kid themselves that much of the post-Second World War government-to-government credit is commercial.

International lending – the background

Investors have long been attracted to foreign securities, primarily because the yields have been higher than on domestic securities. On the principle that 'there's no such thing as a free lunch,' the higher yields were generally associated with greater risks. During the nineteenth century, British investors were severely burned on their loans to US borrowers – first when the canal companies failed in the 1840s, then when state and local governments defaulted in the 1870s, and subsequently when some US railroads went belly-up. French investors incurred substantial losses after First World War on their extensive loans to the Russian tsars and the Austro-Hungarian kings; the successor governments rejected any responsibility for the debts of the predecessors.

By 1920 the risks of international lending were increasingly obvious; in an era of nationalism the political risks were compounding the commercial risks. The European investors' demand for foreign securities declined, partly because of defaults on prewar loans and partly because Great Britain retained exchange controls on the purchase of foreign securities by its residents. In contrast the American demand for foreign securities surged, continuing a development that began during the early years of first World War. American investors paid modest recognition to European experience with foreign loans; during the 1920s the US public acquired billions of dollars of foreign securities. Some were issued by reputable borrowers. Many were issued by German cities and minor rather than major governments. Most of the foreign securities purchased by US residents in the 1920s became worthless during the Great Depression. With the principal exception of purchases of Canadian securities, the international bond market remained dormant for 30 years.

Export credit arrangements

One principal change since the Second World War is that the public institutions – both national and international – have taken the initiative in lending to the developing countries. During the Great Depression, most national governments established export credit or credit guarantee agencies to stimulate exports and promote domestic employment. Today, government loans and loan guarantees are often tied to the purchase of domestic products by foreigners; the US Export-Import Bank (ExImBank) was established in the 1930s to provide cheap credit on sales of US goods to foreign buyers. If buyers are short of cash or if they have domestic money but lack foreign exchange, the availability of export credits may be the crucial factor in the choice among US suppliers, European suppliers, and Japanese suppliers. Indeed, the advantage of easy credit terms may often compensate for the disadvantage of a higher sales price. Suppliers – the export firms within each country and their employees – are subsidized by these credits, since the larger the line of credit, the larger their sales, and the higher the profits and wages in the selling firms.

The process is competitive; consequently, US firms lean on the government in Washington to ease credit terms on export sales, so they will not be a disadvantage relative to their competitors headquartered in Germany, Japan, and other industrial countries. This firms in countries with relatively high prices request their governments provide attractive credit terms to offset their price disadvantage in foreign markets. Their competitors in low-cost countries then lean on their own governments to match these easier credit terms. And so it goes.

One consequence of these export credit arrangements is that foreign customers can frequently obtain loans at a modestly lower interest rate than domestic customers can. The US Export-Import Bank has financed the sales of Boeing 747 jets to various airlines in Western Europe and Asia at an interest rate about 0.5 percent above the interest rates on medium-term US Treasury securities. The interest rates paid by US commercial airlines, when they borrowed to finance the purchase of comparable aircraft, were at least 1 or 1.5 percentage points higher. Some US airlines have purchased the European Airbus because of the attractive credit terms.

Financing economic development

The big change in international lending in the last 50 years has been the establishment of government agencies to facilitate the financing of economic development. The International Bank for Reconstruction and Development (IBRD) or World Bank, set up in the mid-1940s to finance postwar reconstruction in Europe, was the first such agency. After the defaults of the 1930s and the exhaustion of the war, European countries were poor credit risks and could borrow only if some other country cosigned the note. The cosigner was – you guessed correctly – the United States.

The World Bank is an international financial intermediary: it borrows money by issuing its own securities to private parties and to national governments, and then lends these funds to its members. The major reason why the World Bank's securities proved so attractive to private investors was that the US Treasury was the cosigner; as the credit standing in international markets of Germany, Japan, and other countries improved, so did the number of effective cosigners for the World Bank's bonds. If the borrowers failed to repay the World Bank and the Bank proved unable to repay its debts as they matured, then the owners of World Bank bonds had ultimate recourse to the US government and the governments of other member countries of the Bank.

In the years immediately after Second World War, the World Bank made relatively few reconstruction loans, largely because the Marshall Plan placed the financial needs of the European countries on a grant basis. In the 1950s the Bank turned increasingly to development financing as part of a worldwide effort to stimulate economic growth in non-industrial, low-income countries. The development needs of these countries were legitimate; besides, it was only natural – for a bureaucracy – to search for another client when the first client graduated.

Regional multinational lending institutions, such as the Inter-American Development Bank (IADB, headquartered in Washington, D.C.), the Asian Development Bank (ADB, headquartered in Manila), and the African Development Bank (headquartered in Abidjan) were modeled on the World Bank. These institutions are also international financial intermediaries: they sell bonds in the world's capital markets, again on the basis of the guarantees of the United States and a few other industrial countries, and lend the funds to their members. Their success reflects that the credit reputation of each institution is higher than that of the individual borrowers; most borrowers from these institutions would find it virtually impossible to sell their securities directly to private borrowers.

During the early 1950s, much of the financial assistance from the United States to the developing countries was on a grant basis, a carry-over from the Marshall Plan. But in the later 1950s there was increasing pressure within the United States to place foreign aid on a business-like basis; the synonym for business-like was 'loans'. The idea was that the borrowers would then use the funds for productive projects – investments in railroads, ports, and electric power plants that would produce rates of return higher than the interest rates on the loans issued to finance the projects. If development assistance was extended on a grant basis, so the argument ran, then the recipients would not have a strong incentive to use the funds efficiently; they might use the money to finance imports of Coca-Cola or consumer goods. A loan, on the other hand, would force the recipients to pay much more attention to efficiency and costs, since they would be obliged to repay the funds – with interest.

A significant number of countries have successfully made the transition from borrowing from international public-sector institutions to borrowing from private lenders, initially from the major international banks on short-term loans and, subsequently, by the sale of long-term bonds. Taiwan and Singapore have become international creditor countries. Argentina, Brazil, and Chile have been able to sell modest amounts of bonds in New York and London. Similarly Korea – the world's eleventh largest economy before the Asian financial crisis – has been admitted to one rich man's club, the OECD, and has been able to sell bonds in the New York. In time, other countries will be able to borrow from private sources, as their reputations for adhering to their commitments in periods of economic adversity become more established.

The source of developing country debt crises

It is no accident that the developing country debt crisis had its origin in the inflationary 1970s. These countries produce primary products – oil, copper, wheat, coffee, sugar – and so when the prices of these products began to increase in the 1970s, the rates of growth of national income in these countries also began to increase. The projection was that the price of oil and the prices of many other primary products would continue to increase, and hence GDP growth in these countries would remain high.

Surge in bank loans

One story is that the borrowers in the developing countries liked to obtain funds from foreign banks because the terms were generally more favorable than from their domestic banks. The 1960s had been a decade of great expectations about economic development; borrowers incurred substantial external debts because they believed that they would soon be on a self-sustaining growth path. In a few cases, national leaders with imperial ambitions – Sukarno of Indonesia, Nkrumah of Ghana, and Nasser of Egypt – mortgaged the future export earnings of their countries to finance these ambitions.

The popular interpretation of the surge in bank loans to the developing countries in the 1970s was that the banks had experienced a surge in deposits from the various individuals and firms in the OPEC countries, and felt the need to lend these funds. In fact, bank loans to the MBA countries increased much more rapidly than petrodollar deposits. The interest rates on the loans were attractive, especially since the administrative costs of making a large loan to the developing country borrower was only modestly larger than the cost of making a small loan to a domestic borrower. Some banks saw loans to the borrowers in various developing countries as a way to diversify their loans and hence to reduce the risk of their loan portfolios, because of the belief that the defaults of these borrowers would not be significantly correlated with each other or with defaults on domestic loans. Because these loans generally were denominated in the US dollar, the banks believed that they were not acquiring a foreign exchange exposure. And many banks were eager to grow rapidly – and most of the developing countries were eager to borrow.

Moreover while nominal interest rate on US dollar securities were increasing in response to both the increase in loan demand and the increase in the US inflation rate, the increase in nominal interest rates lagged the increase in the inflation rate, with the consequence that the real interest rate (effectively the nominal interest rate *less* the inflation rate) was declining. Indeed, in 1979 and 1980, the inflation rate was higher than the nominal interest rate, so that real interest rates were negative. The lower the real interest rate, the larger the debt-servicing ability of each borrower. (When real interest rates are negative, the optimal amount to borrow is – are you ready – infinite. The story is that the real value of the funds used to repay the loan is less than the real value of the funds initially borrowed.)

The combination of the increase in the rates of growth of income in the developing countries and declines in the real interest rates of their foreign loans meant that the debt-servicing ability of the borrowers was increasing – as long as the anticipated rate of growth of national income and the real interest rate remained unchanged.

Even though their external debts were increasing at a rapid rate, the credit reputations of the developing countries also were improving; more and more of these borrowers always made the interest payments and the scheduled loan reduction payments on a timely basis.

As long as the volume of new loans was increasing at a rate of about 20 percent a year, the borrowers were in a marvelous position to pay interest on a timely basis, since all of the cash necessary to pay the interest on outstanding loans was available from new loans. Indeed, funds available from new loans were more than twice as large as the amount necessary for debt-service payments on the outstanding loans.

From the borrowers' point of view, the situation seemed like heaven – or as close to heaven as any borrower is likely to get. Increases in commodity prices meant high rates of growth of national income. The decline in the real interest rate meant that the real cost of servicing foreign loans – even the much larger volume of loans – was declining. All the cash necessary to pay the interest on the outstanding loans was obtained from new loans.

From the lenders' point of view, the situation also seemed attractive. Because of the decline in the real interest rate, the debt-servicing ability of individual countries was increasing more rapidly than their foreign loans.

The end of inflation

Obviously, loan losses of $200–$300 billion meant that something went very wrong: big money by any test. And the borrowing countries

– the Mexicos, Brazils, Argentinas, and Nigerias – experienced very large declines in their national income as they were forced to adjust to the lenders' demands that they reduce their indebtedness. Both lenders and borrowers failed to realize that all inflations end – some with a whimper, most with a big bang. The 1970s inflation ended with a very big bang; because of the sharp move to a much more contractive US monetary policy, interest rates on US dollar securities soared. The prime interest rate in the United States moved North of 20 percent, real interest rates moved from negative territory to nearly 10 percent – an amazing increase.

The high real interest rates triggered a severe world recession, and the demand for commodities declined. Commodity prices declined sharply and real income growth in the countries that produced these commodities also declined. Because of both the surge in real interest rates and the decline in the anticipated growth of national income, the debt-servicing capacity of the developing country borrowers fell sharply. All of a sudden, the external loans of the developing countries seemed much larger than their debt-servicing capacity. So the lenders stopped making any new loans – which meant that the borrowers lost access to the source of cash that had enabled them to pay the interest on a timely basis.

The losses incurred by the lenders resulted from three big – and very expensive – mistakes. One was the failure to recognize that commodity prices decline as often as they increase, and that the real price of most commodities has not increased in the last 100 years. The second was the failure to recognize that real interest rates *never* remain negative for long – and that in the long run real interest rates have generally moved within a relatively narrow range. The third was the failure to consider where the borrowers would get the cash to pay the interest on the outstanding loans once the cash could not be obtained from new loans.

Once the borrowers in the developing countries seemed unable or unwilling to repay on schedule, fears about the collapse of the banking system escalated. The scenarios usually began with a standstill in the debt service payments of a few borrowers. Argentina wouldn't repay because of ill-will resulting from its misadventure in the Falklands; Mexico couldn't repay because the oil price went down when it was supposed to go up.

The liquidity of the US banks and the foreign banks that had made substantial loans to developing country borrowers then declined – the developing country loans of the US money center banks were twice their capital.

The economics of debt service

The economics of debt service is straightforward (Box 11.2). Once borrowers have sold loans to foreign lenders they frequently sell new loans to get the cash to make interest and loan reduction payments on outstanding loans.

The simple proposition is that the harder the loan terms are, the larger the size of the new loan required each year so that the country can finance the same excess of imports over exports. The higher the interest rates and the shorter the repayment periods, the more rapidly total foreign indebtedness increases. The more rapidly indebtedness increases, the more vulnerable the borrowers in the developing countries become to a credit crunch. The increase in the total indebtedness of the developing countries from 1972 to 1982 amounted to nearly $700 billion. The continuous compounding of the interest on the $120

Box 11.2   Debt Service

Assume that a country needs an excess of imports over exports of $100 million per year for 10 years if it is to achieve its targeted rate of growth of domestic income; the excess of imports over exports would be used to build dams, factories, and schools. The import surplus can be financed in a variety of ways, including grants from various industrial countries, 'soft' loans at long maturities and low interest rates, and 'hard' loans at short maturities and high interest rates. In this example, an annual grant of $100 million per year would enable the country to finance its import surplus. If the country borrows $100 million in year 1 to finance the desired import surplus, then it will be obliged to make interest- and loan- reduction payments in each subsequent year until the loan is repaid. These debt-service payments are a 'charge' against its export earnings. So if the country wishes an import surplus of $100 million in year 2, then it must borrow somewhat more than $100 million in year 2; the year 2 loan must be greater than $100 million by the amount of the interest- and loan-reduction payments on the year 1 loans. Similarly, in year 3 the loan must be greater than $100 million by the amount of the interest- and loan-reduction payments on the loans arranged in years 1 and 2. And so it goes.

billion outstanding at the end of 1972 through the rest of the decade resulted in a cumulative interest bill of about $250 billion: the total interest bill was larger, because interest had to be paid on the loans incurred to finance the excess of imports over exports.

The combination of a larger volume of external debt and harder loan terms meant that a crunch in debt service was inevitable; the major uncertainties involve which country would be the first to be unable or unwilling to repay on schedule. Argentina provided the answer in 1955 – and so its external debts were renegotiated or rescheduled. Rescheduling initially involved the stretching of maturities. Over the next 12 years, eight countries found themselves in a similar predicament of being unable or unwilling to make the interest- and loan-reduction payments on schedule. This meant, of course, that they were unwilling to cut imports or to take measures to increase exports to obtain the foreign exchange to make the debt-service payments on schedule. Rather than incur the domestic political costs of these Draconian measures, they threw the ball to the lenders.

The lenders had relative few options – they wanted to keep the 'borrower in the game' so as to minimize their losses. Moreover they wanted to be able to claim that the loans were performing, even though that meant that they might have to extend $10 million of new money to receive $20 million of interest on the outstanding loans (which meant that they were receiving $10 million of new cash).

The optimal bankrupt

There's a tradition in the markets that bankrupt firms change their names after they have been restructured; there's no point in carrying the negative baggage of a tarnished image. By the beginning of the 1990s, the developing countries had been re-baptized as the emerging market countries.

Emerging market growth

The international investing industry continually is on the hustle for new products and emerging market equities became one of the hot areas in the 1990s. The premise was powerful – the potential economic growth in these countries was much higher than the growth rates in the United States, Japan, Germany, Great Britain, and France, in part because their rates of population growth were significantly higher. The next step in the logic was that there would be lots of rapid-growth firms in the rapid-growth countries. So corporate profits would grow rapidly, and stock prices would soar. Moreover this time the capital flow to these countries would be in the form of stocks, so the countries wouldn't have to worry about paying interest.

As a country's debt-service payments increase relative to its export earnings, a larger and larger share of these earnings are needed to pay interest on the debt. A country's debt-service payments cannot increase forever in relation to export earnings; if they did, eventually all export earnings would be required to service the debt. At some point, the volume of the borrower's external debt reaches a ceiling relative to its export earnings. When this point is reached, the cash from new loans is more or less the same as the cash needed for debt-service payments on the outstanding loans. In this case, these new loans do not finance additional commodity imports or real resources to the country; at this stage, the borrowers have no incentive to pay the interest on the outstanding loans – there is no new money out there that can be used to finance more imports and no prospect of any new money.

The principal reason for any borrower to pay interest on outstanding loans is to maintain its credit reputation – so as to remain an attractive candidate for new loans that will enable it to finance larger investment and consumption expenditures. When the funds available under new loans decline below than the debt-service payments on the existing loans, the incentive not to pay the interest is high. If the borrower reduces the debt-service payments, a larger share of export earnings is available to buy imports. And the borrower may be able to sell more new loans to eager exporters in the industrial countries.

Some of the borrowing countries are practicing the art of optimal bankruptcy. The optimal bankrupt lives well by borrowing often. First the country borrows as much as it can from low-cost lenders, those that charge low interest rates; when that source of funds is exhausted, the country borrows as much as possible from higher-cost lenders. The borrower uses some of the funds from new loans to pay the interest and loan reduction payments on outstanding loans. The only reason the country pays interest on the outstanding loans is to protect its credit reputation – its ability to borrow more. So the borrower will continue to make payments on outstanding loans to ensure an inflow of funds from new loans. If the country's export earnings decline sharply or if the amount of new loans seems too small, the borrower will threaten not to repay.

Officials in some countries will talk about a 'debtors' cartel' – by not paying interest, they could impose large losses on the lenders, perhaps even threatening that the lenders might become bankrupt. At that point, the lenders will usually offer a debt renegotiation to save themselves the embarrassment of being caught with worthless loans.

Of course, the optimal bankrupt knows the creditors are reluctant to throw good money after bad. But the borrowers also know they can injure the lenders by not repaying – or even by threatening not to repay. The larger the possible damage, the larger the amount of new credits the borrower can probably secure. But the larger the volume of new credits the lenders extend today, the more severe will be the borrower's debt-service problems in the future.

Mexico, Brazil, and Argentina are not the only countries that borrow to get the funds to repay maturing loans by issuing new loans; so do the US government and many foreign ones. Even though the developing countries are on a treadmill, it does not follow that they have borrowed too much. Whether an individual country has borrowed too much depends on whether the average interest rate it pays on external loans is higher than the productivity of the investments financed with these loans. Some developing countries have not met this test; the productivity of new investments has been below the interest rate on the loans. Three of the six countries that account for a large part of the external indebtedness of the group – Brazil, Korea, and Mexico – have achieved impressive records in terms of the growth of their economies and of their exports; three others – Argentina, Peru, and the Philippines – have less impressive records.

Problems in debt repayment

As the external debts of the developing countries mount, the obvious question is whether the debts will be repaid. A few countries have succeeded in repaying their international debts – France after the war with Germany in 1870 and Finland after the First World War. And the reconstruction loans of various European countries after the Second World War were repaid. But these repayments were from relatively wealthy countries. Many of the developing countries today have achieved impressive growth records and will be in progressively stronger positions to repay – or more appropriately, to pay a larger amount of the interest on a current basis so the lenders can consider the loans as performing. Some, however, are now so poor compared to the developed countries that refinancing – and eventually some form of cancellation or forgiveness – is inevitable. The banks are going to have to figure out how to secure an effective downward adjustment in the debt burden – or to get the public-sector lenders to provide funds so the borrowers can repay the private banks. Otherwise the borrowers may believe that the real burden of servicing the debt is too costly, and so the borrowers may effectively ignore their obligations, forcing the lenders to capitalize the interest payments, at least for a while.

Increasingly, the borrowers are likely to conclude that they have little to show in the form of new investments as the counterpart for the increase in their external debt. And as they will question the legitimacy of their debts, it will be less likely the lenders will collect 100 cents on the dollar.

Once the borrowers stopped paying the interest on a timely basis, the lenders had a difficult decision: should they 'throw good money after bad', which would mean the loans still could be considered as performing, or should they instead refuse to accommodate to the borrower's predicament? The easy answer was to 'lend' the borrowers just enough money so they could pay the interest. In effect the lenders would write a check to the borrowers, which the borrowers would then endorse, and sign over to the lenders; the borrowers would receive no new cash. The lenders would report the interest received as income, and that the loans were performing.

Some lenders, especially many small lenders, decided that there were more attractive alternatives than participating in this charade. They asked: 'what interest rate would we have to receive before we would make a new loan to Mexico or Brazil or the Philippines or X?' In the context of the crises, some concluded that the minimum interest rate might be 18 or 20 percent – or more – terms comparable to the interest rate on a risky junk bond. So they sold the loans. These loans began to trade at a substantial discount relative to their face value – in many cases, the market value of the loans went to 30 or 40 percent of their face values. As long as market values were so far below book values, lenders had no incentive to provide new finance.

Part of the risk of lending to the developing countries originates with mismanagement; being poor and underdeveloped means they are undersupplied with effective managers and sometimes oversupplied with political demagogues. A larger risk comes from a world recession and declines in the developing countries' prices and volumes of exports. The combination of higher real interest rates and lower export earnings sharply reduces the likelihood of repayment, and greatly increases the likelihood of more debt reschedulings and debt burden adjustments.

Workouts, reschedulings, and bankruptcy

Within the United States and most other industrial countries, there are established procedures for dealing with borrowers that fail to adhere to the terms of the contract. In some countries the creditors take title to the assets of the borrowers in default, the assets are sold, and the cash proceeds distributed among the creditors. In other countries, including the United States, the courts decide whether the borrowers might be able to pay some of the scheduled interest after covering their operating costs; if so, then the capital structure of the firm may be reorganized, and some of the debt may be converted into stock and the interest rates on other debts may be reduced. The rationale for the restructuring is to position the borrowers so that if they are 'able to turn the situation around' by their own heroic efforts, they will receive some of the returns from this achievement.

The external debts of many of the developing countries were restructured in the late 1980s and the early 1990s along the lines of a domestic bankruptcy. The principal amount of the debt was reduced, and the remaining principal was 'guaranteed' by investments in US Treasury securities that would mature when the principal was to be repaid. The interest payments were in the borrower's currency.

The 'lost decade' of economic growth

For many developing countries, the 1980s was a lost decade in terms of economic growth, in that *per capita* income at the end of the decade was lower than *per capita* incomes in 1980. In part, the decline in *per capita* income reflected the increase in population; in many developing countries national income has to grow at 2½ percent a year for *per capita* incomes to remain constant. In part, the decline reflected that commodity prices in 1990 were significantly below commodity prices in 1980: the oil price, for example, was less than half that in 1980. The third factor that explains the decline was that these countries were no longer able to borrow abroad at anywhere near the rate at which they had borrowed in 1970s. As a result of their reduced ability to borrow abroad, they were able to finance a smaller excess of imports over exports, which meant that the supply of goods available in these countries was smaller. Moreover, the reduction in imports relative to exports almost always resulted from a sharp depreciation of the currencies of these countries: the decline in export prices reduced real income.

Growth in domestic debt

The principal borrower in many of these developing countries had been the government. So the decline in the government's ability to borrow from the banks headquartered in New York and London and

Tokyo meant that they had either to increase taxes relative to expenditures or to substitute domestic borrowing for foreign borrowing. Because governments found it politically difficult and time-consuming to raise taxes and reduce expenditures, they had to borrow domestically. Domestic investors in these countries were skeptical about lending to their governments, since the governments had just defaulted on their external debt. So the governments had to promised to pay high real interest rates. Domestic debt of the government began to increase at a rapid rate relative to national income, in part because the interest rates on these loans were significantly above the rate of growth of national income 'Ponzi' finance.

Mexico

The investing community's hero in the early 1990s was President Salinas of Mexico, a Harvard-trained PhD who took heroic initiatives to restructure the Mexican economy – he succeeded in macro stabilization and in reducing the inflation rate from 130 percent in 1990 to less than 10 percent in 1993. Imports were extensively liberalized in the effort to make Mexican firms more competitive, and hundreds of government-owned firms including the airlines, the telephone system, and the banks (but not Pemex, the oil company) were privatized. Foreign capital flowed to Mexico, and for a while it seemed like a self-fulfilling prophecy – the Mexican stock market took off. Mexico became a member of the North American Free Trade Area (NAFTA); tariffs and trade barriers would be reduced on imports and the prospect that import barriers would be eliminated encouraged US firms to invest in Mexico.

There was one minor hitch. Before foreign investors could buy Mexican stocks, they first had to buy Mexican pesos in the foreign exchange market. So the peso tended to become more expensive. Mexican imports increased rapidly, much more rapidly than Mexican exports; by 1993 Mexico had a trade deficit of $25 billion – about 7 percent of its GNP. The economy was growing about 2 – 3 percent a year, so external debt was growing more rapidly than GNP – a non-sustainable relationship. The inflow of foreign capital had positioned Mexico so that it was dependent on $25 billion of new foreign money each year to maintain the foreign exchange value of the peso.

1994 was a tragic year. In January, there was an Indian uprising in Chiapais, the southernmost province. Then in March the leading presidential candidate of the dominant political party was assassinated, and another high-level politician was killed in September. Foreign investors were increasingly reluctant to hold funds in Mexico, and Mexicans concluded that prudence suggested that a larger share of their wealth should be invested abroad. So there was a massive run on the peso, and the currency depreciated sharply; within a few months the peso had lost half its value. The run on the peso had sharp external repercussions in what came to be called the 'Tequila Effect' – capital was moved from Argentina, Brazil, and other countries in Latin America, and the stock prices in these countries also declined sharply.

A $50 billion bailout package was put together to enable Mexico to stabilize the foreign exchange value of the peso. Mexico had to pledge the income from its oil-export revenues as collateral for the loan. Once the peso was stabilized, funds again moved back to Mexico. Mexico repaid the funds advanced from the US government and the other lenders ahead of schedule.

Asia

In 1997, the collapse of the Thai baht triggered a sharp increase in investor concern about the value of their loans and investments in other Asian countries. The risk premium attached to foreign investments in general began to increase. Moreover there was a flight to higher-quality assets and to financial institutions believed safer. Thailand, Indonesia, Malaysia, Singapore, and Hong Kong had experienced real estate booms. Real estate prices were increasing rapidly, much as in Japan in the late 1980s. The rental rate of return on many real estate projects was much below the interest rates on the funds borrowed to finance their construction and property purchase. So the investors had a cash flow problem, in that rental income was much below the interest payments. These investors 'solved' this problem with the cash obtained from new loans; the lenders were comfortable in extending these new loans because the value of the properties pledged as collateral was increasing.

It was too good to last, and it didn't: Ponzi finance once again.

12
Central Bankers Read Election Returns, not Balance Sheets

The grail of monetary reform

For most of the last few years, finance ministers of the world have been pursuing the grail of monetary reform. They have met each other at the annual autumnal meetings of the IMF and at the interim committee meetings every spring, at the monthly meetings of BIS, at the ad hoc meetings of the OECD, at the Group of Ten and the Committee of Twenty, at UNCTAD (United Nations Committee on Trade and Development) in New York and Geneva. The finance ministers of the member countries of the European Union have met in the headquarters of the union in Brussels and on a rotational basis in various national capitals. The presidents and prime ministers of the United States, Germany, Japan, Canada, Britain, France, and Italy have met at Vancouver, Denver, Rambouillet, Puerto Rico, London, Bonn, Tokyo, Ottawa, Versailles, and Williamsburg at annual summit meetings. There have been scores of meetings on a bilateral basis. The prize remains elusive.

Yet without reform, the system survives. Whatever is, is the system. The push for reform is a push for a System with a capital S, a set of rules that would govern the growth of international money and the exchange rate policies – perhaps even the choice of monetary and fiscal policies – of the major industrial countries.

Has floating delivered stability?

The first question is whether the system of floating exchange rates has operated effectively, and delivered on the key promises that the proponents of floating exchange rates made in the 1960s on how the system might operate. As we saw in Chapter 4, their general view was that if currencies were not pegged, then the changes in exchange rates would more or less track the differences in national inflation rates. As a result, there would be only modest (if any) changes in the competitive position of firms producing in different countries as a result of divergent movements from the exchange rate that would have been predicted on the basis of differences in national inflation rates. Moreover the changes in exchange rates would be gradual rather than abrupt. And because of the smoothness of the movements in the exchange rate and the close fit between these movements and the forecasts of these movements based on differences in national inflation rates, changes in exchange rates would be depoliticized.

The surprise over the last 25 years has been that the changes in exchange rates have been larger – indeed, much much larger – than the changes based on differences in the national inflation rates. In the late 1970s the US inflation rate was higher than the inflation rate in Germany by two or three percentage points and yet the US dollar depreciated by more than 10 percent a year. Then in the first half of the 1980s the US dollar appreciated by about 12 percent a year in terms of the German mark, even though the inflation rate in the United States continued to remain higher than the inflation rate in Germany. Another example – from 1995 to 1998 the inflation rate in Japan was several percentage points below the US inflation rate and yet the Japanese yen depreciated by more than 20 percent a year.

So the data on exchange rate movements are not consistent with the view that the changes in them would more or less reflect the differences in national inflation rates. In the long run, changes in exchange rates are consistent with the differences in national inflation rates; this long-run relationship is one of the established facts of international finance. But in shorter intervals of two or three years, there is no systematic relationship between the change in exchange rates and the difference in national inflation rates. Moreover the average annual deviation between the market exchange rate and the exchange rate that would have been predicted on the basis of the difference in national inflation rates has been greater when currencies have been floating than when currencies were pegged. And it follows from the several previous statements that movements in the exchange rates have been far less smooth or gradual than the proponents of floating exchange rates promised.

The major advantage of the system of floating exchange rates is that the national monetary authorities have not had to contend with overvalued currencies and undervalued currencies – they could blame these deviations on the market rather than recognize that these changes reflected the votes of investors on the success and failure of their own policies.

Reform of the monetary system

The member countries of the European Union have reacted to the movements in exchange rates with the decision to adopt a common currency. In part, this bold initiative reflects a political rationale, and in part it reflects the view that a single currency is the appropriate monetary counterpart to a single integrated market. The guardian of international monetary stability, the International Monetary Fund (IMF), has surprisingly largely ignored the systemic problems of monetary arrangements. But the cynics would say that it's more fun and heroic for the managers of the Fund to deal with monetary crises than to develop arrangements that would reduce their likelihood.

It may be that the criticisms that have been directed at the Fund because of its policies toward Korea, Indonesia, Russia and other countries that have severe problems as a result of the Asian financial crisis will induce the Fund to pay more attention to the types of systemic concerns that were the rationale for its establishment 50 years ago. But it is also possible that the Fund has lost so much credibility because of its failure to foresee the crisis and devise policies that were appropriate for countries affected by a global payments crisis that any initiative to deal with systemic issues will occur in a new institutional arrangement.

Reform of the international monetary arrangements could be accomplished with changes in a few key features. A system of pegged rates could be designed to allow for more flexible responses to payments deficits and payments surpluses, while reducing uncertainty about exchange rates felt by international traders and investors. A mechanism could be found to produce the appropriate amount of international money without forcing the United States to incur payments deficits.

The politics of the problem

Stated in this way monetary reform does not sound difficult. Surely it should be possible to obtain the agreement of central bankers and finance ministers to such modest proposals? But this view ignores the politics of the problem.

One of the most dramatic solutions to problems raised by the existence of more than 100 national monies would be to adopt a common worldwide money. Since there would be no exchange rates, crises associated with pending changes in parities and with sharp depreciation of national currencies would disappear. There would be no further need to coordinate the monetary policies of various central banks, for there would be only one central bank and one world monetary policy. Nor would there be any need to be concerned with the relationship between the rates of growth of national monies and of international monies, since the distinction between the two would disappear. Indeed, the advantages of a worldwide money appear so overwhelming that one wonders why national monies are retained.

Once there was a common worldwide money – gold. The move away from the gold standard suggests why the idea of a worldwide money is utopian. One dominant aspect of the twentieth century has been nationalism – three big wars and large military establishments. National governments have given increased priority to domestic objectives, and neither the growth in the power of the state nor the increase in attention to domestic objectives are accidents. At first, monetary policy was manipulated to help finance First World War expenditures. Then, during the Great Depression, national governments geared monetary policy to expand domestic employment.The Second World War was more horrifying than first World War in terms of conflicts among ethnic groups in both Europe and Asia. The Cold War intensified antagonisms. In the final analysis, the attachment to the gold standard faded because governments wanted to manage the national money to achieve domestic objectives, and particularly those of high levels of employment and price level stability: that's where the votes are.

The library shelves are lined with books full of plans for reforming the monetary arrangements and reducing their susceptibility to various crises. These books are full of articles, paragraphs, sections, and subsections which spell out, in detail, when a country could change the parity for its currency and when it could not, when a country would have the right to borrow the currencies of other countries from them or from international institutions, and when a country would be obliged to lend to them. In reality, all of these articles, paragraphs, sections, and subsections are proxies for issues that are rarely discussed formally. For what each national government really wants to know is how the proposed arrangements will affect its ability to achieve its own national objectives – full employment, a stable price level, rapid growth, and control over its own destiny. The leaders in each government want to know how any plan will affect their ability to keep their constituents sufficiently happy to win the next election or forestall the next coup. When adjustments must be made, national governments want to be sure that most of the burden and costs fall on other countries. If some event occurs that adversely affects their constituents, they want to be able to show that the event, like the weather, was imported and beyond governmental control.

Many countries are concerned that an international monetary agreement might limit their freedom to set domestic policies, thus making it more difficult to satisfy their domestic constituencies. Even though Great Britain is a member of the European Union (although not a charter member of the European Economic Community), the British decided not to join the Euro with Germany, France, Italy, and eight smaller members on day 1, because they were worried about employment in Birmingham and Coventry once the bureaucrats in Frankfurt set monetary policy. True, the British would have a voice in selecting these bureaucrats but they prefer – at least initially – that the Bank of England retain its independence rather than become a branch office of a European central bank, much as the Federal Reserve Bank of Atlanta is a branch of the Federal Reserve System in Washington. Every government would readily sign an agreement for international monetary reform if it were allowed to write the treaty, select the managers for the institution, and formulate its policies. Each would then design the arrangements so as to minimize any external constraint on its choice of domestic policies. In this case, membership would impose no cost on the government generating the proposal. The inevitable costs of adjustment would fall on other countries. Naturally, the proposals of various nations would be inconsistent. What is good for France is not necessarily good for Germany – as the Germans have learned, at some considerable cost over the years to their own taxpayers, at meetings of the European Union in Brussels.

Another fact of political life that explains why efforts to establish new rules have not proved very successful is that the interests of residents of different countries frequently conflict. Some produce and export oil, many import oil. Some are interested in price-level stability, others in full employment. Some believe major economic decisions should be resolved by the decentralized interplay of market forces, others believe these decisions should be made in accord with a central plan. Whenever payments imbalances occur, there is sporadic conflict over whether the deficit countries or the surplus countries should take the initiative in making the necessary adjustments to reduce the imbalances. When exchange rates change sharply, the debate is over whether the countries with the appreciating currencies or those with the depreciating currencies should intervene to dampen the movements in the exchange rates. Political leaders talk about the virtues of international cooperation, but domestic factors frequently take priority, especially when the next election may be only months away. Monetary reform has a limited constituency.

The movement toward monetary reform might be advanced if the positions of each of the major countries on the central issues could be predicted: if their proposed arrangements for producing international money and for adjusting to payments imbalances were known in advance. Someplace, somewhere, there may be some systematic knowledge about this question. But in the absence of such knowledge, anecdotal evidence about differing national attitudes toward inflation, bureaucracy, economic openness, and the market must suffice.

Inflation is no accident

Consider how the views of Britain and Germany might differ toward reform of the system. Since the late 1940s the British pound price of the US dollar has more than doubled, while the German mark price of the US dollar has halved. The changes in the foreign exchange values of the British pound and the German mark reflect their price-level performance: prices have risen rapidly in Britain and slowly in Germany. This difference is no accident – in fact, the financial policies pursued by each country during the 1960s and 1970s can be traced to its experiences in the early 1920s. In the interwar period, Great Britain's unemployment rate reached nearly 20 percent. After the Second World War, British economic policy sought to maintain full employment, regardless of the impact on the domestic price level. Germany, on the other hand, has been almost paranoid about increases in its price level, as a result of German experiences with the hyperinflations of 1922–3 (see Box 10.1) and of 1944–8; during both episodes the German mark and most of the financial securities denominated in the mark became worthless. These national experiences foster attitudes that directly affect national monetary policies and indirectly affect positions on monetary reform.

Countries whose prices have increased more rapidly than the average, such as Britain and Denmark, tend to have payments deficits and depreciating currencies; they also have more ambitious approaches toward international monetary rules than do countries with greater price stability, such as Germany and Switzerland, which tend to have payments surpluses and appreciating currencies. The deficit countries want foreign loans and credits available on an automatic basis, without strings and lectures about good financial behavior; they want to avoid the need to devalue, and they hope their currencies will not depreciate. If changes in currency parities are necessary, they want the surplus countries to take the initiative. If the deficit countries must take the initiative, then they want to be able to restrict their foreign payments without subjecting themselves to the criticism or surveillance of other countries or of international institutions.

Countries with payments surpluses, on the other hand, do not want to commit themselves to extending large credits to deficit counties; they fear that if they do, their payments surpluses will become even larger and they will import inflation. Nor do they want to be put in the position of having to revalue to avoid having to inflate.

Substantial payments imbalances or changes in exchange rates result from differences among countries in the rates at which their price levels increase and, indirectly, at which their national money supplies grow. Differences among countries in rates of monetary growth are likely to reflect institutional differences in their tax systems or in their union-management relations.

Demand-pull inflation

The common explanation of rising prices – too much money chasing too few goods – describes a situation known as demand-pull *inflation*. Annual price level increases of 50–100 percent, as in some Latin American countries, are neither mistakes nor accidents: they result from rapid rates of money supply growth. Few governments are perpetually ignorant of the financial policies needed to produce price stability. When price levels continue to increase, it is because anti-inflationary policies are deemed more expensive than those that permit a continuation of the inflation; the belief is that the anti-inflation policies will lead to reductions of both demand and production and to unemployment – and less political support among those adversely affected.

Demand-pull inflation occurs because governments want the profits from the production of money, either to finance their own expenditures or to divert them to its supporters. Because the governments are unwilling to raise their tax rates, expenditures within the public sector are financed with newly produced money. The Vietnam inflation in the United States and the US inflation in Vietnam both reflect increased government spending based on monetary expansion. The Johnson Administration believed that it was less costly politically to finance the full costs of an unpopular war through debasement of the money than by raising tax rates.

Cost-push inflation

An alternative explanation for rising prices, especially in countries with well-organized, independent, and militant labor unions, is *cost-push inflation*. The scenario begins with a strike or the threat of a strike. To obtain labor peace, firms grant large wage increases. Since their labor costs rise, they raise their prices to avoid sharp declines in their profits or, more likely, to avoid substantial losses. The national authorities may decide that the solution to the cost-push problem is to wait until the higher prices reduce the demand for the firms' products and the consequent demand for labor. At that point, the higher unemployment rate might be sufficient to dampen further upward pressure on wages, and the power of the unions might be broken. But the unemployed vote, and elections may occur long before the union structure is weakened. So the authorities may adopt an expansive monetary policy to reduce unemployment; the increase in the money supply leads to an increase in demand for goods and for labor, sustaining the higher prices and the higher wages. When the unemployment rate falls, unions will again be in a good position to strike for another wage increase.

In Britain, which has a large number of decentralized unions, local strikes have been frequent. For a long time British employers were prepared to buy labor peace, knowing they could pass on the higher wage costs by raising prices. Germany, in contrast, can afford its inflation paranoia because its labor force has been relatively docile and traditionally has not pressed aggressively for large wage increases. Moreover, Germany, unlike Britain was a willing importer of foreign labor. Germany could not have achieved its relative price stability with a British-type industrial structure, and the British price level would have risen much less rapidly if its labor unions had resembled their German counterparts. The economic structures in each country have thus reinforced the importance that each attaches to price stability and to full employment.

If the initiatives toward a common currency in the European Union succeed and Great Britain eventually joins the common currency, then either the British or the Germans – and perhaps both – will be in for a shock. There is no one rate of monetary expansion which will leave both happy, and a compromise rate of money supply growth might even leave both unhappy.

National central banks respond to the employment and price level problems that result from their own fiscal and labor market structures. Thus greater harmonization or unification of the economic structures in various countries may be necessary before a comprehensive international agreement, limiting monetary independence in individual countries, can be negotiated. If a comprehensive reform agreement was negotiated while these economic differences remained substantial, the likelihood is high that the agreement would break down when the national views about the appropriate rate of monetary growth diverged sharply. Institutions must adjust to accommodate national diversity, for national diversity will not adjust to institutions.

Bureaucracy is a growth industry

Change is as inevitable in economic as it is in biological life. Individuals go through a sequence of stages of growth. At some stages they grow rapidly; then they mature, stabilize, deteriorate, and eventually die. Throughout the life cycle, they are subject to shocks of disease and accident, which may alter the growth process.

Responding to shocks

Economies also go through stages, although the distinction among the stages may be less clear. Moreover, the length of particular stages in the various economies may differ. Finally, economies are subject to shocks – both structural (such as crop failures) or accidental (such as wars). Technological change is a shock to individuals and firms within an economy, since it may result in a decline in the demand for their products.

Adjustments are necessary whenever shocks occur. Few individuals welcome shocks, and an increasingly large part of governmental activity has involved reducing shocks, and minimizing their effects. Frequently, governments seek to reallocate the costs of a shock among various groups in the economy: the costs and the risks of the shock are 'socialized'. Disaster relief is a tax on the general population to subsidize those who have incurred large losses because of floods, fires, or tornadoes. Unemployment compensation is a tax on the employed to subsidize the unemployed. Social security is a tax on the young to subsidize the aged.

Countries differ sharply in the way they respond to similar shocks. Most countries have a traditional economic style, evident from the different roles played by government in determining price, wage, credit, and investment decisions. In Japan (and in France, to a lesser extent) the bureaucracy plays a major role in setting the target growth rates and the investment levels of particular industries and firms. In other countries these decisions reflect market forces. Americans, for example, favor decentralized decisionmaking: the government should be responsible for monetary and fiscal policy, while households should make the consumption decisions, and business firms the investment decisions. The mix of goods and services to be produced and who is to produce them are the outcomes of millions of private-sector decisions. A few other countries, such as Germany and Switzerland, share the US perspective. Elsewhere governmental authorities are more fully involved in production and investment decisions.

National attitudes toward government intervention closely reflect the prestige enjoyed by the bureaucracy. In Japan and France the brightest graduates of the most elite universities compete for careers in government service; in these countries bureaucratic intervention in investment and production decisions is readily accepted. A strong central government is deemed desirable, and the bureaucrats are regarded as highly competent. In the United States, in contrast, the bureaucracy has low prestige, and pay ceilings on the salaries of bureaucrats have led to a Gresham's Law – the most capable employees leave the bureaucracy for the higher salaries available in the private sector.

As a general rule, the more powerful the bureaucracy, the smaller the scope for market-oriented decisions. Governmental intervention is justified on various grounds, from reducing uncertainty associated with free markets to minimizing excessive competitive waste or reducing business conflict. The bureaucracy affects decisions in several ways – for example, through its influence over the allocation of credit, through taxes, and through the issuance of building, investment, and import permits.

Managing the international economy

The views of most politicians about how the international economy should be managed are an extension of their views about how their domestic economies should be managed. Countries which place a low value on bureaucracy tend to favor an open international economy, with minimal barriers to the free flow of goods and capital internationally. They feel either that exchange rates should be allowed to float freely so as to balance international payments and receipts, or that the supply of international money should be managed so as to satisfy the needs of individual countries. In either case, individuals and firms should be free to choose between domestic and foreign goods on the basis of price, without arbitrary restrictions at the border.

Countries with strong centralized bureaucratic controls over their domestic economies, on the other hand, tend to favor the use of bureaucratic controls to manage international payments. International monetary reform usually has a lower priority for such countries, since their bureaucrats are in a position to correct payments imbalances by tightening or easing controls on purchases of foreign exchange and on imports. Moves toward a more open economy would tend to weaken bureaucratic control and thus threaten the future of the national bureaucracies.

It is thus no accident that US government officials are likely to be more favorable to floating exchange rates than their French and Japanese counterparts. Nor is it surprising that US government officials are more intensely concerned with the adequacy of international money than officials in other countries, for the officials in other countries are more willing to make arbitrary decisions regulating international payments at their borders.

Inevitably, government officials in countries outside the United States are concerned about the costs to the national economies of two types of error: one is too small a supply of international reserve assets, the other, too large a supply. If the supply is too small, as it was in the early 1960s, other countries may still be able to earn payments surpluses by forcing the United States to incur payments deficits. If the supply is too large, as in the late 1960s, these countries import inflation, perhaps from the United States. Foreign bureaucrats believe the cost to their countries of adjusting to too small a supply of reserves is much less than the cost of adjusting to too large a supply. The US authorities, not surprisingly, come to the opposite conclusion.

The new mercantilists

Openness and mercantilism

One of the conflicts in the international economy is over *economic openness*: are foreign residents treated on a par with domestic residents, or are they discriminated against in access to markets, jobs, investments, and tax relief? In earlier periods, nationalism was the opposite of openness, and 'mercantilism' was the term for this nationalistic behavior. The mercantilists were interested in acquiring and hoarding gold to enhance their country's power. An open international economy would threaten, almost by definition, the advocates of nationalism. Nationalism means that the economic interest of domestic producers are preferred over those of foreign competitors – that domestic residents have preferred access to markets, products, and jobs. Tariffs, quotas, and restrictions on the ownership of domestic assets by foreigners reflect nationalist pressures.

The thrust of the last half of the twentieth century has been toward greater openness – toward the reduction of barriers (NTBs) to the free movement of goods and capital. Tariffs and non-tariff barriers to the movement of goods have been reduced. Discrimination against the entry of foreign banks and financial institutions into the domestic financial markets in different countries has been reduced. Controls on international capital flows have been introduced – although there are pressures to restore such controls because of a belief that they have been a major cause of the Asian financial crisis.

Countries subject to strong nationalist pressures are likely to place substantial barriers in the way of imports of foreign goods and services, as well as on the sale of domestic securities to foreigners. Japan has a strong nationalist bias. The Japanese rush toward modernization in the last third of the nineteenth century reflected the fear that foreign imperialists would begin to dismember Japan into colonies or enclaves: Japan developed its industry to resist a perceived external threat. Japanese attitudes toward trade and investment decisions continue to reflect this strong desire to maintain a cultural identify, so Japan resists foreign investments and is reluctant to liberalize its import policies; domestic residents should not be injured or inconvenienced for the sake of international harmony. Japan responded to the problem of tens of thousands of Vietnamese refugees by permitting less than 100 to settle permanently in Japan; in contrast, more than 100,000 settled in the United States. US automobile workers should lose their jobs so that Japanese automobile workers can produce for the US market.

Nationalization and privatization

One pervasive worldwide tendency of the last 50 years has been an increase in the government's role in production. Often, when private entrepreneurs find a particular industry increasingly unprofitable, foreign competition further reduces the number of domestic producers. Yet the government, while reluctant to subsidize private entrepreneurs, usually wants to maintain domestic production. So the activity is shifted to the public sector. Many of the 'private' firms in Italy are owned by one of three large holding companies: IRI (National Institute for Industrial Reconstruction), ENI (National Hydrocarbon Corporation), and ENEL (National Corporation for Electric Energy), each of which has been largely owned by the government. Sometimes national ownership may be justified on grounds of national security. General de Gaulle insisted that France needed a computer industry for national security, and so part of Machines Bull, the largest French computer firm, was absorbed by the government when it would otherwise have been liquidated. Similarly, the Conservative government in Great Britain nationalized Rolls-Royce because the immediate unemployment in areas near the company's factories would have been excessively high had the company folded.

The marked change in the last 15 or so years has been the worldwide move toward privatization. In part this move has occurred as a result of the increased openness of the world economy; government-owned firms as a rule have not been competitive because they have not had to meet a market test. The result is that countries with a large number of government-owned firms in manufacturing are reluctant to reduce barriers to external competition; such moves might jeopardize the survival of these domestic firms or raise the cost of the subsidies to the Treasury.

Although other countries may seem more nationalistic than the United States, the difference is partly an illusion. The large economic size of the United States means that any direct foreign threat to the United States is small; foreign economies have a smaller impact on the level of US business activity than they might on other countries. While Canada and France may worry about US domination of their economies and their national institutions, size alone protects the United States from foreign domination. Foreign ownership of firms – or shares of firms – located in the United States is small. The relatively liberal US position toward foreign ownership would almost certainly change if foreigners tried to acquire a sizeable proportion of major US firms such as IBM or General Motors. Shifts in US foreign economic policy in the last 10 years to more and higher import barriers – such as quotas on imports of textiles, apparel, steel, beef, and petroleum – suggest that the United States is not immune from nationalist pressures.

Reform requires a consensus?

International monetary reform would be a cinch if countries were homogeneous – if each were made in the same image. But most national borders are not arbitrary; rather, they tend to segment economies with differing industrial and institutional structures and electorates with different values. Conflicts in interests are inevitable and complicate monetary reform. Moreover, the increasing priority given to national interests is a worldwide phenomenon; the pull of nationalism intensifies the growth of bureaucracy and domestic demands for monetary flexibility. In time, perhaps, the strength of these national pulls may diminish. In the meantime, efforts at monetary reform which ignore these pressures are not likely to succeed.

13
Monetary Reform – Where Do The Problems Go When They're Assumed Away?

Resolving conflicts among competing interests

A paradox of the last several decades has been the glaring contrast between the problems of the system – the foreign exchange crises and the threats to the domestic banking systems and the trade disputes – and all the good advice in the editorials of *The New York Times* and *The Economist*, in congressional testimony, in international conferences of economists and bankers, in the policy papers produced by the think-tanks in Washington and London and Tokyo, and even in university lectures. Salvation was readily available. The system's problems would be solved if central banks intervened in the foreign exchange market to support their currencies, or if they refrained from such intervention, if there were more coordination of national monetary policies, or if national currencies were eliminated. Or if …

Each of these proposals had the support of eminent authorities. Nearly every expert left the impression that if only his or her favorite proposal were adopted, the system's problems would soon disappear, or at least become much less pressing. Since few of the proposals – other than that of floating rates – have been adopted, the experts' convictions cannot be readily tested. The wide diversity of the 'solutions' is surprising. Some proposals – raise the gold price or demonetize gold, more extensive central bank intervention in the foreign exchange market or less extensive intervention – are contradictory; some of the authorities were wrong if others were right. Some of these proposals are advanced by those at the top of the ministries of finance or their national central banks. So it's a bit curious that their seminal ideas appear only when they are in the private sector – if these proposals were as attractive as their proponents suggested, why were so few adopted? Why was the adoption of floating exchange rates a necessity rather than a move of conviction? The answer to the general question is that the politicians around the world were not convinced about the merits of any one proposal. But if not, why not? Perhaps the national political leaders were unable to understand the proposals. Perhaps vested interests in the various countries prevented their adoption. Or perhaps the proposals were ahead of their time – whatever that means.

The institutional talisman

One feature common to each of these diverse proposals was the belief that changes in the institutional framework of the international monetary arrangements would somehow resolve the problems associated with large trade imbalances or sudden movements in exchange rates. Old problems, however, unlike old soldiers, do not always fade away. Changes in the institutional framework may help countries reconcile some conflicts between their domestic objectives and their external objectives and between their national economic objectives and those of other countries. But some conflicts are inevitable as long as there are separate countries, each with its own set of voters. The poor want to become richer, and the rich want to protect their wealth against losses. The jobless want work, and the employed want protection. Everyone wants to protect his established market share – which makes it difficult for the newcomers to obtain a market share.

So the key question becomes the optimal way of resolving conflicts among competing interests. Changing the institutional arrangements for the foreign exchange market or for producing international money may make it easier to resolve some conflicts. But such arrangements, by themselves, do not eliminate the conflicts of interests; rather, they alter the framework within which the conflicts appear.

A country, after all, is at most a group of individuals with similar aspirations and values. Some countries – such as Belgium, Canada, Malaysia, Switzerland, and Yugoslavia – contain two or three such groups. Some countries in Africa have 20 or 30 tribes; Nigeria has three dominant ethnic groups – the Yoruba, the Hausa, and the Ebos – and many smaller groups. These differences of opinion across groups within a country can be extensive. In a few cases, the country is smaller than the group; this is especially true of a few English Commonwealth countries. In most cases, the country is larger.

Within each country, there are sharp conflicts of interests; this is what political parties, elections, revolutions, and coups are all about. Differences in views and interests and values must be accommodated. If the existing rules seem inadequate to accommodate the desired changes, some groups may have a tea party and set up a new set of rules. And to the extent that the existing rules are designed to obstruct peaceful changes in the structure of the rules, the higher the likelihood of a tea party. For international conflicts, too, there are numerous parties to be heard from when a new set of rules is devised (Box 13.1).

The major features of the new set of rules for international financial relations will almost inevitably be drawn from proposals that are already on the shelf. Most of these proposals can be placed in one of several categories. One set of proposals would have countries submerge their national interests and act as if they shared identical interests. Proposals for a common international currency, a world central bank, monetary unification, and even for the coordination and the harmonization of national policies fall into this category. In contrast, a second set of proposals suggests that countries should concentrate on maximizing their domestic interests: exchange markets should be organized so that any tendency toward payments imbalances would be adjusted by anonymous market forces. The floating exchange rate system would be retained and legitimatized, although rules might have to be adopted to prevent national authorities from fiddling in the foreign exchange market. Someplace between these two groups is a third, which recognizes the conflict among domestic interests in various countries and seeks to find some optimum path between the desires for national monetary independence and the competing desires for a free and open international economy.

In the 1970s, confidence that the problems of the system could be readily resolved by adopting an institutional talisman diminished. A few observers still felt that if their advice had been accepted in the 1960s, the Bretton Woods system might have been retained, and the pressures toward protectionism triggered by sharp movements in exchange rates might have been avoided. The Bretton Woods system was shelved because the monetary authorities were unable to adjust exchange parities to cope with the inflationary pressures. When the pegged exchange rate arrangement became obsolete, the system lost its only effective set of rules, and so there were significantly fewer constraints on the measures that individual countries might take to improve their own national economic welfare, despite the costs that might be imposed on their trading partners.

Box 13.1   The Flat-earthers

Before Columbus, many people believed the earth was flat; it stood to reason that if it were not, everyone on the underside would fall off. The flat-earthers prospered until Columbus sailed to the Indies in 1492 and Newton defined gravity in the *Principia* in 1687. The conclusions of the flat-earthers in other areas – business, language, and money – may be as incomplete as they were in geography and physics; the common sense, intuitive approach does not always produce the right answer.

In business and economic life, it stands to reason that there would be savings in the costs of doing business if systems of weights and measures used in various countries were the same. It is inane that half the world uses gallons, miles, and inches while the other half uses liters, kilometers, and kilos – and that a US gallon is one quart smaller than a Canadian gallon. It stands to reason that savings would be achieved by the standardization on one system of weights and measures, road signs, electrical voltages, bottle sizes, and liquor proofs.

Less than 100 years ago, each local area in the United States was free to set its own time and to decide when noon occurred. In the 1880s, Congress legislated that the country be divided into four standard time zones. About the same time, international convention segmented the world into 24 time zones. Some areas were obliged to move the hands on their clocks ahead, but no area had to change its time-measuring devices or the units. There are inconveniences and costs in having London six or seven hours ahead of Chicago and in trying to remember whether one loses or gains a day when crossing the international date line when flying from San Francisco to Tokyo.

The flat-earthers favor one world time zone; thus, when it is 12 p.m in Washington, it would be 12 p.m in London and Moscow. But because bedtimes and milking hours would have to be rescheduled in much of the world, the change is not imminent, since countries appear unlikely to agree on who incurs the costs and the inconveniences of rescheduling.

Money is a unit of measure or account. Each of the members of the IMF has its own money; most other non-member countries do also. Multiple monies incur costs of foreign exchange transactions, which is the monetary equivalent of language translations.

Box 13.1   continued

Moreover, the exchange of national monies leads to one problem that is not encountered in language translation, for future values are not known; the price of the yen or the mark a year from now – or even next week – is uncertain, largely because national central banks manage their own monetary policies to achieve domestic employment, growth, and financial objectives.

The flat-earthers favor one world money, just as they favor one world time, one world language, one set of measures; it stands to reason that the costs incurred in foreign exchange transactions would be saved if there were only one money. But money differs from distance, time, and language in that it is managed as an instrument of economic policy. The move to a worldwide money means that the flexibility inherent in national monies would be lost.

Politicizing economic conflict: an international money

A frequent observation is that national monies are redundant, since the price of wine in terms of wheat is pretty much the same in each country, after conversion at the prevailing exchange rate. So the argument goes that since relative prices are similar across countries, no economic function is served by having separate national currencies. In fact, the observation is incorrect – or, more politely, insufficiently exact.

The cost of virtually identical Holiday Inn rooms may vary from $25 to $100, depending on whether the room is in a small town in Alabama or in New York City. The United Nations calculates that with the costs for a particular standard of living set at an average of 100 for all the capital cities of the world, the specific cost may range from a low of 50 in Manila to 200 in Tokyo and Paris. The cost of producing the standard Volkswagen in different countries also differs sharply even though the selling price is the same. The prices of goods and services which are less readily traded – haircuts are the standard example – may differ across countries by substantially more than the prices of tradable goods.

Those who believe that national currencies are redundant also sometimes argue that changes in exchange rates are ineffective, since relative prices do not change. Perhaps. But there seems considerable evidence that changes in exchange rates are effective, for when exchange rates change so does the relation between the prices of traded and non-traded goods.

Most – but not all – changes in exchange rates result from differences in national rates of inflation. It might be argued that inflations change only absolute, not relative prices. But if that were the case, no one would be concerned with inflation, except for the minor inconveniences of having to carry more money around – and this inconvenience could be negated by simply printing more large-denomination notes. In fact, inflations change relative prices, at least for a while – which is why inflations occur. In the early stages of inflation, farmers become better off and city folk less well off; borrowers do well and lenders poorly. In a deflation, and even when the rate of inflation declines, the tables are turned: lenders gain and borrowers lose.

The demand for separate national monies has an analogy in the need for national armies. During most years, most countries are at peace. If a country is at peace, it might seem that it has no need for military forces; indeed, its army might be disbanded. But military forces are needed when peaceful means of settling disputes between nations are not deemed satisfactory by at least one party. So, too, a separate national currency may be needed to attain national price level and employment targets.

New problems

Proposals for a common international money as a substitute for separate national monies are attractive. Exchange crises would disappear. There would no longer be a need to debate whether a country with a payments surplus should lend international money or its own currency to deficit countries, for there would be no measurable payments imbalances and no more bickering over which countries should take the initiative in adjusting to payments imbalances. There would no longer be a concern with whether a currency was overvalued or undervalued: the words would no longer have meaning or relevance.

But a common international money would not eliminate the problems of the existing system; it would simply shift their location. Problems of accommodating divergent national interests would be centralized in the management of the international money-producing institution. This institution would have a set of directors who would be ultimately responsive to the political authorities of the member countries. The institution's directors would have to determine how its managers were to be selected, how rapidly the institution should produce money, and when countries might control payments to foreign areas.

The participating countries would also have to agree on the voting strength of each member country. Would the United States, the Netherlands, and Brazil each have the same number of votes, as in the General Assembly of the United Nations and most other international institutions? If not, what criteria should be used to determine the voting strength of each member country? Would the largest countries have veto power over any decisions of the institution's managers, or would they be obliged to follow their mandate? The United Nations principle of one country, one vote would mean that the United States, a nation of 273 million, could readily be outvoted by Trinidad, Jamaica, and other Caribbean countries whose combined population is less than that of Chicago. The costs of adjustment to payments imbalances might be shifted to the United States. At the other extreme, if votes of each country were in proportion to its population (on the principle of one person, one vote), then China and India together would come close to having a voting majority for the world.

Clearly, some accommodation is necessary between these extremes. But what formula would be acceptable to countries with large and small populations, with high and low *per capita* incomes? Until this issue can be resolved, an agreement is virtually impossible. Some countries would be more willing than others to compromise, not because the agreement fully satisfied their needs but because they would know that if the costs of abiding by the agreement were too high, they could ignore their commitments; they could adopt exchange controls or refuse to lend their currencies to other countries. Some countries are substantially more cynical than others when signing international treaties.

Almost as soon as a new international monetary authority was established, a decision would have to be made about how fast the supply of the common international money should grow. Each country would have its own views: some might favor a growth rate of 5 percent a year, others 10–15 percent. This disagreement would reflect differences in national economic structures and priorities. Some countries grow more rapidly than others, perhaps because they have higher savings and investment rates, or because their labor forces expand more rapidly, or because they adapt better to new technologies. Labor unions are much more militant in some countries than in others; these countries may favor a more rapid growth in money supplies to permit sustained full employment. Moreover, some countries are more tolerant about inflation and would be willing to risk more rapid price increases in the belief that they might thus reduce their unemployment rates.

Thus, countries which formerly permitted their national money supplies to grow at a 15 percent annual rate probably would want the supply of common international currency to grow at a similar rate. Countries that had previously favored a slower growth for their own national money would probably also want the international money to grow at a slower rate. Japan, for example, would want a rapid rate of monetary growth, while Germany would want a slower rate. But Japan and Germany cannot each have its way if there is only one money in the world.

Perhaps the directors from different countries could be shown that the differences among them regarding the appropriate rate of money supply growth are unimportant. If so, the rate of money supply growth could be determined by a more or less random process. Then each country could quickly adjust to the new rate, and the costs and inconvenience of forgoing the preferred rate for the community rate would be small. Perhaps. But it is unlikely.

The debates among directors from different countries about the preferred rates of money supply growth would be vigorous, just as they frequently are within individual countries. Countries with similar interests would form caucuses and vote as a club. The small countries would be concerned that their interests might be steamrollered by the large countries. Large industrial countries, on the other hand, would worry about being outvoted by coalitions of the many small countries.

Some countries might devise numerous ad hoc means to limit their international payments – even in defiance of the rules. A few might threaten to secede from the common currency union rather than accept a monetary policy deemed inappropriate to their needs. As long as there is substantial diversity among nations, a common international money and a unified monetary policy are a contradiction in terms. Those who advocate such a union either blithely ignore the real problem or else harbor secret knowledge about how diversity among nations can be readily reconciled – knowledge that is not generally available.

As long as basic structural differences in national economies remain, and countries retain sovereignty, there is little chance that a common international currency might be adopted – and even less that it would work if it were. Control over the production of national money is a large part of what sovereignty is all about. It is not an accident that member countries of the European Community were able to eliminate tariffs on internal trade, accept a common tariff on imports from outside the EC, harmonize their tax policies, and yet still find it difficult to unify their currencies. That countries would give up the flexibility of a national money – and the associated domestic political advantages – to avoid the costs and the newspaper headlines of exchange crises seems unlikely. Perhaps more importantly, such a move would be questionable on the grounds that as long as national economic structures and values differ, countries as a group may gain if this diversity of interests is recognized and accommodated rather than suppressed.

In time, the differences in the national interests of participating countries may diminish and be eliminated. Eventually, business cycles will be in phase across countries, and rates of productivity growth – even attitudes toward inflation and the inflation – unemployment tradeoff – might be more nearly similar. The usefulness of the nation-state as a political unit will then be much lower. However, the date at which interests will become so similar that the nation state can be shelved as an effective decisionmaking unit does not seem imminent.

National monies have been around for about as long as there have been nations. One implication – the most likely, if not the only one – is that national monies will disappear only as the distinctions among nations lose their economic significance. This process is likely to occur on the basis of regional groupings, as countries with similar character-istics merge their currencies. The European Union is one such group; other potential groups are in Southeast Asia, East Africa, Central America, and the Spanish-speaking countries of South America.

An SDR system

The fact is that a move to a common worldwide currency is an extreme solution and a straw-man, and relatively few experts favor the idea. Yet the political problems associated with less ambitious reform proposals are similar to those encountered in this more extreme solution. The smaller the scope that individual countries have in setting their own monetary policies and their own exchange rates, the larger the energies they will inevitably direct to how the international monetary system is managed. The politicians in each country are understandably reluctant to permit international civil servants to adopt measures whose costs they must bear: the civil servants are not obliged to run for office.

A less ambitious approach involves adoption of one international money and the retention of national monies. The US suspension of gold transactions in August 1971 led to proposals for a new interna-tional monetary system to be built around Special Drawing Rights (SDRs) as the dominant international money; the international roles of the US dollar and of gold would phased out. National monies would be retained, and each national currency would have a parity in terms of the SDR. Each country could devalue its currency in terms of the SDR if it had a large payments deficit, or it could revalue its currency – perhaps even be obliged to do so – if it had a large payments surplus.

The SDR producing institution would become an international central bank. Member countries would jointly decide how many SDRs to produce each year and how many newly produced SDRs to allocate to each country. Each country's view about these decisions would almost certainly reflect its view of how best to advance its own interests. The rate at which the supply of SDRs would grow would not satisfy all of the participating countries, any more than all would be satisfied if there were a common international currency which grew at the rate of 3, 5, or 8 percent a year.

Proposing an SDR system, either by that name or by some other, is easier than getting it accepted, for countries are naturally concerned with the future value of the SDR. Gold was acceptable as an international money because of its underlying commodity value. Central banks held gold in the belief that if gold were demonetized their losses would be minimal, since they could sell gold in the commodity market. Similarly, US dollar assets and British pound assets were acceptable as international money because it seemed – once – that these monies could be used to buy gold from the US Treasury and the Bank of England, or at least to buy American or British goods.

Every central bank recognizes that holdings of SDRs are useful only if they can be converted into a national currency. Central banks in a few countries must worry that some other central banks might prove reluctant to sell their currencies for SDRs. US participation is essential to the success of the SDR system, for holders of SDRs would want assurance that they could convert SDRs into dollars to make payments for the purchase of US goods or securities. The United States has the world's largest market in goods and the most comprehensive set of financial markets. Participation in the SDR arrangement by Argentina and Zambia is insufficient for its success if the United States does not participate. Without US involvement, the SDR arrangement would flounder, whereas it makes little difference if Argentina and Zambia do not participate. The reason is that the supplies of goods available in those two countries are not so large that the various central banks would want to hold the Argentinean peso or the Zambian kwacha as international money.

As it is, many countries would probably prefer US dollars to SDRs as international money, for the dollar has greater 'moneyness.' Foreign central banks would hold SDRs because they could be used to buy dollars. Some countries would fear that the United States might at some future date stop selling dollars in exchange for SDRs; in that case, holdings of SDRs would become much less valuable than the dollar. Few countries would accept SDRs if they were not acceptable at the US Treasury. To minimize this concern, the United States could pledge to remain attached to the SDR standard. But this pledge could be broken. The United States could give a super-pledge; but the super-pledge could be broken, as was the US commitment, and a succession of supercommitments, to maintain the $35 gold parity. Many countries would remain reluctant to hold a substantial part of their reserve assets as SDRs, as long as they doubted the commitment of the US authorities – currently and in the indefinite future – to buy SDRs in exchange for dollars.

A paper money or paper gold proposal can succeed only if countries have confidence in the money – that is, in its future purchasing power in terms of goods. This confidence requirement is not likely to be satisfied simply because the members agree to a treaty. For any member might, when it suits its pressing national needs, walk away. And every other member recognizes this reality.

The nonpolitical market solution

A system of pegged exchange rates is much like a fair-weather friend – as long as the major countries are able to achieve reasonable price stability, the system is workable. If the exchange rates were free to float, movements in the rates would be modest. However, if there are substantial differences among major countries in their price-level targets, or even in the strengths of their commitments to realize these targets, floating rates are inevitable, if only because exchange rate movements are inevitable. Investors shift funds to profit from anticipated appreciations and to avoid losses from anticipated depreciations.

The exchange rate as a policy instrument

Proposals for floating exchange rates recognize the divergent pulls of independent national monetary policies. The central bank in each country could produce the amount of money deemed appropriate for its domestic needs. In Japan the money supply could grow at 20 percent a year, in Belgium at 10 percent. Each country would choose the rate of money supply growth that might enable it to achieve its principal economic objectives – high levels of employment and reasonable price stability. If errors occur (which is likely), no country would have to worry about its balance of payments, since market forces would ensure that the country's payments would always be in balance, even if it did not succeed in achieving relative price stability. Exchange rates would change continuously and smoothly, without the volatile movements associated with parity changes.

Developments in the last decade tested these claims. Contrary to predictions, movements in exchange rates have been volatile. Countries have worried greatly about their trade positions and about whether their currencies were appreciating or depreciating. The central banks in many countries have had to intervene in the exchange markets. Paradoxically, the payments imbalances have been substantially larger under the floating-rate system than ever they were under the pegged-rate system. Some of these imbalances were attributable to the surpluses of the OPEC countries (see chapter 9). But the sum of the surpluses of all countries as a group was in some years more than twice as large as those of oil-exporting countries as a group. Some countries have sought to achieve a payments surplus as a basis for growth in their own money supplies; not every country has wanted to follow an independent monetary policy. Other countries have found that the depreciation of their currency the most convenient way to stimulate exports and increase employment; their central banks have bought dollars in the foreign exchange market to limit appreciation of their currencies so as to keep their goods competitive in world markets. Indeed, for some countries, export-led growth may be the preferred way to stimulate the economy. Some countries have a mercantilist preference for exporting goods and importing international money.

The assumption made by proponents of floating exchange rates – that once the rate was free to move in response to market forces, central banks would no longer be interested in the level of the exchange rate – has been proved invalid since 1973. Once the exchange rate is no longer subject to international rules, many governments are likely to manage or manipulate the rate as a useful instrument of policy and as a supplement to their monetary and fiscal policies.

To the extent that central banks intervene in the exchange market, most buy and sell US dollars. For example, the Bank of Japan might permit a depreciation of the yen to increase its exports to the United States. But Germany and France would not welcome this move, since their competitive position in the US market, the Japanese market, and their own domestic markets would be threatened. So they might respond by permitting their currencies to depreciate in terms of the dollar; the Japanese threat to German and French exports would be neutralized. One result would be the flooding of the US market with Japanese, German, and French goods. US exporters, in turn, would find themselves at an increasing competitive disadvantage in the foreign markets. And so the US authorities would be under domestic pressure to depreciate the dollar.

The original objective behind the IMF rules of fixed exchange rates had been to prevent individual members from adopting such 'beggar-thy-neighbor' policies. During the 1960s, when most countries were relatively successful in achieving full employment, this problem appeared unimportant. But it became significant in the worldwide recession of 1970 and 1971, when countries sought to import jobs. There is considerable evidence for the proposition that whenever countries find it difficult to attain domestic targets by changes in domestic financial policies, they will manipulate their international transactions.

In 1974, many countries allowed their currencies to become under-valued; they did not take the initiative to borrow the amounts neces-sary to finance the increase in their net oil imports. Instead, they financed their oil imports on a pay-as-you-go basis, which meant their currencies depreciated – in effect, they increased their exports to earn the dollars to pay for their more expensive oil imports. The lesson of the last decade is that few, if any, currencies float freely; most float subject to considerable intervention. Central bankers are not about to rely exclusively on market forces to determine the foreign exchange value of their currencies; most want to hedge such forces. The temperament of central bankers – and of their constituents – makes them reluc-tant to accept the market's verdict about what the appropriate exchange rate is, and how rapidly it should change.

In both 1977 and 1978, the US payments deficits were so large ($30–$40 billion) that any prediction of their magnitude four to five years before would have been considered lunacy. The explanation was straightforward. The United States was recovering more rapidly from the world recession that its trading partners, and so the US demand for imports – and the foreign supply of exports – was increasing sharply. The dollar tended to depreciate. Yet, most other industrial countries were reluctant to accept the appreciation of their currencies because of the adverse impacts on prices and employment in their export- and import-competing industries.

In 1981 and 1982 by contrast, the US dollar appreciated sharply, to the levels of the early 1970s. Whereas in the late 1970s the European complaint to Washington was that the dollar was too weak, in the early 1980s the complaint was that the dollar was too strong. From the US point of view, it began to seem that no US policies could satisfy the Europeans – although the continual complaints may have instead reflected European apprehensiveness about their economic and financial dependence on the United States. The experience demonstrates that the floating exchange rate system failed to live up to its advertisements.

Most of the minority of economists who favor pegged rates over floating rates would agree that a floating-rate system is workable and feasible, except perhaps in the relatively few periods when individual countries are subject to intense uncertainty about their political and economic futures. But the choice of exchange rate system is made by central bankers and government officials, not by economists. And judging by their behavior, most officials favor pegged exchange rates, with only a few exceptions; the experience with floating rates has been chastening. It is not an accident that the financial officials who favor floating rates are in the larger countries, while those in the smaller countries favor pegged rates.

Rules might be negotiated to prevent or limit central bank intervention under a floating-rate system. The problem, however, is complex – and complex international rules tend not to be workable. Like the US commitment to a $35 gold parity, adherence to such rules would cease when the national interest was deemed overriding.

Before a great deal of progress can be made in devising a new set of rules, the disturbances, including the changes in monetary policy, which have led to the sharp movements in the exchange rates, must be attenuated. Inflation rates will have to be reduced further, at least to the range of the 2–3 percent a year of the 1960s.

The limited scope for reform

Several themes stand out among the events following the suspension of gold transactions among central banks in the last decades.

- First, central banks around the world want to stay in business; few central bankers are interested in phasing out their institutions in favor of an international central bank.
- Second, most central bankers, with the exception of those in Canada and Germany, abhor the uncertainties and the vagaries of floating exchange rates, except as an interim measure; they believe

floating rates have worked far less smoothly than their academic proponents predicted.

- Third, recent events have reduced confidence in national government commitments which are necessary in any type of international system – an international central bank, an SDR arrangement, even floating rates.
- Fourth, within many countries bureaucratic regulation of international payments is now accepted as a means of balancing international payments and receipts. Bureaucrats tend to distrust the uncertainties of the market – indeed, trusting the markets would lead the bureaucrats to the unemployment office.

These factors limit the scope of reform. The difference between ambitious and modest proposals for reform center on two variables. One is the size of payments imbalances that could occur before exchange rates changed or were changed, or before controls on international payments were altered to restore equilibrium, or at least reduce imbalances. The size of imbalances is limited by the ability of deficit countries to finance them and by the willingness of surplus countries to export goods in exchange for international money. The second variable is how the inevitable changes in exchange rates would occur: would they involve explicit changes in the rate, or would the changes be implicit, as bureaucrats tighten and loosen controls on international payments?

The unfavorable outcome, from the point of view of an integrated or open international economy, is a system with small scope for payments imbalances, with international payments balanced by variations in controls on international payments rather than by changes in the exchange rate, and with countries competing with each other to secure export and payments surpluses. One cost of this outcome would be that possible gains in economic efficiency from further integration of markets would diminish because of investors' uncertainties about how the system would evolve. A less measurable concern is that the 'beggar thy neighbor' trade policies would produce political discord: economic problems are too central to be segmented from political relationships.

Economic expertise cannot solve political problems

Each of the systems discussed – an exclusive international money, floating exchange rates, pegged rates, and exchange controls – involves the tug of the international market against the pull of national constituencies. Most politicians win or lose elections on domestic issues or on broad foreign policy issues, not on whether exchange rates float or the price of gold is raised. The first two sets of proposals involve a change in the way countries establish their policies and exchange rates; the third, in contrast, revamps the arrangements to accommodate the pressing needs of individual countries. The fourth approach is less ambitious, although it might be more successful because it acknowledges the diverse interests and preferences of individual countries.

The international money problem reflects the fact that while communications technologies have unified the world of national monies, national economic structures and national values remain diverse. Changes in institutions may provide a more or a less favorable framework for reconciling these national differences, but they cannot eliminate the conflict posed by divergent national interests. The problem appears again and again in determining the rate of growth of international money, in setting appropriate exchange rates, and in determining the allocation and use of international money. The diversity of interests among countries is real. As long as some national monetary authorities have monopoly power, domestic political forces will compel them to exploit it. Crises result when the established 'rules of the game' limit domestic choices.

The historical record suggests that there will be a move back toward pegged exchange rates once inflation rates in the industrial countries decline and converge. This conclusion is reinforced by the extensive intervention of various central banks when currencies have been free to float.

The move toward pegged rates is likely to more nearly resemble pegging under the gold standard than under the Bretton Woods system. Individual countries will peg their currencies when movements in the exchange rates are small; pegging may be the climax of increasing intervention to limit large swings in the rates. Some countries are likely to peg sooner than others. Moreover, countries are likely to differ in the width of the support limits around their parities or central rates. After currencies are pegged, an international agreement might be negotiated formalizing the exchange market arrangements as they exist, rather than forcing sharp changes from the practices then prevailing.

Similarly, arrangements about the future international monetary role of gold will be negotiated after central banks begin to trade gold with each other at or near the market price. Rules will then be developed to formalize the practices. These practices will result from the give-and-take of trading monies and gold.

Part II

The Costs of 100 National Monies

14
The Money Game and the Level Playing Field

One of the great economic clichés of all time is the demand for a 'level playing field.' Government officials in Paris often call on this cliché, especially when their producers lack competitive power in world markets.

Why is the playing field bumpy?

There are a variety of reasons why the playing field may not seem level, and a number have their origin in government policies in Paris, Tokyo, Brussels, and New Delhi. Government regulations are much more extensive in some countries than in others; these regulations raise the cost of doing business and handicap domestic firms. The playing field also is not level because tax burdens are significantly higher in some countries than in others. History is important in the shape of the global playing field; firms headquartered in countries identified with a history of financial stability are likely to have an advantage in world markets. Moreover the firms headquartered in some countries may be younger than firms headquartered in other countries because their populations also are younger.

The economy as bazaar

One useful model of the world economy is that of the bazaar or marketplace. Individuals, firms, and even governments continually buy and sell, wheel and deal, seeking to increase their wealth and their power, esteem, and prestige. The chapters in Part I considered the evolution of international monetary arrangements and the costs and benefits of national monies. The chapters in Part II, in contrast, consider some of the consequences of the segmentation of the world into nearly 200 different currency areas. Some of the consequences are direct and reflect that firms headquartered in countries whose currencies are at the top of the hit parade have significant advantages in international competition because they have a lower cost of capital. Similarly firms and individuals resident in low-tax jurisdictions may have an advantage relative to firms and individuals resident in higher-tax countries. And individuals and firms that are based in countries identified with low levels of regulation have a competitive advantage in the world markets. Young French entrepreneurs have moved the headquarters of their businesses to Ashford, the British terminus of the Chunnel (a hybrid of 'channel' and 'tunnel') to take advantage of the more favorable – read less oppressive – regulatory environment.

Regulation evasion

Government regulations are avoided and evaded in many different countries. In some countries the chatter is about the 'underground' economy, in others of the 'black' economy or the 'moonlight' economy. Regardless of the term, the meaning is always the same – some of the taxes and business regulations are ignored, slighted, circumvented, avoided or evaded. Before the moves to the market economy in Moscow, Warsaw, and Prague, there had been extensive black economies run by individuals with access to goods in short supply, including essential consumer goods like Levis and disco albums of Donna Summer and Michael Jackson. The names of the unregulated economy differ by country, but the meaning always is the same – a set of economic activities is undertaken outside the regulatory framework.

The axiom is that the more severe the regulation and the easier the regulation can be evaded or avoided, the more likely the regulation will be avoided. The implication is that governments will either reduce the scope of regulation to match the regulations in nearby foreign countries or they will have relatively little economic activity to regulate. The significance of the worldwide growth of these 'market economies' for the effectiveness of government policy is discussed in Chapter 15.

Privatization

Every now and then a policy virus gets into the world's water supply, and virtually every country moves its policies in the same direction at more or less the same time. The 1980s and the 1990s witnessed extensive initiatives toward privatization in a wide array of countries. Argentina, Mexico, and Brazil have privatized – or plan to privatize – hundreds of firms in a wide array of industries. Great Britain has privatized its airports and the water-supply systems and parts of the bus and railroad systems. The move from the command economies to the market economies in Russia, Poland, Hungary, and the Czech Republic has involved wholesale privatization. Privatization has been less extensive in the United States than in most other countries, in part because the government sector was smaller; Still there has been some modest moves toward privatization in the United States – Conrail, some local garbage collection services, and even some prisons. The need to privatize is obvious when a country gives up on its planners and chooses to place greater reliance on the market; this need is less obvious in the traditional market economies – but it may still reflect the same motives.

Tax structure

Differences in national tax structures are frequently said to be unfair; firms in nearly every country believe they are at a competitive disadvantage in the international marketplace because their corporate tax burdens are higher than those of their foreign competitors. Corporate taxes, like wages and rents, are a cost, and unless the firms avoid or evade the taxes, they pay the cost and then usually raise selling prices to capture the cash to pay these taxes from their customers. Firms establish subsidiaries in low-tax jurisdictions to avoid or to reduce the costs of taxes; where possible, they shift profits to these jurisdictions by the adroit use of transfer pricing between the firms' subsidiaries in different countries. Similarly they use transfer pricing to shift profits from the countries in which they are headquartered to countries where the tax rates are lower. As a result, the tax payments of these firms are reduced and their after-tax profits are higher. But government expenditures must be financed, and governments need to raise other taxes or shrink their expenditures. The significance of national differences in corporate tax rates and individual tax rates on the competitive position of firms headquartered in different countries is discussed in Chapter 15.

The technology of money payments

The impact of rapid changes in the technology of money payments on the competitive position of commercial banks headquartered in different countries is discussed in Chapter 17. Banking is one of the most extensively regulated industries in virtually every country, and for a variety of reasons. One common feature of regulation is that costs are raised – and Santa Claus and the Salvation Army do not pay for the increase in costs. Regulation of banks means that they will either charge higher interest rates on their loans or pay lower interest rates on their deposits; both measures shrink banks' share in the financial intermediation. Almost inevitably, the banks in the countries with the most extensive regulations are at a disadvantage in the international marketplace; if the transport costs of money are high, then this cost handicap may have a negligible impact on the competitive positions of the more extensively regulated banks. As costs of transporting money internationally decline, banks headquartered in different countries can compete over a wider market area, so the cost differentials attributable to regulation will become more important. The buyers of the commercial banks' services will seek out low-cost producers of money, even if they are abroad. So the question arises whether US, British, or Swiss banks are likely to have a competitive advantage as the costs of dealing with banks in distant locations declines.

Changes in financial arrangements in the 1980s were more extensive than in any period since the substitution of checks for currency notes in the payments process (or perhaps even since the move from commodity to paper monies), so the decade truly can be identified with a financial revolution. One aspect of this revolution was the rapid expansion in the number of new financial instruments – there were interest rate swaps and foreign currency swaps, call options on futures contracts in foreign exchange and put options on futures contracts in foreign exchange, call options and put options on stock market index funds, and zero coupon bonds. A second aspect of this revolution was that the boundaries between commercial and investment banks and insurance companies and asset managers were shrinking; many financial institutions are evolving into 'department stores' even though some specialized 'boutiques' in each major activity will remain. The causes of this revolution and the impacts are evaluated in Chapter 18.

Consider the question: 'how many stock markets are there in the world?' One approach to the answer is to count the stock exchanges; thus in the United States there are exchanges in Boston, Chicago, Philadelphia, Denver, and San Francisco as well as the New York Stock Exchange and the American Stock Exchange in New York as well as the ubiquitous over-the-counter (OTC) market. Similarly there are five stock exchanges in Germany and two in Japan. Consolidation of trading in stocks has been going on for many years in each country, the market share of the New York Stock Exchange has been increasing. An alternative answer is that there is a world stock market, with branches in various countries. The rationale for this view is that large numbers of investors constantly scour the markets for stocks and bonds in each country, hunting for bargains – for securities whose returns are high relative to their risks. The returns on the major securities available in different countries may differ because the securities have embedded country-specific risks.

Outgrowing the market

One characteristic of most business firms is that they want to grow. The motivation is that if a firm ceases to grow, or even if it grows slowly, it may age relative to its competitors; the costs of aging firms tend to increase relative to the costs of firms that continue to grow rapidly. In business, as in biology, aging is a prelude to death – but in business aging can be postponed for an extended period if the growth rate can be maintained. The firms that grow rapidly almost always 'outgrow their traditional market', so the maintenance of their growth rates means that they will either have to develop a new set of products or services for customers in their domestic markets or else grow their sales in foreign markets. The reductions in the costs of economic distance have facilitated the growth of multinational corporations – large, diversified firms with operating subsidiaries in many different countries. Production in these subsidiaries is often integrated across national borders: each plant produces components for its domestic market and for numerous foreign markets. The marketing messages may be similar, although they will be adapted for the local markets and especially for the large national markets. In the late 1960s most multinational firms appeared to be US-based; many Europeans and Canadians feared the eventual domination of their domestic economies by US firms. Yet by the late 1970s, firms headquartered in Western Europe and Japan became very aggressive in the United States; British firms bought Howard Johnson's and Marshall Field & Co. and a German firm acquired A&P – the Great Atlantic and Pacific Tea Co. The big surprise of the 1980s was the surge in the foreign investments of Japanese firms and especially the acquisition of established US and European firms. Sony bought Columbia Records and then Columbia Pictures and Matsushita bought MGM-Universal; Bridgestone Tire bought Firestone Tire. In the early 1990s Japanese foreign investment declined sharply, and some Japanese firms began to sell some of their foreign investments. The change in the pattern of direct foreign investment (DFI) is discussed in Chapter 20.

Japan has been one of the glorious economic success stories of the 40 years before 1990. In the 1950s, national income in Japan was between one-twentieth and one-tenth that in the United States; national income is now nearly one-half that in the United States. In the 1950s there was general skepticism whether Japan could become a competitive industrial economy given its handicaps of geographic isolation, the absence of domestic raw materials, discrimination toward Japanese goods in foreign markets, and its own penchant for exclusiveness. By the early 1970s, Japan was realizing trade and payments surpluses that threatened the stability of the Bretton Woods system; one analyst predicted that the Japanese economy would continue to grow at annual rates of 10–12 percent, so that before the year 2000 *per capita* incomes in Japan would be substantially higher than in the United States and other Western industrial countries such as Sweden and Switzerland. A large number of competing explanations have been offered for the remarkable economic performance of Japan, and these are discussed in Chapter 21. Unfortunately for both Japan and these models and these analysts, Japan has been among the slowest growing of the industrial countries in the 1990s.

Rapid growth in Japan has been associated with equally rapid growth in the several of its smaller neighbors, once grouped as the 'Four Tigers' – Taiwan (sometimes called China Taipei), Hong Kong (formally a British colony that was handed over to China in mid-1997 and now is a Special Administrative Region (SAR) of China), Singapore, and Korea. Each of these countries has benefitted from close economic associations with Japan; firms in these countries often assemble components imported from Japan which are then either re-exported to Japan or more often to the United States. Two of these countries are almost completely Chinese, while Singapore is 85 percent Chinese. Korea shares the Confucian ethic with the overseas Chinese. More recently, the 'Four Dragons' – Thailand, Malaysia, Indonesia, and the Philippines – were touted as the paragons of rapid growth, at least until the advent of the Asian financial crisis in 1997.

For the 30 years of Mao's rule on the Chinese mainland, economic growth was stymied by series of misadventures – first the backyard steel mills, and eventually the Cultural Revolution (see Chapter 22). Since Mao's death in 1979, national income in China has increased at double-digit rates, a phenomenal achievement. Part of this growth has been making up arrears. The key question in Chapter 22 is whether China is likely to continue to grow at these rates, or even slightly lower ones.

Planned and transition economies

Much of the discussion in previous chapters assumed that the world consists of market-oriented economies which have reasonably similar *per capita* incomes. One exception to this view was that the Soviet Union, Poland, Hungary, and the their neighbors in Eastern Europe relied on central planning, at least until the end of the 1980s. The basic economic decisions about what goods should be produced, the amounts of these goods to be produced, and the prices of these goods were determined by bureaucrats. These countries participated in the international economy – they traded extensively both with each other and with the market economies; since private firms could not import and export for profit as in the market economies, other institutional mechanisms were necessary for arranging trade. The financial relations between the planned economies of Eastern Europe and the market-oriented Western economies, as well as the relations between the Soviet and other Eastern European countries, are discussed in Chapter 23. Business was done and bargains were struck. Imbalances in trade were settled by payments of money, frequently the US dollar. Exchange rates were inevitable, although they were not used, as in the West, as a mechanism for balancing receipts and payments. Nevertheless, the question is whether the exchange rate is a fair price. In trade among Western countries, the fair price is the free market price or the official parity. But since there was no free markets within Communist countries, some other mechanism was needed to determine domestic prices, export and import prices, and the exchange rate. And some Eastern European countries believed that the prices used in their trade with the Soviet Union were not in their own best interests.

Russia and its neighbors in what was Eastern Europe are moving toward the market; the encompassing label is now 'transition economies'. Some countries, especially the smaller ones like Slovenia, have made substantial process. But life has been difficult in Russia and the Ukraine, for they have experienced hyperinflations that wiped out the value of the money savings and the pensions of millions of people. Integration of their national markets with the world economy has been a dislocating experience. Fortunes have been made, often by the opportunists who were at the top of heap when the rubric was that of the command economy.

Several themes run through the chapters of Part II. The costs of economic distance are declining; market areas are expanding beyond national boundaries. Differences in business frameworks that were insignificant when the costs of distance were high are now becoming much more significant and are likely to be a cause of friction among nations. There has been a massive move to privatization and a powerful move to reduction of tax burdens – especially tax rates on anything that moves.

While pressures for harmonization and coordination will develop, counterpressures for retaining the advantages of high costs of economic distance will also rise.

15

The Underground Economies and the Cost of Regulation

The role of government

Government inefficiency

One way to get the trains to run on time is to straighten the tracks. Another is to use more powerful locomotives. A less costly way – indeed, the cheapest way – is to lengthen the time allowed for the journey. In the 1920s the trip from Chicago to New York on the Twentieth Century Limited took 15 hours; passengers got rebates if the train was late, with the amount of the rebate scaled to the length of the delay. The same journey on Amtrak now takes 19–20 hours on the Broadway Limited – and there are no rebates if the train is late. The mileage between Chicago and New York is a constant, more or less. If the trains can't adjust to the timetables, then the timetables adjust to the trains. Mussolini's claim to fame was that he got the trains to run on time; but mostly he lengthened the timetables.

Improvements in transport technology should almost certainly have led to a decline in the time required for most trips over the last half-century. 70 years ago, air travel between Chicago and New York took two days with an overnight in Cleveland. Today the same trip takes 90 minutes, more or less. Even with the 65-miles-per-hour speed limit, the driving time from New York to Chicago takes 12 hours.

Japan has its Bullet Trains between Tokyo and Osaka, while France has the TGV between Paris and Lyon with speeds of 300 kilometers per hour. Even Britain has some new, fast trains that travel at 125 miles per hour – not quite as fast as the TGV. The Chunnel – the rail tunnel under the English Channel between Great Britain and France – has reduced the travel time from London to Paris to a bit over three hours.

(The economy airfare between Chicago and London is lower than the rail fare between London and Paris but that's another story.) Yet even where the trains run faster, they usually run at a loss – and when they run slower, they almost certainly do.

The Darwinian view of economics is that the efficient survive and expand, while the inefficient shrink and die. Nevertheless from the 1950s to the 1980s the roles of government in most countries increased – as measured by the government spending as a share of GDP – even though there was a general view that government was becoming less efficient in delivering goods and services and the mail. The US Immigration and Naturalization Service finds it difficult to prevent illegal entry into the United States; it is estimated that there are 3–7 million 'illegals' in the major US cities and on the farms – but no one knows. Some estimates place the number at 20 million – modestly smaller than the populations of California or of Canada. The Internal Revenue Service finds it difficult to collect all the taxes owed the US government – tax revenues would be 10 percent higher if there were 100 percent compliance. There are horror stories of the John Smiths who continue to collect Social Security checks 10 years after they've passed away and the John Does who can't manage to collect their unemployment compensation checks because the system has lost their employment records. The Food Stamp program was established to reduce government-owned surplus food stocks and at the same time to provide better nourishment for the poor; subsequently food stamps became a second US currency and a source of considerable fraud.

There are horror stories about the shortcomings of large organizations in the private sector, so horror stories are not unique to government. Patients occasionally get lost in hospitals; someone goes into the hospital needing a tonsillectomy and leaves sans an appendix. The power companies turn off the electricity at the wrong house. Deliveries are made to the wrong apartment. There are oil spills off the California Coast, and tankers run aground in the Delaware River. Commercial airline pilots land at the wrong airports.

Yet governmental inefficiency may be unique, and for several different reasons – the governments in the industrial countries are usually much larger than private firms and employers, and government agencies are responsive to a variety of different political interests rather than to profit motives in their decisions. Government-owned airline firms and steel mills and railroads and telephone systems have generally operated at a financial loss; the money necessary to finance the loss has almost always come from general taxation. Moreover the money necessary to pay for the new investments of these government-owned firms has come from general taxation. One reason for the loss is that the wages of the employees in most government agencies have generally been higher than the wages for similar labor skills in the private sector, and the government employees generally have more job security than their counterparts in private firms, and usually have much more attractive medical benefits and retirement pensions. The government is more or less a monopolist; traditionally government-owned firms haven't had to worry about competition, at least in their domestic activities. But there are lots of exceptions – increasingly the US Postal Service has to worry about competition from Fed Ex (formerly Federal Express), as well as from the telephone companies, the fax services, and even the Internet. And government-owned airlines have had to compete with private-owned airlines on many international routes.

One reason for the apparent inefficiency in the government sector is size – and the increase in size – which is evident in Table 15.1 and 15.2. The government's share of GNP is smaller in the United States than in any other large industrial country: the government sector in Japan has expanded more than twice as rapidly as the government sector in the United States – maybe it's those fast trains. The government sector in Germany is half again as large as that in the United States. The only significant decline in the size of government sector is that in Great Britain in the 1980s – and that change was reversed in the first half of the 1990s.

Table 15.1 General government expenditures/GNP, 1965–98

	1965	1970	1975	1980	1985	1990	1995	1998
United States	27.9	31.6	34.6	33.7	32.8	32.9	36.4	
Japan	20.0	19.4	27.3	32.6	31.6	31.3	35.7	36.4
Germany	36.7	38.6	48.3	48.7	47.0	45.1	49.5	46.5
France	38.4	38.9	43.5	46.4	52.2	49.8	54.3	53.1
Italy	34.3	34.2	43.2	41.6	51.2	53.1	52.1	49.2
Great Britain	36.4	39.0	46.3	45.0	44.0	39.9	43.0	38.9
Canada	29.1	34.8	40.1	40.5	45.3	46.0	46.5	40.1
Total				37.2	38.2	37.7	39.5	38.0
Total: smaller countries				40.0	42.1	42.1	43.9	41.0

Table 15.2   General government total outlays, 1960–95 (percent of nominal GDP)

	1960	1970	1980	1990	1995
United States	25.5	31.6	31.8	33.3	33.5
Japan	13.6	19.4	32.0	31.7	36.4
Germany	27.7	38.6	47.9	45.1	51.6
France	30.9	38.5	46.1	49.8	54.5
Great Britain	29.9	39.0	43.0	39.9	43.9
Canada	25.4	34.8	38.8	45.8	47.3

The expansion of the role of government almost always has been associated with noble purposes – providing medical care, housing, education, roads and income support, as well as national security and defense. And everyone wants more of these activities, for the value or at least the cost of services provided by the government has almost always been larger than the price paid for them. (Consider the mirror-image statement – if the price paid for the services provided by the government were higher than the value of the services, no one would buy the services.) In effect, governments specialize in 'loss leaders' – if the production activities were profitable, the odds are high that the activity would be in the private sector.

Since government expenditures must be financed, it follows that the larger are government expenditures as a share of national income, the higher must tax revenues be as a share of national income. Few individuals want to pay higher taxes. Governments always can borrow to pay for these expenditures but there are severe limits to the share of total expenditures that can be financed by borrowing: government borrowing implies higher interest payments in the future and future rather than current taxes. For a few years a government may be able to borrow to get funds to pay the interest on its outstanding debt; however, as government indebtedness increases relative to GDP, the interest rates that the government must pay on its outstanding loans increases. So it's a safe rule of thumb that the higher the level of expenditures, the higher the level of taxes.

Very few government taxes are directly related to the value of services provided – the exceptions are the 'user taxes', the tolls on the highways, the gasoline taxes, and the airport departure taxes which may be somewhat related to the cost of the services provided. In the private sector individuals and firms set prices to cover production costs; if prices remain below costs for long, a trip to the bankruptcy court is inevitable. If instead prices are significantly above costs, then new firms are almost certain to enter the industry, and their efforts to increase market share may lead to a decline in prices.

There is a large disconnect between the taxes paid by individuals and firms, and the end services provided with the funds from these taxes. So there's an incentive on the part of Jo Public to reach for the services and skip the taxes. That's also true on the part of the politicians – there are more votes out there promising and providing more and better services to the public, and higher wages and salaries to the teachers and policemen and army officers and civil servants than in raising taxes to pay for these goodies. The consequence is that there is an inevitable tendency for the size of government sector to grow because of the lack of a connection between government expenditures and taxes. The other side of the coin is that those who are taxed do not associate particular benefits with the taxes they pay.

Reduced effectiveness of government

As taxes have increased, the incentives to avoid, evade, ignore, sidestep, forget, escape, and non-comply have increased. One measure of the reduced effectiveness of government is the growth of 'underground' economies – the 'moonlight' economies or the 'black economies' in the United States, Great Britain, France, Germany, Russia, and many other industrial nations. The story is pervasive. Government taxes income so it's worthwhile to avoid or evade the taxes. Individuals engage in barter in the belief that the services provided and consumed aren't income. Government rules restrict or prohibit profitable activities, so the rules are evaded or avoided; sometimes it's the production of, sometimes the provision of, moonshine.

One set of transactions in the underground economy includes those that lead to legal incomes for firms and individuals that are not reported to the tax collector. Much of this undeclared legal income is in cash. Many individuals and small firms want to be paid in cash – they don't want the paper trail associated with payment by credit or debit card, or by check. The chatter is that those involved in home-repair services in many countries prefer cash payments. But occasionally, some of this taxable income may be 'in kind', a form of barter – the optometrist swaps a set of contact lenses with his car mechanic for a motor tune-up. Doctors, dentists, and pharmacists treat each other to professional discounts, frequently of 50 percent. Cooks and waitresses may get several free meals per day along with their money incomes – these meals are a form of income but the value of the income reported to the tax collector may be below the full value. (There are other forms of legal income that are not considered taxable by governments. The parish provides the minister with a house; the services of the house are income but the income traditionally has not been considered taxable. The air transport services obtained with the use of mileage awards are a form of income but the Internal Revenue Service hasn't figured out how to tax it. There are lots of seminars on cruise boats and in seaside resorts that are considered business expenses and reduce taxable incomes, even though a large part of the activity seems more nearly like a vacation than an investment in education.)

In some firms and in some countries, employees have 'rights' to fiddles or perks or other benefits; it's recognized that they will use the company's samples, or its stamps, or its phones, for their personal use. Such goods are part of their pay. Using the company phone for personal calls is undeclared, illegal income; so is using the company car.

Finally, there's the (illegal) income associated with illegal activities – transactions in heroin and marijuana and other drugs, prostitution, production and sale of 'white lightning' and other alcoholic beverages.

Because these economies are underground, there's no good way to measure their significance, or how the size of the underground economy differs across countries. The general view is that the underground economy is larger, the higher the tax rates and the more severe business regulation. In some countries, especially in what had been the command economies in Russia and in the Ukraine, unreported income has been estimated to be 30–40 percent of GDP. There is a strong belief that the underground sector has grown rapidly, even though the data aren't available to prove – or disprove – the point. The rapid growth of these activities might partially offset the slow measured growth in the legitimate or above-ground economy. Each government generally has an incentive to provide a low estimate of the size of the underground economy in its country – at least until they want more resources for tax collection and law enforcement. Underground transactions are more pervasive where individuals traditionally deal in cash – in rural areas and in low-income areas in central cities.

Where the activity is illegal, the transactions almost always involve cash. Some estimate that illegal drugs are a $20–$30 billion a year business in the United States, or about 1 percent of GDP. Marijuana is said to be the second or third largest cash crop in the US economy, after soybeans and wheat. Prostitution is valued as a $1–$2 billion a year activity. These estimates are significantly smaller than those for unde-clared legal incomes – the amount of tax evasion. But even if estimates of illegal incomes are half or a third of their 'true value,' the total is small in terms of the above-ground economy. Even if these transac-tions have increased very rapidly, the amounts involved are so small that the impact on the aggregate level of economic activity is negligi-ble.

The growth of the underground economies reflects the decline in the effectiveness of government regulation – and in respect for these regu-lations. In many countries, tax bracket creep increased with inflation; tax bites have increased more rapidly than increases in income. The smaller the effectiveness of government in implementing its own rules and collecting its taxes, the larger the likelihood that firms and indi-viduals will shift some of their transactions into the underground economy. The counterpart to the reduced ability to collect taxes is the reduced effectiveness in the allocation of expenditures. When govern-ment distributes money, there are more and more instances of fraud; every major city has had a 'welfare queen,' who managed to collect 14 checks a month under 14 different names.

Why don't the trains run on time?

Decline in infrastructure quality and tax base

It might have been Yogi Berra who said 'A three cent stamp doesn't cost three cents anymore.' The cost of the three-cent stamp (that is, the stamp for delivering first-class mail) has increased from three cents in 1950 to 32 cents in 1998. The US price level increased by a factor of five during this same period, so the 'real cost' of first-class mail doubled. Actually, the real cost increased even more, for the quality of mail service has almost cer-tainly declined – there are fewer mail deliveries each day, there are fewer post offices, the mail deliveries take longer, and there is more lost mail.

Consider some of the other elements in the decline in the effective-ness of government management. The quality of government pro-duced services has decreased. In Britain, individuals have opted out of the socialized medical system and bought private services either to reduce waiting time or to acquire medical services that they believe to be of higher quality. Within the United States, the concern about the decline in the level of public education has led to an increase in expen-diture on private education, especially in cities and at the elementary and secondary school level. Stores, universities, colleges, churches, and businesses have developed their own police forces – which frequently include many part-timers whose primary employment is with a public police force.

A second element is the decline in the quality of the public infrastructure. Libraries are closed because the governments cannot pay for both books and salaries. There are more potholes in the roads and the quality of roads and sewers decline because government is caught between its limited ability to tax and the demands of government employees, almost always organized into unions, for higher salaries. For a long time safety on public transportation in the major US cities declined. The paradox is that the quality of government provided services declined even as salaries in the public sector increased. The increase in salaries in the government sector has been even more rapid than in the private sector. There appears to be a cost-push element in the public-sector wages, because the employees are organized into unions. The unions favor similarity of salaries for individuals, and salaries tend to vary with the seniority and experience of individual workers rather than with their productivity. So it follows logically that those workers with the highest productivity are likely to be attracted to the higher salaries available in the private sector.

Fiscal deficits are associated with inflation, which leads to overvalued currencies. Overvalued currencies require exchange controls – barriers or tariffs or other controls that separate the domestic market for goods and services from the world market. Such controls enable the governments (and their friends) to buy foreign exchange on more favorable terms than the 'run-of-the-mill' business firms and individuals. Lots of countries have used these controls – Great Britain, the United States, France, Italy, Japan, and a large number of developing countries. But these measures are effective only to the extent that earners of foreign exchange are not tempted to jump the fence and sell their export earnings at the higher price available in the free market. Hence at times a pegged exchange rate can become like a tax on the earnings of foreign exchange. If the currency is overvalued, of course, countries with floating currencies might also use these taxes to increase their own earnings.

The governments with the largest expenditures tend to finance part of their expenditures by relying on the printing press: the tax base isn't sufficiently large. And, for a while at least, they tend to borrow internationally as well as domestically. Thus, when the United States has a large fiscal deficit and the US dollar tends to be weak in the foreign exchange market, foreign governments lend to the United States; high interest rates mean that the US securities are attractive to foreign investors.

One link between the underground economy and international money flows is the movement of 'suitcase money'. Individuals move currency from high-tax to low-tax jurisdictions; this shifting of money out of the country makes it much more difficult for the tax collector to prove that individuals have under-reported income. Or they move currency in suitcases to circumvent domestic exchange controls: they want to get the funds into some other currency area. There are other links – one is that the underground economies flourish in countries with high tax rates, because these countries have high levels of government expenditures. But the authorities find it easier to increase expenditures than tax revenues. So they borrow. Both taxing and borrowing take money from the public – although taxing is more directly coercive than borrowing.

Privatization

One remarkable change that has been on-going for the last 20 years has been privatization, which has affected government-owned airlines and telephone systems and numerous other government-provided services. Governments have also outsourced the suppliers of a variety of services as a way to reduce costs; these services include garbage collection, the management of prisons, and operation of libraries.

Initiatives toward privatization can be viewed in terms of developments in particular industries (such as airlines, telecommunications, and banking) or in terms of particular countries (Great Britain, Mexico, Argentina, Japan, and the United States). (Privatization in Russia, China, Hungary, and other countries that are on the trip to the market from a command economy are discussed in Chapter 25.)

Probably one of the most extensive approaches toward privatization in a traditional industrial country has occurred in Great Britain. British Airlines was privatized. So was the phone system, gas distribution company, electric power production and distribution, railroads, steel mills, and water supply companies. Prime Minister Thatcher did much much more than undo the legacy that the Conservative government had inherited from the Labour governments of the 1940s and the 1950s, which had nationalized steel and coal, the health system, and much of the housing stock. Clearly one of the motivations was ideological – Mrs Thatcher's view was that the government should provide law and order and arrangements for the enforcement of contracts for consenting adults. A second motivation was financial. If government-owned firms could be sold to the private sector, then the government would no longer have to subsidize operating losses (although in some cases the governments might subsidize operating losses for a set number of years). Nor would the government have to provide the cash to finance new investments. And there would be a one-time increase in government revenues when these firms were sold to private investors. Because of the government's interest in securing a large (if not a maximum) gain from the sale of these firms, they had to 'prepped' – converted into profitable enterprises. In some cases, thousands of employees were induced to leave, perhaps by taking early retirement. The motivation was that the higher the anticipated profits associated with a firm about to be privatized, the higher the price the potential buyers would pay for it, and the greater the windfall to the government selling the firm.

Argentina began its privatization effort in the early 1990s, and privatized a large number of firms, including airlines and oil-production firms. Mexico privatized more than 500 firms.

Privatization was far less extensive in the United States than in other countries, in part because the government sector was smaller. Conrail – which had been assembled as an East Coast freight-hauling railroad from the carcasses of some bankrupt railroads – was privatized. TVA (Tennessee Valley Authority) and the various government-owned power producing firms in the Northwest remain in the public sector. Amtrak continues to be government-owned; the commuter railroads and the bus systems in many systems are still in the public sector. The Japanese privatized Nippon Telephone and Telegraph and parts of their railroads.

That so many different and varied goverments privatized firms in so many different industries at more or less the same time cannot be a coincidence. Each government benefitted fiscally, both from the reduction in the drain on the government's budget to finance operating losses and the one-shot proceeds from the sale. In many countries there was recognition that government-owned firms could not compete in the global market. Consider airlines. The US airline industry has 8 or 10 national firms and a much larger number of regional firms. Four of these US firms compete extensively across the continental United States – and they have paid attention to reducing and controlling costs. This focus on costs has been valuable in competing against government-owned foreign firms that have traditionally been under lesser pressure to reduce costs. Or consider telecommunications, which is essentially a global industry: firms were privatized to reduce the losses that government firms would incur.

16
Tax Avoidance – A Game for the Rich

Tax havens

Superstar Miss X is a nubile factor of production that has engaged in tax avoidance. She lived in Switzerland and worked elsewhere – Hollywood, London, Rome, and Budapest. Her dramatic abilities resulted in a magnificent income, nearly all from sources outside Switzerland. Because she was a Swiss resident, her income was not taxed in the United States or London or Italy. Swiss taxes on her income were much lower than US taxes would have been if she had lived in Hollywood, or than British taxes would have been if she lived in London.

Miss X and the Swiss had struck a bargain. The Swiss sold Miss X tax-avoidance services – the right to live in a low-tax jurisdiction. Miss X bought this service because she liked the higher after-tax income; better to live where taxes are low than where they are high. The Swiss profited from the transaction, for the taxes paid by Miss X greatly exceeded her demand on local public services for schooling and plowing the snow from the roads to her home. In effect, Miss X was subsidizing the Swiss, and as a result other Swiss – the Swiss Swiss rather that the Vagabond Swiss – paid lower taxes. Had she lived in London, Swiss tax revenues would have been lower, and the Swiss would have had to raise tax rates on the Swiss Swiss to provide them with same level of public services.

Switzerland is also a tax haven for mobile as well as for nubile factors of production, for the tax rates in Switzerland are substantially lower than tax rates in most other developed countries. Indeed most taxes in Switzerland are levied by the various cantons like Zug and St Gallen rather than by the federal government in Bern. Liechtenstein, Panama, the Bahamas, the Netherlands Antilles, and the Cayman Islands provide similar services. Tax havens are established to attract income from foreign sources – and then to tax this income lightly. One common feature of the tax havens is that they tend to be small geographically. Most – Switzerland is an exception – have modest if any defense expenditures. Expenditures on welfare also are modest. Competition among tax havens keeps the tax rates on foreign-source income low. If the tax rate in the Cayman Islands were increased relative to the rates in other havens, most foreign-source income would be diverted from the Caymans to the Netherlands Antilles, or to Bermuda, or to some other tax haven.

Low-tax jurisdiction

Tax havens are only one example of tax avoidance. England's richest lords leave London for low-tax jurisdictions in Bermuda, the Bahamas, and the Channel Islands to avoid high British inheritance taxes. US firms and German firms issue bonds in Luxembourg because interest income there is not subject to withholding tax; buyers of the bonds want to avoid having part of their interest income taxed at source – in effect, withheld. US professors teach in Canada for two years and avoid both US and Canadian income taxes; residence outside the United States for more than 18 months means they than were not subject to US taxes, and Canada does not tax foreign professors on their Canadian income during the first two years that they live in Canada.

Most individuals, however, cannot move to low-tax jurisdictions without suffering a serious loss in income; their occupations tie them to a particular city or region. Only when the possible tax savings are large relative to the costs of shifting residences do individuals move to a foreign tax jurisdiction. (Within the United States individuals and especially those who are retired move to Florida and Arizona–the states that have low income taxes and low state inheritance taxes.)

Transfer pricing

One alternative to moving to a low-tax jurisdiction is to shift income there. Some London-based professors have their royalty and consulting incomes paid to bank accounts in Zurich and in Liechtenstein. When a US firm or a British firm uses an Antillian or a Zugian (Zug is a Swiss canton near Zurich, one of the busiest tax havens in Europe) tax haven, the transfer price – the price at which its affiliates in several countries buy and sell goods and services from each other – is frequently set to shift income to the low-tax jurisdiction. For example, a US firm may export goods to its German affiliate, and arrange the documentation for the transaction so the goods are first sold to one of the firm's sales subsidiaries in Bermuda. The parent company charges the Bermudan subsidiary an unusually low price, thereby income is shifted from the United States to Bermuda; the Bermudan subsidiary charges a modestly higher price when it in turn sells the goods to the German subsidiary, so income is shifted from Germany to Bermuda. The firm's taxable income in Bermuda increases, while its taxable incomes in both the United States and Germany decline. The goods never get to Bermuda – indeed, neither the documents nor the money go there.

Both the US and the German tax collector know about tax havens. They scan the prices used in transactions between foreign subsidiaries and domestic offices of the firm to forestall flagrant attempts to shift income. They relate the stated prices on these intra-firm transactions to the prices of similar goods that are sold in markets, which provide an effective benchmark for a 'fair price'. But many intra-firm transactions have no readily available commercial counterparts and no ready-reference market prices, so firms can be somewhat arbitrary in their pricing – within reason. Similarly, firms can be somewhat arbitrary in their allocation of common overhead costs among their branches and subsidiaries in various countries; again to the extent they have discretion, they want an exceptionally large share of these costs to be incurred in jurisdictions with high corporate tax rates.

Tax havens are profitable despite the ever-watchful eyes of the tax collector; sales subsidiaries based in tax havens are not established unless the probable savings in taxes more than compensates for the legal fees charged by high-priced lawyers (lawyers, incidentally, who frequently received their most valuable legal education about the ins-and-outs of the taxation of foreign income while working for the Inland Revenue Service or the local tax collector before they move to the private sector). If the use – or abuse – of tax havens were so extensive that governments felt a serious loss from runaway income and foregone taxes, transfer pricing would be examined more closely.

Members of the US Congress have complained that the corporate income tax payments of the US subsidiaries of foreign firms have been much too low; they note that many of these subsidiaries stopped paying taxes once they had been acquired by a foreign firm. It's possible that the subsidiaries ceased being profitable soon after the change in ownership (which raises the question of why the foreign firms acquired these US subsidiaries – but that is a different topic). And it's also possible that the new foreign owners were shifting income from the United States to Zug, or to some other tax haven.

Economic impact of taxation

This transfer-pricing issue has become particularly intense with respect to the US subsidiaries of Japanese firms which have paid virtually no tax to the US Treasury, apparently because they had no US income. Most of these subsidiaries had been profitable before they had been sold to the Japanese firms. Thus the 700 Japanese subsidiaries of US firms paid more tax to the Japanese government than the 3700 US subsidiaries of Japanese firms paid to the US government. In part, this difference could be explained by differences in the 'ages' of these firms – the Japanese subsidiaries of US firms have generally been significantly older than the US subsidiaries of Japanese firms; newly established foreign subsidiaries may not secure profits in their first few years of operation. The British subsidiaries of Japanese firms also have reported very low profits. Several officials of the Nissan subsidiary in Great Britain were jailed because of tax fraud.

Even without tax havens, differences among national tax systems might have a significant impact on the pattern of international transactions. All governments tax, but in different ways and at different rates. Governments tax income, both personal and corporate, they tax interest income, dividend income, and capital gains on securities and real estate. Governments tax real property like houses, land, machinery, and even clothing. Governments tax transactions – retail sales, purchases, imports and exports, births and deaths.

Most governments have a virtually unlimited need for revenues; the larger revenues are, the larger expenditures can be, and large expenditures enhance political support. But taxes have a cost, for they diminish political support. So each government seeks to increase its tax revenues at minimal cost in terms of the loss of political support. Ideally, governments would like to tax foreigners to get the funds to undertake expenditures that benefit domestic residents, which is what tax havens are all about.

Not unexpectedly, the tax rates differ sharply among countries. Similarly the tax base – the types of income and the types of transactions that are taxed – also differ. These differences are frequently used to explain why some nations grow slowly and others grow rapidly, why the exports of some countries grow more rapidly than those of others, and why investors move money from some countries to others. In nearly every country, businessmen allege that they are at a disadvantage in international trade because they are taxed more heavily than their foreign competitors; they believe that they would be better off if their tax burdens were smaller. (We all would be better off if our tax burdens were lower, but the second statement in the previous sentence doesn't necessarily follow from the first.)

Taxes, like wages, interest rates, and the cost of electricity, have an economic impact; many firms raise the selling prices of the goods and services they sell to get the money to pay the taxes. The key question is whether differences among countries in tax structures and tax rates have a significant economic impact on the international competitive position of firms producing in various countries.

Why tax rates differ

The revenue needs of countries differ because the sizes of their public sectors differ. The larger the public sector within a country, the higher its tax rates and the larger the range of incomes and transactions which are taxed.

Americans have been fond of saying – especially to the Japanese – that US tax bills are higher because US forces have been 'defending' the free world. US military expenditures have been 6–7 percent of national income; in Japan, the constitution limits these expenditures to 1 percent of national income. In most other industrial countries the military budget is in the range of 1–2 percent of national income.

The size of the government sectors in different economies was summarized in Table 15.1 and 15.2 (pp. 241, 242); the striking fact was that the government sector was significantly larger in Germany, Japan, and other industrial countries, even though these countries spend a smaller share of their national income on defense. In general, they spend a larger share of their national income on social welfare, including health care and housing. Because their government sectors are larger, they need more tax revenues. Either they need higher tax rates on the same types of income and transactions, or they need to tax more incomes and more transactions.

Everyone agrees that taxes should be fair. Fairness, after all, is like motherhood. The disagreement arises over what is 'fair' – over the amount of taxes to be paid by those with low incomes relative to the amount of taxes to be paid by those with higher incomes. Governments differ from private businesses in one important aspect:

governments supply certain goods and services below their cost of production. Many of these goods and services are given away; some are sold, but at prices substantially below cost. But while particular goods and services can be sold below cost, the total supply of goods and services cannot be sold below production costs, unless a country can borrow abroad indefinitely. To the extent that some goods and services are available below cost, the prices of other goods and services must exceed their costs of production, and the subsidy to the buyers of goods produced by the first group must be financed by the tax on the buyers of the goods produced by the second. In a crude way, the net tax revenues on the second group must more or less match the subsidies to the first group. An individual can get a 'free lunch'; society as a whole cannot. Someone must pay for the goods and services produced by the government. One reason the size of the government sector has expanded is that 'everyone' – well, nearly everyone – wants that free lunch from the government; the implicit view is that someone else will pay most or all of the cost. A free lunch at school is cheaper than a cash lunch; attractive as the free lunch may be, however, someone has to pay for it.

The size of government is a good measure of the amount of goods and services that individuals consume collectively. In Western societies, the amount of goods and services supplied by the government ranges from 20 to 60 percent of the total goods and services produced in the economy. The cliché has it that the amount of goods and services supplied by the government is a response to the demands of the society. But the cliché is a cliché; some part of the government output reflects the ability of firms in different industries – the farmers, the producers of defence goods, small businesses – to get support for increased output. Most of the benefits of government produced goods and services go to selected groups – farmers receive agricultural extension services and price supports, students get free school lunches, and professors receive research stipends from organizations like the National Science Foundation – while the costs fall broadly on taxpayers. Many firms are extremely fond of military expenditures – because they produce military goods. Each group sees its own interests advanced if the government spends more on the goods and services it produces; the value of these benefits will almost certainly exceed their share of costs. For as long as the production of additional government goods and services is dissociated from their costs, advantages may accrue to the government and to those members of the bureaucracy associated with the extension of new services.

Corporate tax rates in industrial countries

Invisible taxes

One characteristic of the ideal tax from the point of view of the tax collector is that the tax be buried and not visible to the individual paying it. The corporate income tax satisfies this test, for the tax is embedded in the prices of the products sold by the firm. Most buyers of virtually any good or service – an automobile, a new home, an airplane trip – would be hard pressed to answer the question of the size of the tax payment associated with the purchase. (The corporate tax has several major disadvantages – one is that profitable and efficient firms are penalized relative to unprofitable less efficient firms, and another is that shareholders may be subject to double taxation, once when the firm is taxed and again when the shareholders are taxed on their dividends or capital gains.)

Corporate income tax payments are larger as a share of both national income and total tax payments in the United States than in any other industrial country. Someone might conclude from this data that the US corporate income tax rates are higher than tax rates in other industrial countries. Similarly someone might conclude that since personal income taxes account for a larger share of national income and total taxes in the United States than in these other countries, then their personal income tax rates must be higher than the personal income tax rates in the United States.

Neither conclusion is not warranted. It would be a mistake to infer tax rates on corporate income and personal income from the share of government receipts from each type of tax.

Corporate tax and income tax

One reason why the ratio of corporate tax receipts to total taxes is lower in most foreign countries than in the United States is that foreign governments spend a higher proportion of their country's national incomes than the United States does and so they have larger revenue needs. Even if they had the same corporate tax rates, the yield of the corporate tax would be lower as a percentage of total taxes.

The principal reason that the ratio of corporate income tax receipts to GDP is lower in most foreign countries than the United States is that the corporate income is a smaller share of GDP, and for two different reasons. One is that the corporate sector is a smaller share of the economy – many of the public utilities like railroads, the telephone companies, the electric power producers may be government-owned firms; another is that there are relatively more small firms, and these firms are frequently not incorporated. If, for example, corporate tax rates were identical in each country, then revenues generated by the corporate profits tax would be smaller in various foreign countries than in the United States because the corporate sectors are smaller abroad. Moreover, corporate profits relative to corporate sales may be lower abroad, so the corporate income tax base would be smaller even if the corporate sectors in these other industrial countries were as large as the corporate sector in the United States.

Similarly, the tax base for personal incomes is smaller abroad; a much larger proportion of taxpayers have incomes too low to pay personal income taxes. Tax rates on personal incomes are higher in Great Britain than in the United States, in that tax payments are larger for each level of personal income. But since personal incomes are lower, revenues from taxes on personal income are smaller relative to both GDP and to government expenditures.

Comparison of national tax rates is a necessary first step in determining the impact of taxes on the competitive position of the firms producing in each country. The US corporate income tax rate, now 36 percent, is generally lower than the corporate tax rates in most other industrial countries. However, definitions of taxable income differ, largely because some countries permit their firms to depreciate their plant and equipment more rapidly than others. When governments permit firms to depreciate plant and equipment rapidly, expenses are higher and so profits are smaller, and tax liability and tax payments are lower – even if the tax rates are the same. Moreover, countries differ in the scope of investment tax credits extended to business firms; investment tax credits reduce the effective tax rates for those firms that can take advantage of them. Rapid depreciation and investment tax credits both reduce the effective tax rate significantly below the posted rate.

Taxes can be avoided, evaded, or paid. Avoidance is legal, although there are costs. Subsidiaries in tax havens have to be established, and lawyers are expensive. Evasion of taxes – which is illegal – incurs costs and risks; in some countries, payments to the tax collectors in their personal capacity may obviate the need for much larger payments to the collectors in their official capacity. Still, evaders are sometimes caught, fined, jailed, and in some cases ostracized.

Despite all the attention to corporate tax rates, only individuals pay taxes. Corporations may have an infinite life, but they do not feel, suffer, breed, or smile; only people do. Corporations do not 'pay' taxes – they collect funds to pay these taxes from their customers, their shareholders, their employees, and their suppliers. The burden may fall not on the corporation's owners (as a decline in their after-tax incomes), but on the customers, who pay higher prices, or on the suppliers, who receive lower prices. General Motors pays a tax of 36 percent on its corporate profits; until 1971 it also paid a sales tax of 7 percent on its sales of automobiles. Ostensibly, the corporate tax fell on the profits, while the excise tax fell on the customer. But GM probably raised its selling prices to obtain funds to make its corporate tax payments. Similarly, firms do not 'pay' social security taxes – they collect the funds to pay these taxes by paying their employees lower wage and salary rates.

The large variety of taxes befuddles many taxpayers: if they were aware that 20, or 30, or even 40 percent of their income was taxed, they might be more cautious about proposals for increases in government expenditures. And if all of their taxes were collected by a straightforward income tax or consumption tax or value-added tax, they would have greater incentive to calculate the payoffs from tax avoidance or evasion.

Economic impact of corporate taxation

The legal form of these taxes should be distinguished from their economic impact. The corporate tax and sales tax fall directly on the consumer if the demand for the product is sufficiently strong. Consider the impact of a possible increase in US corporate income tax rate by about 10 percent – say, to a rate of 40 percent. GM, Ford, and DaimlerChrysler would probably raise their selling prices to offset higher corporate tax payments, so that the after-tax returns earned by their shareholders would remain pretty much the same in the long run if not immediately. Similarly, the resource-depletion allowance, which allowed oil companies to reduce their tax payments, almost certainly meant a lower price for gasoline; when the allowance was reduced in 1975, the gasoline price went up modestly so that the oil producing companies would have more or less the same after-tax rate of return.

But taxes are only part of the story. Governments tax to spend. And while taxes raise costs to firms, government expenditures (or at least some of them) may lower those costs. Public expenditures can reduce the need for private expenditures, reducing a firm's costs. Thus government expenditures on roads and airports reduce transportation costs for manufacturing firms. Expenditures on fire departments reduce the need to purchase similar protection privately, while expenditures on education reduce the need for firms to train their own employees. The

Box 16.1   Tax Rates and Corporate Profits

A simple example demonstrates that the increase in the tax rate on corporate profits is not likely to have a major impact on selling prices of automobiles produced in the United States. Assume that an automobile sells for $10,000, that the profits-to-sales ratio for US auto firms is 10 percent, and that the corporate tax rate is 36 percent; the ratio of tax to sales would then be 13.6 percent. Because these firms will raise their selling prices to pass the increase in the tax bite forward to consumers, then the pre-tax profits-to-sales ratio must rise to 14 percent to cover the increase in the firms' tax liabilities; the firms' selling prices will increase by less than one-half of 1 percent. If, instead, the profits-to-sales ratio is 20 percent, then the increase in the selling prices will be about 1 percent.

Now assume that the corporate tax rate is increased to 40 percent.

Note that the impact of the imposition of the corporate tax on the final selling price varies with the profits-to-sales ratio – the higher this ratio, the larger the impact. Profits-to-sales ratios vary by industry; within the United States, the average for many industries falls within the range of 2–6 percent. For firms with a 4 percent ratio, the impact of the introduction of a 50 percent tax – from a tax rate of zero – would raise the final selling price (again assuming all of the tax is passed forward to the consumer and that previously there had been no corporate income tax) by 4 percent.

Changing the corporate income tax rate is thus likely to have a modest effect on the competitive position of firms in different industries. Assume another extreme example – the corporate income tax rate is completely eliminated. Eventually, after a period of adjustment, firms would reduce the prices at which they sold their products, so their after-tax profits would be the same as the after-tax rate of return before the tax was eliminated. One consequence would be that reduction in final selling prices in industries with high profits-to-sales ratios would be larger than the price reductions in the industries in which these ratios are low; as a result the first group of industries would probably expand their sales relative to the second. A second consequence is that the ability of the most profitable firms in an industry to cut prices would be enhanced relative to the ability of the less profitable firms, and so the failure rate for these less profitable firms would increase.

impact of changes in the corporate tax rate on the prices of goods thus depends on how much of the tax is passed on in the form of higher prices and on whether there is any cost-reducing impact of associated government expenditures. Most economists believe that a substantial part of corporate tax is shifted forward to consumers, except perhaps for a brief interval after the tax rate is changed.

Corporate tax rates are likely to have a significant impact on international trade only if the tax rates are much higher in some countries than in others. The differences in corporate tax rates among industrial countries are generally smaller than 10 percentage points. For most industries, differences in tax rates can explain only a small part of the differences in selling prices among countries, except for a few industries in which the profits-to-sales ratios are very high. Much of the pattern of international trade and investment reflects differences in real costs: bananas can be produced in Ecuador at a lower cost than in Chicago because nature has been more generous with the requisite climate and soil in Ecuador. But steel can be produced at a lower cost in Chicago, since the iron ore is near the Northern end of Lake Michigan and the coal is near the Southern end. The differentials in real costs attributable to the uneven beneficence of nature and variations in capital accumulation are much more significant in explaining national differentials in costs of production than differences in national tax rates.

An increase in corporate tax rate in a country, like an increase in wages, may affect its international competitive position in the short run; its economic position in the long run will be unaffected, for the exchange rate will change to offset the price-raising impact of higher taxes on the demand for domestic products. Assume that the corporate tax rate is increased from 30 percent to 40 percent, and that the profit-to-sales ratio *averages* ten percent. Then the average firm will increase the selling price for its goods by 1 percentage point – say from 100 to 101 – for the firm to have the same after-tax profits. Firms with high profit-to-sales ratios will increase their prices somewhat more, firms with low profit-to-sales ratios will increase their prices somewhat less.

Customers will respond to the increase in the average selling price by reducing their demand; the country's currency will depreciate. Depreciation by itself will tend to enhance competitiveness, and thus offset the impact of the higher domestic prices. The competitive position of some firms may improve and than of other firms may worsen, but the overall impact on the country is not likely to be economically significant. True, if national cost structures become more nearly similar then differences among national tax systems will become increasingly important. The reduction of any barrier to mobility of goods and capital would make the differences in national tax systems more significant: the search for low-tax jurisdictions would be more intense. Increased attention would undoubtedly be given to tax harmonization and tax coordination among governments, so as to minimize shifts in productive activities among jurisdictions. Inevitably, international arrangements would be established to harmonize national tax structures and prevent competitive tax practices.

Taxes on foreign income

Tax collectors have a voracious appetite. They continually hunt for new sources of revenue. So they tax firms and individuals on a wide range of their domestic activities. In some countries, they tax firms and individuals on their foreign income. The US government taxes the US income of foreign firms and foreign citizens, much as if they were domestic residents. The US branches and subsidiaries of foreign firms calculate their tax liability to Uncle Sam using the US definition of income and the US tax rates. The US government also taxes the foreign income of US firms and US citizens, much as if they were domestic residents. The income of the foreign subsidiaries of US firms becomes an effective US tax liability only when the subsidiaries pay a dividend to their US parents. (The incomes of the foreign branches of US firms become an effective US tax liability when the incomes are earned – which means that there is an incentive to organize the foreign activity as a subsidiary when it becomes profitable.) These firms and individuals have almost certainly paid taxes to the governments of the countries in which they earned this income; the US taxpayers then receive a credit against their US tax liability for foreign income taxes paid, as long as the foreign tax rate is not above the US tax rate. Because of this credit foreign tax payments reduce domestic tax liabilities on a dollar-for-dollar basis. Many foreign governments follow the same approach; occasionally governments, especially in the developing countries, may give tax concessions so that foreign investors are spared paying domestic taxes for 5 or 10 years; some of these concessions are known as 'tax holidays'. These tax holidays are significant only if the U.S firm can find some way to shield the foreign income from the US tax authority

The US Treasury participates in bilateral tax treaties with many foreign governments; these treaties provide that the total tax payments to both governments will not be higher if the higher of the two tax rates is applied. No government attempts to tax the foreign income of nonresidents, except insofar as they buy domestically produced products and pay the tax that is implicit in the prices of these products. The opportunity to delay the tax payments on foreign income, known as tax deferral, is like an interest-free loan from the US Treasury to the firm. In effect, the right to delay this tax payment means that the effective tax rate on foreign income is below the posted tax rate. At an interest rate of 10 percent, a tax liability of $100 has a present value of $50 if the payment to the US Treasury can be delayed for seven years. The combination of tax deferrals and tax havens like Zug provide firms with attractive and flexible opportunities. Thus, the profitable foreign subsidiaries of a US firm might be tiered – organized as the subsidiaries of a Swiss or Bahamian subsidiary. Profits in high-tax countries could be diverted to subsidiaries based in tax havens, and the funds could in turn be invested in another subsidiary which is rapidly growing and needs additional funds. Transfer pricing can be used to divert profits to the tax haven; the taxes on these profits are then deferred.

A perennial issue is how to tax domestic residents with foreign income relative to domestic residents with domestic income. The equity approach is that domestic taxpayers should be taxed on the same basis, regardless of the source or type of their income. Domestic income and foreign income, earned income and unearned income, interest income on state and local securities and corporate dividends would all be taxed at the same effective rate.

It is hard to disagree with the general equity principle. But practical problems arise when the taxable foreign income must be defined. Is it foreign income before taxes are paid to the foreign tax collector, or is it after-tax income? If it is foreign income after taxes, what recognition should be given to foreign income taxes paid? An alternative to providing a credit for foreign taxes paid is to consider these tax payments as a deduction or cost in computing domestic tax liability: foreign tax payments of a dollar would reduce domestic tax liability by about 50 cents. In this case, the total taxes paid to the two tax authorities would be higher than if the credit approach were used. Foreign investment would thus be discouraged, and for two reasons. first, income on foreign investments would be taxed more heavily than income on domestic investments and, second, income earned by US firms in various foreign countries would be taxed more heavily than if the same income were earned by firms resident in this country. So the foreign affiliates of US firms would be at a tax disadvantage relative to their host-country competitors – and relative to firms headquartered in countries that follow a relaxed approach to the taxation of foreign income of domestic firms.

From the US point of view, it might seem desirable to discourage foreign investment, since the income accrues to the United States – both to the owners of the investment and to the US tax authorities – only after taxes have been paid abroad. In some cases the after-tax return to the United States might be larger than if the same funds had been invested in the United States; in most cases, however, the after-tax return on the foreign investments is likely to be below the before-tax return on domestic investment. But there may be a wash, since the same argument is likely to hold with respect to the US investments of foreign firms.

The US firms that invest overseas are not impressed with this logic; their own interests are best served by maximizing their profits on their after-tax income. From their point of view, when you've seen one tax collector, you've seen them all. Given that they must pay a given amount of tax, they are largely indifferent to whether they pay taxes to Uncle Sam or to his foreign colleagues. So the firms engage in a marketing campaign, stressing the favorable effect of their foreign investments on the US balance of payments and US foreign policy.

So there is an inevitable conflict in the design of international tax policy, depending on whose interest is to be served. The cosmopolitan or world economic welfare is served if investment funds are allocated between domestic and foreign alternatives on the basis of their pre-tax rates of return; the implication is that taxes on foreign income should be the same as those on domestic income. The national economic welfare is served only if the rates of return to the economy on foreign investment, after payment of foreign taxes, exceed the pre-tax return on domestic investment. From the firm's point of view, it should be sufficient that it pays taxes to the countries in which it operates; there should be no residual tax liability to US authorities. From the point of view of US taxpayers, the taxes on foreign income should be the same as on domestic income; if foreign tax rates are lower than US rates, then an additional tax is due the US Treasury.

Taxes on money

Kings in medieval times had a simple technique for raising money. They filled a leather bag with gold coins and shook the bag vigorously. The edges of the coins began to wear away, and gold dust began to collect in the bag. The gold dust was then sent to the mint for manufacture into new coins – and the coins which had been in the bag continued to circulate at their face value. In effect, the king was taxing the holders of gold coins by shaving their commodity value. Sovereigns have been taxing the holders of money ever since.

Currently, sovereigns are more sophisticated in their approach to taxing banks: they provide banks with a monopoly position by limiting entry into the banking business, and then they tax the monopoly profits in the form of the requirement that the banks hold reserves at the central bank in the form of a non-interest-bearing deposit; so the income of banks is lower. (See Chapter 16 for a discussion of competition among banks.) As a consequence, borrowers pay higher interest rates on their loans than if competition were more extensive. Similarly, depositors receive lower interest rates and a smaller supply of 'free' services than if banks competed more aggressively for deposits. Bank profits are higher than they would be if banking were a competitive industry with unimpeded entry of new firms.

The 'excess' profits resulting from barriers to entry are 'taxed' by requirements that banks hold certain assets – usually government securities or deposits – at the central bank. For example, US commercial banks must hold from 3 to 18 percent of their assets as deposits in the Federal Reserve System; they earn no interest on these deposits. Without such a requirement, these commercial banks would have more income-earning assets, and the banks' revenues would be greater, and higher revenues would permit the bank to pay higher interest rates on deposits. So the banks would gain in the first instance; however most of these gains would then be competed away and be received by depositors.

The significance of this implicit tax on banks' earnings depends on the proportion of bank assets invested in non-interest-bearing funds and on the interest rates available on other assets. Assume the Federal Reserve requires that US banks hold 14 percent of their assets in non-interest-bearing reserves or deposits while the Bank of England has a similar requirement of 4 percent; assume also that the average interest rate on bank assets in both countries is 10 percent. The revenues of commercial banks in Great Britain are 10 percent higher than those in the United States – so the interest rates paid depositors might be

10 percent higher. If US banks pay an average interest rate of 6 percent to their depositors, those in Great Britain can pay 6.60 percent and still be no worse off. If commercial banks hold non-interest-paying deposits in the central bank, the central bank in effect receives a loan from these banks on which it pays no interest. And so the central bank can then lend the funds to the government at a low interest rate, since it has no need for interest income.

The system has some of the characteristics of a Rube Goldberg device. Restrictions on entry into banking produce monopoly profits for the commercial banks; the central bank then taxes these producers of money. In the United States, commercial banks increase their reserves or deposits at the Federal Reserve by selling US government securities. And the Federal Reserve in effect buys these securities. So the interest paid by the Treasury on the US government securities owned by the Federal Reserve is subsequently returned by the Fed to the US government. In recent years, this payment has exceeded $15 billion.

Differences among countries in the way banks are taxed might have a significant impact on the competitive strength of banks in different countries. What remains to be determined is their impact in intensifying or neutralizing the competitive advantages of banks in different countries in the international marketplace.

Tax anything that can't move

The first axiom for the fiscal authorities is to bury each tax so that it isn't visible to the taxpayer. The second axiom is to tax heavily the incomes and transactions of those taxpayers who aren't readily mobile – and by implication to tax lightly the incomes and transactions of mobile taxpayers.

As costs of communication decline, the costs of mobility decline. The pressures will be increasingly intense to harmonize tax rates – and, indeed, tax codes – within the European Union. Similarly there will be pressures to unify tax codes within the various states in America. Tax harmonization is likely to mean pressures to reduce taxes in the high-tax countries and states.

17
Banking on the Wire

Q: Why are Swiss bankers rich?
A: They compete against Swiss bankers.

Banking competition

A revolution is hitting commercial banks. The technology of money payments is changing; the transfer of pieces of paper as parts of the money payments is being replaced by transmission of electronic impulses and computer tapes. As a result, the geographic scope of banking markets is increasing; formally protected regional markets are increasingly subject to competition from banks headquartered in other countries and areas. The effectiveness of national cartels in limiting competition among banks is declining. In the 1960s, US banks expanded rapidly abroad; in the late 1970s and 1980s, foreign banks and especially banks headquartered in Japan became extremely aggressive in the US markets for deposits and loans.

Consider – you have an ATM (Automatic Teller Transfer Machine) card – a card that lets you obtain cash and make deposits at the local supermarket or at the airport or at almost any bank. Now you need no longer choose a bank because it has a branch or office near where you live or where you work. You can use your ATM card to obtain cash when you're in a foreign country, often in that country's currency. Most readers of this book in the 1990s are likely to have an ATM card; few readers in the early 1970s had such cards. An ATM card means you can obtain cash at more than 60,000 locations in the United States – and tens of thousands of locations in various foreign countries.

Traditionally, the domestic banking market in each country was protected from foreign competitors by the high costs that foreign banks encountered in establishing branches on someone else's turf. Moreover, the difficulty of operating in foreign currencies deterred expansion abroad. And regulation, informal as well as formal, has limited expansion of banks into foreign countries.

Banking has been a highly regulated industry; initially these regulations were adopted to protect depositors against loss because the banks miscalculated. Commercial banks have been required to hold reserves in their central banks. Ceilings have been placed on the interest rates they can pay on different types of deposits. Banks have been required to hold certain types of assets and have been prohibited from owning other types of assets. Bank loans to any one customer have been limited to a small fraction of the capital of the banks. And their loans to all customers are limited to a given multiple of their capital. Regulation was originally intended to protect the small savers from losses they might incur if the banks in which they held deposits were to close; depositors lost $2 billion when banks closed in the Great Depression of the 1930s. Regulation is also designed to protect the economy from the collapse of the banking system.

Measures adopted to limit bank failure constrained competition among banks. So regulation has helped the less efficient banks to be more profitable than they otherwise would have been in a more competitive environment. Regulation constrains the growth of the more efficient banks and their ability to increase their market share.

Branching/acquisitions

Competition among banks based in different countries takes several forms. More than 50 US banks once had branches in London, primarily to sell US dollar deposits and buy dollar loans; these banks were generally willing to sell deposits and buy loans in the German mark, the Swiss franc, and a few other foreign currencies. A few of these London branches do a significant business in British pounds in competition with British banks. Indeed, if regulations were changed so that US dollar transactions in London were forbidden, most of the US banks that still have London offices would close them. Similarly, if US banks were prohibited from selling dollar deposits and making dollar loans outside the United States, the number of branches of US banks in Luxembourg, the Bahamas, Singapore, Panama, and other offshore centers would decline sharply. Three US banks would retain large numbers of overseas branches; a few more would have branches in the major foreign financial centers.

British, Swiss, and Japanese banks have opened offices in New York, Chicago, and San Francisco. Lloyd's Bank bought first Western Bank & Trust in California. European-American Bank, owned by a consortium of six banks in six European countries, acquired Franklin National Bank; subsequently European-American was acquired by ABN–AMRO, the leading Dutch bank. ABN–AMRO has been extremely aggressive in expanding its banking activities in the Mid-West and is one of the largest banks in the United States. National Westminster Bank has bought National Bank of North America in New York. Hong Kong & Shanghai Banking has acquired Marine Midland and then Republic National in New York (as well as Midland in Great Britain). The branch system of Bankers Trust in New York was sold to the Bank of Montreal, Bank Leumi (Israel), and Barclays. Mitsubishi Bank bought the Bank of California. Bank of Montreal acquired Harris Bank and Trust in Chicago.

US banks have also purchased shares in foreign banks. And when the establishment of branch offices or the purchase of shares in banks abroad has been prohibited or constrained, foreign customers have been invited to do business in the bank's home office or in a convenient regional office. Thus Canadian nationalism has constrained US banks from competing aggressively by limiting their market share, but those Canadian individuals and firms who desire less costly banking services than those available in Montreal and Toronto have been welcome in New York and in Chicago.

Entry into foreign markets by branching or acquisition enables aggressive banks to circumvent the regulations of the national authorities that limit their growth in their domestic markets. Many commercial banks have sought to grow rapidly, in part because they believe their profits increase with size and in part because they may be on an ego trip. Every central bank, however, directly limits the growth of commercial bank liabilities denominated in its currency – and hence the growth in commercial bank assets – to limit inflation. The upper limit to monetary expansion may be 6, 10, or 20 percent a year, but at each moment every central bank has a limit. So an individual bank within a country can grow more rapidly than banks as a whole only if it can increase its share of the domestic market; if it succeeds, the market share of some other banks must decline. Aggressive banks expand into new or ancillary businesses that produce fee income – ownership of mutual funds, travel, leasing, and computer services. Banks trade government bonds and foreign exchange. And they can seek to penetrate the domestic banking market in some foreign countries, either by setting up branches near the foreign customers or by attracting foreign customers to their home offices. An aggressive bank is likely to expand abroad, for the costs of obtaining customers in a market which it has not previously entered are likely to be smaller than the costs of increasing its share of the domestic market.

Changes in technology

Changes in the technology of money payments are affecting the structure of the banking industry, just as the shift from propeller craft to jets altered the structure of the airline industry. Expanding into foreign markets is becoming progressively easier as changes in the technology of the payments process reduce the costs of economic distance between the banking offices and their customers and their potential customers. As more and more payments are made by electronic funds transfer, the market areas in which an individual bank can compete is being enlarged because the costs of moving money are declining sharply. To the extent banks in some countries are more efficient or have other competitive advantages – perhaps because they have a cost advantage – they are likely to increase their share of the world market for bank deposits and bank loans.

What banks produce

Most firms have a highly visible product – General Motors produces Cadillacs and Chevrolets and Saturns, AT&T produces telephone services, IBM produces mainframe computers and personal computers. But confusion surrounds what banks actually produce, partly because the product is not visible and partly because the banks, when they sell their products, 'pay' interest to their depositors.

Depositors and borrowers

Basically, a commercial bank produces demand deposits and time deposits; the bank 'sells' deposits in exchange for cash. The cash received from the sale of a deposit enables the bank to buy loans, mortgages, bonds, and securities, each of which carries an interest income. Banks also have numerous other activities for which they receive fixed-fee payments: they rent safe-deposit boxes, sell bonds and stocks, and manage trusts. But the bread-and-butter activity for most banks – and much of the jam – involves selling demand and time deposits and buying loans.

Banks deal with two groups of customers, depositors and borrowers. (The terms 'depositors' and 'investors' are close synonyms.) These roles overlap – virtually every borrower is also a depositor, and some depositors are also borrowers. Business firms tend to be predominantly borrowers and households tend to be primarily depositors. Banks are intermediaries or brokers between the depositors who want a safe, secure, and convenient place to store some of their wealth, and borrowers, who want to expand their current production or consumption more rapidly than they can on the basis of their current wealth and income. The spread or markup between the interest rates that banks pay depositors and the interest rates they charge borrowers covers their costs and is the major source of their income.

Profits in banking

Profits in banking depend on three factors: marketing skills in selling deposits, investment skills in buying loans and other types of assets, and skills managing the enterprise. Since selling deposits by paying higher interest rates – that is, through price competition – is usually limited by the authorities – or, in many countries, by a gentlemen's arrangement among the banks, – banks often compete by offering toasters, TV sets and pretty checks as bonuses when they seek to sell deposits and by providing assurances about their safety and stability. The skill of a bank in selling deposits determines how rapidly the bank can grow.

Investment skills involve matching the yields on loans, mortgages, and other securities with the risks of each of these securities – both the risk of default and the risk that the price of the security may change. Within each economy, riskier loans and securities usually offer higher returns. Banks – at least the successful ones – seek those securities that offer the highest return for the risk – or, alternatively, the lowest risk for the return. The banks that are best able to determine which securities are underpriced relative to their risks earn the highest profits. And the more profitable banks are better able to increase the interest rates they pay on deposits, so they can grow more rapidly.

In many ways, commercial banks are like other financial intermediaries – mutual savings banks, savings and loan (S & L) associations, even life insurance companies. Each sells its liabilities to the public and uses the money obtained to buy loans, securities, and other income-earning assets. From the point of view of households, owning the liabilities of each type of institution is one way to store wealth. A life insurance policy, a pension, or a passbook deposit are the symbolic forms of wealth; the wealth is the financial claim on the institution.

Thus, the loss of the policy or passbook does not lead to any loss in wealth, for the institution will issue a replacement policy or passbook.

Commercial banks differ from other financial intermediaries in one important way, however: their demand deposit or checking account liabilities are used in payments and hence are considered money. Money – by definition – is transferred to pay for the purchase of goods and services and securities, and to settle debts. As a group, banks operate the payments mechanism, which provides for the transfer of money. Checks are messages or signals from depositors to their banks to transfer ownership of part of the bank deposit to whoever's name follows the phrase 'Pay to the order of.' The check is the symbolic form of money, but not the money itself; the money is the bank liability or deposit.

Banks generally pay much higher interest rates on time deposits than on demand deposits. Selling demand deposits thus would appear to be more profitable than selling time deposits, since interest rates are lower. In fact, however, banks incur substantially higher costs in managing their demand deposits, for they must process billions of checks and shift money from the payers' to the payees' banks; these costs are so high that the sale of demand deposits is only marginally more profitable than the sale of time deposits.

The payments mechanism

The bank's market area

In the early nineteenth century, the major product of banks was bank notes – engraved prettified pieces of paper that were promises to pay the bearer in lawful money. Each bank produced its own distinctive notes; the countryside was full of competing bits of paper. Industrial states chartered banks to finance the building of roads, canals, and railroads. The payments process involved the transfer of bank notes in hand-to-hand circulation. The market area for each bank was limited to its immediate vicinity, largely because individuals lacked confidence in the value of notes issued by banks in distant locations, and so they were reluctant to accept these notes. If a bank failed, the notes issued by it would become worthless. Firms and individuals in Chicago were reluctant to accept New York bank notes, because they were wary about the credit standing of banks 700 miles away. Banks in New York were even more reluctant to accept notes issued by Chicago banks. Indeed, bank notes frequently sold below their face value in distant cities; thus a $1 note issued by a New York bank might sell for 95 cents in the Chicago market, while $1 bank notes issued by banks in Chicago might sell for 90 cents in New York. Since the transport costs of money were relatively high, the price of the notes varied inversely with the distance from home office of the bank that produced them. The discount below the face value reflected the risk that buyers were taking on both the legitimacy of the note and the financial standing of the bank that issued it.

The size of the market area of each bank was limited by the costs that potential borrowers and lenders incurred in dealing with it: the time and financial inconvenience of dealing with a bank located in a distant city was higher than those in dealing with a nearby bank. Some banks, especially in the smaller cities and country towns, had a neighborhood monopoly: no other bank was within convenient walking – or riding – distance.

Checks and branching

When checks began to replace bank notes as a means of payment in the latter part of the nineteenth century, the market area of banks expanded. Checks had several advantages over bank notes. One piece of paper could be used for large payments and for payments of odd amounts. The money transfer process was less risky; the theft of checks, unlike the theft of notes, involved little risk, for payment on the check could be stopped. Checks could safely be sent through the mail; so the transport costs for checks were much lower than the transport costs for bank notes. Hence the use of checks facilitated transactions between buyers and sellers separated by great distances. The increased use of checks coincided with the development of a comprehensive railroad system and improvements in the postal systems. The decline in transport costs associated with the expansion of the railroad system also enlarged the size of the market area for goods, so individuals had more occasions to pay firms and individuals located at greater distances.

By bringing depositors and borrowers from various locales into the expanding market area of a large number of more distant banks, the change in the technology of payments reduced the monopoly position of each local neighborhood bank. The size of the market was limited by the speed and efficiency of the check transfer process and by the costs of acquiring information about distant banks. Of course, borrowers still found personal contact with their bankers useful and, at times, necessary, for loans had to be negotiated in person, and so bankers found it convenient to stay in their offices to meet borrowers. But even then, the loan negotiations could occur elsewhere – in the borrower's office, or on the golf course.

Banks began to develop branches as checks replaced notes. Large banks are more efficient than small banks because there are economies of scale in the basic banking functions – selling deposits, buying loans and other securities, and operating the payments mechanism. Processing the flow of checks within one institution is less costly than moving these checks among numerous institutions. And branching enables banks to marry offices located in residential and suburban areas, which primarily serve depositors, with those in downtown areas, which primarily serve borrowers. As business firms expanded rapidly and became concentrated in fewer and fewer cities, the demand for large loans from banks increased sharply. In the growing industrial centers, business firms wanted to borrow much more money than banks in the vicinity of their offices could lend on the basis of local deposits. Banks located near these firms found that the business demand for loans exceeded their lending capacity. Households, in contrast, were spread over a larger residential area. Banks within the residential areas frequently received more money in deposits from households than they could readily lend in their local area. A mechanism was needed so that the money received from the sale of the deposits of banks in residential neighborhoods could be available for loans in business areas. Banks in residential areas could simply lend money to banks in business areas, or banks from each area might merge to internalize the transfer of funds within one firm. The growth of branch banks suggests that internalization was more efficient.

Electronic banking

The move to electronic banking means that checks – and paper – will no longer be used in the money-transfer process. With the electronic transfer of funds, when Joe Doe wishes to pay his electric utility bill or his taxes, he will signal his bank by instructions on his personal computer, which will be connected to the computers in the bank. Doe will call the bank, then enter his social security number, his bank account number, his Personal Identification Number (PIN) to prevent the misuse of his account by someone else (the coded number serves the same function as the signature on a check), a number that represents the account of the electric utility to be paid, and the amount of the payment. A synthesized voice will repeat this information to Doe. The signal will then go to the computer in Doe's bank and from there to the computer in the utility's bank; these computers are linked electronically.

Much of this system is already in place. The banks already have machine tellers that accept deposits and distribute cash; a plastic card and a four-, six- or nine-digit code enables depositors to obtain cash in the evening and on weekends and at other times when the bank is closed. When the bank is open, the automatic tellers are like an express line at the supermarket; customers with simple transactions process themselves quickly. Cash can readily be drawn against the overdraft limits on Mastercard and Visa and other credit cards. These consoles are now usually located at the doorstep of the bank – and increasingly they are being placed in supermarkets and at airports and in shopping centers.

The electronic banking system has several advantages. Postage costs are avoided. The transfer process is instant: there is no delay between sending and receiving funds. The monthly or weekly balancing of checkbooks is redundant; Doe can determine the balance whenever he dials a particular number. And there is no equivalent of a bad check; if Doe wants to pay Roe $100 and has only $50 in his account, the computer balks. The printing, transfer, and identification of billions of pieces of paper becomes outmoded.

Wire transfers mean that many traditional credit cards will be replaced by debit cards. When John Doe fills up his car at the corner gas station or checks out of his motel room, his use of the debit card sends a signal to the bank, and payment will be made immediately, regardless of the time of day or the day of the week. Bankers may work from 9 to 3, but computers work around the clock.

Individuals who make relatively few payments will continue to use checks. And notes and coins will still be used for small payments. But those who make a large number of payments will find the electronic system less costly and more convenient. Electronic banking will further enlarge the market area for deposits beyond national boundaries. The distance between the customer and the bank will be irrelevant. The neighborhood becomes the world. Banks headquartered in New York will advertise in Frankfurt for mark deposits and loans, while banks headquartered in Frankfurt will compete for New York deposits and loans. Banks will be able to attract foreign customers without the cost of establishing offices abroad. Canadians will be able to bank as easily in Chicago or New York as in Toronto.

Competition among international banks

Banking has been an international industry for centuries. The Rothschilds and the Fuggers were extended families with banking offices in several different countries; however, they were essentially investors rather than producers of money. In the latter part of the nineteenth century, British banks established foreign branches to finance the overseas trade and investment of firms based in London and Liverpool. But these branches were primarily set up in the outposts of the empire which were poorly served by domestic banks. Thus, relatively few branches of British banks were established in the United States, for British firms could use US banks. Similarly, US banks, when they began to go overseas in the early years of this century, followed US business primarily to Argentina, Brazil, and other areas not adequately served by existing banks.

In recent years, the motive for overseas expansion has shifted. Initially, a handful of New York, Chicago, and San Francisco banks followed US firms to Europe, competing for the foreign business of these firms in the hope of gaining more of their US banking business. The expansion of the overseas branch networks of the three largest US banks – Citibank, Bank of America, and Chase Manhattan – was especially rapid. The sudden increase in the number of US banks with branches abroad was partly a defensive response by the first US banks that went overseas; the Chicago banks moved abroad to protect their established relationships with various US firms from the competitive threat posed by the New York banks that were already operating abroad. In 1960 about eight US banks had 130 foreign branches. By 1980, 126 US banks had nearly 1000 foreign branches. In the 1990s, some US banks closed their foreign branches, especially in the smaller financial centers.

Over the same period, more than 50 foreign banks set up branches in the United States, nearly all in New York. These banks wanted to participate directly in the largest financial market in the world; their direct interest was retaining the US business of their domestic customers – and to attract some US customers.

US banks operating abroad and foreign banks operating in the United States share a common problem: they lack the deposit base essential to providing them with the funds to make loans. They can borrow these funds from their home offices, they can borrow in the interbank money market, and they can borrow from the offshore market. And they do all three. If they have the deposits, they can buy the loans. In the loan market, both borrowers and banks are mobile; major US banks, once limited by legislation against branching in other states, set up loan production offices in major cities across the country.

Many countries have been reluctant to admit foreign banks, because they wanted to protect the domestic banks from the challenges of foreign competitors. Thus, Norway and Denmark traditionally did not permit foreign banks to establish branches. At one time Peru and Chile closed the local branches of foreign banks, and Venezuela applied discriminatory legislation. For years, US banks found it impossible to establish branches in Mexico. (Mexican policy was reversed when the Mexican banks incurred large loan losses and became severely undercapitalized.) Even when a US bank establishes a branch abroad, the price is often a commitment that the bank will not compete actively for domestic business. As a result, most of the Tokyo branches of US banks have been only modestly profitable.

Such attempts by governments to protect their own banks from having to compete with the local branches of foreign banks will become increasingly irrelevant. The move to electronic banking, by reducing the importance of national boundaries as a limit to the size of the market, will diminish the need to establish foreign branches. With electronic banking, instructions to make payments will be handled over the wire. Thus, banks outside Switzerland, for example, can deal in Swiss francs on the same terms as banks inside Switzerland – perhaps on even more favorable terms.

Money havens will follow the tax havens. The computers may be placed in the Cayman Islands or Bermuda, or some other safe offshore banking center; the terminals attached to this computer will be next to the phone. When face-to-face contact between the bank and the customer are necessary, the bank will send a representative to the customer's office. As the effective size of the market increases, some banks whose domestic markets had been protected will find themselves subject to more intense competitive challenges from foreign banks.

The competitive edge

The speed of the shift to electronic banking on an international scale is unpredictable. Assume, however, that the system is in place next Monday morning. Some banks will compete vigorously to maintain or enhance their share of the world market for deposits and loans, and several will succeed in increasing market share. Others will lose market share. Whether an individual bank is in the first group will depend partly on how efficient and competitive it has been in the domestic context.

In this new international market, US banks will have three advantages: size, efficiency, and identification with a money that is at the top of the currency hit parade. Not only is size important in making very large loans, but it also confers a competitive marketing advantage, for depositors often equate safety with size. In the credit crunch of 1974, and again in 1982, the competitive positions of the largest US banks improved relative to those of smaller ones; investors reasoned that the Federal Reserve might permit the 20th largest US bank to fail, but it was quite unlikely that the Fed would permit any of the 10 largest US banks to close, and impose losses on depositors. And the largest US banks are generally bigger than most of their foreign competitors, with the exception of banks headquartered in Japan.

Changes in the ranking of banks in the size hit parade frequently reflect mergers. Banks in Europe – and, to a lesser extent, Japan – have merged in response to the competitive threat posed by US banks. In Great Britain, Barclays (the largest bank) merged with Martin's Bank, while Westminster and National Provincial combined into National Westminster. Lloyd's has merged with the Trustee Savings Bank. In Canada, the Royal Bank and the Bank of Montreal are merging. In Belgium, Banque Lambert, the fourth in size, merged with Banque de Bruxelles, the second largest. In the Netherlands, the number 2 and number 3 banks have merged. Yet, by international standards, the largest banks in many European countries are still relatively small. The entire Belgian banking system is smaller than Citibank. If European banks want to be as large as one of the three or four leading US banks, they will almost certainly have to merge across national borders. But national differences in ownership and regulatory structures make such mergers extremely difficult – although they should become easier as banking regulation is made at the regional level in Brussels.

US banks are probably more efficient than those in most foreign countries – a result of the greater competition in the banking markets in the United States. More banks compete for deposits and for loans in most markets, except those in the smaller cities and towns. There are nearly 10,000 banks in the United States, more than in the rest of the world combined. The large number of US banks reflects the nineteenth-century populist fear of centralized money trusts, which led to prohibitions against branching across state lines, branching across county lines in Indiana, and for many years branching across the street in Chicago. The reason US banks are both more numerous and larger is that the US economy is such a large part of the financial world. There are more financial assets in the United States *per capita* than in any other country. Demand deposits in Chicago exceed those in all of France

Since restrictions on branching constrain US banks from expanding geographically and setting up branches in other states, other means are used to attract customers. The contrast between the relatively uninhibited growth of US business, both nationally and internationally, and the sharp restrictions on the domestic expansion of US banks has forced them to become innovative and adaptive. Many of the US banks headquartered in one of the Eastern cities attract deposits from and make loans to firms headquartered on the West coast. Similarly, the market for bank loans and deposits in New York includes banks headquartered in Newark, Boston, Pittsburgh, Chicago, and Los Angeles. New York banks participate in the Chicago market. Competition has prevailed, despite the earlier regulations against interstate banking; the result is that US banks in the major cities have been more fully subject to competitive pressures than banks headquartered in most foreign countries.

One measure of bank efficiency is provided by the spread between the average price the banks pay on their deposit liabilities and the average price they receive on their loans – that is, by the markup between the interest rates the banks pay on deposits and the interest rates they receive on loans. Within a country, competition ensures that spreads among banks are similar; significant differences in markups are not sustainable, otherwise, the banks with larger spreads would lose deposits, and their share of the market, to more efficient banks. Among countries, however, spreads tend to differ: they tend to be larger – in some cases, substantially larger – in Continental Europe than in the United States. The differences among countries are sustainable only as long as the national market is protected from external competition; gradually, banks in the countries with the higher markups will lose their share of the market.

In this new worldwide market, banks based in countries where larger spreads prevail will be under great competitive pressure. If, in order to hold deposits, they offer higher interest rates to depositors while their spreads remain unchanged, their minimal lending rate will be so high that the least risky domestic borrowers will seek funds at foreign banks, which will be charging lower interest rates. If, instead, they set rates on loans competitive with those charged by foreign banks, then their deposit rates will fall below those paid by banks that operate with smaller spreads. They may try to reduce their spreads, but to do so they must pay lower wages or induce their employees to work harder, or find some magical approach to become more efficient.

Some banks will discriminate by charging a different set of interest rates to those customers who have more attractive opportunities abroad. But such price shading can be only a partial response to the problems raised by the higher costs of European banks. In the final analysis, either costs will be cut or the less efficient banks will lose market share.

The second advantage of US banks in the new international market is that their domestic currency – the US dollar – is likely to remain the preferred currency brand name. Indeed, the share of world banking business denominated in the US dollar may increase relative to the share denominated in most foreign currencies. This currency preference provides US banks with a competitive advantage, for if depositors prefer dollar-denominated deposits, many will also prefer that these deposits be issued by US banks. Combined with their lower costs, US-owned banks are likely to end up with a larger share of the world market for deposits.

Banking is generally viewed as a sensitive industry, because banks both produce financial wealth and operate the money payments mechanism. Governments are wary of allowing a substantial part of the banking services demanded by their residents to be supplied by foreign banks. If banks in a country are largely foreign-owned, or even if the larger customers of the banks have ready access to foreign banks, then the effectiveness of national regulation and of national monetary policies will seem threatened. Efforts will be made to limit the access of foreign banks to domestic borrowers and lenders, measures that will counter the thrust toward an open international economy.

18

Zeros, Swaps, and Options – The Revolution in Finance

A hole in the hedge

Orange County, California, one of the richest in the United States, sits on the Pacific Coast, and abuts Los Angeles to the North and San Diego to the South. The county is one of the politically most conservative in the United State – strong voter sentiment for larger military expenditures (lots of retired naval officers live there), a balanced budget, sending illegal immigrants home, limiting tax increases, and reducing the size of the government.

The new world of finance

In December 1994 Orange County went bankrupt as a result of the efforts by its chief financial officer to increase the rate of return on the county's portfolio by several sophisticated financial transactions. One was the use of leverage: borrowing short-term funds and using the borrowed monies to buy longer-term securities that carried higher interest rates (which meant that Orange County increased its interest income by the excess of interest rates on long-term securities over the interest rates on the borrowed short-term money funds). Another was the purchase of esoteric financial instruments that had been invented only a few years earlier.

The losses incurred by Orange County amounted to $1.6 billion. Since there are about 4 million people in the county, the losses *per capita* amounted to $400. Not small change. There may or may not be a relationship between the wealth of Orange County, its voting preferences, and the losses. A cynic might say that this was an expensive way for a conservative citadel to learn that 'there's no such thing as a free lunch.' It may take longer to learn this lesson in a rich county than in a poor one. In previous years when interest rates on US dollar securities had been declining, Orange County had increased the return on its portfolio from the use of leverage. The decline in long-term interest rates meant that the prices of long-term bonds were rising, so Orange County benefitted from both the capital gains and the excess of interest rates on long-term securities over the interest rates paid on the borrowed short-term funds. 1994 was not an especially comfortable year for investors, for interest rates increased quite rapidly – which meant that the prices of long-term bonds declined sharply, so much so that the capital losses from the decline in their prices was much greater than the excess of long-term over short-term interest rates.

It's probable that the additional returns that Orange County realized from this strategy in the 1993 and earlier years had been larger than the losses incurred in 1994. So the strategy had been profitable over an extended period. But the additional income from these earlier years had been spent, and wasn't available to forestall the move into bankruptcy court.

Orange County had good company in taking a bath in the new world of finance. Gibson Greeting Cards incurred losses of $20 million on its purchases of some esoteric securities from Bankers Trust in New York; Gibson was not pleased by the loss and claimed it was led astray by the sophisticated Wall Street city slickers. Gibson filed a lawsuit claiming it was the victim; there was an out-of-court settlement. Procter & Gamble (some might say aptly named) was reported to have lost $120 million following the guidance of the same city slickers. Piper Jaffray of Minneapolis was one of the small city slickers and its investment managers lost millions of the hard-earned money of the widows and orphans of the Twin Cities in what was supposed to be a conservatively managed money market fund. Baring Brothers one of the oldest investment banks in London reported a loss of $1.4 billion as a result of transactions by a rogue trader in Singapore who had been dealing in option contracts; because of this large loss, the firm was forced out of business.

In August and September 1998 the various hedge funds – supposedly the most sophisticated investors around – reported their recent investment results. George Soros' Quantum Fund reported losses of $2 billion on its various Russian-related investments. Long Term Capital Management in Greenwich, Connecticut – the whiz kids of finance with the most sophisticated computer models around – reported that it had lost about $2 billion of the $4 billion that it had had under management during August 1998; the firm indicated that was going to investors for additional funds and would reduce its management fees. Several weeks later the Federal Reserve arranged a $3 billion bailout by the lenders to Long Term Capital to delay or forestall the liquidation of its highly leveraged positions. Nomura Securities, the largest investment bank in Japan reported losses of more than $1 billion; a significant part of these losses were from activities in Russia and the emerging markets. Other investment banks and commercial banks with groups that mimic the trading activities of the hedge funds also reported large losses on their trading activities.

What are hedge funds?

The losses incurred by the hedge funds were so large that the name seems a bit of a misnomer. These funds generally combine the capital of their owner-managers with those of various large and wealthy private and institutional investors who seek above-average returns; the hedge funds then borrow additional money, often in the ratio of $9 or $10 of borrowed funds for each $1 of their own and investor capital. The managers of the hedge funds then invest in a wide variety of different financial instruments, often on margin. For example, if the hedge funds were to buy a commodity futures contract on the Chicago Board of Trade, or the Chicago Mercantile Exchange, or the London International Futures Exchange (LIFE), then they might be able to develop a $1 million position on the basis of a $50,000 cash investment. And $40,000 or $45,000 of this cash investment might have been borrowed; $10,000 or $5,000 of this investment would reflect the capital of the fund obtained from the manager-owners and their investors.

So the leverage of the funds – at least some of the funds – was extremely large. Long Term Capital is reported at one time to have had positions of $200 billion on its capital of $4 billion – leverage of 50: 1.

The name 'hedge fund' comes from the idea that the risks attached to the different assets in their portfolios are somewhat offsetting – in effect, the funds have diversified portfolios. For example a hedge fund might go long Italian government bonds and short German Government bonds in the belief that in the move to the Euro, the interest rates on these two bonds should converge: the interest rate on the Italian bonds would decline sharply and the interest rate on the German bonds would increase. Often the funds would seek profits from very small price movements – still, the product of a small number (a very small price movement) and a large number (the size of their position in these securities) can be a large number. In some cases, however, these funds were attracted by the high yields available on the stocks and bonds available in the emerging-market countries. A few hedge funds had gone broke prior to 1998. But many reported annual rates of return of 30 or 40 percent. So the owner-managers became very rich in a short period of time. And the high returns attracted lots of others who wanted a piece of the money machine. Obviously Bankers Trust, Piper Jaffray, Soros and Long Term Capital didn't set out to lose their clients' money – and, more importantly, their own. Indeed they almost certainly anticipated that their clients would profit from these transactions, so that their own incomes and reputations would be enhanced.

Sophisticated financial instruments are rather like the automated luggage system of the new airports in Denver and Hong Kong – if it's very new and very large, it's a good bet that initially it won't work quite the promised way.

Where do financial revolutions come from?

The decade of the 1980s was most exceptional in terms of the changes in financial arrangements, and particularly in the rapid increase in the number of new financial instruments – zero coupon bonds, futures contracts in foreign exchange, options on futures contracts in foreign exchange, collateralized mortgage obligations, foreign exchange swaps, interest rate swaps – the list goes on and on. The comprehensive buzz-word was *derivatives* – the meaning was clear, the new set of instruments were derived from, or based on, the traditional bonds, stocks, and foreign exchange.

Inflation and financial instruments

One factor behind the explosion in the growth of financial instruments was the sharp changes in the prices of stocks, bonds, and currencies in response to the acceleration of inflation rates in the 1970s and then the decline in inflation rates throughout the 1980s as a result of the contractive monetary policy adopted at the end of 1979. The large changes in the prices of these assets meant that the risk attached to the ownership of these assets increased sharply. So lots of banks and other financial institutions and individuals wanted the high yields attached to these securities, but also wanted some way to reduce their exposure to risk of large loss should the price of the securities decline. The risk was inherent in the system as long as interest rates were changing sharply; if some investors were successful in reducing their exposure to these price risks, then either their exposures would be offset by the mirror-image exposures of another group of investors, or these risks would be transferred to others more willing to carry them. The second factor was the continuing decline in the costs of information, attributable to remarkable developments in communications and personal computers, which meant that the costs of evaluating these risks and trading them also declined sharply. The third was the surge in business-school graduate specialists in finance, who became skilled in relating the prices of these instruments to their risks.

Debt, stock prices, and junk bonds

Moreover, the financial environment was changing sharply. There was an explosion in the growth of debt in the 1980s; US Treasury securities outstanding increased from $800 billion at the end of 1979 to $2900 billion at the end of 1989. The debt of most national governments increased at comparable rates; the major exception was the British government, which successfully reduced its debt, thanks in large part to receipts from privatizing a number of large government-owned firms such as British Airways and British Telecom. Household debt and corporate debt also increased rapidly in the United States, the increase in corporate debt resulting from the financing associated with massive leveraged buyouts. The privatization initiatives in many countries, and particularly in emerging-market countries like Mexico and Argentina resulted in a sharp increase in the number of stocks that could be traded.

There was a surge in stock prices, led in part by the increases in New York and in Tokyo; the Dow Jones index of equity prices increased by a factor of three in the 1980s, while the counterpart Nikkei 225 increased by a factor of more than six. (It's only a coincidence that the percentage increase in the Dow more or less matched the percentage increase in the US Treasury's debt.) Because the decade was identified with declines in inflation rates and in anticipated inflation rates, the prices of bonds generally were increasing – although bond prices in the United States declined sharply in 1987. The price of commercial real estate in many large cities in the United States and abroad surged, which led to construction booms in London, New York, Tokyo and Toronto; in some of these cities the supply of usable office space doubled. There was a explosive growth of 'junk bonds' – so-called because they had not been rated by the credit-rating agencies that customarily ranked the riskiness of individual bond issues. The king of junk bonds was Michael Milken who both 'invented' and developed the market for trading them; his success in selling these bonds boosted his firm Drexel Burnham close to the front rank of investment banks. Milken showed that the returns on these bonds were extremely high relative to the risk, and so the investors in these bonds would earn an 'excess return'. The end – and there always is an end – was that the junk bond market collapsed and the owners of these securities incurred large losses, which appear to have more than offset the higher interest rates they had earned in earlier years. Drexel went bankrupt and Milken was indicted by the US government on several different charges and spent several years in jail.

Financial engineering and securitization

'Financial engineering' was one of the buzzwords of the period. The firms in the financial services industry – the brokerage firms, the investment banks, the banks, even the life insurance companies – make a lot of money when they have new products to sell. Initially the profit rates for the firms that first developed the new products were high, before the followers and imitators had entered the market to increase market share by driving down returns. Milken became a billionaire as a result of his success with junk bonds.

One of the terms under the financial engineering banner was 'securitization', which involved a bank or some other firm taking a large number of somewhat similar types of securities – home mortgages, car loans, student loans, credit-card debt – and bundling them, which then became the basis for issuing a new security which might be attractive to particular investors. A pension fund might be interested in acquiring credit-card debt or car loans because the interest rates would be higher than on traditional securities; the pension fund would not have the facilities to manage the monthly collection of interest on these loans. So the bank that initially made the student loans or the auto loans would become an originator and a bundler, and it would invest its own monies as it arranged these loans into bundles that would be attractive to institutions that were willing to hold these securities for the long-term. Even after the bundles were sold, the bank might continue to service the loans – it would collect the monthly interest payments and forward the money to the pension funds. Securitization was made possible by the sharp reductions in the costs of collecting and organizing information and data. As a result relatively more money would flow into housing loans, auto loans and other types of loans that could be easily packaged.

The mirror image of bundling lots of $10,000 and $20,000 loans into a large loan was that a traditional security such as a $100,000 US

Treasury bond could be unbundled into a number of different securities. The traditional long-term bond issued by the US Treasury pays interest twice a year; the owner of the bond would be repaid the principal in 30 years. The security has 60 coupons; each coupon is like a dated check from the US Treasury, and provides for the payment of interest on a stipulated date, for example January 15 and July 15 during each of the next 30 years. The investors would frequently put their bonds in a safe deposit box at a bank and then visit the bank every six months to clip the interest coupon that represented the interest payment that was currently due; this coupon would then be deposited in the bank as if it were a check from the US Treasury.

The investment banks and the brokerage firms like Goldman Sachs and Merrill Lynch would buy these bonds and then 'strip them' – they would sell each of the interest payment coupons as a separate security. Similarly the 'corpus' of the bond – the body that stipulates the terms for the repayment of the principal – would also be sold as a separate security. So the 30-year bond would become 61 different securities – the first interest coupon, the second interest coupon, the third interest coupon, all the way to the 60th interest coupon; the corpus of the bond would be the 61st security. Each of these securities would be sold separately, although individual investors might buy several of them. The investment banks anticipated that the total revenues from selling the 61 separate securities (zeros) would be higher than the revenues from selling the bond with the attached coupons – and higher than the price they paid when they bought the bonds; otherwise why go through the activity of stripping the coupons?

The income to the investors that bought the zeros came from the difference between the low initial price they paid for them and the face value of the zero on the date that each interest coupon could be deposited.

Investors were attracted to zero coupon securities for one of several different reasons. Zeros provide an easy way to match the date when a payment will be made with a particular security. For example, a grandparent of a newly born child might buy a zero that would mature in 18 years, when the child might be expected enter college. Or a couple in the 50-year-old age cohort might buy a coupon that would mature in 20 years, soon after the date of their planned retirement. Moreover zeros were convenient; there was no need to go to the safe deposit vault to clip the interest coupon because the effective interest rate was built in to the general increase in the price of the bond on its journey to maturity. In addition, zeros provide a marvelous way for the investor to implicitly reinvest the interest income, which was especially attractive in a period when interest rates were high and expected to decline. Finally, for a while, the income attached to ownership of a zero was treated as a capital gain, and hence the tax payment would be delayed until the security was sold; subsequently the Internal Revenue Service ruled that each year's capital gain would be taxable even if the gain had not been realized.

Various corporations realized they could issue zero coupon bonds at somewhat lower interest rates than the traditional bonds; zeros provided an easy way to raise funds without an immediate cash outlay. When the bonds matured, someone else would have to worry about the source of the cash to pay the bondholders. Caveat emptor.

Index funds

One of the perennial questions in finance is whether 'stock pickers' can beat the market – whether over an extended period individuals and firms can choose a portfolio of stocks that will have a higher rate of return than 'the market.' Much of the finance industry is based on the view that there is a positive rate of return to picking stocks – thousands of analysts earn their living from seeking to outperform the market, and a few earn a very good living. The cynics would say that their high incomes reflect that the fact they have generated lots of commission income for their firms, and that the number of yachts owned by the clients of these firms should be compared with the number of yachts owned by the managers of the firms.

Some of the studies show that 50 percent or so of the mutual funds fail to achieve the average rate of return on the market as a whole. As a result of the combination of the skepticism about the skills of stock pickers and the low cost of computation, a new section of the financial services industry has developed that enables individuals to buy 'a share of the market.' These index funds mimic the market, they choose the stocks to buy based on the ratio of the market value of an individual firm like Exxon or GE to the market value of all stocks as a group. A big advantage of the index-fund approach is that transactions costs are much lower than those for the average mutual fund, in part because there is relatively little trading compared with the run-of-the-mill mutual fund. Research and administrative costs also are lower.

The index fund approach has been extended to different segments of the market. For example, a mutual fund might take the index approach to the 30 stocks included in the Dow Jones or the 100 largest firms or to the firms in a particular industry on a national or a global basis.

Swaps

Foreign currency swaps and interest rate swaps also were among the major new financial instruments developed in the 1980s. Consider first a foreign currency swap. Assume Lufthansa has bought a Boeing 747, with the part of the purchase price financed by the US Export–Import Bank (ExImbank); the loan terms entail semi-annual payments of principal and interest for the next eight years. So Lufthansa may conclude that it has a foreign exchange exposure in the US dollar. And the airline may take the view that it is in the business of moving individuals in slender aluminum tubes rather than in speculating in foreign exchange and so it may seek to reduce its foreign exchange exposure.

At the same time a number of US airlines have bought jets from the European consortium, Airbus; part of the purchase price was financed by borrowing from government-owned export credit agencies in Germany and in France – their counterparts of the US Export-Import Bank. The payment terms are likely to be similar, with the difference that the US airlines have to make semi-annual payments in German marks and French francs. These US airlines almost certainly wish to hedge their foreign exchange exposures.

The foreign exchange swap enables Lufthansa and the US airlines to offset their foreign currency exposures. Lufthansa enters into a foreign exchange swap with Deutsche Bank, or J.P. Morgan, or Bankers Trust, or National Westminster, or another of the top 30 commercial banks; Lufthansa is guaranteed the exchange rates at which the bank will convert German marks into US dollar for each of the two yearly payment dates over the next eight years. United Airlines enters into a mirror-image swap with the same bank; the bank guarantees the exchange rate at which United can obtain marks for dollars on the two annual payment dates for each of the next eight years. So each firm hedges its foreign exchange exposure with the bank, and the bank enters into two swaps that have mirror-image features. Provided the bank has done its homework correctly, the bank has incurred no foreign exchange exposure.

Swaps tend to have somewhat standard features. Payments tend to be twice a year. Maturities tend to be eight years. The swaps are quoted in nominal values, but the principal amounts are never swapped – only the effective interest payments. The banks as middlemen love the income that is the difference between the prices at which they buy and sell the payments in different currencies. The banks acquire two risks – there is the credit risk that one of the parties to the swap may go bankrupt and not be able to deliver the foreign exchange. (There is an asymmetry, in that the bankrupt firm may fulfill the swap if the swap is 'in the money' because the currency that it has agreed to purchase has risen in price above the price implicit in the swap contract.) And because of the inability of the firm to complete the contract, the bank may have a foreign exchange exposure.

Interest rate swaps share the same feature – the parties to the swap contract to exchange a set of future payments. Consider a typical saving and loan (S&L) association in the United States, which holds a number of fixed-interest rate 20- and 30-year mortgages; the interest rates on these mortgages cannot be changed during the life of the contract. In contrast, the interest rates on the deposit liabilities of these S&Ls change frequently. So the S&L has an interest rate risk; this S&L would enter into a swap contract to pay a fixed interest rate and to receive a floating interest rate as a way to reduce its exposure to interest-rate risk. The success of the S&L depends on the success of the banks as middlemen in finding a firm that would like to receive a floating interest rate and pay a fixed interest rate – the mirror-image of the payments and receipts of the S&L.

Some long-term lenders such as the World Bank are in this position. So each of these firms enters into a swap with a bank as a middleman. Both the foreign exchange swaps and the interest-rate swaps tend to reduce the risk of the participating firms.

Derivatives and options

One of the new products that had been developed extensively is the *option*; option contracts are readily available on bonds, stocks, and futures contracts in foreign exchange. Consider an option that John Doe buys when he is interested in buying a large house at the corner of Fifth Avenue and Main Street; the price of $300,000 is agreeable but he needs several weeks to tie up some loose ends before he fully commits to the purchase. So he pays the owner the property $2,500 for a 30-day option to buy the house at the $300,000 price. This option contract has three features – a money payment (the premium) from the buyer of the option to the seller (or writer) of the option, an expiration date (30 days), and the price that the owner of the option will pay the owner of the property if the option is exercised (the strike price).

Call options and put options

Call options on foreign exchange are one example of these new instruments. Assume that ABC Manufacturing believes that the German mark is going to increase in price in the foreign exchange market. ABC can buy German marks in the spot exchange market or it can buy German marks in the forward exchange market; if, instead, the German mark should decrease in price, then ABC will lose money. So ABC buys a call option on the German mark. ABC pays First National Bank a premium of $300 for the right to buy 50,000 German marks within three months at the price of 1.75 German marks per US dollar. In this case, if the German mark should depreciate, then ABC loses no more than the premium paid for the option. If, instead, the German mark appreciates above the strike price, then ABC exercises the option and receives the 50,000 marks at the strike price of 1.75 marks per dollar.

The seller of the call option often owns the German marks and is motivated by the premium received from ABC. Or the seller of the call option might believe that the German mark will depreciate, so there is little likelihood that it will be obliged to deliver German marks: the seller again is motivated by the premium income. (In the former case, the seller is writing a 'covered option' and in the second, the seller is writing a 'naked option'.)

Assume, instead, that ABC owns securities denominated in the German mark and is concerned that the mark might depreciate. To limit its losses, ABC could buy a put option on the German mark. ABC pays a premium to the seller of the put option; if the German mark should depreciate, then ABC delivers German marks to the seller of the put option at the strike price so its loss from the depreciation of the German mark is limited. The seller of the put option is motivated by the premium income. In some cases, the seller of the put option may have a short position in the German mark; in this case, the seller is hedged because the gain from the decline in the value of its short position will offset the loss from taking delivery of the German marks. In other cases, the seller may believe that the German mark is unlikely to depreciate, and so the seller writes a 'naked option.'

Call options and put options on the German mark are available with different maturity dates and different strike prices. At times, the strike price may be below the market price of the option, and so the option is said to be 'in the money'. But there is no immediate profit, because the difference between the strike price and the market price is smaller than the premium charged for the option. If the strike price differs significantly from the market price, the option is 'out of the money'. The more distant the maturity date, the larger the premium for a given strike price.

Options are available on a large number of currencies, government bonds, the shares of individual firms, the shares of a portfolio of firms, Treasury bills, Eurodollar deposits, gold, silver, and a variety of other commodities. The banks and the other financial firms trade options because they provide a substantial and additional source of income. Individual firms and investors like options because they provide a way to shuffle risks – especially the risks of large changes in the prices of securities and commodities – on to others who are more willing to carry these risks – for a price. Competition among the firms that sell options is expected to keep these prices reasonably low. Investors can also buy options based on the market as a whole; if the option is exercised, then the investor receives a share in an index fund that owns a portfolio of stocks.

'The collapsing house of cards?'

One of the observations about hedge funds in the 1990s was that as a group they were reporting phenomenally high returns. Since the 'no free lunch' cliché applies to financial markets, the general inference was that these funds must be taking exceptional risks. The exceptional returns to the owners of the funds and their investors reflected the large leverage of the funds. Every time a new financial instrument is developed there is concern that the system is becoming riskier, and the metaphor of the 'collapsing house of cards' is again brought out of the closet; earlier the metaphor of the 'inverted pyramid' had been applied to the Eurodollar market. The fear was that one or two of the cards at the bottom of the pyramid would buckle, and the cards above them would tumble even though these cards had individually been well positioned.

How fitting is the metaphor?

One aspect of the answer depends on whether the risks that are inherent in a market system are being concentrated in a smaller number of firms and individuals and whether the risk in the portfolios of these firms and individuals is increasing or decreasing. The innovations allow individuals and firms to reduce their risks, often by allowing them to hedge their exposure to risk at much lower cost. Yet the financial innovations also enable some firms and individuals to acquire more risk, particularly by writing naked options for premium income. If the changes in the prices of the underlying securities differ sharply from anticipated, then they will incur large losses, and some (or even many) may go bankrupt. One of three largest Swiss banks, the Union Bank of Switzerland, is said to have lost more than $1 billion from mispricing options and as a result of the erosion of its capital position was forced to seek a merger with another of the large Swiss banks.

If a large market participant incurs losses and becomes bankrupt, then the losses will be incurred by the firms and individuals on the other side of its contracts. It is possible that some of these firms and individuals might be forced into bankruptcy because the contracts are not fulfilled. The more likely case, however, is that the counterparties will be able to absorb the losses. For years the hedge funds earned exceptional returns because they were earning the risk premium inherent in the higher yields on riskier assets. As the funds prospered, they increased in size and number, and so they had to take on larger positions in particular trades. One analogy is provided by the market in junk bonds: for years, investors in junk bonds earned exceptional returns because few of the firms that issued these bonds tanked. Yet during the recession a large number of the firms that had issued these bonds failed, and the owners of junk bonds incurred losses that were substantial relative to the high levels of interest income in the earlier fat years. Milken's fortune remained largely intact.

Another analogy is provided by the firms that sell insurance against losses due to floods. Floods tend to be infrequent in many areas, so that for many years – indeed, until the floods occur – the premium income of these funds will be very large relative to the money paid out in the settlement of claims to those who incurred losses as a result of the floods. When the floods occur, however, watch out.

When the funds are profitable, their capital tends to increase; since they are highly leveraged, their purchases tend to raise asset prices. Moreover, there is a bit of a herd instinct in their behavior, so they may purchase the same or similar securities at the same time. When the funds incur losses on particular contracts, they may be subject to margin calls, and they may either then have to sell part or all of their positions, or else provide their counterpart with additional capital. The usual response to a margin call is to sell the most liquid assets or positions first, as a way to minimize the adverse price movement associated with these sales. If the capital of the large hedge funds should shrink because of adverse price movements and they sell assets to raise cash, the probability is high that they will sell their most liquid assets – which will cause the prices of these assets to decline.

The rate of return

There is a fundamental proposition in finance that, in the long run, the rate of return on financial assets cannot exceed the rate of return on real assets. The rate of return on financial assets is the sum of the dividends, capital gains, and interest that investors earn on their holdings of stocks and bonds and deposits and other financial instruments, and through their ownership of shares in mutual funds and pension funds relative to the value of their investments at the beginning of the year. The rate of return on real assets can be viewed as the profits and interest payments of firms relative to their productive assets. The logic behind the statement is that the cash secured by investors as dividends, realized capital gains, and interest must come from someplace; those who pay out this cash must earn the money from profitable investments. So the real rate of return is based on the underlying productivity of the economy, and can be viewed as the rate of growth of national income – actually the rate of growth of national income adjusted for the increase in the labor force.

A large part of the income to investors in particular years comes from capital gains – the increase in the price of stocks and bonds and real property. The general basis for these gains is that the buyers of these stocks and bonds and real property seek either the future cash income attached to these assets, or the gains to be made from selling these assets to someone else who seeks the cash income from the future gains. In some cases, firms provide cash to the stockholders by buying back shares, either as a substitute for dividends (the capital gains are taxable at a lower rate) or as a complement to dividends. In the end, the investors want cash or paper that can be readily converted to cash.

Our fundamental proposition seems inconsistent with the data for the 1980s and the 1990s, – at least, the data for most countries – for the rates of return on stocks and bonds and real property appear to have averaged 15 or 20 percent or more, while the real rates of growth were in range of 3–6 percent. Part of this discrepancy is that the rates of return on stocks and bonds and real property are in monetary terms while the rates of return on the real assets include an adjustment for inflation; comparability suggests that the rates of return on stocks and bonds and real property be adjusted downward by the inflation rate – or, alternatively, that the rate of return on real assets be adjusted upward by the inflation rate.

Even after this adjustment, however, the rates of return on stocks and bonds and real property would be significantly higher than the rate of economic growth. Part – perhaps a substantial part – of this discrepancy can be explained by the fact that in the inflationary 1970s the rates of return on stocks and bonds (but not on real property) were substantially below the real rates of economic growth, as a result of the decline in the prices of these assets. So the high rates of return on stocks and bonds in the 1980s and the 1990s partially reflects a form of 'catching up'.

It's possible that the high rates of return on stocks in the United States and some other countries reflect 'irrational exuberance' and that investors were buying stocks because they expected that stock prices would continue to increase at 20 percent a year forever. This approach to investing in stocks was evident in Japan in the late 1980s; for the 1990s as a whole, the rate on stock prices and real property has been negative while the real rates of return have been modestly positive.

The financial services industry blossomed in the 1980s and the 1990s because high rates of return on stocks and on bonds and real property led to lots of trading activity. The incomes of these firms surged as a result of the combination of commissions associated with their brokerage function, their own trading profits, and the capital gains associated with owning inventories of stocks and bonds in a environment of rising asset prices. Investors have been willing – perhaps reluctantly willing – to share some of their gains with the investment banks, brokerage firms, and hedge funds. During this extended period of rising asset prices, the hedge funds have had exceptional returns because the prices of risky assets have increased relative to the price of less risky assets and the capital structure of these funds and their high leverage suggests that they will have more long than short positions.

When the period of secular increases in the rate of return on financial assets relative to the return on real assets ends – and it's a safe bet that it will end – the returns to the firms in the financial services industry will decline, and perhaps sharply. In this new environment asset prices will decline more often, even though on average the prices of stocks and real property may increase more frequently than they decline. It will then be fun to develop the scorecard on the hedge funds to determine whether they have earned exceptional returns, or whether instead their great success in the 1980s and the 1990s reflected simply the combination of high leverage and a rising asset-price environment.

19

The World Markets for Stocks and Bonds

Consider two questions:

Q: How many stock markets are there in the world?

Q: Where have investors been able to earn the highest rates of return on stocks over an extended period?

The implications of globalization

One way to answer these questions is to rely on anecdotes, and particularly the stories of the market participants. An alternative approach is to rely on the data. The answers to both questions are more ambiguous than they seem. Consider the answer to the second question at the end of 1989. Investors who owned Japanese shares had a higher rate of return higher than investors who owned shares of firms in other industrial countries over the previous 10 years, the previous 20 years, and even the previous 30 years. The high rates of return on Japanese stocks reflected both the sharp increase in stock prices in terms of yen (in the 1980s stock prices in yen terms increased by a factor of six) and the fact that over the previous 20 years the yen had appreciated by 4 or 5 percent a year.

The comparison of the rates of return on stocks and the bonds denominated in different currencies requires that the returns on the various national currencies be compared in terms of a *common currency* – which might be the US dollar, or the Japanese yen, or even the nascent Euro. The need for a common currency benchmark leaves unsettled a major question – should the returns be compared after investors have hedged their exposure to risk of changes in currency values, or should they be compared on an unhedged basis. In the second case, the return to investors involves a change in the currency values between the date the foreign bonds or stocks are first acquired and the dates these securities are sold. The globalization theme suggests that the various stock exchanges in the world are little more than geographic extensions of an integrated world market for stocks and bonds. One analogy is that there is a world market for gasoline, even though prices are not identical at each of the gas pumps in different countries, these differences in prices for a more or less identical product reflect differences in transport costs to several markets, in local and national taxes, and in the scope of competition in each local market. The analogy suggests that the world market for stocks is not be very different from the world markets for photographic film, or for automobiles, or for petroleum. The implication of the globalization theme is that the rates of return on stocks traded in each national market should not be significantly different once an adjustment is made for the differences in the risks of the securities traded.

Is the world stock market integrated or segmented?

How many stock exchanges?

One answer to the first question above is to count the number of stock exchanges in various countries – thus there are 10 or 12 stock exchanges in the United States, including the New York Stock Exchange, the American Stock Exchange in New York, the Boston Stock Exchange, the Philadelphia Exchange, the Midwest Exchange in Chicago, and the Pacific Stock Exchange in San Francisco as well as smaller exchanges in cities in the mountain states. In Canada, stocks are traded on exchanges in Toronto, Montreal, Calgary, and Vancouver. Tokyo has its stock exchange, and so does Osaka. There are five stock exchanges in Germany. Each country has at least one stock exchange, and several large countries may have more than one.

In addition, in virtually every country stocks are bought and sold in over-the-counter (OTC) transactions. Indeed, initially stocks were bought and sold in informal markets; then someone had the idea that trading would be facilitated if stocks were traded in an organized exchange with formal rules. Firms would pay a small fee to have their shares listed on the exchange – but the belief was that this fee would be modest relative to the increase the price for the firms' shares.

That there are 10 or 12 stock exchange in the United States reflects its regional history – the local firms were traded on the exchanges in the major city in each region. The reduction in the significance of the regional stock exchanges partly reflects the fact that as business firms have consolidated and become national and multinational, the number of firms that were listed on the various regional exchanges declined, and several of these exchanges have merged while others have gone out of business. Moreover, since the managers always want their shares to trade at the highest possible prices, they may have the shares listed on other exchanges or even shift the exchange on which their shares are traded. (Their rationale is that the higher the price at which the shares trade, the easier it is for the firm to raise additional capital. Moreover, as share prices increase, existing shareholders experience capital gains and become richer.)

The significance of the regional exchanges within a country can be evaluated by comparing the market value of the stocks listed on the various exchanges in each country. Thus the market value of the 2,400 stocks traded on the New York Stock Exchange is sixty times larger than the market shares traded on the American Stock Exchange. Investors could still trade national firms on the regional exchanges. The exchanges in Chicago and on the West Coast have one major advantage relative to the exchanges in New York – namely, that they are open later.

One world stock exchange?

The implication is that there is only one significant stock exchange in each country whenever more than 85 or 90 percent of stocks, as represented by market value, are traded on one exchange. The logical extension of this proposition that there is only one stock market in each country is that there is only one stock market in the world. The distinction is between the term 'stock exchange' and the term 'stock market': the stock market is more inclusive and includes the various countries. The rationale for the view that there is a world stock market is that a significant number of investors and large financial firms compare the anticipated returns on foreign bonds and foreign stocks with the anticipated returns on domestic bonds and stocks.

Investors in London have more or less the same knowledge and information that investors in New York have. Of course, not every London investor has the same information about the New York market – some investors prefer to buy stocks of the firms that are close to home. Many professional investors – the mutual funds, pension funds, investment banks – cover the major stock markets in the search for bargains. So if 10 or 15 percent of the investors resident in a country compared foreign securities with domestic securities, the markets would be effectively integrated. Many of these firms and investors are resident in large countries including the United States, Great Britain, Germany, and Japan and seek to diversify the securities in their portfolios to reduce their risk. Some of these firms and investors resident in small countries – Switzerland, the Netherlands, Sweden, Saudi Arabia, Hong Kong, Singapore – have 'outgrown' their countries and invest abroad because there are so few opportunities to diversify at home.

Obviously most investors do not compare the anticipated returns and risks on foreign securities with those on domestic securities. The key question is whether enough investors compare the risk and the return on foreign securities with those on domestic securities so the markets can be considered integrated. The answer varies, depending on currency pairs and the dates the comparison is made. For example, the US and the Canadian bond and stock markets have been integrated for an extended period. The Swiss and the German and the Dutch markets have similarly been integrated.

Segmentation or integration?

So the question is whether the national markets are segmented or integrated, or – perhaps more appropriately – the extent to which the markets are integrated and the extent to which they are segmented. Just as firms headquartered in Illinois, Texas, and California arranged to have their shares listed on the stock exchanges in New York, so firms headquartered in Great Britain, Germany, and Japan have had their shares listed on the New York Stock Exchange.

The argument that the national financial markets are segmented has two major components. The first is that most of the profits of most of the firms traded on the stock exchanges in each country are based on their domestic sales. The second is that most of the investors in most of the countries hold a very large share of their wealth in domestic securities, and a very small share in foreign stocks and bonds.

So the debate has the characteristics of 'the glass is half full – the glass is half empty 'conundrum. Moreover, the thrust of the declines in the cost of communication and control is that the markets are becoming less segmented even if they are not yet fully integrated. And there are the asymmetries between markets in the large countries and markets in the small countries – changes in the prices of stocks and bonds in large countries are likely to have a larger impact on prices of stocks and bonds in small countries, whereas changes in these security prices in small countries are far less likely to have a significant impact on the prices in large countries.

Consider now the nature of linkages among financial markets in different countries. Why do stock prices rise? One story is in terms of investor optimism about the future; the cliché that a 'rising tide lifts all ships' might be applied to the impacts of changes in US stock prices on stock prices in every other country, quite independent of underlying economic conditions. Or this cliché might be applied to the impact of buoyant economic conditions in the United States on economic conditions in Canada, Mexico, Japan, and the other countries that are large trading partners of the United States. Both stories might be relevant.

Anecdotes are helpful. The bubble in stock prices in Japan appeared to have reflected impacts on the financial markets in Taipei and Seoul, but not on the US and the European markets.

A cousin to the question of whether the stock markets in the various countries and the bond markets in various countries are integrated is whether the stock and bond markets within each country are integrated. In effect, the question is whether the border between different types of financial instruments within a country are higher or lower than the borders between the same type of financial instruments across countries.

The cliché that a 'rising tide lifts all ships' can be applied to both stocks and bonds within a country. Periods of economic optimism are associated with increases in both bond and stock prices. As bond prices rise, interest rates decline (this is the same statement, not a statement about cause and effect) and some investors in search of higher returns buy stocks. A more scientific version of the relationship is that when interest rates decline, the anticipated returns associated with the cash flows of stocks are discounted at a lower interest rate, which means that stock prices increase.

Within a country, many investors specialize in buying bonds and others specialize in buying stocks. But there are a few investors who choose between stocks and bonds on the basis of the anticipated returns on each type of security.

In a world of perfect foresight, the rates of return on the bonds denominated in the different national currencies should be similar after adjusting for the realized changes in exchange rates. As long as the perfect-foresight assumption is made, then the interest rates on bonds denominated in the currencies of the countries with the higher inflation rates will be higher. And the difference in interest rates will reflect both the differences in inflation rates and the anticipated and realized changes in exchange rates.

Box 19.1   Investing the Lottery Prize in Bonds

Consider now that you won the lottery, with the caveat that you are to search for bargains among the bonds available in different countries and denominated in different currencies.

Investors increasingly compare the anticipated returns on foreign stocks with those on domestic stocks.

Assume that you have won the $10 million lottery prize and that you have decided to invest in long-term bonds, so it's a horse race between bonds denominated in the US dollar, bonds denominated in the Japanese yen, bonds denominated in the German mark, and bonds denominated in any of 10 or 15 other currencies. First note that the US bond market is much the largest in the world.

Consider interest rate relationship in the absence of international trade in bonds in a zero inflation world. Interest rates will be high in those countries identified with high rates of economic growth and high rates of investment relative to their savings rates.

Now relax the assumption that prohibits trade in bonds. Investors will move funds to buy the bonds in those countries where interest rates are higher, with the result that interest rates will not differ significantly as long as inflation rates remain similar.

Now relax the assumption that inflation rates are similar. Interest rates will increase in those countries with the higher inflation rates, and their currencies will depreciate in the foreign exchange market.

The world of perfect-foresight assumptions is a useful benchmark. But the real world is characterized by lots of unanticipated shocks – oil shocks, inflation shocks, crop failures, financial bubbles, banking crises. One basic proposition in finance is that investors want to be compensated for holding risky securities or for holding securities denominated in currencies deemed riskier.

The intuition is that the rates of return on the bonds denominated in most foreign currencies will be higher than the rates of return on bonds denominated in the US dollar after the purchase of the foreign exchange on the date the race begins and the purchase of US dollars on the date the race ends. The story is that investors want to be compensated for incurring cross-border risks: especially the risk of changes in exchange rates.

Because the interest rates on securities denominated in the currencies of countries experiencing high rates of inflation are likely to be higher to compensate investors for the decline in the purchasing power due to the increase in the consumer price level, the comparison of the returns on bonds denominated in different currencies must necessarily occur only after adjustment for the realized changes in exchange rates.

The size of 10 largest bond markets at the end of 1996 is shown in Table 19.1. The US market is nearly 50 percent of the world total.

The return on the bonds denominated in each currency is the sum of the interest payments and the changes in the price of the bond between the beginning and the end of the period. The US dollar rate of return includes the own-currency return *plus* the adjustment for the change in the exchange rate between the beginning and the end of the period. Both the own-currency and the US dollar rates of return for bonds denominated in different currencies for different holding periods are shown in Table 19.2.

First consider the choice among bonds denominated in different currencies. Should you buy the domestic bond, or should you buy bonds denominated in a foreign currency? If you buy the foreign bonds, you are first going to have to buy that country's currency in the foreign

Table 19.1   The world bond market, 1996 (US dollars billion or equivalent)

	Total ($)	Central gov.	Local gov.	Corp and other	Institution
US dollar	9583	2682	1050	2257	960
Japanese yen	3666	1962	97	1075	355
German mark	2303	699	83	1161	309
Italian lira	1274	976		187	88
French franc	1044	510	3	153	162
British pound	662	446		33	183
Canadian dollar	446	203	110	62	71
Dutch guilder	401	197	3	120	81
Belgian franc	367	219		127	38
Danish krone	288	104		175	9
Other					
Total	21547	8748	1393	5735	2431

Source: Salomon Brothers.

Table 19.2 Bond market return

Local Currency Bond Return

Country	1970–1980	1980–1990	1990–2000	1970–2000
Canada	5.9%	12.5%	10.9%	9.7%
France	6.0%	13.3%	9.9%	9.7%
German	7.7%	7.2%	8.7%	7.9%
Italy	7.2%	16.6%	13.3%	12.3%
Japan	6.3%	7.5%	7.6%	7.1%
Netherlands	7.0%	8.9%	9.1%	8.3%
Sweden	6.0%	11.2%	13.2%	10.1%
Switzerland	5.7%	3.3%	6.2%	5.1%
United Kingdom	9.3%	12.5%	11.6%	11.1%
United States	5.1%	12.1%	8.2%	8.4%

US$ Bond Returns

Country	1970–1980	1980–1990	1990–2000	1970–2000
Canada	4.7%	12.5%	8.3%	8.4%
France	8.9%	10.5%	7.0%	8.8%
German	15.5%	8.5%	5.8%	9.8%
Italy	3.9%	12.7%	7.1%	7.8%
Japan	11.3%	12.4%	10.8%	11.5%
Netherlands	13.6%	9.9%	6.2%	9.8%
Sweden	8.2%	7.6%	8.4%	8.0%
Switzerland	16.2%	5.3%	4.2%	8.4%
United Kingdom	9.0%	9.5%	9.8%	9.4%
United States	5.1%	12.1%	8.2%	8.4%

exchange market before you can buy the bond; at a subsequent date, probably at the end of the holding period, you sell the bond and convert the proceeds in the foreign currency into the US dollar by purchasing the US dollar in the spot exchange market.

The horse race is between the rate of return from holding US dollar bonds with the rate of return from holding bonds denominated in the foreign currency, after first having purchased the foreign currency in the foreign exchange market. The outcome of the horse race is sensitive to the date the race begins and the length of the race – the length of the holding period. There is a foreign exchange transaction at the beginning of the horse race, and one at the end. The outcome, incidentally, is not sensitive to whether your benchmark currency is the Japanese yen, or the German mark, or the Swiss franc, since in each case you would begin by buying a foreign currency before buying the bond denominated in the foreign currency and then buying the initial currency at the end of the holding period. Note that to keep the experiment simple the interest income is reinvested in the foreign country. And similarly to keep the experiment simple also assume that you buy the least risky government bond in each country.

Throughout the 1950s and 1960s the interest rates on bonds denominated in the Swiss franc were below those on securities denominated in the US dollar. Then in the late 1970s the interest rates on US dollar bonds increased above interest rates on bonds denominated in the German mark, the Dutch guilder, and the Japanese yen as these foreign currencies were appreciating relative to the US dollar. As long as these currencies were appreciating, the total return on these foreign bonds was generally higher than the return on US dollar bonds. An alternative version of the same statement is that the returns on US dollar bonds were lower than the returns on foreign bonds because the foreign currencies were appreciating in the foreign exchange market.

The difference between interest rates on the foreign bond and interest rates on US dollar bonds adjusted for the realized change in the price of the US dollar in terms of the foreign currency is shown in Figure 19.1 for various holding periods. A minus sign means the return on the foreign bond is below the return on the US bond. During each of the five year periods, the difference in these returns primarily reflects the change in the exchange rate. Thus in the 1970s the return on these foreign bonds was significantly above the return on the US bonds because of the sharp appreciation of these currencies. In the first half of the 1980s, when these currencies depreciated, the returns on these foreign bonds were below the return on the US bonds. For the

25 year period, the return on the foreign bonds averaged modestly above the return on the US bonds, primarily because of the appreciation of these foreign currencies in the 1970s

The horse race in stocks

Again you've won the lottery, and this time the investment choice involves the market basket of the stocks available in the several countries. The size of the various national markets in stocks shown in Figure 19.1. In the late 1990s the market value of US stocks was greater than the combined market values of all other national markets. The ratio of market valuation of stocks to GNP in the United States is higher than in most foreign countries for four reasons – the corporate sector is a larger part of the economy, the US corporate sector is a large part of some foreign countries' economy because of the role of US multinationals, the earnings of US firms have been higher as a share of GDP and stock prices have been higher in relation to earnings – the price/earnings (P/E) ratio of US firms is higher than the comparable ratios for most non-US firms.

The return on stocks in each country is the sum of the dividend payments and the change in the price of the stock between the beginning and end of the period. The market valuation data are readily available but the dividend data are not available for the stocks in each country; for most countries, samples of dividends suggests that they are small in relation to the price of stocks.

There have been lots of examples of sprinters in the horse race that faltered in the home stretch. In the 1980s, stock prices in Japan increased by a factor of six, while US stock prices were increasing by a factor of three. There was lots of chatter about the stellar performance of the Japanese economy, and the pace of research and development (R & D) of Japanese firms, the high savings rate in Japan, the concern of Japanese investors for the long run rather than quarterly changes in corporate earnings. By the early 1990s, it became clear that the sharp increase in Japanese stock prices in the late 1980s had been a 'bubble' – in the late 1990s, Japanese stock prices were more or less where they had been in 1984.

The intuition is that the rate of return on the stocks in individual countries should reflect their rates of economic growth. Thus stocks of the firms headquartered in rapid-growth countries like Hong Kong and Korea should have high rates of return because the earnings of these firms will be growing rapidly, and investors will pay an

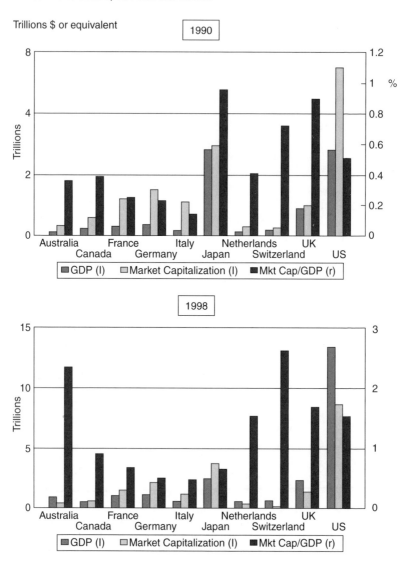

Figure 19.1   Stock market valuations and GDP, 1990 and 1998

increasingly higher prices for these stocks. A second element in the economic intuition is that since many investors consider stocks and bonds to be substitutes for each other, then the countries with high interest rates will tend to have low stock prices. However, the rate of growth of stock prices should tend to be high because the anticipated rate of growth of GDP, and hence corporate profits, should be high.

Consider Hong Kong, truly a phenomenal example of rapid growth. Hong Kong's *per capita* GDP is not much below *per capita* GDP in the United States. In 1960 and 1970, *per capita* GDP in Hong Kong was way below that in the United States. Moreover, Hong Kong's population has increased much more rapidly than the US population. So the GDP growth argument suggests that returns from holding Hong Kong stocks should have been considerably higher than the returns from holding US stocks.

There is a third story, which is that the return on the stocks available in a particular country will increase as foreign investors in their search for bargains become intrigued with these stocks and add these stocks to their portfolios in their search for bargains.

The rates of return on US stock prices and foreign stock prices for various holding periods are shown in Figure 19.2; the returns on foreign stocks are US dollar returns.

The returns on US stocks generally were higher than the returns on the stocks available in most of the foreign countries. In the mid-1990s and in the late 1990s, year-to-year increases in US stock prices were

---

Box 19.2   Stocks and Bonds

Now consider a horse race in stocks comparable to the horse race in bonds – you've again won the lottery and the choice is to buy the representative US stocks, or the representative stocks in each of 10 or 15 foreign countries. If you buy the foreign stocks, you first must buy the foreign currency in the foreign exchange market, and then at the end of the horse race or holding period, the total value of your investment in the foreign stocks must be sold in the foreign exchange market.

Because stock prices are much more variable than bond prices, the outcome of the race will be much more sensitive to the choice of the date when the race starts and when the race ends.

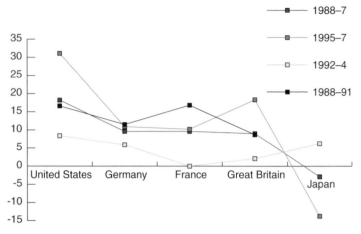

Figure 19.2   US dollar returns on national stock markets, 1988–97

exceptionally high. Once again there were lots of explanations – there was a new US economy, investors had a long-term orientation and were far less concerned with short-term blips in corporate earnings, there was billions of new cash in retirement plans that had to go someplace, and the managers of firms were paying much greater attention to reducing costs and increasing profits.

These explanations may prove to be much more stolid than the explanations offered 10 years earlier for the boom in Japanese stock prices. And then, again, …

20
Why are Multinational Firms Mostly American?

A note to the reader: The title of this chapter, taken from the first edition may seem dated in view of the rapid pace of acquisitions of US firms by firms headquartered in various foreign countries – especially in Japan and to a lesser extent in Great Britain. Sony acquired Columbia Records and then Columbia Pictures. Matsushita bought MCA–Universal, another of Hollywood's major studios. Bridgestone Tire acquired Firestone Tire. These were the types of transactions that made the front pages of the major newspapers. In the latter part of the 1980s, there were usually more than a thousand of these acquisitions each year; and 30–40 percent of the acquisitions of US firms by firms headquartered abroad were by firms headquartered in Japan. US firms were continuing to expand their foreign investments, but the rate of growth of these investments was swamped by the investments of foreign firms in the United States. One striking feature was that a very large part of these new foreign investments in the United States involved the acquisition of established US firms; when US firms have gone abroad, in contrast, they often have built new factories on 'greenfields.'

So it may seem strange keeping the chapter title from the first edition. Read on.

The American challenge?

In the late 1960s one of Europe's best-selling books was *Le Défi Americain (The American Challenge)*. The author was Jean-Jacques Servan-Schreiber (JJ-SS), publisher of *L'Express* (the French imitation of *Time*) of *L'Expansion* (the French version of *Fortune*), and, for a while, of *European Business* (the French counterpart of the *Harvard Business Review*). Servan-Schreiber was energetic, if not original. By 1981, *Le Défi*

Americain was obsolete; JJ-SS came forth with *Le Défi Mondial*, next, *Le Défi Intergalactic*.

The central thesis of *Le Défi Americain* was dramatic. After the United States and the Soviet Union, the third economic power in the world was US business firms in Europe. As evidence, JJ-SS cited the increasingly important position of the subsidiaries of US firms in European industry, especially in such technologically advanced fields as computers and electronics.

The striking feature of these US firms was that they then were far ahead of their British, French, and German competitors in integrating their production and marketing across European borders. International Harvester's (now Navistar) French plant produced transmissions for tractors, while its German plant produced tractor motors; each of these plants exported its product to the other. IBM–Europe produced its computers using components made in various plants across the Continent; indeed, its production line in Europe was seven countries long.

Servan-Schreiber advocated numerous changes to help Europe meet the US challenge. European business should become more like American business – more graduate business schools like Harvard, more professional managements like that of Exxon, greater decentralization of corporate decision-making as at ITT, and more expenditures on R&D as at IBM.

One of the not-so-best-selling books in London in 1902 was *The American Invaders*, by F. A. McKenzie, a Scot worried by the American threat to British industry. Americans, he wrote, were 'succeeding in Europe because of advantages in education, their willingness to accept new ideas, and their freedom from hampering tradition.' In part, the supremacy of US firms was reflected in US exports, in part by the growth of the European subsidiaries of US firms. McKenzie noted the dominance of US firms in the new industries: 'applications of electricity to traction, the typewriter, the automobile, and the machine tools.'

Servan-Schreiber never acknowledged McKenzie or *The American Invaders*. If he had, he would have had to explain why 65 years and two world wars after 1902, US firms owned only 5 percent of corporate assets in Europe and accounted for 10 percent of European imports. And he would also have had to explain why the ratio of US foreign investment to US national income in the early 1970s was significantly below the ratio in 1913.

McKenzie was somewhat premature in predicting American dominance of European industry. So was Servan-Schreiber. While a few US firms had set up branches in Europe as early as 1850 and direct foreign investment increased at the end of the nineteenth century, direct US foreign investment was modest until the 1920s, and largely confined to firms engaged in mining and producing crude petroleum; these firms had integrated 'upstream' to source for the US market. In the 1920s US investment in manufacturing abroad jumped sharply, and especially in Europe. From the 1930s through most of the 1950s, foreign investments were modest because of the Great Depression and the Second World War; indeed, in the 1930s many US firms sold the European subsidiaries that they had acquired in the previous decade. But beginning in the late 1950s, direct US foreign investment soared; US firms purchased many foreign firms and set up new plants of their own.

Direct foreign investment

By 1970 a substantial part of total manufacturing in Canada was foreign-owned, especially by US firms; indeed, in some Canadian industries more than three-quarters of the local plants were foreign-owned. US firms in the 'new' industries continue to invest abroad extensively, much as they did in McKenzie's day; the major difference is that the new industries were pharmaceuticals, computers, and electronics rather than the application of electricity to traction. But US firms are well established abroad in traditional industries, such as hotel-keeping and food processing, automobiles, soaps and toothpaste. The numbers of Hilton Hotels and Holiday Inns and McDonald's and Wendy's outside the United States are growing rapidly. (Holiday Inns is now owned by a British firm.)

Altogether, direct foreign investment (DFI) for firms headquartered in all countries totaled about $75 billion in 1960, of which slightly more than half was undertaken by US firms and 10 percent by British firms. Forty percent of US foreign investment was in manufacturing, 30 percent in petroleum, and nearly 10 percent in mining. Foreign investments by Germans and Japanese firms were small until the late 1980s, when they began to increase rapidly (one cost of losing wars is that the foreign subsidiaries of domestic firms almost always are expropriated). From 1973 to 1978 the value of US direct investments abroad increased by two-thirds; during the same period, foreign investments in the United States doubled. US direct foreign investment continued to grow in the 1980s at about the same rate as in the 1970s; in contrast, foreign investment in the United States surged, and especially in the second half of the decade. Much of the investment in the United States was undertaken by firms headquartered in Japan and Great Britain – and, to a lesser extent, in Germany, Switzerland, and the Netherlands. Firms based in a small number of countries – the United States, Great Britain, the Netherlands, Switzerland, Sweden, and Japan – account for most of the direct foreign investment. Foreign investment is extensive in some industries (aluminum, petroleum) and minimal in others (textiles and steel). Dutch firms (Unilever, Shell, Phillips) are large investors abroad, while Belgian firms are not. Swedish firms are big foreign investors, while Danish and Norwegian firms are not.

In the late 1970s foreign firms began to increase their investments in the United States at a rapid rate: they were prepared to compete in the US firms' backyards. British Petroleum acquired Sinclair Oil and then began to buy Standard of Ohio. Imperial Chemicals, the leading British chemical firm, acquired Atlas Chemical, which then ranked about 20th in the United States in sales; BASF (a German chemical company) acquired Wyandotte Chemical. The chemical industry is truly international, in that a very large share of the investment of US firms is in foreign countries; similarly a very large share of the investment of European firms is in other countries. (Curiously, the foreign investments of Japanese firms in the chemical industry are relatively small compared to the foreign investments by Japanese firms in other industries.) Panasonic, one of the top three Japanese electronics firms, bought the Quasar Division of Motorola while Sony bought Warwick Electronics. A subsidiary of Nestlé, a Swiss firm, successfully bid for Libby, McNeill & Libby, a Chicago-based food processor. Grand Union, one of the largest food retailers in the United States, was acquired by a French–British firm. The Imperial Group in London bought Howard Johnson's – and then sold it. Volkswagen set up an assembly plant in Pennsylvania to turn out 200,000 cars a year. Toyota, Nissan, Honda, Mitsubishi, and Mazda established plants to produce autos in the United States. Three of the major drug suppliers in the United States – Ciba–Geigy, Hoffmann–La Roche, and Sandoz – are Swiss. Petrofina, the Belgian petroleum firm, is beginning to refine and distribute in the United States. The European penetration of the US market has gone so far that the Good Humor Company is part of the Liverpool-based Thomas Lipton tea empire.

Despite the recent surge in foreign investment in the United States, the foreign investments of US firms are slightly larger than the US investments of foreign firms; foreign firms have not yet overcome the head start that US firms developed in the 1920–70 period. US foreign investment surged in the late 1950s and the 1960s, not in response to any plan, but rather in response to market forces. Many US firms were sometimes viewed as playing 'follow-the-leader' in their industries; if this observation is correct, then the motivation for the foreign investment by the 'leader' would have to be explained. The 'follow-the-leader' strategy is likely to be expensive if the market opportunities are inappropriate. One attraction to the US firms was that the rate of economic growth of Western Europe appeared likely to be higher than in the United States, partly because of the bounce-back from the Second World War and partly because of the optimistic expectations generated by the development of the Common Market.

Then, in the late 1960s, the growing overvaluation of the US dollar, caused by more rapid inflation in the United States than in Europe, further induced US firms to invest more abroad to source for their export markets; initially, these firms had supplied foreign markets from US plants. But as US costs increased relative to foreign costs, these US plants lost their competitive edge – in the US as well as in the foreign market – and firms needed to produce abroad to protect their market share. Then some US firms began to invest abroad to protect their market share in the US market because production costs in the United States were increasing rapidly; thus US electronics firms set up manufacturing and assembly plants in the Far East to protect their position in the US market from the competitive thrust of Japanese firms.

The depreciation of the US dollar relative to European currencies and the Japanese yen in the 1970s reduced the incentive for US firms to invest abroad. German and Japanese firms then began to invest more extensively in the United States; Volkswagen, which had previously supplied the US market by exporting from Germany, then decided to protect its market share in the United States by establishing a US assembly line. Volvo committed itself to a $100 million assembly plant in Tidewater, Virgina – and then backed off. Just as US firms had increased their foreign investment as the US dollar became overvalued, so German, Japanese, and other foreign firms increased their investment in the United States as the US dollar became increasingly undervalued. Foreign investment in the United States began to grow three times as rapidly as US investment abroad. The foreigners were coming.

A new imperialism?

The relation between foreign investments and the national interests of the host – and of the source – countries came under critical attack as nationalist pressures increased. By the late 1960s, when Servan-Schreiber's book was published, ownership of domestic factories and resources by foreign firms – especially by US firms – had become a sensitive political issue in many countries. Was Canada worse off because such a large part of manufacturing facilities in Canada were owned by US firms? Many Canadians, including a non-trivial number of Canadian economists, thought so. Canadian and other host countries feared that the activities of the giant multinational firms, especially those based in the United States, were a new form of imperialism, more insidious than the gunboats of the late nineteenth century. Nationalists in many countries – primarily in developing countries, but also in France and Canada – complained about a loss of sovereignty to the large international companies. Nationalist pressures were especially directed against firms engaged in extracting resources in developing countries. Peru expropriated International Petroleum, the local subsidiary of Exxon and also some of the local properties of W. R. Grace. Bolivia took over the local operations of Gulf Oil. In Chile, the Christian Democratic government of Eduardo Frei purchased 50 percent of Anaconda Mines; subsequently, the Marxist government of Salvador Allende nationalized the rest of Anaconda as well as the mines of most other foreign companies. Mexico and many other developing countries restricted foreign ownership to participation in joint ventures with Mexican partners.

From time to time the countries in which firms that have been investing abroad are headquartered are also concerned about foreign investment, especially about its possibly harmful effects on the balance of payments, on unemployment, and on tax revenues. The labor unions in the United States – and many of their friends in the US Congress – believed that Mexican entry into the North Atlantic Free Trade Area (NAFTA) would mean that US firms would increase their investments in Mexico, both to source for the Mexican market and to source for the US market.

Patterns of market penetration

What needs to be explained is why the pattern of direct foreign investment changed so sharply, beginning in the late 1970s but especially in the latter half of the 1980s. In 1988 or 1989, Servan-Schreiber might have written *Le Défi Japonais* as son of *Le Défi American*. Indeed, many others did. Unfortunately the Japanese threat evaporated, because the foreign investments of Japanese firms in the 1990s declined almost as abruptly as they had surged. In the mid-1990s the foreign investments of a handful of firms headquartered in Korea surged in a pattern similar to the Japanese pattern a decade earlier. Then after the advent of the Asian financial crisis in 1997, these Korean firms had to retrench, and a significant number of the investments that they had acquired a few years earlier went up for auction.

Why produce abroad?

Why a firm acquires productive facilities in one or several foreign countries cannot be answered without first considering its unique qualities. A firm consists of a set of individuals engaged in production and in marketing; their diverse activities are coordinated by central management. The managers buy certain inputs to produce a variety of outputs. Most of the productive activities within the firm could be purchased, in modular fashion, from other firms. The managers might hire one company to develop new products, a second to produce them, and a third to market them. The choice of whether to conduct an activity within the firm or to acquire the product of the same activity 'in the market' is usually made on the basis of cost; competition forces the firm to choose the low-cost alternative. Some magazines – for example, *Playboy* and *Penthouse* – are primarily cut-and-paste jobs in that a small editorial staff buys most of the stories and photos from freelancers. *Time* and *Newsweek*, in contrast, maintain much larger staffs who write virtually all of the stories. US truck firms are rather like *Playboy*, in that they assemble components manufactured by other firms; US auto firms, in contrast, tend to produce most of the basic components of autos. (Traditionally, there have been sharp differences among the US automobile firms, in that Chrysler did more outsourcing than General Motors, although more recently General Motors has increased its outsourcing.

Each type of firm has certain advantages – managerial and financial skills, marketing and engineering know-how, and customer loyalties. Firms are identifiable as collections of production skills, marketing skills, financial skills, or organizational skills; these tags denote their advantages relative to their competitors. Each firm continually seeks to exploit its advantages in the most efficient way. Since its competitors are constantly trying to erode its advantages, the firm must continually strive to maintain its market position by developing new advantages and exploiting its established advantages in new, including foreign, markets.

When a firm considers expansion into foreign markets, it must decide on the most efficient way of exploiting its advantages: it might export from domestic plants, produce in the foreign market, or sell its know-how and other advantages to firms with productive facilities in these foreign countries. If the firm decides to produce abroad, it must consider whether to enter into a partnership with a host-country firm in a joint venture. The choice will depend on a variety of economic – and perhaps political – considerations.

Initially, the firm may supply the foreign market by exporting the output of its domestic plants. Then, after the foreign sales have become sufficiently large the firm may establish a plant abroad to produce for the foreign customers. Or the firm may acquire an established firm headquartered in the foreign country. At first, the production in the foreign country may involve only the assembly of imported components, so as to save on transport costs and tariffs. The drug companies, for example, repackage drugs from large containers into smaller bottles; the auto companies assemble cars and trucks from kits and then from imported components.

As the size of the foreign market expands, a large-share of the inputs to the product may be locally produced, although the parent may continue to supply senior management, technical knowledge, and some financial assistance. Increases in the scale of output in the host-country plant are likely to be associated with declines in unit production costs; the output of this subsidiary may supplement, and perhaps ultimately supplant, exports from the home-country plants.

At some point, the costs of production in the foreign subsidiary may fall below those of domestic plants, and the firm may begin to supply part or all of the domestic market from foreign subsidiaries. Ford imports the Escort for the US market from its Mexican subsidiary. Some US electronics firms produce part or all of the components for particular products in Taiwan, South Korea, Singapore, and Malaysia; these components are then shipped to the United States for assembly into the final product.

Integration of manufacturing

The extensive integration of manufacturing activities in different countries is a recent innovation. Initially the market for many products was local or regional, and most of the local needs were satisfied from nearby production. Imports were minimal. Every town had its butcher, baker, and candlestick-maker, as well as its cobbler, tailor, cigar maker, and brewery. The potential for cost reductions associated with large-scale production was small. And even where savings in production costs were possible, the extra costs of controlling a large-scale operation with activities in widely separated locations dominated the savings.

The change in the last 150 years is that technological developments have both greatly increased the savings associated with large-scale production and reduced the costs of coordinating distant activities. Thus bauxite mined in Jamaica is shipped to eastern Venezuela for refining to take advantage of extremely low-cost electricity produced on the Rio Caroni. At one time some US electronics companies sent partially assembled radio receivers to South Korea by air freight for further processing by skilled, relatively inexpensive labor. The combination of increasingly sophisticated products – higher unit values – and sharp declines in costs of transportation and communications has reduced the pressure on firms to locate productive activity near either the market or the source of raw materials; instead, production can be shifted to those sites where unit production costs will be the lowest. As in banking, these changes in technology have increased the size of the market; regional markets are grouped into national markets, and national markets into the international market.

Expansion of national markets has encouraged firms to integrate their activities in different countries. In some countries, a firm may both produce and market, in others it may only market, and in still others it may only produce. It is thus necessary to distinguish between the share of the world's market for a product held by US firms, British firms, and Swiss firms, and the share of total production in each country undertaken by domestic and by foreign firms. The factors which explain where particular goods are produced are likely to differ from those which explain shares of a particular national market held by domestic and by foreign firms. Servan-Schreiber focused on output shares, which is what US industry in Europe is all about. Whereas US firms produce largely in Europe to satisfy the European market, European firms traditionally have sourced for the US market by exporting from their domestic plants. General Motors and Ford have major subsidiaries in Britain and Germany, which were acquired in the 1920s. In the 1980s the larger Japanese auto firms – Toyota, Nissan, Honda, and Mitsubishi – began to establish plants in the United States.

Why firms invest abroad

The prospect of profits motivates most business investment decisions. There are a few exceptions: some decisions are made for vanity or to show the flag. General Leonard Wood established Sears, Roebuck stores in Mexico and elsewhere in Central America because he wanted to plant the US flag South of the Border. Air France maintains some money-losing routes for the glory of the country. A few firms may invest abroad because the corporation president likes those twice-a-year trips to Madrid or Florence. The list of ad hoc explanations for these non-economic investment decisions is long, and some individual investments may indeed be explained by one or several factors. Most of these non-economic investments are, however, likely to be a small part of the firm's activities, otherwise they would be too large an drag on the firm's ability to maintain its market share relative to aggressive competitors.

Since the patterns of foreign investment do not appear to be random among countries, there almost certainly must be a systematic explanation for most – but not necessarily all – foreign investments.

Compensating advantage and superiority

US firms competing in the European market are usually at a disadvantage in relation to their host-country competitors, since they incur costs their host-country competitors do not. Similarly Japanese firms producing in the United States generally incur higher production costs than their US competitors – unless they've sited their plants in areas with relatively low wage rates and tax rates relative to their established US competitors. The activities of the European subsidiaries of US firms must thus be managed from New York, or Los Angeles, or Des Moines if they are to be integrated with those of the US parent; the costs of plane travel across the Atlantic and international phone calls mount. The salaries and expenses of US managers in Europe may be several times higher than those of comparable European managers; the US managers receive housing allowances, and travel allowances, and educational allowances. Because of this cost disadvantage, firms with foreign subsidiaries must possess some offsetting advantages if their profit rates are to be comparable to those of their host-country competitors.

Similar statements might be made about European and Japanese firms which have bought subsidiaries in the United States. These firms believe that it is more profitable to satisfy the US market by producing in the United States than by exporting. The implication is unless they have a compensating advantage, their profits will be below those of their US competitors.

Three possible and non-exclusive advantages are attributed to the source-country firms – firms that establish productive facilities abroad. According to Servan-Schreiber, the US advantage is the product of the combination of managerial know-how and a flexible business system; US businessmen may be exceptionally competitive. The problem of superiority theories is that they imply that Mother Nature has favorites in the distribution of talent. If Americans were superior managers, the low-cost response for European firms would be to hire more American managers. Some do, and the success of the US management consulting firms in Europe – the McKinseys, Booz Allens, and Boston Consulting Groups – is a substitute for hiring American managers. Other objections to the superiority hypothesis include its failure to provide insights about why foreign investment is so large in some industries and so small in others – and its failure to explain why the Dutch and Swiss invest extensively abroad, unless the Dutch and Swiss are also superior. Moreover if this view is correct, it implies that the superiority of US businessmen declined sharply in the 1980s while the superiority of Japanese businessmen increased. And the would-be superiority of the Japanese firms must more or less have stopped in the early 1990s.

Indeed, this 'theory' is really a tautology. All it really says is that the managers of firms based in some countries are superior, and the evidence of their superiority is that they invest abroad.

A second explanation is that source-country firms have an advantage in the form of a patent or technical know-how, or marketing skills, or other firm-specific advantages. In a few industries, these advantages may derive from large US government programs in defense and space; however, this argument is irrelevant for the foreign investment activities of Ford and General Motors, Playboy Clubs, Holiday Inns, Coca-Cola, money center banks, firms in food-producing industries, and the like. Of course, the advantages might reflect the fact that relatively high US wages compel US firms to give greater attention to reducing their costs by developing labor-saving processes, while intense competition forces US firms to develop new products for both old and newly created needs. So US firms tend to develop 'advantages' more rapidly than firms in other countries. Once these new products and processes have been developed to satisfy the US domestic market, these firms then seek to exploit these advantages to satisfy demands in foreign markets. So the explanation is directed to the market-share question.

Presumably, the factors which explain why US firms develop these advantages might also explain why firms headquartered in the Netherlands, Switzerland, and Sweden also develop advantages which they then use to increase their sales abroad. The question of what source-country firms headquartered in different countries have in common becomes a question of the identification of the shared characteristics of the firms that develop advantages that have value in foreign countries.

The shortcoming of explanations of international ownership based on firm-specific advantages is their incompleteness about why firms in some countries develop more of these advantages than firms in other countries. Moreover, US firms, and Swiss firms, and Dutch firms could sell their patents, know-how, and product advantages to foreign firms rather than incur the costs of managing subsidiaries located abroad. Indeed, many US firms do exactly that by licensing their advantages. Coca-Cola sells franchises and its concentrate to foreign bottling companies. Most McDonald's outlets in foreign countries are licenced. If the sales prices for advantages were sufficiently high, few US firms would ever incur the cost of establishing subsidiaries abroad.

So the reluctance to sell the firm-specific advantages to host-country firms must be explained. One suggestion is that firms fear that such sales might facilitate the growth of foreign firms which would later become their competitors. An alternative suggestion is that firms may find it difficult to sell the advantages, perhaps because they are ill-defined, especially if R&D leads to continuing changes in the advantages or if they involve marketing know-how. Thus each time the 'know-how' changes, a new negotiation between producer and buyer might be necessary. The more general reason for their reluctance to sell their advantages is that these firms believe their income will be higher if they exploit their advantages through wholly-owned subsidiaries rather than if they sell them.

Maintaining rate of growth

A third explanation is that firms invest abroad when maintaining the rate of growth of sales within their traditional industries in the domestic market becomes increasingly difficult or expensive. One reason might be that domestic demand for their products is growing more slowly, perhaps because the domestic market has become saturated. The intuition is that the firm's sales grow rapidly in the areas approximate to the garage or shop or store where the firm was established initially; then in response to the rapid increase in the market share in these nearby areas, the firm begins to increase sales in more distant geographic areas. The motivation is that it is easier or less costly to achieve a given increase in sales if the market share is small than if the market share is large. The firm realizes that if the growth rate of sales slows, the firm is likely to age; both its employees and the plant and equipment are likely on average to become older. The logic is that the when the firm is expanding its sales at a rapid rate, the newly hired employees will be relatively young and there will be substantial investment in new plant and equipment. As the growth rate slows, then the labor force is likely to become older, and the unit labor costs may increase because the increase in wage rates will exceed the increase in productivity. Similarly as the growth rate slows, the rate of investment in plant and equipment is likely to decline, and the average age of the productive facilities will increase; other firms in the same industry that have been able to maintain more rapid growth rates will invest in plant and equipment that may incorporate the newest technologies.

In this situation, the firm might expand into other industries in the domestic market – that is, the firm might cross the borders between industries. Alternatively, the firm might cross national borders and expand abroad with its traditional products. And, of course, the firm might do both. For many firms, crossing national borders may be easier than crossing industry borders at home, given their expertise in producing and marketing particular products.

The proposition that the firm wishes to maintain its growth rate to prevent or limit aging may explain why the firm continues to hunt for new markets as its share of the established markets increases; eventually some of these new markets will be in foreign countries. This view might explain why firms seek foreign markets, but not why they produce abroad – it might explain *market* shares, but it does not explain *output* shares.

The shortcoming of this group of explanations is that they tell a story about why the firm may wish to expand and why it may wish to expand its sales in foreign countries, but they don't identify the advantage of the source-country firms that enable them to compensate for the costs of economic distance. And these approaches don't provide a handle for explaining which countries are the source and which are the host countries, and why the United States appears to be becoming a host country at a rapid rate after having been a dominant source country.

Capital market advantages

A fourth explanation of the country pattern of direct foreign investment – the capital market view – is that US firms and those based in other source countries have an advantage in the world capital market. One form of this advantage is that these firms can borrow at lower interest rates than their competitors headquartered in countries identified with higher interest rates. An even more important form of this advantage is that shares of these firms headquartered in countries identified with low interest rates sell at higher prices than the shares of firms in the host countries – the countries identified with higher interest rates. These firms benefit from a country-specific advantage in the form of a lower cost of capital.

Interest rates on US dollar bonds have been lower than those on comparable securities denominated in nearly every other currency for most of the last half-century, and especially during those periods when US firms invested abroad extensively. Since the US dollar is their domestic currency, US firms generally have been able to borrow on more advantageous terms than their foreign competitors. Canadian and European firms have come to New York to issue US dollar bonds, not because they want to spend the funds in the United States but because interest rates on US dollar securities were sufficiently below their domestic interest rates to justify incurring the risk of loss from depreciation of their currencies relative to the US dollar.

One consequence of the general preference of investors for US dollar securities was that US firms were willing to pay a higher price for an advantage – such as a technological innovation – than non-US firms. And given an opportunity to increase its income by undertaking a new project, a US firm would generally pay a higher price for the same anticipated income stream than a non-US firm. The other side of the coin is that if a US firm buys a French firm, even though the earnings of the French subsidiary remain unchanged, investors would be willing to pay more for the shares of the US firm because of their preferences for US dollar-denominated securities.

This view suggests that the advantages of US firms are inherent in investor preferences for securities denominated in the US dollar, just as the advantages of Swiss firms are inherent in investor preferences for securities denominated in the Swiss franc. US firms are identified with US dollar equities, just as Swiss firms are identified with Swiss franc equities, and Dutch firms with guilder equities. A firm cannot change the currency denomination of its equities without changing its national identity. And firms almost never change their nationalities. (Some British firms that were primarily involved in Malaysia shifted their domicile from London to Kuala Lumpur after Malaysia became independent, and one or two firms headquartered in Hong Kong moved their main offices elsewhere in anticipation of the British departure from Hong Kong in 1997.) As long as interest rates on US dollar securities are low relative to those on comparable securities denominated in other currencies, US firms will have a country-specific advantage – an advantage that firms headquartered in most foreign countries cannot buy since it is inherent in the system rather than in the behavior of individual firms.

The implication of this capital market explanation is that the source countries for foreign investment are those with relatively low interest rates. Casual observation suggests that the countries other than the United States which have been large exporters of direct foreign investment – Switzerland, the Netherlands, and Great Britain – have traditionally been low-interest rate countries. The Netherlands was the low-interest rate country in the eighteenth century, when the Dutch empire was expanding abroad and Dutch trading firms were setting up overseas offices. In the nineteenth century, Great Britain was the low-interest rate country, and British firms followed the expansion of the empire. Even though both empires have shrunk markedly, the large international businesses such as Unilever and Shell in the Netherlands and in Great Britain have continued to flourish.

The capital market view also explains the pattern of ownership in different countries – whether individual countries will be source or host countries. As long as the US dollar is the preferred currency, US firms will establish foreign branches and buy up foreign firms. Foreign ownership of plants in the United States and foreign takeovers of US firms may increase, but the capital market explanation suggests that the growth of US investment abroad will be substantially larger: more importantly, the output shares of US firms will increase.

Exchange rate changes

The test of any theory is its ability to explain observed events. One of the most demanding phenomena to explain is the surge in investment in the United States by Japanese and European firms in the late 1970s and again in the second half of the 1980s. How capable are these theories of explaining the takeovers of Howard Johnson's and A & P and Marshall Field & Co. by firms headquartered abroad? The Servan-Schreiber view would be that – all of a sudden – the Europeans and the Japanese developed superior abilities to combine technical and managerial skills. In contrast, if the theories that emphasize firm-specific advantages are correct, the implication is that Japanese and European firms must have surged ahead of US firms in developing such advantages – yet the relevance of these advantages to the foreign takeovers of US firms is questionable.

There are newspaper stories which suggest that foreign firms invested extensively in the United States because they wanted to participate in the largest consumer market in the world; however, many participate in the US market by exporting their domestic production. Some firms are said to have invested in the United States as political insurance; they feared that military events in Europe or moves toward governmental ownership would handicap their survivability. Yet the advantage of these foreign firms relative to US firms in the US market remains unexplained.

Few theories therefore do a good job of explaining why the incentive of US firms to invest abroad declined in the 1980s, while the incentive for German and Japanese firms to invest abroad increased. The change in the low-cost location of investment is explained by the changes in exchange rates, which have been larger than the changes in relative costs of production. During the same period that the German mark and the Japanese yen appreciated, interest rates on assets denominated in these currencies fell; and so firms headquartered in both countries had less of a disadvantage – and more of an advantage – than firms based in the United States.

US dominance of multinationals

Several factors explain why US firms still seem to dominate the lists of multinationals, despite the surges in the foreign investments of Japanese and German firms in the 1970s and the 1980s: dominance on the list of multinationals might be measured by total sales or aggregate assets. One is that the domestic US market for most goods is large, more than twice as large as the Japanese market, and more than three times as large as the German market. So US firms become relatively larger by producing just for the domestic market. At some stage, however, the domestic market tends to become saturated, and the opportunity to maintain the rate of growth of sales in the domestic market diminishes, so if firms are to maintain their growth rates, then they must begin to sell abroad. Partly because the levels of *per capita* income in the United States have been higher than in most other industrial countries, this limit tends to be encountered in the United States before it is met abroad – even though the foreign countries are smaller. For example, the rate of growth of auto sales in the United States slowed in the late 1950s and the 1960s because most families already had a car; the similar limit in Japan was encountered only in the 1980s.

Partly because US wages in many industries were higher than wages in the same industries in other countries, production costs in the United States were generally higher than production costs in these other countries for much of the period from the 1920s to the 1970s. US firms were obliged to invest and produce abroad if they were to be competitive in foreign markets. The result of the real depreciation of the US dollar relative to the German mark and the Japanese yen in the late 1970s and the late 1980s is that the locational advantage changed in favor of the United States. Firms headquartered in Europe and Japan realized that they had to establish US factories to be able to continue to supply the US market on a profitable basis; both Mercedes and BMW, for example, established automobile factories in the Southeastern part of the United States. (Some Japanese firms have invested in the United States because of a fear that their access to the US market might be constrained by various import barriers.)

A third reason for the US dominance is that US firms have generally had an advantage in the international capital market throughout most of the period since the end of the First World War, with the exception of the late 1970s and the 1980s; the cost of capital for US firms was below the cost of capital for firms in most foreign countries, with the exception of Switzerland, the Netherlands, and (in the 1980s) Germany and Japan. This cost of capital advantage reflects the fact that the US dollar has been the currency at the top of the hit parade for most of the twentieth century, with the exception of the brief period when the US inflation rate seemed out of control and then when a tough anti-inflationary policy was adopted to move the United States back to price level stability.

Paradoxically US firms seem dominant in the industries associated with rapid technological change such as biogenetics and computer hardware and software. At the same time, US firms have a major market share in fast foods and soft drinks – industries identified with economies of scale and marketing skills.

One question that follows is why foreign firms are so eager to invest in the United States, even though they frequently first enter the United States by acquiring established US firms, and often pay premium prices for these firms. One reason is that the US market is the largest and generally the most open in the world, so that a foreign firm entering the US market is less likely to elicit a direct challenge from domestic competitors than if the firm enters some other foreign market with the same level of foreign sales. A related reason is that the lessons developed in the US market are like a postgraduate course in marketing and strategic development; the lessons that German firms learn in the US market will be useful in competing with US firms in the German and other European markets.

The costs of direct foreign investment

One of the paradoxes of recent decades is that both home-country and host-country governments have questioned the economic advantages attached to the activities of multinational firms. That these firms have grown and expanded suggests efficiencies greater than those of the smaller domestic firms they have replaced. The benefits of these efficiencies must be distributed among their employees in the form of higher wages and salaries, or among their customers in the form of lower prices, or among their shareholders as higher profits and dividends. And if wages and profits are higher, then the tax collectors will gain, since the tax base will be higher. All four groups may gain. And the source country or the host country may gain as a result of their activities, or both may gain; it is implausible that both home and host countries could be worse off at the same time.

Source countries

The source countries have several major criticisms of multinationals. One involves runaway jobs; unions often find that the multinational firms circumvent their national monopoly over the supply of labor. Foreign investment affects the distribution of jobs among countries, just as changes in trade patterns do. Belatedly – 50 years belatedly – the unions are becoming interested in the international labor situation. Hence, the choice for the unions in the source country is whether to merge with unions in the host countries or to develop some other fraternal relationship with them.

A second criticism involves taxes: the foreign income of the multinational firms headquartered in the United States is taxed initially by the foreign government, and in most cases there is little left over for the US tax collector. The United States has double-taxation agreements with many other countries; these agreements provide that the income is taxable first in the country in which it is earned, and that the combined tax rate of the foreign host and the US government cannot exceed the higher of the two national rates. Assume the British tax rate is 40 percent and the US rate is 50 percent. If a US firm invests at home, each dollar of profit generates 50 cents for the US tax collector. If the firm invests in Britain, each dollar of profit generates 40 cents for the British tax collector and only 10 cents for the US tax collector.

A third concern involves the adverse balance-of-payments consequences of multinationals' activities. Foreign investments mean that exports decline and imports increase more rapidly than might otherwise occur. While the payment of dividends may counter the loss of exports, the offset may be partial rather than complete.

These criticisms of multinationals imply that the source-country firms face a choice between producing at home or producing abroad, when the effective choice for some firms may be producing abroad or not producing at all. The shift in the production of many electronics products to Southeast Asia occurred because production costs there were much lower than in the United States; if US firms had not joined German, Dutch, and Japanese firms in this move, they would have lost both their export markets and the domestic market. The loss of US jobs, the shortfall in US tax revenues, and the adverse impact on the US balance of payments would have been even sharper. Even if US firms might have retained a domestic market, at least for a while, without shifting to offshore production, their long-run competitive position would have been weaker.

There are other criticisms. During the dollar crises, the multinationals moved funds to avoid losses from changes in exchange rates; some may have also sought to profit from these changes. Some critics even suggest that the dollar crises resulted from the behavior of these firms, and not from the mismanagement of the system. An even more sensitive issue involves the alleged political involvement of multinationals in the host countries. Multinationals may contribute to political parties, much as host-country firms do. ITT tried to forestall the election of Allende in Chile; many foreign firms retain representatives in Washington. Again, the firms say they act to protect their interests. The criticism is that the interests of the multinational firms may not be identical with US national interests nor with the interests of the host countries – but then the interests of US firms may not be identical with that of the US government.

Host countries

Host-country governments – or at least the US government – may be embarrassed and inconvenienced by disclosure of the political activities of multinationals. But the managers of the firms are paid to protect the firm's interests, and they have on occasion found that the methods of decisionmaking and persuasion that are typical, or at least not uncommon, in the host country would not be generally accepted at a New England town meeting.

Host-country attitudes toward multinational firms are ambivalent. Many countries compete to attract foreign firms, for they bring employment, on-the-job training, and tax revenues. In many products, these firms provide access to world markets. Yet foreign investment has been much criticized within the host countries. Some of these criticisms are vague and reflect simple-minded xenophobia; foreign investment is equated with imperialism. Having nationals work for foreigners or having foreigners own domestic resources is said to demean the nation. Other criticisms are more specific: the foreign firm exploits the nation's patrimony of non-reproducible petroleum, or copper, or bauxite, or tin, or reduces employment, or evades taxes, or stifles domestic entrepreneurship. The host-country government may feel that foreign-owned firms diminish its sovereignty and may resent these firms' involvement in the domestic political process.

Appraisal of these criticisms requires a benchmark – a view of what would have happened to growth, income, employment, and corporate development in the host country had foreign investment not taken place.

One of the major concerns of small countries is that they might become technological backwaters; these countries fear that because their own science and technology and industries do not offer attrac-

---

Box 20.1   If There Were No Foreign Firms in Canada

Assume that the Canadian government had progressively restricted the operation of foreign firms in Canada. More of the Canadian market would not be supplied by the domestic production of Canadian firms, but by imports. And Canadian imports from the same US firms which do not have Canadian subsidiaries would increase. Canadian incomes would be lower, or at least would increase less rapidly, since the supply of capital and knowledge would be smaller or more expensive. But determining the relative size of each of these adjustments is virtually impossible on an *a priori* basis. The Canadian firms that replaced the US firms would import some of the resources that the Canadian subsidiaries of US firms now get from their parents, and they might pay higher prices. As a group, Canadians would be worse off. But whether they would be worse off by 1 percent or 5 percent is difficult to estimate. Perhaps they might gain more control over their destiny – or their culture might remain purer – but these factors too are difficult to measure – probably because they are trivial.

tive careers, highly educated and trained nationals will migrate to the larger countries. (People in Kansas feel the same way.) Multinational companies often centralize their R&D activities in a relatively few locations, which is why government officials sometimes conclude that the multinational firms impede the development of a viable local scientific community. The presumption is that in the absence of the multinational company, domestic firms would undertake R&D comparable to that done abroad by the foreign firm. Perhaps. But it is equally possible that the domestic firms might import their R&D because the costs of imports would be less than domestic production costs.

Host-country governments worry that multinational firms diminish their sovereignty. Occasionally the head office of a multinational firm may, in response to pressures from its own government, direct the subsidiary to cease exporting to certain markets or to shift funds to the home office. Host countries fear that the power and influence of the state may not be used directly against a foreign firm, perhaps because it enjoys the backing of its more powerful government. The host-country government would like to be able to rely on foreign as well as on domestic firms to increase exports or boost employment, or to take other measures that may not be in the firm's interests. Foreign firms may be less amenable to such measures than domestic firms would be. Perhaps. But foreign firms know they can be asked – or forced – to leave the country; for this reason, they may be less able than domestic firms to withstand government pressures.

To the extent that multinational firms offer access to the world market, they are likely to be the 'pawns' of competing national governments. For example, when Canada adopted a set of measures to induce US auto companies to produce more cars in Canada, US employment and US tax revenues declined. When Malaya adopted a set of measures to attract foreign electronics firms, Singapore and Taiwan began to worry, much more than the United States and Japan did.

Foreign firms are sometimes accused of making excessively high profits, especially in the extraction of non-reproducible resources. Host-country governments know that mines or wells will eventually be exhausted, so they want to maximize national gains from these resources. Typically, the host-country governments have auctioned concessions to exploit the resources; they may receive a lump-sum payment or a contingent payment based on profits. If a concession proves attractive and profitable, then a host country may seek to revise the contract in its own favor. But the game is asymmetrical; if the firm fails to discover oil or the concession proves unprofitable, the company never gets a refund. In some cases, of course, the arguments for reopening the contract may be strong; perhaps the state issued the concession under duress, or a minister may have been bribed and have thus betrayed the interests of his government. Since most resource-owning countries manage to attract foreign firms to exploit their resources, the threat of contact renegotiation cannot be too severe. And, increasingly, the firms may recognize the likelihood of expropriation as they determine how much – or how little – to bid.

In manufacturing, the profits earned by a foreign company reflect its efficiency. High profits mean that the firm can satisfy the market demands more efficiently than its domestic competitors. High profits also mean higher taxes to the host-country government. And greater efficiency allows the firm to use fewer domestic resources, which are thus available for other uses. Most governments, of course, would like to get the taxes and the efficiency, but at a lower cost in terms of profits to foreign firms.

The arguments are inconclusive. At various times (like nearly every other year), the Canadians have set up study groups to determine whether Canadian interests have been served by the presence of multinationals. There is a supply of anecdotes about their misbehavior; the critics have a point or two, if not a case. The virulence of the criticism is more evidence of the increasing nationalist sentiment so evident in national monetary policies. Various governments have set up foreign investment review boards to screen desirable foreign investments from less desirable proposals. The United Nations has developed a code of conduct for multinational firms, a sort of Miss Manners' guide to 'correct' behavior. Why the code should apply only to multinational firms is unclear; fairness suggests that all domestic firms should also follow the code.

Whither the conflict?

The conflict between governments and multinationals is likely to become more intense. Problems arise because the firms are dynamic organizations and respond to developments in technology and markets, while political organizations – states – remain largely static. Firms grow and consolidate and expand their activities around the world in response to changing profit opportunities, while states are locked into a more or less fixed set of boundaries. Reductions in the costs of transportation and communication increase the mobility of business firms, but this increased mobility may be viewed as a threat by the of host-country governments.

In many industries the growth and expansion of multinationals has increased competition and reduced the monopoly power of the dominant domestic firms. The US automobile industry is much more competitive because of the eagerness of foreign firms to export to the US market, and the German automobile industry is more competitive because of the presence of General Motors and Ford. Sony and Panasonic have greatly increased competition, so there is now an international electronics industry. In drugs, chemicals, and numerous other industries, trade and investment have substantially increased the number of participants. Evidence of unusually attractive profits induces other firms to enter the market. Inevitably, pressures to regulate the multinational corporations – and to regulate the capacity of states to regulate these corporations – will develop. Because the issues are complex and the interests of various states and corporations highly diverse, ambitious efforts at a regulatory code are not likely to succeed.

Three changes are possible.

- The first is an agreement among governments to limit their reach into the foreign activities of firms which they identify as 'their corporate citizens' – or into the extraterritorial span of national control. This change would be directed primarily at the United States.
- The second, a set of rules governing the entrance of foreign firms into manufacturing, would be much like the rules governing the access of foreign goods to the domestic markets. These rules might specify when access should be unimpaired and when the firm might be required to join with a local partner.
- The third is a set of rules about compensation for foreign firms when their property is expropriated or when they are otherwise deprived of the full value of their advantages.

Yet the likelihood of meaningful rules is small, at least in the near future. And the reason is that governments in both the source and host countries appear to find more political support in what is effectively an ad hoc approach to regulation – in other words, the economic issues interest them less than the domestic votes.

21
Japan – The First Superstate?

In 1970 Herman Kahn, physicist and nuclear theorist, predicted that Japan would become the first superstate – that Japan's GNP would double between 1970 and 1975, and again between 1975 and 1980 – a fourfold expansion in a decade. Between 1970 and 2000, annual average growth rates would reach 9 percent a year, so that by the year 2000 GNP in Japan would be nearly 16 times the 1970 levels. The news was heartening to the Japanese and frightening to most other countries because of the competitive impact of Japanese goods in world markets.

The Japanese challenge

No country has presented more of a challenge to international trade and monetary arrangements in the 1970s and 1980s than Japan. Yet a prediction in 1950 or in 1960 that Japanese industry would present a major threat to US and German firms in relatively few years would have seemed absurd. Japan had been bombed extensively in the last several years of the Second World War, its factories ravaged. Japan had lost its colonies in Manchuria, Korea, and Taiwan. Japan had very few raw materials and imported most of its energy and much of its food. It almost seemed as if Japan would remain forever on the international dole – if there had been any willing donors.

Within a generation, Japanese exports were the most rapidly growing component of international trade. Japanese producers dominated world markets for steel, ships, autos, electronic products, and photo optics.. By the early 1970s the Japanese firms in many industries seemed a threat to their foreign competitors, more insidious than during the Second World War, for the Japanese seemed to be playing by the rules of the system and winning. By the late 1970s, Japanese automobile production was larger than US automobile production. The major Japanese automobile firms – Toyota and Nissan – began to produce superb up-scale cars, the Lexus and the Infinity. Then the Japanese auto firms began to establish production and assembly facilities in the United States.

Early in the 1960s the Japanese government had adopted a 10-year 'Doubling National Income' plan. With a population growth rate of 1 percent a year, per capita incomes would double in a decade if productivity gains – increases in output per person employed per year – averaged 7 percent a year. Actual economic performance beat the targets of the plan, in contrast to most other countries, where economic performance has almost always lagged behind the target. In the 1960s *per capita* incomes in Japan were increasing at a rate of 10 percent a year, so that in 1967 *per capita* incomes were twice as high as in 1960.

Kahn's prediction was based on the extrapolation of the growth rates of the 1960s through the next 30 years. In the 1960s, Japan had grown at the rate of 12 percent a year; in contrast, the United States had grown at the rate of 3 percent, and Germany and France at rates of 6–7 percent a year. Simple arithmetic suggests that if a country with a lower level of GDP grows more rapidly than countries with higher levels of GDP, then eventually the GDP in the rapid-growth country will eventually surpass GDP in the slow growth countries, no matter how large its initial disadvantage.

Secrets of the miracle

In the early 1980s, a new industry appeared – books which offered the secrets of the Japanese economic miracle. The story in *Japan as Number One*, by Ezra F. Vogel, is one of tradition, literacy, social cohesion, and a Puritan or Confucian work ethic. *The Art of Japanese Management*, by Richard T. Pascale and Anthony G. Althos, and *Theory Z*, by William Ouchi, emphasized the skill of industrial managers in developing a consensus among workers before introducing change. *The East Asia Edge* highlighted the 'Four Tigers' – Korea, Hong Kong, Taiwan, and Singapore – who were achieving gains in economic well-being about as rapidly as Japan. *Shogun*, by James Clavell, had its own story, at least by implication; business firms in various industries competed extensively for market share, just as several centuries earlier feudal war lords had competed for power and turf, fame and attention.

Some explanations gave priority to 'Japan, Inc.,' asserting that the economic success was a result of industrial policy in Japan, which involved cooperative planning between business and government leaders about developing new products and entering new foreign markets. The general idea was that the heads of the large firms in each industry met with the senior officials from the Ministry of Finance and from the Ministry of International Trade and Industry (MITI) in the 'special situations' room in the basement of the Imperial Palace to decide how to dominate world markets. Probably each of these explanations had some validity – and so the question is to determine their relative importance.

Increases in national income result from increases both in the number of hours worked, and in labor output or productivity per hour. Increases in the volume of capital equipment and technological improvement lead to increases in productivity: the workers are smarter and have more powerful machines to work with.

In most industrial societies, labor supplies grew rapidly during the 1960s as members of the post-Second World War baby boom graduated from school and entered the labor force. Yet in all of these economies, the work week was becoming shorter, vacations were becoming longer, there were more holidays with pay, and the retirement age was lowered. All these changes were normal economic responses to growing material affluence, so the number of hours of work per year declined. Increasing absenteeism and more voluntary unemployment also led to a reduction in the effective labor supply. So the differences among countries in their growth rates largely reflected differences in productivity growth. Somehow the Japanese did something better – while they may have worked harder, they could not have worked progressively harder year after year for a decade and a half, or else they should have been able to run the mile in two and a half minutes.

The arithmetic of economic growth should be distinguished from the economics of growth. What was needed was a story that explained why Japanese firms invested so much, and whether the high productivity growth rate was closely tied to the high rates of household saving and business investment. The high personal savings rate – three times as high as in the United States – was explained in institutional terms; because the benefits of government's social security program were so modest, individuals saved to provide for their old age. And because the real rate of interest earned by savers – the money interest rate adjusted for the inflation rate – was negative, individuals needed to save a very high proportion of their income to achieve an increase in the purchasing power of their cumulative savings.

Then the willingness of Japanese firms to invest had to be explained. One story centered on the Japan, Inc. concept – that the business and government leaders planned the penetration and takeover of world markets. The usual story was that the Japanese facilitated business investment, especially into new products that offered higher value added. Moreover, the Japanese took advantage of the low tariffs abroad, but foreign firms found it difficult to sell in the Japanese market because of a variety of formal and informal import barriers. There were continued suggestions that the Japanese government provided various subsidies to firms that were developing new products – but documenting this view proved difficult. And the officials in the Ministry of Finance had rigged the credit system through ceilings on interest rates; indeed because real interest rates were negative, business borrowers were implicitly subsidized by individual savers.

For fans of the market system and free trade, these ideas were heretical; it was an article of faith that government intervention in the economy would lead to a lower growth rate because of the distortions to the efficient use of resources caused by the regulations. There was a lot of empirical support for this view. The view that a planned economic system could deliver a higher growth rate than a market system was disturbing. So was the idea that a country could gain if it maintained tariffs and other barriers to imports; the free trade argument that dates back to Adam Smith's *The Wealth of a Nation* in 1776 claimed that such barriers retard growth.

Slowdown in growth

Soon after Kahn's book appeared, the Japanese economy began to falter; there was a sharp recession in 1971. At the time of the first oil shock in 1973–74, the Japanese price level increased by 30 percent in one year. In 1974, Japan was hit by the world recession. It began to appear that the cyclical behavior of the Japanese economy mimicked the swings of the world business cycle, but in an exaggerated fashion. When world business was booming, the Japanese economy purred. But when the world economy burped, the indigestion in Japan was severe. Despite these burps, the Japanese economic growth rate in the 1970s was higher than in the other industrial economies. But the excess of the Japanese growth rate over the US growth rate in the 1970s was significantly lower than in the previous several decades.

The slowdown in the Japanese growth rate was almost certainly inevitable. Those who had projected a continuation of rapid growth had failed to recognize that no element in the system can grow more rapidly than the system itself for an extended period. Rapid growth in Japanese income requires a corresponding rapid growth in Japanese imports, because Japan lacks raw materials and also imports many of its foods. The growth in imports must be financed by an approximately equal rapid growth of exports. If Japanese exports grow at 8 percent a year while world exports grow at 4 percent a year, then Japanese exports would eventually be larger than world exports – and that would be a neat trick.

The second factor that is usually overlooked is the contrast between Japanese economic growth in the 1950s and the 1960s and the growth record before the Second World War. From the late nineteenth century until the beginning of what has been euphemistically called 'The Great Pacific Confusion' in Tokyo, economic growth in Japan averaged between 4.0 and 4.5 percent a year. The increase in the growth rate in the several decades before 1900 resulted from a commitment to industrialize, undertaken to prevent or withstand the rapacious Western powers who coveted spheres of influence and turf in Japan as they had in China. This economic growth rate, which consisted of productivity gains of about 3 percent a year and increases in the labor force of about 1 percent a year, was modestly higher than the growth rates of most other countries during the early stages of their industrialization.

Per capita incomes in Japan did not change significantly during the Second World War. Immediately after the war, however, cut off from supplies, extensively damaged by massive bombing, short of foods and raw material, and bereft of foreign markets, *per capita* incomes fell sharply. Because they could not export, they could not earn the foreign exchange necessary to buy raw materials; and without raw materials, they could not produce for export. So it was Catch-22.

In the late 1940s and early 1950s, economic growth in Japan began to increase rapidly, more so than at any time in the previous 60 years. But much of this growth was 'making up arrears' and recovering from the calamitous economic consequences of the war. By replacing the railway switches, the railway system was put back to work; small investments in a few strategic locations led to a large increase in output. So the productivity growth was phenomenal. However, not until the mid-1950s did *per capita* incomes in Japan reach 1940 levels. Incomes in the United States had more than doubled during the same 15 years.

Assume, in the absence of war, that Japanese income had continued to grow at the historic rate of 4 percent a year. Then *per capita* income would have doubled from 1940 to 1958 and doubled again from 1958 to 1976. However, in the mid-1950s, *per capita* incomes were one-half of what they would have been had there been no war. The rapid growth in the 1960s meant that Japan actually achieved the income levels it would have attained had there been no war, if the pre-1940 growth rate had continued into the 1940s, the 1950s, and the 1960s.

Thus far, the story is one of arithmetic. A number of stories might explain why the growth rate was so much higher after the war than before. One is that once the labor force, the savings rate, and competitive spirit were organized to achieve an 8 percent growth rate, that momentum alone would lead to a continuation of this rate. The increase in the growth rate in the early postwar years could be viewed as a counterpart to the increase in the growth rate in the late nineteenth century, when the campaign to industrialize was first undertaken.

The competing scenario is that the Japanese economy had tremendous excess capacity immediately following the Second World War, and that rapid growth could be maintained as long as there was some excess capacity and no severe bottlenecks. Rapid growth meant more effective use of the existing capacity rather than the rapid expansion of capacity. In the early postwar period there was in fact substantial idle capacity in industry because of the shortages of switches, spare parts, raw materials, and markets. But as this idle capacity became utilized, continuing the growth momentum would become progressively more difficult. Similarly, the skills of the labor force may have been less than fully utilized if many individuals were working at jobs below their potential as gauged by their education. Once the skills of the labor force were fully utilized, maintaining the growth rate would prove more difficult.

Japan, Inc.

All economies face the same questions – what goods and service should be produced, in what volumes, and by what techniques? In some economies, decisions about what to produce and how to produce are made in a highly decentralized way by the managers in tens of thousands of firms, in response to their views about consumer demands and industrial demands. In other countries a few government officials – perhaps at a planning agency or the finance ministry – make these same decisions; if they err, some goods will be in short supply and others will pile up in the stores. In both cases there is always the concern that if too many firms invest in the plant and equipment designed to produce similar goods, productive capacity will be excessive, prices will be cut to levels below total costs, anticipated profits will evaporate, and some firms will incur substantial losses.

Adam Smith observed that businessmen rarely meet without deciding how to 'carve up' markets – these businessmen want to avoid the type of competition that might lead to declines in the prices of the goods they sell. In the United States, legislation is intended to limit various practices that might lead to a decline in competition. Few other countries have such pro-competitive legislation. The concern is that as a consequence of the more stringent US antitrust policies, foreign firms have an advantage – they can be confident that their investments will be profitable, and that the supplies of goods produced will not be so large as to depress prices sharply, because they can meet and discuss the measures to limit cut-throat competition. In contrast, managers of US firms are subject to greater uncertainty about whether contemplated investments will prove profitable, and so they are more reluctant to make the investments in new plant and equipment.

Unfair competitive advantage?

Somehow the view became pervasive that the Japanese success in penetrating the world markets with textiles, steel, autos, TVs and VCRs reflected the fact that Japanese firms had an unfair competitive advantage. Partly the criticism centered on trade imbalances, and in particular the Japanese trade surpluses in commodities such as electronics, autos, computers. Japanese imports were largely raw materials, and most of these products were non-competitive with anything produced in Japan. In contrast, Japanese exports to the industrial countries were manufactured goods, and almost always competitive with goods produced in those countries. The ratios of Japanese imports of manufactured products to domestic consumption of these same manufactures was much below the comparable ratios in any other industrial country, leading to the charge that import barriers were both formal and hidden in Japan. Moreover many Japanese imports of manufactured goods were luxury items like BMWs, Mercedes, and French crystal – goods which had few Japanese counterparts. There was also continuing concern that the Japanese were subsidizing exports or otherwise 'dumping them' – selling these goods in the United States and in other foreign markets at prices significantly below the sum of the prices of these same goods in Tokyo, Kobe, and Osaka, and the transport costs for these goods from Japan to the United States. Or perhaps the

Japanese had an unfair advantage in the way their business system was organized.

The Japan, Inc. metaphor developed while Japanese economic growth was flourishing. Businessmen and officials of two powerful government agencies were supposed to meet to formalize market-sharing arrangements. The Ministry of Finance (MOF) supposedly controlled the supply of credit, and hence was in a powerful position to secure business cooperation because of its ability to supply credit to the commercial banks, which in turn allocated credit to individual firms that needed to borrow to expand capacity. The second agency, the Ministry of International Trade and Industry (MITI), controlled import licenses and hence was in a strong position to influence the investment decisions of individual firms. If these firms didn't listen, MITI would stall on requests for import licenses. Thus the Japan Inc. story was that businessmen responded readily to government initiatives, suggestions, and requests – to ensure that they could obtain credit and import licenses. According to this story, government officials were relatively strong and in a powerful position to affect business decisions.

An alternative model of competition within Japan is a twentieth-century version of struggles among feudal warlords for power, authority, and prestige. According to this view, the descendants of these war lords, the *zaibatsu* or *keiretsu* – the Sumitomos, the Mitsubishis, the Mitsuis – are a family of related firms in a variety of industries. Each family is centered on a bank and includes a trading firm, a steel firm, a shipping line, a petrochemical firm, a subset of textile firms, and so on. Each family of firms engages in extensive mutual support, favoring other members of the group in buying inputs and in supplying credits. There are interlocking share ownerships, which sharply reduce the likelihood of hostile takeovers. Moreover, within each industry, every firm is extremely conscious about its market position – whether it is the number 1 or the number 5 firm. Each firm accepts its market position, but is very reluctant to see any decline in its position because its prestige – and hence the prestige of the group – would diminish. Finally, unlike other competitive industrial countries, very few large firms go out of business, and mergers in most industries have been very infrequent.

The second model differs sharply from the first. The first suggests that rapid growth is a result of effective central planning or coordination. The second implies that rapid growth is a result of extensive competition, which may be more pervasive than in other industrial countries.

The role of capitalists and bankers

Consider the number of firms in the major industries in Japan, which almost always is much larger than the number of firms in each of these industries in the United States and in Europe. There are eight or nine major automobile firms in Japan, whereas there are only two large automobile firms in the United States and four large firms and only a few boutiques in Europe. The Japanese motorcycle industry includes Honda, Suzuki, Kawasaki, and Yamaha; Harley-Davidson is the only significant US producer of motorcycles. Kenwood, Matsushita, Sony, Toshiba, Hitachi, Sanyo, Sharp, AIWA, Yamaha, Denon, Nakamichi, Onkyo, and Luxman compete for market share in consumer electronics. Industry by industry, there are many more firms than in the United States and in Western Europe, even though the Japanese economy is less than half the size of the US economy. Economic growth has not led to a sharp reduction in the number of firms in Japan as it has in other industrial countries.

To maintain its market share, each firm in Japan must obtain the funds necessary to finance new investment in plant and equipment. If the firm incurs losses, financial support can be obtained from related firms. And the workers know that their futures are intimately linked with the success of their firm, so they accept smaller than average wage increases and smaller than average semi-annual bonuses. If their firm were to go bankrupt, the future of the employees would be bleak because the lifetime employment system means that job mobility is low.

The implication of these two factors – the emphasis on maintaining market share and lifetime employment – is that the roles of capitalists and bankers and workers in Japan are reversed from those in other market economies. In the United States, Britain, and Germany, the workers have the first claim on the revenues of the firm; firms go out of business when the wage rates they pay and their labor costs are too high relative to revenues for there to be enough left over to repay the bankers and other lenders, and to finance new investments. In Japan, by contrast, the firms first make the investments necessary to maintain their market share, and they pay interest to the bankers; the funds left over are divided among the workers, usually on the basis of age. So there is substantial difference among firms in wages paid individual workers with similar skills. This is possible because wages within each firm are determined by seniority rather than by job classification. Moreover, part of the wage payment consists of a semi-annual bonus, and the size of the bonus can be varied as revenues vary: if revenues are modest, then the bonus will be small.

The stability of market shares of individual firms in particular industries might seem consistent with the planning model or with the competitive model. If the planning model were the better explanation, it might be inferred that government would have attempted to rationalize the business system by encouraging mergers. Such mergers have occurred – but only to a modest extent – and often among banks to 'save' other banks that have been crippled by large loan losses. To the extent that the planning model is relevant, the Japanese growth rate has been reduced and the impact of Japanese competition in world markets has been dampened.

The asset price bubble

One of the surprises in the 1980s, and especially in the last several years of the decade, was the rapid climb of Japanese firms in their ranking on various world financial hit parades. Japanese banks dominated the hit parade of the world's largest banks – usually seven or eight or the 10 largest banks in the world were Japanese. The market value of Japanese firms increased sharply relative to the market values of firms headquartered in every other country; indeed, at the end of the decade the market value of Japanese firms was more than twice the market value of US firms. Since national income in Japan was then about half of US national income, the ratio of the market value of Japanese firms to Japanese GNP was four times the comparable ratio in the United States. The value of real estate in Japan increased to twice the value of US real estate – and Japan is about the size of California, and much of the country is mountainous. Newspapers were full of stories of the membership costs at various new golf courses in the country – in some cases the prices were in the range of $200,000 to $300,000. Japanese investors were massive buyers of real estate in the United States and Europe, especially of trophy properties – Rockefeller Center, the Pebble Beach Golf Course on the Monterey Peninsula in California. Japanese hotel groups and individual Japanese were large buyer of real estate in Hawaii; one new hotel was so costly that the average daily room rate was projected at $800 a day. Japanese firms went on a massive acquisition binge in the United States and Europe.

The Japanese appeared to have all the money: It seemed as if Herman Kahn's forecast was coming true. The Japanese were beginning to count the month and years before the forecast implicit in the title *'Japan as Number One'* would come to pass.

Moving into recession

From the beginning of January 1990, Japanese stock prices began to decline; by mid-1992 equity prices were 40 percent of their peak December 1989 values. Real estate prices began to decline, although at a slow rate. The buyer of the Pebble Beach Golf Course – who had paid $760 million – sold the course for $480 million to another Japanese. Japanese real estate and construction firms began to go bankrupt. Many of the real estate loans held by the Japanese banks became non-performing, because the rental incomes were significantly below the interest payments. The loss in personal wealth from the decline in stock prices and in real estate prices was phenomenally large. For the previous 40 years investment in real estate was a sure way to make money, because the price of real estate always seemed to be rising. As a result of the decline in real estate prices, individual investors began to reduce their spending. Because so many office buildings were less than fully occupied, the banks were reluctant to lend for new construction, with the result that new construction spending declined sharply.

The Japanese economy began to move into a recession; from 1992 to 1997 the growth rate in Japan was significantly below the growth rate in the United States. Because of the sluggish growth in consumer demand, business firms were reluctant to invest. So it seemed like a New Japan: and Kahn's forecast looked far less brilliant. In part, the slowdown in the economy was an inevitable result of the implosion of asset values and the resulting decline in personal wealth. Moreover, the government's sluggish response in recapitalizing the banks in a formal way compounded the problem; banks have not been aggressive lenders because they were increasingly concerned that their outstanding loans were too large relative to their capital.

The key question was whether Japan would recover its former growth momentum, or whether instead the Japanese economy would continue to limp along. The story told by those who believe that the sun is setting on Japan is that the country's population is aging at a rapid rate. Each female in Japan has only 1.8 children, in part because of the very cramped living accommodations in the urban areas and in part because young women have tasted the freedom associated with their own incomes and are reluctant to become homemakers. The absolute size of the population will begin to decline. As the population ages, consumption expenditures are declining because older populations buy less in the way of durables, and clothing, and even entertainment. Their savings tend to increase, at least until their final illness.

The paradox is that concern about the adequacy of funds for retirement led to an increase in the household savings rate. Sluggish growth in demand and the economy meant that interest rates declined far below those in other industrial countries; indeed, such low interest rates were last observed in the Great Depression of the 1930s. Because of a large part of the income of the retired Japanese comes from the interest on their savings accounts, the decline in their interest rates meant that their incomes declined, and as a result so did their consumption spending. The result was that the private virtue of a high savings rate had become a public vice because spending levels had declined below the levels necessary to keep the economy fully employed and growing at a rate higher than 2 percent a year.

Demographics or negative wealth?

So demographics might explain the sharp slowdown in the rate of economic growth. As much of the population begins to save for retirement, the level of domestic saving seems inordinately high relative to the domestic investment opportunities.

A second explanation for the sluggishness in economic growth resulted from the direct effects of the negative wealth impacts associated with the sharp declines in stock prices and real estate prices, and the indirect effects of these declines on the capital of Japanese banks. By almost any measure, the loan losses of these banks were significantly larger than their capital; some estimates indicated that these loan losses were between 15 and 20 percent of Japanese GNP. Even though these banks were under water in any strict 'mark-to-market' test, there was little indication that the banks might be closed with loss to depositors; everyone acted as if they had full confidence that the government would bail out the banks, or at least the depositors. Yet the banks themselves acted as if they were reluctant to extend loans, so observers came to the conclusion that there was a credit crunch.

The guarantee that the banks could not fail meant that they had been informally recapitalized by the government; the government had become the silent, major stockholder. But there was a stalemate: the government appeared unable to get sufficient agreement among the banks to move to a formal recapitalization – which would have meant that the losses incurred by these banks would be recognized. One problem was that best-managed of the banks – those with the smallest losses relative to their capital – did not want to be seen in the same group with the banks that had much higher ratios of loan losses to capital. But there almost certainly are other explanations for the sluggishness in the move from informal to formal recapitalization. The Japan, Inc. planning model suddenly appears largely irrelevant – and perhaps it was irrelevant even during the period of rapid growth.

And yet there is a paradox – despite the shortcomings of the Japanese economic performance as shown in the data on the relatively high rate of unemployment (for Japan), the sluggish rate of growth, the decline in industrial production, there was relatively little urgency in development of new government policies. Washington had a varied menu of measures that the Japanese government should adopt, including tax cuts, increases in government spending, and reduction of government regulation of firms in the financial services industry. In part, the lack of urgency in the development of such policies may have resulted from the lack of evidence about hardship in the streets.

The external impact of Japan

Cushioning the swings in the business cycle

The rapid increase in the size of the Japanese economy has had an increasingly disruptive impact on the economies of its major trading partners – and especially on the US economy. In the 1950s and 1960s, during the pegged-rate exchange system period, Japan had a stable balance of payments cycle: three years of progressively larger payments deficits attributable to an acceleration in the rate of economic growth were followed by a year of tight money, slow growth, and a payments surplus. The story is that as the business expansion in Japan developed momentum, the rate of growth of imports increased while the rate of growth of exports declined, so that the annual payments deficits became increasingly larger. These payments deficits were financed by increases in the amounts borrowed abroad from commercial banks in the United States and Europe. As the ability to borrow decreased, the Bank of Japan was forced to contract domestic credit, and the growth in Japanese demand and income become sluggish. Import demand dropped sharply and exports soared, for firms were much more eager to sell abroad once domestic growth slackened.

The Japanese payments balance responded quickly and a large payments surplus developed; the funds from the payments surplus were used to repay the loans incurred in the years with the payments deficits. And, because export sales were usually only 20 or 30 percent of domestic sales, a small reduction in domestic demand led to an increase in exports that was several times larger. The story was straightforward: once Japanese firms had the productive capacity in place, goods could be produced; if these goods could not be sold at home, they would be sold abroad at the prices necessary to clear the market. Better to sell at discount – or even at distress prices – abroad than to engage in price competition in the domestic market, or not to produce at all.

Thus whenever the rate of growth of domestic demand in Japan faltered, the United States and many other industrial countries experienced an increase in their imports from Japan. The growth of Japanese exports was counter cyclical to the growth of Japanese domestic income. The ability to divert productivity capacity from the domestic to the foreign markets enabled Japan to cushion the swings in its business cycle. Japan was exporting inflation to its trading partners when its own economy was booming because of the surge in its demand for imports, and it was exporting deflation to these same countries whenever its own growth slowed significantly because of the decline in its demand for imports.

In the 1950s and 1960s, the international monetary system could readily adjust to the payments deficits that resulted whenever the Japanese wanted to have payments surpluses because Japan still was a reasonably small country. Many of its exports were directed to the United States, which was the national market most open – or least closed – to Japanese goods. Moreover, marketing in a large open economy like that of the United States was substantially easier than trying to sell the same volume of goods in smaller countries. Individuals firms and groups of firms in the United States complained about unfair competition: they asserted that the prices of these goods in the US markets were substantially below the prices of comparable goods in Japan. The Japanese had two responses – that they were not dumping, but even if they were dumping, cutting prices was the only way they could increase their sales in the US market. So the US response was to lean on Japan to follow 'orderly marketing procedures.'

Export of payments imbalances

In the 1950s and most of the 1960s, after contractive monetary policy had shifted the payments balance into a comfortable surplus position, the Bank of Japan relaxed its monetary policies and the economy resumed its rapid growth rate. However, in the late 1960s, there was sharp change; when the Bank of Japan moved to a more expansive monetary stance, the increase in effective domestic demand was weaker. Because domestic demand in Japan was not growing nearly as rapidly as productive capacity (or as rapidly as domestic demand had grown in the 1960s), Japan continued to realize large payments surpluses as exports boomed. In effect the Japanese were selling Toyotas and Sonys abroad and using some of the funds from their export earnings to buy US Treasury Bills – not because this was intended, but because they could not manage their exports relative to imports.

In both 1969 and 1970, Japan's current account surpluses were 4–5 percent of it national income; in 1971 And 1972, the ratio approached 10 percent. Since for evey surplus there is a deficit, the inability of the Japanese to manage domestic demand relative to its productive capacity meant it was exporting very large payments deficits to its trading partners, principally the United States.

For the US consumers, increased availability of goods from Japan was a tremendous advantage in two very different ways. The variety of goods available in US markets was extended by imports from Japan, and, for an extended period, the quality of many of the goods available to them improved sharply. US producers responded by improving the quality and variety of their own products – the quality improvement was especially evident in automobiles produced by US firms. But for US producers of goods competitive with imports from Japan, the story was less hopeful: the increase in imports from Japan meant a decline in market share, output and employment, and profits – and a large number of US firms went out of business.

The large Japanese trade surplus in 1970 and 1971 and the resulting US payments deficits were a major factor in the breakdown of the Bretton Woods system. Even in the absence of more rapid inflation in the United States than abroad, the Japanese surpluses would have threatened the stability of the system. The revaluation of the Japanese yen in response to the excessively large Japanese payments surplus would have reduced this surplus somewhat; the tentative 'somewhat' reflects the fact that Japanese imports are not especially price-sensitive because such a large part of these imports are industrial raw materials and energy. And Japanese exports are not especially price-sensitive because Japanese firms are reluctant to reduce production and sales, even when net selling prices fall: the story is that many of their costs are fixed (because of their commitments to employ their workers for a 'lifetime') and so marginal costs are generally low relative to total costs. If a small revaluation would not have been effective, than a larger revaluation might have succeeded. In 1971, however, Japan was reluctant to revalue the yen: any decline in exports relative to imports would have intensified unemployment in Japan. A large part of the Camp David initiative in August 1971 was directed at inducing Japan to revalue the yen or to permit it to float; the German mark and the Canadian dollar had been floating for several months.

In 1973, as the world economy boomed and prices of raw materials imports increased, Japan's trade surplus declined. Japan's oil import bill increased by $15 billion a year. Japan had a modest payments deficit in 1974. When the world recession hit in 1975, domestic demand in Japan grew sluggishly, and once again Japanese producers began to ship more abroad. Comparisons across countries indicated a much greater cyclical variation in the payments balance in Japan than elsewhere. The story was simple – when the growth in Japanese income was rapid, Japan's exports would grow slowly, and when Japanese income grew slowly Japanese exports would grow rapidly. Variations in the growth of domestic income were the major factors in explaining the changes in Japanese trade balance.

With the move to floating exchange rates in the early 1970s, the textbooks predicted that Japan would always be in payments balance. But officials in the Bank of Japan had apparently not read the textbooks, for from time to time the Bank was a large buyer of US dollars in the foreign exchange market; the motivation was to limit the appreciation of the yen. Paradoxically, these Japanese payments surpluses were much, much larger than had ever been experienced under the pegged-rate system; when the rules of the Bretton Woods system were abandoned, the system was left without rules. Without intervention, the yen would have appreciated sharply, and Japanese exporters would have been obliged to cut export prices sharply, or else forgo sales. The problem was the same as under the pegged-rate system – if domestic income was growing sluggishly, then excess productivity capacity would have to be geared to export sales.

In the mid-1980s, Japanese investors concluded that US dollar securities were attractive, largely because the interest rates were 3–4 percentage points higher than the interest rates on comparable Japanese securities. One result of large imports of US dollar securities by various Japanese investors was that the Japanese yen depreciated extensively; another was that Japan again developed very large trade surpluses and very large current account surpluses. The counterpart of these surpluses was large US trade and current account deficits.

The world's largest creditor country

During the 1980s Japanese foreign investments began to increase at a rapid rate; by the late 1980s Japan had become the world's largest creditor country (which meant that the excess of Japanese-owned foreign assets over foreign-owned assets in Japan was much larger than the comparable ratios for other countries), displacing the United States from the position it had achieved during the first World War. The counterpart of the increase in Japanese-owned foreign assets was that Japan developed a persistently large trade surplus. About half of the total Japanese trade surplus was a result of its bilateral trade surplus with the United States. Japan had trade surpluses with many of its neighboring countries that were large exporters to the United States; many of their exports contained large Japanese components. So on a multilateral basis the US trade deficit was about three-quarters of the Japanese trade surplus.

The counterpart of Japan's move to the world's largest creditor country was that the United States became the world's largest debtor country. The result of the Japan's new role as an large international creditor is that each year the country receives an increasingly large amount of interest income and profits on its foreign investments. Part of this investment income flows to Japan and part is reinvested abroad; the part that flows to Japan tends to lead to an appreciation of the yen. The paradoxical result is that the stronger yen handicaps the ability of firms producing in Japan to export on a profitable basis – which increases their incentive to invest abroad.

In a mercantilist world, the Japanese trade and payments surpluses might represent the success of economic policy. But the proposition is not convincing: the excessively large surpluses represent the failure of policy. The managers of Japan, Inc. have failed to design a system which is able to cope with cyclical imbalances without placing great strain on its international trading relationships. The likelihood that Japan will bear out Herman Kahn's prediction is low.

22
China – The 800lb Gorilla

China is 'big history'

In the last few years there has been a remarkable expansion in the product line of Chinese restaurants in America and Europe. The traditional Cantonese cuisine that dominated the restaurant menus in the 1950s and the 1960s has given way to cooking in the Mandarin, Sczechwan, and Hunan styles. These differences in cuisine reflects the immense size of China, and the fact that basic foodstuffs available on the seacoast differ from those available inland – the Cantonese chefs worked around rice dishes; seafood is an important component of the menus. Mandarin cooking is Northern with wheat the basic starch. Meats were important in the cuisine of Hunan and of Sczechwan; and because the meats were not always fresh, hot spices were added to distract from the taste of the basic ingredients. The North–South wheat rice distinction is more or less the Yangtze River, which bisects China; 400 million live north of this river and 800 million south of it.

China is a big country, physically larger than the United States. And like the United States, Brazil, Russia, and Australia, the other large continental economies, China has an abundance of raw materials and the ability to produce the basic foods for 1200 million people – almost twice the combined populations of Europe and North America.

China also has a 'big history,' which begins in the third millennium before the beginning of the Christian era. Its early industrial achievements were impressive – bronze, porcelain, moveable type, and paper were first developed there. China had a well organized governmental bureaucracy at a time when much of Europe consisted of tribes warring to expand their turf. Marco Polo, the Venetian-based adventurer, traveled to

China in the thirteenth century and on his return reported on their superior achievements. Until the seventeenth century or perhaps even the eighteenth century, *per capita* incomes in China were higher than those in Europe. China missed the Industrial Revolution for more than a hundred years, and fell far behind a rapidly developing West. European power was brought to bear on China in the middle of the nineteenth century, and parts of the country were colonized by Great Britain and Portugal. During the first half of the twentieth century the internal struggle for power dominated politics: an imperial family dynasty that had ruled for three centuries was challenged by republicans, who in turn were challenged by the Communists. In the late 1930s the seaboard provinces were occupied by the Japanese in the prelude to their more ambitious adventures throughout Southeast Asia.

The hermit kingdom

The Communists consolidated their power in 1949; the remnants of the Republican government moved to Formosa or Taiwan, along with several million others who feared for their future in a communist-controlled state. China was self-absorbed in the first 30 years (1950–1978) of Communist rule; initially Chairman Mao went for backyard steel mills in the misnamed 'The Great Leap Forward' which proved to be an economic disaster. Then he sent tens of millions of the urban middle class into the countryside to feed the pigs in what was euphemistically called the 'Cultural Revolution'. There was a strong effort to obliterate individualism; everyone wore the same tufted blue cotton suit which came in two different sizes. China was a hermit kingdom for the 30 years of Mao's leadership. Contact with the West was extremely limited. There were more extensive contacts with the Soviet Union, but then the inherent conflicts between the national interests of the Soviet Union and of China came to dominate what passed for ideological affinity. Economic growth during the Mao period was modest, probably less than 1 percent a year. Much of what passed for industrial China seemed organized like medieval manors; a large factory would own the housing for its workers, and provide medical care, vacations, even much of their food. Several of the major armies had their own business units, which included hotels and manufacturing plants. The various government ministries and the central bank had their own universities. One university reportedly owned the factories that produced desks, chairs, and other classroom furniture.

Opening the door

China's economic policies changed dramatically after Mao's death. Deng Xiao Peng, Mao's successor after a brief struggle for power, opened the door for the move toward greater reliance on the market and increased trade with other countries. Foreign firms were encouraged to invest in China, but they were required to participate in joint ventures with Chinese firms. Some of the state-owned firms were privatized. Individual Chinese had much greater opportunity to study and visit abroad, and the Overseas Chinese were encouraged to visit and invest in China.

In the last 20 years the rate of economic growth in China has averaged around 10–12 percent – a remarkable achievement. Despite this rapid growth, *per capita* GNP in China is less than $1000 because the level was so low at the beginning. As a result, China's GDP is less than one-sixth that in the United States. Growth has been much more rapid in the seacoast provinces where much of the new industrial investment is located; *per capita* incomes of the 250 million people that live there is four–five times the average for the country. The rapid growth-provinces include Guangdong, which is up the Pearl River estuary from Hong Kong, and Fujian, which is opposite Taiwan. If the growth rate for the next 20+ years continues at the level of the last 20 years, then in 2025 China's GDP will be not much below that in the United States, even though *per capita* incomes will still be much lower. Long before that, China will have surpassed Japan as the dominant Asian power. If the growth rate continues for the next 50 years, then *per capita* incomes in China in the middle decades of the twenty-first century will be approaching those in the United States, and China will be one of the dominant economic powers, if not the predominant one.

The experience with projecting that Japan would surpass the United States as the dominant economic power demonstrates the risk – and the potential embarrassment – in making long-term growth projections. Still the next 20 or 30 years are a blink in Chinese history; the dates are less important than the trend, and whether the trend can persist.

In 1965 some analysts said that if Japan continued to grow at 8 or 10 percent a year when the rest the world was growing at 2 or 3 percent, then eventually *per capita* income in Japan would exceed *per capita* income in the United States. That prediction has not yet been proven correct. Japan has achieved growth rates sufficiently high so that the United States has more trade frictions with Japan than with any other country; indeed, US trade frictions with Japan are more significant with those of all European countries as a group. These trade frictions are represented by the exceedingly large Japanese trade surplus, whose counterpart is the US trade deficit.

Problems of Chinese growth

During the last few years China has been the country with the second largest trade surplus. China, however, is not the only Chinese country with a large trade surplus – Hong Kong has a trade surplus and so does Taiwan. If these countries continue to grow and if they continue to have trade surpluses, it's a safe bet that the US trade deficit with China will increase. Chinese growth has already presented problems for the United States and its other trading partners. There is a modest tradition of intellectual property rights. China has the second largest holdings of international reserve assets. Now that sovereignty over Hong Kong has been transferred from London to Beijing and Hong Kong has become a Special Administrative Area (SAR) of China, China has the largest foreign exchange reserves in the world – almost twice those of Japan. One insight into China's growth potential might be based on the economic success of the 'fifth most populous country in the world' – The Overseas Chinese.

The economy of the overseas Chinese

The national income of the overseas Chinese is much larger than China's national income. Hong Kong, Taiwan (or, as it sometimes called China Taipei), and Singapore are largely Chinese. The business communities in many other countries in Southeast Asia – Vietnam, Malaysia, the Philippines, Thailand, and Indonesia – are largely Chinese (and would be even more extensively Chinese if the governments in Kuala Lumpur and Jakarta had not adopted affirmative action-type policies to favor the Malays in their business activities). Within the United States the Chinese have been remarkably successful in terms of academic achievement and business success, especially in small family businesses.

The 'Little Tigers'

Hong Kong, Singapore, Taiwan, and South Korea are grouped as the 'Little Tigers', a response to their high and sustained rates of economic growth of 6–8 percent for about 30 years. Singapore and Hong Kong are both small island economies, whose only natural resource is their remarkable harbors. Singapore has a population of $2^3/_4$ million while Hong Kong has almost twice as many people. Both are extensively involved in transit trade as well as manufacturing (although most of the manufacturing in Hong Kong has moved across the Chinese border to the various sites along the Pearl River estuary). Singapore's imports are 50 percent larger than its national income – a large part of imports are processed or assembled, or refined, or somehow modified and then reexported.

Hong Kong and Singapore

The role of the Hong Kong government toward managing its economy differs from the approach of Singapore. Hong Kong has been about as freewheeling an economy as possible; the economic role of government has been trivially small, and limited primarily to providing law and order, building an efficient infrastructure, expanding educational facilities, and developing public housing. Until the handover to China the Hong Kong government might have been described as a benevolent dictatorship; the citizens had little if any say in their choice of leaders or of policies. In contrast, the government of Singapore was involved in extensive economic planning; individuals were forced to save a very large share of their incomes partly in government funds, which were then invested to contribute to economic growth. Extensive efforts were undertaken to attract foreign firms and to upgrade the technological skills of the labor force. The government was not tolerant of criticism and dissent: a facade of democratic institutions was maintained but the dominant political party had total control.

Much can be made of the differences in the political arrangements in Hong Kong and Singapore. Still despite their differences both have been remarkable success stories – which suggests that the political arrangements may not be all that important as long as their economic and political environments are stable.

Taiwan

Taiwan also has been an amazing economic success story, despite the lack of natural resources and large defense expenditures. In 1949, *per capita* income in Taiwan was about $100 a year (although the number is uncertain because of the large immigration from the Mainland); currently the level is about $10,000. Taiwan ranks 10th–15th on the world list of GDPs, an amazingly accomplishment in terms of its inherited handicaps and an unfriendly neighborhood. The economy consists of tens of thousands of very small firms and relatively few large firms comparable to those in Japan and Korea. Taiwan's foreign exchange reserves are larger than those of any country in Europe and exceeded only by those of Japan – and on a *per capita* basis, Taiwan's foreign exchange reserves are almost three times those of Japan.

South Korea

The economic success of South Korea is even more remarkable than that of Taiwan. When the Korean War ended in 1954 much of the country was in shambles; most of what is now South Korea had been overrun twice by the armies from the North. Prior to the war and the division of the country in 1945, most of the country's industry had been in the North. Since the war the country has maintained a large army: its defense expenditures account for nearly 10 percent of GDP. Partly because South Korea is larger than the other three 'Tigers' combined and partly because of the strong sense of national identity, Korea has tried to develop its economy on the basis of its own firms. So Korea has been unfriendly to foreign investment, although it has sought to adapt technologies that had been developed abroad. A very large share of productive activity occurs in one of the 30 large chaebols – family-based holding companies that may own controlling interests in 40 or 50 different operating companies in a wide range of industries.

Insights from the success of the overseas Chinese

The economic success of these 'Tigers' is clear, even though Korea and to a lesser extent Hong Kong have become enmeshed in the Asian financial crisis. Their economic success has been achieved even in the absence of raw materials or the capacity to grow the food necessary for their peoples.

What are the common factors that might explain the economic success of the 'Tigers'. Each country has a very high savings rate. Each country has made a large investment in upgrading its educational system and labor skills; literacy rates are high. Each country has had a very strong export orientation. The role of government in productive decisions is modest, although the governments have a strong investment orientation. And each more or less started with a 'clean slate' – there was a trivial industrial structure.

China has several of the factors associated with the economic success of the 'Tigers'. The savings rate in China is high. China – at least the China of the 1980s and the 1990s – has a strong orientation toward increasing exports and participating in the world economy, much like the 'Tigers'. Indeed, the ratio of imports to GDP is extremely high for a large country with a rich and varied resource base, and more or less self-sufficiency in agriculture.

What are the differences between China and the four 'Tigers' and how might these differences affect China's economic growth?

- One is size; China has more than 15 times the population of the four tigers combined. Large countries are more difficult to manage than small countries. Regionalism has been a pervasive problem in Chinese history; from time to time the central government often has found it difficult to control the very disparate regions. As in so many other countries, the wealthy regions are reluctant to share resources with the poorer ones. There are elements of informal provincial trade barriers.

- A second is geography; the 'Tigers' are close to the sea and have relatively easy access to foreign markets. Much of China is far from the sea; the implication is that industrial development in the inland areas will be more difficult and hence growth potential is lower because of the higher costs of developing the infrastructure.

- A third that China is resource-rich. China can feed itself despite its extremely large population. And China has most of the resources necessary for its industrial development, which means that it has less need to export to earn the foreign exchange to import these materials than any of the 'Tigers'.

- A fourth is recent history and ancient history. China has international political ambitions that none of the 'Tigers' has. Much attention is given in Beijing to recovering the 'lost province' of Taiwan. Almost certainly China will wish to become an even more important regional power, with stewardship over the overseas Chinese. Their ambitions may extend to becoming a global power, with the implication that military expenditures may increase as a share of national income.

- A fifth is recent industrial history. The 'Tigers' started with a clean slate. In contrast, China has an industrial base that has been inherited from its 30 years under Mao. There are more than 100,000 medium and large state-owned firms, which together employ more than 110 million people. These firms are highly inefficient, with employment levels are extremely large relative to their levels of output – some estimate redundant labor may total 50 million people. These firms are in debt to the state-owned banks, which have made many loans that will never be repaid – the estimate is that the accumulated loan losses of these banks may be $500 billion, a third of China's GNP.

One challenge to China is to provide good jobs for those now effectively unemployed and for the tens of millions who will become unemployed as agriculture in China becomes more efficient. The inference from the high level of foreign exchange reserves and the large trade surplus is that domestic supply capabilities in China are significantly higher than domestic demand. This problem is common to a number of countries in the neighborhood (except Korea) that have high savings rates. And China's supply capabilities will be even greater because there are tens of millions of workers who are underemployed. The difference is that the problem of excess savings in these other countries occurred when their levels of *per capita* income were much higher than the level of *per capita* income in China. It may be that the savings rate in China will decline or that the domestic investment rate will increase; there are abundant opportunities to invest in housing and other components of the infrastructure. Otherwise part of the excess saving will tend to flow abroad, and China will continue to have large trade surpluses. Small countries like Taiwan can have trade surpluses that are large relative to their GDPs without inviting a hostile reaction from their trading partners and the countries that might be expected to have the counterpart trade deficits. It is likely to be exceedingly difficult for a large country like China to develop a trade surplus as it grows because the counterpart trade deficits are too large to be acceptable to its trading partners. China may yet emerge as the '800 lb gorilla', a annoyance, or a challenge, or even a threat to its trading partners. A major problem that China must resolve is to find a larger number of attractive domestic investment opportunities if its savings rate does not decline.

One limit to the continuation of a rate of economic growth of 6 or 8 percent a year is external; China will find it increasingly difficult to grow its exports at these rates because its share of foreign markets for textiles, footwear, toys and sports equipment, and apparel already is large. Continued rapid growth of exports is necessary to obtain the foreign exchange to pay for imports – and the need for imports might increase as domestic supplies of various raw materials become depleted, or need to grow commensurate with the growth of the economy.

There are also several possible domestic limits to factors that might lead to a sharp decline in the growth rate. Many of the state-owned industrial firms may wither, unable to recover costs by making attractive products and unable to retain their most productive employees. Tens of thousands of these firms may remain active even though their losses are subsidized by loans from the state-owned banks that will never be repaid. At some point these banks must be recapitalized, or a new set of private banks must be established to provide credit for the profitable and productive enterprises.

China has appeared largely immune to the Asian financial crisis, although its growth rate declined from 8 percent to 6 percent in the 1990s; the irony of China's development prospects from the economic view point is that its savings rate may be too high to provide the growth in demand necessary to provide the jobs for those in industry. As in Japan, an increase in economic uncertainties may lead to an increase in saving. So the economic conditions for the continuation of a rapid rate of growth include broadening the mix of exports to include a larger share of high-value-added products, the continued dismantling of the tens of thousands of inefficient enterprises, the development of an efficient banking system, and a modest reduction in the savings rate. Even if these conditions are satisfied, the political developments may constrain growth. Regionalism is an ever-present source of friction because of the sharp differences in *per capita* income. Growth is likely to require some decentralization of decision-making, and the monopoly of power held by the Communist Party is likely to be challenged.

23
Zlotys, Rubles, and Leks

The new Central Europe

The most remarkable change between the fifth and sixth editions of this book has been the collapse of 'The Evil Empire.' The Berlin Wall has disappeared, East Europe has been rechristened Central Europe, and the USSR – the Union of Soviet Socialist Republics – is no more, replaced by the CIR – the Committee of Independent Republics. The Baltic Countries – Estonia, Latvia, and Lithuania – have regained the independence they lost in 1939. Ukrania and Russia squabble over who owns the Black Sea fleet., and there is a continual concern over the command and control of hundreds of nuclear missiles in countries that often appear to be on the edge of disintegration.

Ethnic unrest

Ethnic unrest seems pervasive. The Azeris and the Armenians shoot at each other on a regular basis. Yugoslavia has fractured; Slovenia, Macedonia, Croatia, and Bosnia-Herzegovina have become independent countries, while the Belgrade government has been supporting the Serbs who have been seeking to annex Serbian enclaves in Croatia and Bosnia to a Greater Serbia. Serbia – sorry, Yugoslavia – almost certainly will see an independent Kosovo. Estonia and Latvia and Uzbekistan are trying to decide what to do with the millions of ethnic Russians that were settled in their countries by Stalin in the 1920s and the 1930s. The Uzbeks and the Kazaks are making life unpleasant for the 'Volga Germans,' resettled among them by Stalin. The Czechs and the Slovaks have had a peaceful divorce.

It is as if each nation state from the Rhine to the Pacific can contain only one ethnic group. The fit between the national borders and ethnic identities is crude; there remain large enclaves of Hungarians in Rumania and Slovakia, Greater Hungary has 15 million people, of whom 10 million are in Hungary. Similarly there are hundreds of thousands of Turks in Bulgaria, and 50 million Russians live outside Russia. So there may be more 'ethnic cleansing'.

Economic change

One consequence of the rearrangement of political borders is that monetary arrangements have changed. Before the breakup of the Soviet Bloc, the currencies of Poland, Hungary, and other satellites were pegged to the Russian ruble, and the Russian ruble was pegged to gold, at least nominally. For the most part, inflation rates in the USSR and the other Communist countries were low. Most goods were in short supply, and the waiting lines were extremely long. The change in political arrangements means that Poland and its Central European neighbors no longer peg their currencies to the ruble. Most of these countries have had very high inflation rates; Poland and Ukraine and Russia have had hyperinflations. These countries now are in the midst of transitions from the command economy to market economies. In some countries – the Czech Republic and Hungary – this transition has been rapid. What had been East Germany has been absorbed into a rich West Germany, at a very high cost to the West Germans. Elsewhere the pace of the transition is slower. Rumania struggles. One of the major issues in the transition involves the process of privatization of state-owned assets – the railroads and the electric utilities and the housing stock and the factories. A second issue involves the relation between the large countries in the area and their smaller neighbors.

Schachtian economics

Hjalmar Schacht was Hitler's chief financial adviser, a wizard of money. The term 'Schachtian policies' has become a synonym for economic policies used by a large country to exploit its smaller neighbors. Under Schacht, the Eastern European countries paid above-market prices for their imports from Germany and received below-market prices for their exports to Germany. Schachtian policies lived on long after Schacht died. In the 1950s and the 1960s, the Soviet Union exploited its smaller neighbors in Eastern Europe. Then after the surge in the petroleum prices in the 1970s Russians were subsidizing their richer neighbors in Poland, Czechoslovakia, and East Germany. Paradoxically, the change did not occur because the Russians became good guys, remorseful about their past, but rather because they were sluggish about raising the price of petroleum to the world level. Despite the strictures of Marx and Lenin, those who believe in the classic propositions of the market economy believe that exploitation is inevitable in planned economies – as long as prices in the world economy are used as a benchmark.

It's arguable that the fall of the Berlin Wall resulted from an insight that Gorbachev developed that it was silly for poor Russians to subsidize rich East Germans, Czechs, and Hungarians. Russia was subsidizing its clients to the West by paying them above-market prices for their products and charging them below-world market prices for petroleum produced in the Soviet Union. Once Gorbachev began to reduce the subsidies, the self-interest of these countries in remaining clients rapidly declined.

Market prices and the planned economy

Marxist doctrine predicts that the Socialist societies would one day function without money. Stocks and bonds went out with the tsars, and most productive assets – and many non-productive assets – were owned by the state. But government-owned banks in the Soviet Union and in Eastern Europe produced money, workers received much of their income in the form of money payments, and much of their consumption expenditures (excluding housing, heath care, and education) were financed by money payments. Indeed, within Russia, Poland, and the neighboring countries, the banks were among the most efficient of the enterprises. They could produce money much more rapidly than the farms and factories could produce the food and consumer goods that the workers wanted to buy with their money. The result was queues of shoppers, and stores full of empty shelves. A lot of the money went into the mattress because it took too much time to spend it. Individuals accumulated cash because they had little to spend their money on.

Prices and costs

In the West, with a few exceptions – postal services, railroad passenger services, and other government-provided goods and services – prices are set to cover costs. The core of a market economy is the belief that a good should be produced if the consumers will pay a price sufficiently high to cover its production costs. And in competitive industries, profit-maximizing firms expand output as long as selling prices are higher than the costs of production. Within planned economies, in contrast, government bureaucrats determined which goods and services would be produced. Then they would make an independent decision about the prices at which these goods would be sold: the prices set for goods that were deemed 'important' for consumer welfare were low. If the planners set the prices too high, then the goods would pile up on the shelves waiting to be sold. If instead the planners set the prices too low, then queues and shortages developed and a large number of customers would remain unsatisfied. In planned economies, selling prices covered production costs on a much smaller range of goods than in market economies. There were many more 'loss-leaders' – goods whose prices were far below their cost of production. The planners recognized the needs and the preferences of the public, although they believed that they knew what the public wanted better than the public did – which is why they were chosen to be the planners.

Thus in the planned economies, many goods and services were sold at nominal prices – at prices much below their production costs. Housing, medical services, university education, and air transport were cheap in the Soviet Union. So were tickets to the Bolshoi Opera and the Kirov Ballet. But not all goods and services could be sold at prices below their cost. Indeed, for the economy as a whole, the excess of revenues over costs in some industries must match the excess of costs over revenues in other industries. A large part of government fiscal revenues came from the excess of revenues over costs on various consumer goods – shoes, clothes, and housing. Thus, as a general rule, for every loss there had to have been a corresponding 'profit' on some other group: in effect, the profits on the second group financed the losses on the first. Except that, as in the West, if the losses dominated, the planners went to the central bank to get newly produced money to finance the losses.

Trade

The differences between market and planned economies in their approaches to setting prices become important when they trade with each other. Within the West, international trade reflects the decentralized decisions of thousands of firms in more than 150 countries. Firms export if their costs are low enough for them to be able to undersell the domestic producers in foreign markets, and they import if foreign prices are sufficiently below the prices of comparable goods available from domestic producers. The planned economies imported and exported for the same reasons the market economies do – it was cheaper to import some goods and to pay for them with exports than to produce these goods domestically.

So the planned economies imported industrial products, raw materials including gold and petroleum and hams, machinery, computers, turbines and other high-technology items, wheat, coffee, and tea, as well as goods which might be temporarily in short supply. Their exports consisted largely of raw materials, a few industrial products, and IOUs – promises to pay in the future because they were not able to pay in the present. Like good capitalists, they were eager to borrow to finance their purchases; they needed more imports than they could pay for from their current export earnings.

In the planned economies, prices were not very useful as guidelines for deciding which goods to import and which goods to export. If prices were used as guidelines, then the goods exported would be those that were priced far below their production costs, while the imported goods would be those which were sold at prices much above costs. 'Arbitragers' – or smugglers – made a fortune exploiting the differences between prices for the same good in the market economies and in planned economies. So planners decided which goods could be imported and which goods could be exported.

The centrally planned economies (CPEs) conducted their foreign trade through state trading organizations (STOs). When the CPEs traded with market economies, they dealt at world prices, more or less; their exports were sold at or below prices of comparable Western goods, regardless of the cost of producing them. Similarly, the planned economies paid world prices for imports from the market economies, unless they were successful in negotiating special price deals. The monetary counterpart to the monopolization of imports and exports in state trading organizations was that consumers in the Soviet Union and its Eastern neighbors were not permitted to hold US dollars, German marks, and Swiss francs. Firms and individuals in the West were not permitted to hold money and securities in the East. Both the monopoly on trade and the monopoly on money were necessary complements to ensure that private decisions of the consumers could not undercut the public decisions of the planners.

One of the fixations of the planners in Moscow – although it may be a Russian fixation that became institutionalized under the planners – is the belief in the economies of scale, so much so that the lowest unit production costs can be achieved if only one factory produces each type of good. The planners agreed that all the fork-lift trucks for the planned economies of the East would be produced by the Bulgarians. The Russians would produce the airplanes and the big ticket military hardware items.

Much of the trade between countries in Eastern Europe involved a series of bilateral exchanges – Russia sold 1000 3-ton trucks to Czechoslovakia in exchange for 1650 6-inch lathes. World prices could be attached to these barter exchanges to determine whether Czechoslovakia got a better deal than if it had sold the lathes in the West at world market prices and used the proceeds to buy trucks from Italy or Germany.

The Eastern Europeans believed that the prices they paid the Soviet Union for their imports were generally higher than the prices the Russians would get for the same goods if they sold them in the world market. And they also believed that the prices they received on their exports to the Russians were generally below those they might receive in the world market. Paying more for imports and receiving less for exports is what Schachtian policies are all about. And the Rumanians and Bulgarians participated in these policies in the 1960s and 1970s for the same reason they did in the 1930s – the big bully next door didn't give them much choice.

While STOs were a logical counterpart to central planning, the individual STOs are not branches of the Salvation Army – each was a maximizing agent, constantly calculating whether it was more profitable to sell in the Western markets than to STOs in other Eastern European countries, and whether it was cheaper to buy in the West than from other STOs. Trade between STOs in the various planned economies was on a barter basis. Each STO could calculate the world market price of the goods it wished to export and the goods that it might import from other STOs, so Western market prices became the benchmark. As political barriers declined, the STOs undertook more trading with the West and less with each other; the ability of the Russians to exploit their smaller neighbors declined. Indeed, when the world price of oil increased in the 1970s, the Russians did not raise the price on oil exported to their East European neighbors correspondingly, so the East Europeans benefitted by being able to obtain oil at lower prices than most other oil-importing countries.

East European finance

The ruble was a heavy currency

Financing trade

The Russian currency – the ruble – and the currencies of other Eastern European countries were not included in the world hit parade of currencies, since individuals were not free to sell rubles and zlotys against US dollars, Swiss francs, and German marks. Transactions in Western currencies by residents of East Europe were strictly controlled – which meant prohibited: the governments wanted to monopolize the holdings of US dollars, German marks, other convertible currencies. Investors did not buy rubles because they expected that the ruble might be revalued nor did they sell rubles because they anticipated that the ruble might be devalued in terms of the US dollar or the German mark. Comparisons of interest rates on bank deposits in the Soviet Union and in the United States were not meaningful, since the interest rates on bank deposits in Communist countries were set by the plan, usually at levels of about 2 percent. Because the state banks were monopolies, they had no incentive to raise interest rates to attract funds from other financial institutions, spending on current consumption, and mattresses.

When the Russians and the Eastern Europeans exported to the West, they were paid in US dollars, German marks, or some other major currency; they were apt to deposit these funds in the Moscow Narodny Bank in London or the Banque Commerciale pour L' Europe du Nord in Paris or Wozchod Commercial Bank AG in Zurich, or in another Western branch of one of the Russian banks. Similarly, when they imported, they wrote checks against their deposit balances in one of these banks. Trade with market economies was financed in one of the Western currencies, largely because Western firms did not have any incentive to hold ruble money balances.

Perhaps a better indication of the Russian position in finance was its large grain purchases in the 1970s. Whenever harvests in Russia were poor, wheat imports were necessary. Much of wheat imports came from the United States in its role as the residual supplier in the world grain market. Part of the wheat purchases were financed by credit, part by sales of Russian gold. In bad crop years Russian gold sales were unusually large. Gold sales were last-resort financing, for when it came to gold, the Russians were at the top of the list of mercantilists.

Dollar-mark pegging and currency reform

The Russians fantasized that the ruble was at the top of the currency hit parade – the financial market counterpart to their claims to having invented the sewing machine, the typewriter, and baseball. The ruble needed a price in terms of the US dollar, the German mark, and other Western currencies. Foreign embassies in Moscow and Warsaw needed rubles and zlotys to pay for local staff and food. Similarly Western tourists in these cities needed to buy the local currency. Moreover, the ruble needed a parity in terms of some other asset, because the ruble could not float in the exchange market since the necessary conditions for a floating exchange rate – that buyers and sellers meet freely to exchange national monies – were not present. Since no Western country was willing to peg its currency to the ruble, the Russians had to peg the ruble to a Western currency.

In 1937 the Russian ruble was pegged to the US dollar at the rate of 4 rubles to US$1. During the Cold War, the Russians did not appreciate the implication that the US dollar was four times as valuable as the ruble. So in 1950 they pegged the ruble to gold at a rate of 140 rubles per ounce of gold. Actually the peg could have been 1 ruble per ounce of gold or 1000 rubles per ounce of gold; in the Soviet Union the price of gold was irrelevant in determining how much gold was produced, how much the gold miners were paid, the uses of newly produced gold, and when gold was sold abroad. But once the ruble was pegged to gold, a ruble–dollar exchange rate could be readily calculated from the ratio of the US and Russian gold parities. Given the then US gold parity of US$35, the exchange rate was, once again, 4 rubles to the dollar.

In 1961 the Soviet Union underwent a currency reform; all outstanding ruble notes were declared worthless and had to be exchanged for new notes at the rate of 1 new ruble for 10 old rubles. (This 'reform' was really a tax on holders of bank notes, especially those who held large amounts of notes.) At the same time, the Russians set a gold parity for the new ruble at 32 rubles per ounce. Then the exchange rate between the new, heavy Ruble and the US dollar could be calculated as the ratio of the price of 1 ounce of gold in terms of each currency. And so the new exchange rate was US$1.11 equals 1 ruble.

Now the ruble was worth more than the dollar – or at least so it seemed. Since the ruble price of gold had no economic significance, the Russians in effect had first decided on the dollar–ruble exchange rate they wanted, and then set the ruble price of gold accordingly. If they had set a gold parity for the new ruble at 7 rubles per ounce, the exchange rate would have been US$5 to 1 ruble; with a gold parity of 1 new ruble to the ounce, the exchange rate would have been US$35 to 1 ruble.

The currency reform at the ratio of 10 old rubles for 1 new ruble suggests that all ruble prices should have fallen by a factor of ten; each new ruble would then be ten times as valuable as each old ruble. Thus, the ruble price of gold should have fallen from 140 rubles per ounce to 14 rubles; the dollar–ruble exchange rate would then have been $2.50 per ruble. But in terms of purchasing power, the ruble would have been grossly overvalued. So the Russians used the commotion of the currency reform as a smokescreen to devalue the ruble in terms of the dollar from 1 ruble equals US$0.25 to 1 ruble equals US$0.11, a 125 percent increase in the ruble price of the US dollar.

This dollar–ruble exchange rate was largely symbolic: no one in Moscow or Kiev could buy US dollars at this price. Since Soviet trade with the West largely consisted of swapping bundles of exports for bundles of imports, the exchange rate was irrelevant for balancing Soviet payments and receipts with other countries. The new ruble–dollar exchange rate was primarily important for tourists and diplomats in Moscow. The ruble was clearly overvalued for both groups; at this exchange rate, the goods available in the stores in Leningrad and Moscow were expensive. But then many of the services – opera tickets, domestic transportation, restaurant meals – that these groups purchased were remarkably cheap, because they were implicitly subsidized. When the US dollar price of gold was increased in 1971 and 1973, the ruble got heavier relative to the dollar, since the ruble price of gold was unchanged. Moscow gloated. But the Russians had an exchange rate problem: they had to decide whether to peg the ruble to the US dollar, thereby allowing their currency to float in terms of the German mark, the Swiss franc, and the British pound, or to peg the ruble to the German mark and allow the ruble to float in terms of the US dollar and the British pound. One thing was clear. The planners could not rely on market forces to bail them out; they had to decide. So they stuck with gold and revalued the ruble in terms of the dollar, first by 8 percent at the end of 1971, then by nearly 10 percent in early 1973. The Russians were striving to make the ruble respectable. But at the same time they were revaluing the ruble, the price of the US dollar was increasing significantly in terms of the ruble in the black market.

The lek and the leu are not heavy currencies

The Albanian lek and the Rumanian leu also were greatly overvalued; their purchasing power was much less, at the official exchange rates, than that of Western currencies. From the point of view of the planners, overvaluation had the advantage of taxing the foreign diplomats and tourists who had to acquire these currencies. Because the exchange rates in the Soviet Union and other Eastern European countries were so out of line with market reality, their governments had set up special exchange markets for tourist transactions where the rates were half or less than half the official rates. Moreover, a black market developed in US dollars. Thus, the official rate for the Bulgarian leva was 0.97 per US$1, the tourist rate 1.32 leva per US$1, and the black market rate 2.57 leva per US$1. The official rate for the Albanian lek was 4.14 leks per US$1, the tourist rate 12.5 leks per $1. The premium in the black markets – the percentage spread between the black market rates and the official rates – varied from 200 to 400 percent, and suggested how unreal the official rates were. That the exchange rates for tourists from capitalist countries were 150–250 percent higher than those for tourists from Socialist countries was one indication that each Eastern European country recognized how grossly overvalued were the currencies of its neighbors.

The ruble-dollar seesaw

From time to time, individual Eastern European countries made cautious moves toward increased trade with Western countries, moves which might be associated with an increased role for market-determined prices in their economies. Yugoslavia had gone much further in this direction than the others. Yugoslavia belonged to the International Monetary Fund (IMF) and sought to make its currency convertible. The Yugoslav dinar was readily traded, and Yugoslavs could hold foreign currencies and readily travel abroad. The foreign exchange value for the dinar was set at a level which – together with a variety of import controls – balanced Yugoslavia's payments and receipts with the rest of the world. Several extremely large devaluations of the dinar were necessary in the early stages of Yugoslavia's opening to the West to offset the previous substantial overvaluation.

On occasion, the Russians and other Eastern Europeans, stimulated or threatened by the success of the European Economic Community (EEC), announced plans for a common market of their own. For planned economies, a 'common market' might mean free trade within the associated economies; stores and factories in each country could import from foreign as well as domestic sources. But this approach would require that each factory know the foreign as well as the domestic demand for its product. A common market for planned economies would have required integration of the planning systems of the member countries.

The exchange rate relationship between the Soviet Union and its Eastern bloc neighbors would have little significance once such planning systems were integrated. The currencies of other Eastern European countries – the Polish zloty, the Hungarian forint, the Romanian leu, and the Albanian lek – had parities, usually expressed in terms of gold or occasionally in terms of the Russian ruble. However, expressing parities in terms of gold (like the ruble's parity in terms of gold) was meaningless, since no individual, firm, or agency could deal in gold at this price. But the exchange rate for the zloty in terms of the ruble might be computed from the parity of each of these currencies in terms of gold. Given the parity of the Polish zloty in terms of the dollar – about 3.4 zlotys to US$1 – and the ruble–dollar rate of US$1.24, the price of the ruble in terms of the zloty should have been 4.2 zlotys to the ruble. But the Poles pegged the zloty at 13.8 zlotys to the ruble. Zlotys were cheap in terms of rubles, which was good for the Russians. Nearly all of the Eastern European currencies were cheap in terms of the ruble, which was even better for the Russians. The foreign exchange costs of the Russian diplomatic establishment in Eastern Europe – the 38 divisions of the Russian Army that sat between the Vistula and the Oder – were thus reduced. Poland collected a large supply of rubles from its sale of zlotys to the Russians. And these rubles were used to settle imbalances in the barter trade – to pay for Russian oil and steel. The exchange rate structure was favorable to the Soviet Union and costly to the smaller Eastern European countries. Capitalism may have gone out with the tsars, but imperialism did not.

The move to the market-economy

Barter, credit, and détente

In the 1970s Moscow had a Pepsi-Cola franchise – Pepsi had arranged a barter deal and agreed to import Russian vodka for sale in the United States while the Russians imported Pepsi. The US demand for vodka had been growing rapidly so it seemed like a set-up to increase Pepsi's market share in its eternal struggle to catch up with Coke. Pepsi for vodka was only the icing on a much larger cake: there were extensive efforts to facilitate industrial growth in the Eastern bloc. Fiat built a massive automobile plant in the Soviet Union, and the Russians began to export the Russian Fiat – not to be confused with the Polish Fiat, or the Spanish Fiat, or the Fiat Fiat. Mack Trucks was involved in a similar program to build a turnkey factory. For numerous industrial products in Eastern Europe, Western firms built the plants from scratch and trained the local managers.

In a few cases, the Eastern Europeans paid for these imports by exports to the West; in many cases, however, credits available from the West were the financing mechanism. The Hungarians, the Poles, and other Eastern Europeans were nibbling at the fringes of the Eurocurrency market. Initially, the largest source of financing was Western governments, which were eager to promote exports – and the employment associated with such sales. While the same credits might have been used to finance investments in the industrial countries themselves, the demand was inadequate: there already were enough automobile and steel plants in the West. Subsequently, commercial banks, especially those headquartered in Germany, France, and Italy supplied the credits.

The breakdown in the Polish economy associated with the Solidarity crisis of the 1980s led to an external debt crisis; labor unrest led to significant declines in production on the farms and in the mines and factories, so that Polish exports did not increase as rapidly as anticipated. Yet it seems likely that Poland would have had an external debt crisis even without its labor problems, for it would not have been able to earn the foreign exchange to pay interest on its external debt. The debts to the Western banks and governments continued to increase because of compound interest.

Privatization

Russia, Poland, and even Albania have made the commitment to move from a command economy to a market economy. One aspect of this move involved privatization of various enterprises, from large industrial conglomerates to local stores and houses, apartments, and banks. Another aspect of this change involved developing the institutional framework of a market economy – officers in banks to do credit analysis, a legal framework for the settlement of commercial disputes (including an impartial judiciary), accounting firms to audit and report on the integrity of the data of individual firms.

The problem for Russia and Poland and their neighbors was that these features of a market economy could not be ordered fully assembled from Sears Roebuck. Rather, the arrangements evolved in response to demand and these countries had to go through a transition from a controlled to a market economy with minimal disruption to living standards for their populations.

These transitions were largely unplanned; no one had been there before. Once regulations limiting prices began to be relaxed, prices began to rise. And once prices began to rise, the value of the currency holdings of households began to decline. And individuals (who had previously hoarded money because they were tired of waiting in line to spend their money) began to spend accumulated currency, with the result that inflation began to accelerate. As prices began to rise, these individuals began to spend at a more rapid rate. Some individuals began to buy US dollars, or German marks, or Swiss francs. The result was that the zloty and the ruble began to depreciate, and in some cases at an accelerating rate.

Privatization was handicapped by the lack of clear title to the ownership of property. Who owned the steel mills in Gorky – The Ministry of Industry or the City of Gorky? Who owned inventories of raw materials like aluminum? There was a great deal of spontaneous privatization. One aspect of the move to privatization was that receipts of the large industrial enterprises remained with these firms; the firms were reluctant to deliver these receipts to the government. The consequence was that the government receipts declined, and the share of government expenditures that were financed by government borrowing increased sharply. So inflation accelerated. Demand for the output of many of these large enterprises declined sharply with the move to the market economy, but the enterprises were reluctant to lose labor. Many of these enterprises had been producing for a captive market; their ability to capture or even maintain market share in a competitive economy was handicapped because the quality of the goods they produced was so shoddy.

Structure and size

Tourists to the Kremlin have the opportunity to view the world's largest bell and the world's largest cannon. The bell developed a large crack in the casting process; fortunately, the cannon was never fired – if it had been, it would have exploded, since the charge required to propel the cannon shot would have ruptured the barrel. Size seems to be a Russian fixation. The Russians have the largest airplanes and the largest rockets; Aeroflot has been the world's largest airline. This emphasis suggests there is something in Russian psyche about the virtue or payoff from size – a belief in the economies of scale. This same belief has been reflected in the industrial structure – each factory was designed to be able to produce a sufficiently large output to satisfy the demand in the Soviet Union and in its Eastern European clients, so in many cases there was only one factory to produce each type of good. Moreover, for political reasons many factories had been located far from the markets.

Many of these plants were vertically integrated; they produced the inputs or components for the factories. The factory that produced the autos produced the bumpers and the steering wheels and the windshield wiper motors. The factories also provided housing for their employees and schools for the employees' children. In effect, they were self-contained, like medieval manors. Labor markets were non-existent. People were told where they would work, and in effect they were told where they might live – they needed permits to move from one city to another. This system was designed to make life easy for the planners and the controllers, not for efficiency.

The move to a market economy has meant a radical change in structure. It is easy to list the key features of the market economy – private ownership of property, consumer sovereignty. The problem is to figure out the best path from here to there. No one had been there before. And the path that would work best for a Poland or a Hungary might differ from the best path for a Russia. One reason the paths differ is that the size of these countries differs, as does their experience with command economies.

24
Transition Economies: Who Lost Russia?

Q: What is a transition economy?
A: A country on the move from a command economy to a market economy.
Q: Which countries are considered transition economies?
A: The big ones are Russia, Ukraine, and Poland; there are 20 smaller ones, including what had been East Germany, the three Baltic countries of Lithuania, Latvia, and Estonia, the Czech Republic, Hungary, Belarus, Armenia, Albania, and Tajikistan.
Q: What is the best way to move from a command economy to a market economy?
A: Who knows?

The command and the market economy

Consider several of the differences between a command economy and a market economy:

- In a command economy the means of production – the factories and airlines, the banks and retail stores, the houses and apartments, are owned by the state; in the market economy the factories *et al.* are owned by companies and individuals.
- In a command economy prices are set by the planners in the central government and are only tangentially related to the costs of production; in the market economy the price of each good and service is closely related to its costs of production.
- In the command economy the funds necessary to finance the costs of government are collected in the prices of goods (which is essentially a form of indirect taxation); in the market economy the taxes

necessary to finance the costs of government are added to the prices of goods and a significant part of taxes are direct individual incomes and corporate incomes.

- In the command economy the major task of the factory manager is to produce the volume of goods necessary to satisfy the targets set by the central planners; in the market economy the major task of the factory manager is to design the goods that the consumers are eager to buy.
- In the command economy everyone had a job and there was full employment; in the market economy there have been high levels of unemployment because some individuals wanted to take more out of the pot in the form of wages than they were contributing to the pot in the form of productivity. In effect they weren't earning their keep – which meant that they had discovered a free lunch or a partial free lunch.
- In the market economy each worker receives the value of his or her marginal product – at least, that is what the textbooks say.
- In the command economy engineers are at the top of the decision-making hierarchies; in the market economy the marketing specialists or the finance MBAS are at the top of the hierarchies.
- In the command economy of what had been the Soviet Union and its allies in Eastern Europe, there was a strong belief that the most efficient pattern of production involved extremely large factories, so that each major good would be produced in only one or several plants. The factories that produced certain inputs would at times be at a considerable distance, and even in different countries, from the factories that used these inputs.
- In the command economy there are no commercial disputes because there is no private property; in the market economy there is a need for a system of courts – and of lawyers and independent judges – to resolve disputes between producers and consumers and among different producers.
- In the command economy those who get to the top have sharp elbows; in the market economy those who get to the top have sharp elbows.

Russia, Ukraine, Poland, the Czech Republic, Hungary *et al.* have all faced the same set of problems of getting from there to here – the objective has been to move to the market economy with minimum decline of GDP and minimum hardship for the pensioners and others who had a secure standard of living – if at a very low level – because of the safety net in the command economy. The success of Russia and its neighbors in making a successful transition to the market economy has differed substantially. One way to rank these countries is in terms of the changes in GDP and *per capita* GDP on the transition road. Another way to rank them is in terms of how the pensioners and the defenseless have fared. The Czech Republic ranks high on the scorecard of the countries that have made a successful transition. So have the Baltic Republics – Estonia, Latvia, and Lithuania. In contrast, Russia and Ukraine have had many more problems in the transition, so much so that the remarkable democratic reforms that had occurred in Russia are threatened by the return of Communists to power.

During the command economy period, *per capita* incomes differed sharply among these countries. *Per capita* incomes were higher, the closer a country was to Paris, London, and Rome. Standards of living in most of these countries probably were significantly higher – in comparison with similar standards in Western Europe–than the data on *per capita* incomes suggest. There were two arguments, which were partially offsetting. GDP estimates would have been significantly higher if the various goods and services had been valued at Western prices (Table 24.1). The currencies were partially overvalued prior to the move to the command economy.

Table 24.1   GDP *per capita* in US dollar, 1990 and 1995

	1990	*1995*
Bulgaria	1343	1538
Croatia	5106	3992
Czech Republic	3126	4814
East Germany	9000	16000[a]
Hungary	3179	4286
Poland	1630	3055
Rumania	1257	1573
Russian Federation	2554	2455
Slovenia	8706	9372
Ukraine	n.a.	864

Notes:
[a] After Reunification.
n.a. = Not available.
Source: European Bank for Reconstruction and Development, *Transition Report* (1998).

The history of what had been the Democratic Republic of Germany –
more popularly known as East Germany – differs sharply from every
other command economy because Germany was reunified in 1990 (the
first German unification occurred in the 1870s) and the Bonn government spent $100 billion a year – roughly $5000 per individual – to
increase the living standards of the 17 million people who lived there.
The West Germans felt that the alternatives to this massive subsidy
(which was intended to induce the East Germans to remain in their
home towns) were either to accept millions of immigrants or raise the
counterpart to the Berlin Wall to prevent the East Germans from
moving West. The increase in *per capita* incomes in what has been East
Germany is primarly a result of the subsidy rather than the increase in
productivity; unemployment rate in what had been East Germany is
nearly 20 percent.

The transition economies have received various types of financial
transfers, including credits from the World Bank and the European Bank
for Reconstruction and Development (EBRD), the International
Monetary Fund (IMF) as well as investments by firms headquartered in
Western Europe, the United States, Japan, and Korea. German firms
invested extensively in the Czech Republic: Skoda, the Czech auto firm,
was acquired by Volkswagen. General Electric purchased the large elec-
tric-light bulb factory in Hungry. Various Western petroleum companies
invested in Russia. The financial transfers from the West Germans to the
East Germans are several hundred times larger than the transfers to the
more than 20 countries that have made the same journey.

One of the key questions is why some countries have made a more
successful transition than others. A related observation is that the score
on the transition appears related to geographic location – the further
west the country, the more successful the transition. The basic problems include development of market institutions, privatization, fiscal
reform and macro stabilization, and industrial efficiency.

Where do market institutions come from?

One of the pervasive observations is that the desire of individuals to
trade is universal. There are street markets in virtually every country in
the world, and such markets were extensive in the command
economies. The move from street markets to a market economy is not
linear – a market economy has a lot of institutional arrangements that
are more or less taken for granted; street markets demonstrate the

entrepreneurial instinct or spirit is universal, but these markets cannot simply be extrapolated into a market economy.

Accountants, lawyers, and credit

A market economy has a set of accountants who compute the profits of individual firms and their tax liabilities. These accountants provide information to the shareowners about the profits of individual firms; they are a check on the statements of the managers. Moreover, the accountants compute the tax liabilities of both firms and individuals. There are few, if any, accountants in a command economy, since there is little need for estimation of profits or of tax liabilities The cash associated with the sales of the output of individual firms goes to the bank accounts of the state rather than to the bank accounts of the firms, so the firms lack the cash to upgrade their factories or even to keep them in good repair.

A market economy has a set of lawyers who facilitate the resolution of commercial disputes. Disputes are inevitable when property is privately owned. Mechanisms – especially low-cost mechanisms – are needed to resolve these disputes. Moreover a market economy has a set of judges that are deemed impartial. These lawyers and judges and the set of laws cannot be readily obtained from a mail order catalog.

A market economy has a set of banks with credit officers or loan officers who help allocate household savings. Training individuals to estimate the profitability of individual borrowers and the likelihood that they will honor their financial obligations is complex. There's a bit of a chicken and an egg problem here: borrowers can't develop their credit reputations until they have received loans, but their ability to develop a reputation for repaying on time can be determined only after they have received loans.

The common feature of accountants, lawyers and judges, and credit officers is that they involve *trust*. Trust has always been in short supply in command economies, which relied on coercion to implement the decisions made at the center. Decision-making in a command economy was not transparent; the consequence of the centralized approach to decision-making was that the citizens developed a cynical approach to the state.

Industrial restructuring

One of the major problems of the former command economies involved restructuring their industry so that particular firms could be competitive in a global economy. Most of those firms that produced raw materials and primary products would be able sell these products in world markets, despite their high costs. They might rely on Western firms to assist in reducing costs. A few of the former command economies may be able to make their way in the world by exporting raw materials, much like some of the countries in the Middle East, Africa, and Latin America. Several earn and will continue to earn lots of foreign exchange from tourism; several will earn foreign exchange from the remittances from nationals who are guest workers abroad. Russia, Hungary, and the Czech Republic somehow have to become competitive in parts of industry. The key question involves the efficiency of industry – the steel mills, auto and truck factories, textile and apparel factories, food producing factories, factories that produce machine tools, light-bulbs and toothpaste. The managers of these plants are caught in the classic 'Catch-22' situation. To update the plants, they need lots of investment capital. Even though the savings rates in these economies are not low, the countries lack the institutional mechanisms for allocation of these savings among the firms with the greatest productive potential.

The costs of the manufacturing firms in these former command economies are so high and the industrial plant so obsolete – by Western standards – that the efficient solution often is to abandon the enterprise. The problem is then the lack of employment opportunities for the workers who will be displaced; the labour in many of these factories is large relative to the value of output – they have not had a tradition of trying to minimize costs. The quality of the products from many of these factories has been low by the standards of Western goods, and the workers in the factories have not had the experience that their incomes will depend on the quality of the goods they produce.

Macro stabililization and the price level

Most of the former command economies have experienced a hyperinflation – inflation rates of more than 50 percent a month for a year or two – in the process of transition to a market economy. In contrast, each of these countries generally had a very low inflation rate during the years of the command economy. The dominant reason for the low inflation rate before the transition from the market economy was that prices were controlled, and did not 'clear markets' – rather, 'queuing time' cleared the markets. Those with the sharpest elbows, the greatest patience, and close friends in high places got the goods while the others allowed their money holdings to accumulate. There were black markets in both domestic goods and imported goods, and the prices in these markets were not included in the measurement of the inflation rate.

Part of the increase in money holdings consisted of the increase in savings deposits in state banks and the rest of the increase in holdings of currency notes. Some of the individuals increased their holdings of US currency and Germany currency; the purchases of these foreign currencies were illegal. Changes in relative prices were inevitable as these countries moved to a market economy. The alignment of the prices of particular goods and services changed to match the alignment of prices of the same goods and services in the world economy. The price of petroleum and various petroleum products rose to the world price level, or else various investors bought oil in the East to sell in the West. Similarly goods which are cheap in the West – manufactures such as automobiles and various electronic goods – would be imported. Tariffs and other trade barriers could drive wedges between the prices in the West and the prices in the transition economies – and these wedges might be 30 or 40 percent.

The change in relative prices inevitable in the integration into the world economy should be distinguished from the increase in general price levels which resulted from the combination of a self-fulfilling prophecy and the problems of developing a tax system appropriate for a market economy – and collecting the taxes necessary to finance the government expenditures. During the command economy period, government expenditures varied from 60 to 80 percent of GDP; the ratio was higher in those countries in which agricultural production occurred on state-owned farms. Because these high taxes became embedded in the prices of goods, the prices of these goods were extremely high compared with the prices of similar goods in Western economies. Footwear, clothing, and household goods had much higher prices than their Western counterparts, but a large component of the high price was the indirect tax.

The cliché in the West was that the workers in the East had to work 15–20 times as long to buy a pair of shoes. The major reason shoes were so expensive was that shoes were heavily taxed – the difference between the price of the shoes and the cost of their production was used to finance the subsidies for housing, medical and health care services, the military, and the general costs of government. With the move to the market economy, the decline in the price of shoes meant that the major source of tax revenues declined. No one would have continued to buy these shoes given that shoes produced in the market economies could be imported. So the governments needed to increase taxes to finance their expenditures. At the same time, they needed to reduce the subsidies to those factories and other enterprises whose revenues were below their costs.

So these countries need to develop a new tax system. Because spending by the government sector remained high as a share of GDP, tax rates had to be high. The taxes could be direct or indirect. There is little tradition of paying taxes: individuals were reluctant to pay taxes because they had lots of evidence of government waste. But the governments were reluctant to reduce waste quickly because that meant that they had to reduce the 'hidden unemployment' on the factory floor.

Privatization

In command economies the means of production are owned by the state, while in market economies the means of production are owned by individuals and by firms. So the problem was to transform ownership of factories, airlines, banks, homes and apartments, land, local bus systems, corner grocery stores, gas stations, butchers, bakers, and the candlestick makers.

Consider the basic alternative approaches toward privatization. One is to give the factories and shops to the workers, another is to give the assets to the citizens at large, and a third is to sell the assets for the highest possible or the second highest possible price. These approaches can be combined – 10 or 20 percent of the shares might be given to the employees, 30 or 40 percent might be given to the citizens, and the remaining shares might be sold to the highest bidder. These ratios might differ by firm and size of the business unit.

In the West, governments that have privatized have often first reorganized the productive enterprise into an independent government-owned firm; the reorganization identified the assets owned by the firm. Various measures were then undertaken to reduce the firm's costs, often by inducing employees to take early retirement. Then shares in the firm were sold, usually to the highest bidder in an auction. Once the firm was profitable, buyers could easily be found; there were few serious potential buyers for firms that were not profitable, the potential buyers being reluctant to incur the turmoil associated with reducing employment so that the firm might be made profitable.

Consider the range of possible buyers. One is the public at large; since all the factories had been owned in common, shares in these factories might be distributed to the public much like an income tax refund, except that each citizen would get the same number of shares.

(Of course there are problems – would children qualify? What about citizens that are living in foreign countries?) This broad-scale distribution would not work well for apartments, but then individuals might be given the apartments that they are living in and perhaps even the small shops where they worked. Or, alternatively, the plants might be given to the employees; the employees would then have to decide on each one's share of the total ownership. Or the shares might be sold to citizens at large.

The practical difficulty in selling the shares is that relatively few individuals would have had the cash to buy them. Moreover, a non-trivial number with the cash may have acquired it in ways that 'bent the rules' under the old system. Because cash was so limited the amount offered for these firms would generally be low relative to the intrinsic value of the enterprise. The shares in a particular enterprise might be sold in stages – 20 percent in the first year, and then 20 or 30 percent in each of the next several years. If shares were to be sold, will foreigners be allowed to bid for the shares – if not, will foreigners be allowed to buy the shares in the secondary market?

There is an asymmetry in the privatization process. The demand would be relatively strong for those productive activities that would be immediately profitable to the new sets of owners and weak for those activities not likely to operate profitably – indeed, one of the problems is that these newly privatized firms may not be able to count on funds to cover their losses.

The débaâcle in Russian finance

The major shock to the transition economies occured in Russia in the summer of 1998. Russia's fiscal deficit was between 5 and 10 percent of its GDP. Various types of wage and payments arrears had developed because tax collections increased too slowly and the government could not reduce its expenditures. The interest rates on the ruble debt, which had been 30 percent in April, increased to 60 and 90 percent; at these levels the surge in interest payments meant that the government debt would double in less than a year. So there was a race between the ability of the Russian government to reduce its fiscal deficit before interest rates and interest payments surged. The sharp increase in interest rates reflected two concerns – one was that the ruble might be devalued, and the second was that the Russian government would default on its debt. The Russian government was caught between a rock and a hard place. Tax rates were extremely high because tax collection was so low. No one – well, hardly anyone – could afford to pay all the taxes they were supposed to pay.

The Russians tried to reduce the crunch in two ways. The first was that the ruble debt was swapped into US dollar debt, which reduced the amount of the ruble debt to be financed. The second was that the IMF provided loan commitments of more than $20 billion; the actual cash would be available as the Russians succeeded in reducing their fiscal deficit.

The Russian government both defaulted and devalued, and the ruble lost more than half of its value. The paradox was that individual Russians had stashed US$50–$100 billion outside their own country. The flow of funds from Moscow was several times larger than the flow of foreign loans to Moscow. The Russians – at least the rich Russians with access to cash – had relatively little trust in their own banks and their own government.

25

Fitting the Pieces Once Again

Someday, perhaps, the international money problem will disappear. Perhaps the nation-state will be phased out as the basic political unit. Or independent countries may merge their currencies into a common international currency.

A common international currency?

Neither event seems imminent. Over the last 50 years the number of countries has increased sharply as colonial empires have broken up. Nearly all the newly independent countries have opted for their own currency, and some of them have gradually moved to monetary policies directed at their domestic objectives. Many other countries, long independent, have also oriented their monetary policies to domestic objectives. Now there are 140-plus members of the IMF, three times the initial number.

The nation-state appears unlikely to disappear in the foreseeable future as the basic unit for organizing political activity – for supplying law and order, and deciding on income distribution and economic priorities. Nor is there any indication of a broad-based movement toward the merger of national monies, except in the context of the European Union. No other group of nations seems close to planning seriously for a common money.

A merger of national monies makes economic sense only if the economic structures of the participating countries are similar – if their business cycles have similar phasing, if their labor forces grow at a similar rate and are similar in terms of skills, and if their preferences for price stability and full employment are also similar. Even then, vested interests within the several countries, both economic and political, would strongly oppose the merger, since the use of a national money is closely linked with the exercise of sovereignty. Control over the growth of the money supply is one of the most effective measures available to government leaders as they seek increased support from their constituents.

National monetary policies reflect political forces within individual countries – the level of interest rates, the rate of growth of the money supply, and the rate of increase in the price level are still issues in national elections. For this reason, prices rise more rapidly in some countries than in others, so payments imbalances are inevitable. Usually the countries with the most rapid increases in their price levels incur payments deficits. Eventually adjustments are needed to restore payments balance. Either exchange rates change, or else some other variable that will balance international payments and receipts must be altered.

Inevitably, the anticipation of changes in exchange rates leads to conflicts, for profit-oriented business firms, anticipating these changes, seek to achieve profits or at least avoid losses from such changes. But if some firms earn profits, then losses must be incurred by someone else – either the central banks, the commercial banks, or individual investors. And these shifts of funds across borders sometimes take the initiative away from the authorities; they may be forced to alter their exchange rates, economic controls, or monetary policies earlier than they had planned. Moreover, authorities in the deficit countries and in the surplus countries are frequently at odds about who should take the initiative in reducing the imbalance. And they also disagree about the best policies to use, especially whether market forces are superior to bureaucratic decisions.

Collapse of rules of behavior

The increasingly domestic focus of national monetary policies led to the breakdown and collapse of the IMF rules in the early 1970s. These rules were a guide to national behavior: they indicated when countries could change their exchange rates and when they could not, and when they could use controls on international payments and when they could not. The purpose of the rules was to ensure that in attempting to solve its own economic problems, a country would not dump them in the laps of its neighbors.

That the IMF rules became obsolete should not be a surprise, for the history of most international agreements is that they last for only a decade or two. Then, when the economic circumstances for which the rules were intended change, the rules become passé. (Although the institutions established to manage the rules live on.) While it might be possible to design sets of rules sufficiently broad to cope with changes in all circumstances, such rules would almost certainly be so general that they would have no bite or impact. What the rules can do is increase the confidence that each country can have about the future policies of its trading partners – modestly. Few countries, however, are likely to accept severe constraints on their future freedom of actions – or to abide by the constraints if doing do is expensive to their domestic objectives.

Two events occurred in the 1970s that were not contemplated when the IMF rules were drafted 30 years earlier. One was the world inflation and the unwillingness of Germany to accept an increase in its inflation rate comparable to the increase in the US inflation rate. The second was the decline in the relative economic position of the United States, evidenced by the more rapid growth in Germany and Japan.

New rules or international monetary institutions?

New sets of rules may be negotiated to deal with a variety of issues. Such rules could be directed to exchange market intervention practices of national central banks, even in the context of a continuing inflation. Or they might be directed to the rate of growth of international money. In the absence of new rules, ad hoc approaches will be adopted to cope with problems. Then each country will adopt the measures that suit its immediate needs and interests, with minimal regard for the external consequences. The new rules would have to provide for greater flexibility among national currency areas; the rules would have to mediate between enabling countries to follow policies appropriate to their domestic objectives and minimizing the likelihood that some countries would pursue 'beggar thy neighbor' policies and complicate the price, employment, or payments problems of others.

Designing the arrangement most likely to work requires foreknowledge of the types of economic problems that are likely to be dominant in the next five, 10, and 20 years. Unemployment? Inflation? Unemployment and inflation simultaneously? Will recessions and booms occur at the same time in the United States and Western Europe, or will they occur at different times? Will nationalism continue to become more powerful, or will the pendulum swing? And what about national attitudes toward market forces and bureaucratic regulation? Will the worldwide move toward more conservative policies continue? The types of rules most likely to be effective vary with the answers to these questions.

One frequently mentioned alternative to new rules is to rely on authority: to endow those who manage the international monetary institutions – the IMF and its successors – with the power to make the necessary decisions. But this approach seems untimely, for one counterpart to the increased attention to domestic objectives is most countries' increased reluctance to delegate substantial decisionmaking power to an international institution because of constraints on their domestic policies. The IMF has not emerged from the Asian crisis with glory, and so there will be increasing reluctance to delegate more power to the institution. Almost inevitably, the important decisions are likely to be made in national capitals. The managers of international institutions are increasingly responsible to committees of representatives from national capitals; the international civil servants will police the rules, but they will not make the rules, nor will they determine when the exchange rates must be changed, or by how much. The counterpart to the increasing concern with domestic objectives is that power has moved from international institutions to national capitals.

Crises – especially over changes in exchange rates – are inevitable in a multiplecurrency world. While US authorities, German authorities, and many economists continue to favor floating exchange rates, many countries, especially the smaller ones, appear committed to a return to pegged rates. The more important foreign trade is to a country's economy, the stronger this commitment is. The authorities in many countries have concluded that floating rates have worked less well than they had hoped – and far less well than they had promised. The United States and the Europeans believe that a return to pegged rates will impose constraints and complicate the attainment of their employment and price-level objectives, the Germans are concerned that once again they will import inflation from their more expansive neighbors, while the Americans are concerned about once again taking on an external constraint on domestic policies. And they are also concerned that the smaller countries will tend to free-ride.

Exchange controls?

The alternative to changes in exchange rates as a way to balance international payments and receipts are direct regulation of international payments through one or another form of exchange controls. One attraction of this approach to the authorities is that the political costs are smaller. The objection to increased reliance on an exchange-controls approach is that it fragments the international economy, for each type of transaction tends to be subject to its own form of control, especially if relatively few transactions are controlled. The more comprehensive and uniform the controls over imports and exports of goods as well as securities, the more nearly this approach is equivalent to changes in exchange rates. The distinction is that bureaucrats rather than market forces determine when the effective exchange rate is changed. But while academicians talk about the attractions of controls as long as they are comprehensive, the bureaucrats and politicians are likely to find compelling reasons for numerous exceptions to comprehensive controls. Eventually, the rules must deal with the issue: what are the acceptable forms of controls, when can they be used, and how do they relate to changes in exchange rates?

The role of gold

As the system moves from floating rates toward some form of pegged rates, the adequacy of international money will again be of great concern, despite the surge in the dollar holdings of central banks in Europe, Japan, and the various developing countries. Central bankers will again struggle with the problem of whether gold should have a monetary role. A closely related issue is whether the US dollar holdings of foreign central banks will be convertible into gold or some other asset. Now, any central bank is free to acquire gold, but at the prevailing price in the private market.

As long as foreign central banks hold more than $400 billion in liquid dollar securities, the US Treasury will be reluctant to accept convertibility of the dollar into other international monies because of the fear that if conversion is possible, there will be a run to convert. Either gold will increasingly lose its monetary role or central banks will tend to formalize arrangements to deal in gold at prices nearer the market price. Gold demonetization could occur passively: central banks in deficit countries would sell their gold in the private market, rather than to each other at the monetary price. Such sales are likely to be minimal until the conviction spreads that gold will be demonetized. Some central banks might even be buyers in the commodity market.

The gradual demonetization of gold would require agreement on a comprehensive arrangement to produce a new international money;

otherwise there will eventually be a severe shortage. The paradox is that the decline in credibility resulting from US gold demonetization may make it more difficult to obtain agreement on alternative means to produce international money. In any negotiations, the Europeans would be preoccupied with the concern that if the United States could effectively demonetize gold they might later 'demonetize' the new international money by refusing to buy it in exchange for the US dollar.

The alternative to gold demonetization – a worldwide increase in the price of gold – seems less impractical and unlikely than it did 20 years ago, even though most economists and editorial writers deplore the use of a 'barbarous relic' as money. While the continued use of gold as money may be barbarous, the continued demand for gold reflects the fact that many nations lack faith in the commitments of their major trading partners, and so they put more value in a commodity money than in a paper money. Their decision may be wise or unwise – but it is their decision. Most of the objections that stalled the inevitable increase in the monetary price in the 1960s are irrelevant because of the sharp increase in the market price of gold. Relatively little attention was given to the implications of a higher gold price (or of gold demon-etization) for monetary arrangements. And while taking gold out of the mines of South Africa and Russia to bury it again in the vaults of central banks is stupid, at least those who acquire the gold pay most of the costs. If once again there were a monetary price for gold, more gold would be available to satisfy the monetary demand. The increase in the monetary value of existing gold holdings would enable central banks to move toward the preferred combination of gold, dollars, and SDRs in their international reserve holdings. An increase in the gold price would not resolve all international monetary problems forever; no price can be fixed forever and, on the international scene, no agree-ment lasts forever. A US initiative to increase the world gold price has some strong arguments in its favor, however. Many Europeans prefer this solution, and they would bear nearly all the economic costs. There may even be some favorable impacts on the relationship between the US dollar and other currencies, for the ratio of US gold holdings to foreign holdings of US dollar securities would increase.

European preferences are conditioned by the monetary events of the last several decades and especially by their dependence on the United States – and their interpretation of this dependence. The countries in Western Europe want greater control over their own monetary policies, but their attitudes are ambivalent: they want to achieve payments surpluses while ensuring that the United States does not have a deficit. Such attitudes are inconsistent. They want to achieve price stability while maintaining pegged exchange rates, two objectives which are consistent only if the United States also achieves price stability.

Just as no price can be fixed forever, no currency is likely to be at the top of the hit parade forever. The shift from the US dollar into gold and other currencies in 1970 and 1971, a result of US inflation and speculation against the dollar, may suggest that the dollar's tenure as the top currency may be over. Yet the shift from US dollar may have been short-term phenomenon, largely an anticipation of the appreciation of the German mark. Some diversification in reserve holdings is likely, primarily to supplement rather than replace the dollar.

Political pressure will certainly develop to diminish the dollar's international role. The Europeans would like the Euro to be 'an equal' to the dollar, but in the absence of a major US inflation or financial débâcle, such an outcome seems highly unlikely. Foreign countries do not like the asymmetry of having to revalue or devalue their own currencies relative to the US dollar, in effect, they hope that a revision of the arrangements might protect them from US inflation – they hope for an external constraint on US policy. The move toward a paper gold arrangement is an effort to use political power – the force of numbers – to provide an external constraint on the United States and to reduce the impact of US policies on other countries. The political route is taken because economic forces are still likely to keep the US dollar at the top of the hit parade.

The conflict is not unusual; it is what the international money game is all about. National interests conflict, on both major issues and minor issues, and the bureaucrats and politicians know that their own roles require that they achieve gains for their constituents. So each will agree to modify institutional arrangements only if its constituents gain. Conflict is inevitable as long as there are national monies; changes in the rules and structure cannot eliminate it. The various solutions – eliminating gold, raising the gold price, relying on paper substitutes for gold, or letting exchange rates float – do not resolve the conflict; instead, they shift the arena in which the conflict will occur.

Index